# THE WORLD ALMANAC FOR KIDS
## 2010

**WORLD ALMANAC® BOOKS**
An Imprint of Infobase Publishing

# THE WORLD ALMANAC FOR KIDS 2010

**2010 Edition New Content:** RJF PUBLISHING

**Project Management:** Robert Famighetti

**Contributors:** Brian Fitzgerald, Amanda Hudson,
William A. McGeveran Jr.

**Photo Research:** Edward A. Thomas

**Design:** BILL SMITH GROUP

**Chief Creative Officer:** Brian Kobberger

**Project Directors:** David Borkman, Shaunna Coon

**Design:** Geron Hoy, Ron Leighton, Jennifer Basilio, Tamara English

**Production:** Eric Murray, Bob Horvath

### INFOBASE PUBLISHING
**Editorial Director:** Laurie Likoff

**Senior Editor:** Sarah Janssen

**World Almanac® Books**
An imprint of Infobase Publishing
132 West 31st Street
New York NY 10001

Hardcover
ISBN-13: 978-1-60057-127-5
ISBN-10: 1-60057-127-5

Paperback
ISBN-13: 978-1-60057-128-2
ISBN-10: 1-60057-128-2

For Library of Congress cataloging information, please contact the publisher.

The World Almanac® for Kids is available at special discounts when purchased in bulk quantities for businesses, associations, institutions, or sales promotions. Please call our Special Sales Department in New York at (212) 967-8800 or (800) 322-8755.

You can find The World Almanac® for Kids on the World Wide Web at http://www.worldalmanac.com

Book printed and bound by RR Donnelley, Crawfordsville, IN
Date printed: November 2009
Printed in the United States of America

RRD BSG 10 9 8 7 6 5 4 3 2 1

The addresses and content of Web sites referred to in this book are subject to change. Although The World Almanac® for Kids carefully reviews these sites, we cannot take responsibility for their content.

# CONTENTS

# Television

## XOXO

The second season of *Gossip Girl* followed Serena, Blair, and the rest of "Manhattan's elite" through more rumors and scandals.

## FRESH IDOLS

Kris Allen (center) beat out runner-up Adam Lambert (far left) in the eighth season of *American Idol*.

## HILARIOUS HANNAH

Miley Cyrus starred as Hannah Montana in the third season of the successful Disney show.

## AMERICA THE BEAUTIFUL

Audiences tuned in for laughter and drama with Betty Suarez (America Ferrera) in *Ugly Betty*.

## GLEEFUL CAST

The first season of *Glee* charmed both viewers and critics with its fresh combination of humor, romance, and song-and-dance numbers.

7

# Movies

## TOGETHER AGAIN

The second movie in the Twilight series, *New Moon*, reunited stars Kristen Stewart and Robert Pattinson.

## BACK TO HOGWARTS

Harry and his friends faced down new adventures—and heartbreak—in *Harry Potter and the Half-Blood Prince.*

## ABOARD THE *ENTERPRISE*

Director J.J. Abrams brought an updated version of *Star Trek* to movie screens—and found a whole new generation of fans.

9

# Movies

## UP AND AWAY
Available in 3D in many cities, the animated film *Up* was a hit with adults and children alike.

## THE X-MEN RETURN
*X-Men Origins: Wolverine* starred Hugh Jackman (left), Ryan Reynolds, and Taylor Kitsch (right). The successful movie was the fourth in the X-Men series.

## STILL PRIME

Starring Shia LaBeouf and Megan Fox, *Transformers 2: Revenge of the Fallen* was a Summer 2009 hit.

## SEEKING FAME

A new group of teens sang and danced their way through an update of the classic movie *Fame*.

# Music

## FEARLESS TAYLOR

In early 2009, the song "Love Story" from Taylor Swift's *Fearless* album became the country song with the most paid downloads in history.

## KING OF POP

Michael Jackson's tragic death in 2009 led many fans to re-discover his music. Radio stations played his music around the clock for days after his death, and his *Number Ones* album shot to the top of the charts.

## MORE DEMI

Demi Lovato's second album, *Here We Go Again*, went to No. 1 on the Billboard 200 chart.

## BAND OF BROTHERS

The Jonas Brothers released their fourth album, *Lines, Vines and Trying Times*, in June 2009. Fans were also able to see the band in movie theaters with the release of *Jonas Brothers: The 3D Concert Experience*.

# Sports

## BIG BEN WINS AGAIN
Quarterback Ben Roethlisberger led the Pittsburgh Steelers to a thrilling 27–23 victory in Super Bowl XLIII in 2009. It was Big Ben and Pittsburgh's second Super Bowl win in four years.

## UCONN IS UNDEFEATED
The University of Connecticut women's basketball team completed a perfect 39–0 season by crushing Louisville 76–54 in the championship game on April 7, 2009.

## LIGHTNING BOLT

The world's fastest man was at it again in 2009. In July, Jamaican sprinter Usain Bolt ran the fastest times ever in the 100 meters and 200 meters—shattering the world records he had set at the 2008 Olympics!

## DYNAMIC DUO

Pittsburgh had another reason to celebrate in 2009. Young stars Evgeni Malkin (71) and Sidney Crosby (87) led the Pittsburgh Penguins to their first Stanley Cup championship since 1992.

# Sports

## X-CELLENT PERFORMANCE

No 2009 sports champion was a greater inspiration than teen motocross star Ashley Fiolek. She became the first deaf athlete to win a medal at the X Games, taking home the gold in the Women's Moto X Super X.

## L.A. STORY

Kobe Bryant averaged more than 30 points per game during the 2009 playoffs and led the Los Angeles Lakers to their fourth NBA title of the decade.

## GRAND CHAMPION

Swiss tennis star Roger Federer won the Wimbledon men's singles title in July 2009. It was his 15th Grand Slam (major tournament) title—a new record for most Grand Slam wins by a men's player.

## AWESOME ALBERT

In 2008, slugger Albert Pujols of the St. Louis Cardinals was named the National League Most Valuable Player (MVP). He was even better in 2009, hitting more home runs, knocking in more runs, and leading the Cards to the playoffs.

# Animals

Will a cat always land on its feet? ➡ page 24

Furry or scaly, creepy or crawly, schoolbus-sized or microscopic—animals fascinate people of all stripes. Here are some facts about the Animal Kingdom.

## WEIRD ANIMAL FACTS

### DEEP-SEA ANGLERFISH

Deep-sea life is full of pressure! Creatures that inhabit the ocean waters one-half to two miles below the surface must resist the pressure of all that water weighing down upon them. Their environment is only a few degrees Fahrenheit above freezing and dark because little of the sun's light can reach that far.

Not many animals can survive at such depths. The ones who do, have evolved in unique ways. Deep-sea anglerfish are one common species in this harsh environment. They sprout a growth from their heads that they use like a fishing rod. They make the end of it glow using **bioluminescence**. Bioluminescence is the ability of some animals to create light. Deep-sea anglerfish use this glow to lure prey so they don't waste energy swimming around looking for food.

### ANTS AND APHIDS

Species within an ecosystem depend on one another for survival. Sometimes, however, odd couples can be found. When animals of different species form a relationship that benefits all involved, it's called mutualism. Ants and aphids have this kind of relationship.

Aphids are insects that feed on plants. As part of digestion, they produce a sugary waste called honeydew. Ants will protect and take care of aphids in return for honeydew, which they eat. They will even carry aphids into their nest so they will survive through the winter.

# LIFE ON EARTH

This time line shows how life developed on Earth. The earliest life forms are at the bottom of the chart. The most recent are at the top of the chart.

| | Years Ago | | Animal Life on Earth |
|---|---|---|---|
| **Cenozoic** | 10,000 to present | | Human civilization develops. |
| | 1.8 million to 10,000 | | Large mammals like mammoths, saber-toothed cats, and giant ground sloths develop. Modern human beings evolve. This era ends with an ice age. |
| | 65 to 1.8 million | | Ancestors of modern-day horses, zebras, rhinos, sheep, goats, camels, pigs, cows, deer, giraffes, elephants, cats, dogs, and primates begin to develop. |
| **Mesozoic** | 144 to 65 million | | In the Cretaceous period, new dinosaurs appear. Many insect groups, modern mammal and bird groups also develop. A global extinction of most dinosaurs occurs at the end of this period. |
| | 206 to 144 million | | The Jurassic is dominated by giant dinosaurs. In the late Jurassic, birds evolve. |
| | 248 to 206 million | | In the Triassic period, marine life develops again. Reptiles also move into the water. Reptiles begin to dominate the land areas. Dinosaurs and mammals develop. |
| **Paleozoic** | 290 to 248 million | | A mass extinction wipes out 95% of all marine life. |
| | 354 to 290 million | | Reptiles develop. Much of the land is covered by swamps. |
| | 417 to 354 million | | The first trees and forests appear. The first land-living vertebrates, amphibians, and wingless insects appear. Many new sea creatures also appear. |
| | 443 to 417 million | | Coral reefs form. Other animals, such as the first known freshwater fish, develop. Relatives of spiders and centipedes develop. |
| | 542 to 443 million | | Animals with shells (called trilobites) and some mollusks form. Primitive fish and corals develop. Evidence of the first primitive land plants. |
| **Precambrian** | 3.8 billion to 542 million | | First evidence of life on Earth. All life is in water. Early single-celled bacteria and achaea appear, followed by multi-celled organisms, including early animals. |
| | 4.6 billion | | Formation of the Earth. |

# ANIMAL KINGDOM

The world has so many animals that scientists looked for a way to organize them into groups. A Swedish scientist named Carolus Linnaeus (1707-1778) worked out a system for classifying both animals and plants. We still use it today.

The Animal Kingdom is separated into two large groups—animals with backbones, called **vertebrates**, and animals without backbones, called **invertebrates**.

These large groups are divided into smaller groups called **phyla**. And phyla are divided into even smaller groups called **classes**. The animals in each group are classified together when their bodies are similar in certain ways.

## Vertebrates
### Animals with Backbones

| | |
|---|---|
| FISH | Swordfish, tuna, salmon, trout, halibut, goldfish |
| AMPHIBIANS | Frogs, toads, mud puppies |
| REPTILES | Turtles, alligators, crocodiles, lizards |
| BIRDS | Sparrows, owls, turkeys, hawks |
| MAMMALS | Kangaroos, opossums, dogs, cats, bears, seals, rats, squirrels, rabbits, chipmunks, porcupines, horses, pigs, cows, deer, bats, whales, dolphins, monkeys, apes, humans |

## Invertebrates
### Animals without Backbones

| | |
|---|---|
| PROTOZOA | The simplest form of animals |
| COELENTERATES | Jellyfish, hydra, sea anemones, coral |
| MOLLUSKS | Clams, snails, squid, oysters |
| ANNELIDS | Earthworms |
| ARTHROPODS | |
| Crustaceans | Lobsters, crayfish |
| Centipedes and Millipedes | |
| Arachnids | Spiders, scorpions |
| Insects | Butterflies, grasshoppers, bees, termites, cockroaches |
| ECHINODERMS | Starfish, sea urchins, sea cucumbers |

## Homework Tip

How can you remember the animal classifications from most general to most specific? Try this sentence:

**K**ing **P**hilip **C**ame **O**ver **F**rom **G**reat **S**pain.

**K** = Kingdom; **P** = Phylum; **C** = Class; **O** = Order; **F** = Family; **G** = Genus; **S** = Species

# WHAT IS BIODIVERSITY?

The Earth is shared by millions of species of living things. The wide variety of life on Earth, as shown by the many species, is called "biodiversity" (bio means "life" and diversity means "variety"). Human beings of all colors, races, and nationalities make up just one species, *Homo sapiens*.

## Species, Species Everywhere

Here is just a sampling of how diverse life on Earth is. The numbers are only estimates, and more species are being discovered all the time!

### ARTHROPODS (1.1 million species)
insects: 1,000,000 species
moths & butterflies: 175,000 species
flies: about 122,000 species
cockroaches: about 4,000 species
crustaceans: 40,000 species
spiders: 35,000 species

### FISH (24,500 species)
bony fish: 21,000 species
skates & rays: 450 species
sharks: 350 species
seahorses: 32 species

### BIRDS (10,000 species)
perching birds: 5,200-5,500 species
parrots: 353 species
pigeons: 309 species
raptors (eagles, hawks, etc.): 307 species
penguins: 17 species
ostrich: 1 species

### MAMMALS (9,000 species)
rodents: 2,000 species
bats: 1,000 species
monkeys: 242 species
whales & dolphins: 83 species
cats: 37 species
apes: 21 species
pigs: 16 species
bears: 8 species

### REPTILES (6,000 species)
lizards: 4,500 species
snakes: 2,900 species
tortoises & turtles: about 294 species
crocodiles & alligators: 23 species

### AMPHIBIANS (4,500 species)
frogs & toads: 4,000 species
newts & salamanders: 470 species

### PLANTS (260,000 species)
flowering plants: 250,000 species
bamboo: about 1,000 species
evergreens: 550 species

## Biodiversity Q&A

**What percentage of all known living species are vertebrates (with backbones)?**
About 5%. Although they all have backbones, vertebrates can differ greatly in form, size, and habitat. They range from blue whales in the ocean to birds and of course humans.

**True or false? Snakes aren't found naturally in the wild in Ireland.** True. According to legend, St. Patrick banished snakes from Ireland. More likely, ancient snakes never migrated to the Emerald Isle, which doesn't have much biodiversity. Snakes are also not found in the wild in Iceland, Greenland, and Antarctica. Not only is the ground frozen year-round in these places, they're completely surrounded by water, like Ireland.

**Why is biodiversity important?** Forms of life are interlinked. If one species of plant or animal becomes extinct it affects other life forms. Studies have shown that biomes, or environments, with wider varieties of life forms can better survive difficult conditions, such as drought.

# BIGGEST, SMALLEST, FASTEST

## IN THE WORLD

### WORLD'S BIGGEST ANIMALS

**Marine mammal:** Blue whale (100 feet long, 200 tons)

**Heaviest land mammal:** African bush elephant (12 feet high, 4-7 tons)
**Tallest land mammal:** Giraffe (18 feet tall)

**Reptile:** Saltwater crocodile (20-23 feet long, 1,150 pounds)

**Heaviest snake:** Green anaconda (16-30 feet, 550 pounds)
**Longest snake:** Reticulated python (26-32 feet long)

**Fish:** Whale shark (40-60 feet long, 10-20 tons)

**Bird:** Ostrich (9 feet tall, 345 pounds)

**Insect:** Stick insect (15 inches long)

### WORLD'S FASTEST ANIMALS

**Marine mammal:** Killer whale and Dall's porpoise (35 miles per hour)

**Land mammal:** Cheetah (70 miles per hour)

**Fish:** Sailfish (68 miles per hour, leaping)

**Bird:** Peregrine falcon (200 miles per hour)

**Insect:** Dragonfly (35 miles per hour)

**Snake:** Black mamba (14 miles per hour)

### WORLD'S SMALLEST ANIMALS

**Mammal:** Bumblebee bat (1.1-1.3 inches)

**Fish:** *Paedocypris progenetica* or stout infantfish (0.31-0.33 inches)

**Bird:** Bee hummingbird (1-2 inches)

**Snake:** Thread snake and brahminy blind snake (4.25 inches)

**Lizard:** Jaragua sphaero and Virgin Islands dwarf sphaero (0.63 inch)

**Insect:** Fairyfly (0.01 inch)

## HOW FAST DO ANIMALS RUN?

This table shows how fast some animals can go on land. A snail can take more than 30 hours just to go 1 mile. But humans at their fastest are still slower than many animals. The human record for fastest speed for a recognized race distance is held by Usain Bolt, who set a new world record in 2009 in the 100-meter dash of 9.58 seconds, for an average speed of about 23 miles per hour.

| MILES PER HOUR | |
|---|---|
| Cheetah | 70 |
| Pronghorn antelope | 60 |
| Elk | 45 |
| Ostrich | 40 |
| Rabbit | 35 |
| Giraffe | 32 |
| Grizzly bear | 30 |
| Elephant | 25 |
| Wild turkey | 15 |
| Crocodile | 10 |
| Tiger beetle | 5.5 |
| Snail | 0.03 |

# *HOW LONG* DO ANIMALS LIVE?

**M**ost animals do not live as long as humans do. A monkey that's 14 years old is thought to be old, while a person at that age is still considered young. The average life spans of some animals in the wild are shown here. An average 10-year-old boy in the U.S. can expect to live to be about 75.

Galapagos tortoise .... 100+ years
Box turtle............. 100 years
Blue whale ........... 80 years
Alligator ............. 50 years
Chimpanzee........... 50 years
Macaw............... 50 years
African elephant ...... 35 years
Bottlenose dolphin...... 30 years
Gorilla............... 30 years
Horse ............... 20 years
Periodical cicada....... 17 years
Tiger................. 16 years
Lion.................. 15 years
Lobster............... 15 years
Cat (domestic) ........ 15 years
Cow .................. 15 years
Tarantula ............. 15 years
Dog (domestic)........ 13 years
Camel (bactrian)....... 12 years
Moose ............... 12 years
Pig................... 10 years
Squirrel .............. 10 years
Deer (white-tailed)....... 8 years
Goat ................. 8 years
Kangaroo.............. 7 years
Chipmunk.............. 6 years
Beaver ............... 5 years
Rabbit (domestic)....... 5 years
Guinea pig............ 4 years
Mouse ............... 3 years
Opossum ............. 1 year
Worker bee........... 6 weeks
Adult housefly........ 1-3 weeks

## ANIMAL WORDS

| Animal | Male | Female | Young |
|---|---|---|---|
| bear | boar | sow | cub |
| cat | tom | queen | kitten |
| cattle, elephant, moose, whale | bull | cow | calf |
| deer | buck, stag | doe | fawn |
| donkey | jack | jenny | foal |
| ferret | hob | jill | kit |
| fox | reynard | vixen | kit, cub, pup |
| goat | buck, billy | nanny, doe | kid |
| goose | gander | goose | gosling |
| gorilla | male | female | infant |
| hawk | tiercel | hen | eyas |
| horse | stallion | mare | foal, filly (female), colt (male) |
| kangaroo | buck | doe | joey |
| lion | lion | lioness | cub |
| pig | boar | sow | piglet |
| rabbit | buck | doe | kit, bunny |
| swan | cob | pen | cygnet |
| turkey | gobbler, tom | hen | chick, poult |

# WHAT ARE GROUPS OF ANIMALS CALLED?

**Here are some (often odd) names for animal groups:**

| | |
|---|---|
| **BEARS**: *sleuth* of bears | **KITTENS**: *kindle* or *kendle* of kittens |
| **CATS**: *clowder* of cats | **LEOPARDS**: *leap* of leopards |
| **CATTLE**: *drove* of cattle | **MONKEYS**: *troop* of monkeys |
| **CROCODILES**: *bask* of crocodiles | **MULES**: *span* of mules |
| **CROWS**: *murder* of crows | **NIGHTINGALES**: *watch* of nightingales |
| **FISH**: *school* or *shoal* of fish | **OWLS**: *parliament* of owls |
| **FLIES**: *swarm* or *cloud* of flies | **OYSTERS**: *bed* of oysters |
| **FOXES**: *skulk* of foxes | **PEACOCKS**: *muster* of peacocks |
| **GIRAFFES**: *tower* of giraffes | **RAVENS**: *unkindness* of ravens |
| **HARES**: *down* of hares | **SHARKS**: *shiver* of sharks |
| **HAWKS**: *cast* of hawks | **SQUIRRELS**: *dray* or *scurry* of squirrels |
| **HYENAS**: *cackle* of hyenas | **TURTLES**: *bale* of turtles |
| **JELLYFISH**: *smack* of jellyfish | **WHALES**: *pod* of whales |

# PETS AT THE TOP

Here are some of the most popular pets in the United States and the approximate number of each pet in 2009:

| | | | |
|---|---|---|---|
| 1. Freshwater fish | 171,700,000 | 5. Birds | 15,000,000 |
| 2. Cats | 93,600,000 | 6. Reptiles | 13,630,000 |
| 3. Dogs | 77,500,000 | 7. Equine | 13,300,000 |
| 4. Small animals | 15,900,000 | 8. Saltwater fish | 11,200,000 |

Source: American Pet Products Manufacturers Association's
2009/2010 National Pet Owners Survey

## PETS Q&A

Will a cat always land on its feet? **Not every time, but often. Cats are extremely flexible compared to many other animals, and they can easily turn their bodies as they fall. One lucky cat survived after falling 42 stories!**

True or false? Dogs and cats are color-blind. **False. Despite the myth, dogs and cats can see in color, though not all the colors humans can see. For example, dogs can see blues but not greens.**

What breed of dog was the most popular in the U.S. in 2008? **The Labrador Retriever. According to the American Kennel Club, the Labrador retriever has been the most popular breed of dog in the U.S. for many years.**

# URBAN WILDLIFE

Opportunistic Species/Urban Wildlife are animal species that have taken the opportunity of their closeness to humans to increase their chances of survival. A species can be native to one area but opportunistic as it spreads to another.

**Pigeons** are the typical urban bird. Almost everyone recognizes this wild neighbor. The pigeon's diet consists primarily of seeds and grains, as well as insects and some greens. They are not picky and are known to accept human food scraps and leftovers when they are offered. Pigeons live in groups called flocks, and are comfortable in human-built structures.

**Canadian Geese** are associated with lakes and ponds, however they also spend time on land and will nest some distance from water if the site seems safe. Artificial ponds and lakes and good grazing places like those found in parks, corporate and school campuses, and golf courses are ideal habitats for geese. This is the main reason they have settled in to year-round residency and have grown in numbers in suburban and urban areas.

Adult **American Black Bear** range from five to six feet long and between 250 and 330 pounds. For such large animals, they can run fairly quickly—up to 25 miles per hour—and are skillful tree climbers. A common assumption is that bears are exclusively meat eaters, however ripening fruits, berries, and nuts make up the bulk of their diet. Animal material eaten by bears includes insects, carrion, and occasional small prey, such as deer fawns. Around homes and in passing through suburban neighborhoods, bears may stop to sample the fare in gardens, compost bins, trash cans, birdfeeders, beehives, and outdoor barbecues.

# ENDANGERED

When a species becomes extinct, it reduces the variety of life on Earth. In the world today, 7,725 known species of animals (and even more plant species) are threatened with extinction, according to the World Conservation Union. Humans have been able to save some endangered animals and are working to save more.

## Some Endangered Animals

**Western Lowland Gorilla** Western lowland gorillas live in regions of Africa near the equator, specifically Angola, Cameroon, Central African Republic, Congo, Equatorial Guinea, Gabon, and Nigeria. Gorillas get around on all four limbs, placing their weight on the knuckles of their hands and their feet. Following chimpanzees, gorillas are the second closest relatives of humans.
**Reasons for population decline:**
• Disease caused by Ebola virus
• Chopping down of trees in their habitat has made it easier for people to illegally hunt these gorillas for food.

**Wellington's Solitary Coral** The Wellington's Solitary Coral is found in Galápagos Archipelago in Ecuador. There has been a decline of more than 90% in the population since the 1982 El Niño—an unusual weather/ocean event that occurs every few years. The rapid decline in the numbers of Wellington's Solitary Coral following the 1982 El Niño leads scientists to believe the coral are very sensitive to temperature changes.
**Reasons for population decline:**
• El Niño
• Global warming
• Pollution

**Yangtze River Dolphin** The Yangtze River dolphin, also know as the Baiji, lived in the Yangtze River, in China. The Yangtze River dolphin is probably the world's most endangered aquatic mammal. The last documented sighting of a Yangtze river dolphin was in 2002. Since then, scientists have been unable to find proof the dolphins are still around. It is possibly extinct.
**Reasons for population decline:**
• Fishing methods, including use of nets and hooks, that indirectly harmed dolphins
• Loss of habitat due to increased development
• Collisions with large ships
• Pollution

# SPECIES

**Townsend's Shearwater** The Townsend's shearwater is a rare seabird of the tropics. They are found on the Revillagigedo Islands in Mexico. Efforts are being made to remove introduced species from these islands.

**Reasons for population decline:**
- Decline in quality of habitat due to overgrazing by sheep, which were introduced to Socorro and Clarion islands
- Preyed upon by cats, which were introduced to Socorro Island
- Destruction of nests by pigs and rabbits, which were introduced to Clarion Island
- Volcanic eruption on San Benedicto Island

**Kakapo** They live on Anchor Island and Codfish Island, New Zealand. Scientists transferred all remaining known kakapo to these two sanctuaries because of the threat of invasive predators on other New Zealand islands. As of March 2009 the remaining population of kakapo was 103. The kakapo, which cannot fly, is the world's largest parrot. It can weigh up to 13 pounds.

**Reasons for population decline:**
- Habitat loss
- Hunting by humans
- Preyed upon by introduced predators, including cats, dogs, weasels, and rats
- Competition from possums, deer, which feed on similar items
- Low rate of reproduction

**Panamanian Golden Frog** The Panamanian golden frog is from Panama. The remaining population in the wild is not known. Some scientists think there may be none left. There are about 1,000 of these frogs in zoos. Since amphibians—including frogs, toads, and salamanders—absorb water through their skin, they are especially vulnerable to changes in the environment. Scientists estimate about one-third of all known amphibian species are threatened or endangered.

**Reasons for population decline:**
- Disease caused by a fungus
- Habitat loss and decline in habitat quality because of deforestation
- Pollution, exposure to chemicals such as those in fertilizers
- Over-collection to sell as pets

# FACTORS THAT CAN MAKE A SPECIES ENDANGERED:

**HABITAT DESTRUCTION.** As human populations grow, they need places to live and work. People build houses and factories in areas where plants and animals live. Filling in wetlands and clearing forests (**deforestation**) are examples of this threat.

**OVERHARVESTING.** People may catch a kind of fish or hunt an animal until its numbers are too low to reproduce fast enough. Bison, or buffalo, once roamed the entire Great Plains until they were almost hunted into extinction in the 19th century. They are now protected by law, and their numbers are increasing.

**ALIEN SPECIES** are plants and animals that have been moved by humans into areas where they are not naturally found. They may have no natural enemies there and can push out native species. Red fire ants and zebra mussels are examples of alien species in the U.S.

**POLLUTION** in the air, water, and land can harm plants and animals. It can poison them or make it hard for them to grow or reproduce. Factories are not the only source of pollution. Oil, salt, and other substances dumped on roads can wash into streams, rivers, and lakes. Acid rain can damage or kill trees.

# GET BUGGED

**What's a really heavy insect?** The African goliath beetle only gets to be about 4 to 5 inches long compared to the stick insect, which can grow up to 15 inches long. But the goliath can weigh nearly a quarter of a pound.

**What characteristics do all insects share?** Insects do not have backbones. They have three pairs of walking legs. (Spiders, which have eight legs, are arachnids, not insects.) Also, insects' bodies can be divided into a head, thorax, and abdomen. Another thing they lack is lungs. Instead, insects breathe through tubes that open directly onto the surface of their bodies.

**True or false? Malaria, a disease transmitted through mosquito bites, kills more than one million people each year.** True. You could say the mosquito is one of the most dangerous creatures in the world. Malaria can be prevented and cured, but over one million people still die from it each year. Most of the victims are younger children in Africa, where people often lack the resources to prevent the spread of the disease.

**How fast can a cockroach move?** 4 miles per hour. Cockroaches are one of the fastest insects on land. At their top speed, over short distances, they run only on their two hind legs. That's because those legs are longer than their front legs.

# ANT COLONY

"Soldier" ants defend the colony. Other ants forage for food.

"Nurse" ants watch over unhatched eggs and larvae (young ants) in a nursery chamber.

Food found by worker ants is stored in a chamber.

Some ants are responsible for digging tunnels and chambers to enlarge the nest.

Garbage and ants that have died are kept in a separate chamber.

The colony begins with a queen. She digs a chamber in which to lay eggs. These eggs produce the colony's first ants. (Practically all the ants in a colony are female. Male ants survive only long enough to mate.)

# THE WORLD ALMANAC FOR KIDS
# ON THE JOB: VETERINARIAN

## A veterinarian, or vet, is a physician for animals.

### What veterinarians do?
There are more than 62,000 veterinarians in the United States. Most of these vets care for small pets such as cats and dogs. Others care for large farm animals, including horses, sheep, and cattle. These vets usually make house calls! Vets also do research for companies that make food or medicine for animals. The U.S. government even hires vets to be food inspectors. These vets help make sure that the meat and poultry we eat are safe. Some adventurous vets work in zoos and circuses.

### Would you like to be a veterinarian?
If you are thinking about being a veterinarian, here are some questions to ask yourself:
1. Do you like animals and want to help them?
2. Can you imagine staying calm when an animal is hurt or scared?
3. Are you interested in science?
4. Would you be comfortable dealing with blood and giving shots?
5. Do you like working with people, too?
If your answer to these questions is "yes," a career as a veterinarian could be for you!

### How can you become a veterinarian?
To be a vet, you must have a Doctor of Veterinary Medicine (DVM) degree. Getting this degree takes a lot of hard work. After four years of college, students must be accepted to a veterinary school. There are only 28 veterinary schools in the United States—compared to 131 medical schools—so it can be difficult to be accepted to one. It takes four years to graduate from veterinary school. Students spend three of these years learning about animals, diseases, and medicines. They spend the last year working with an established vet in an animal hospital or clinic. Here they can work with patients and their families. Some vets take more time to become specialists in a specific area—such as animal cancer or allergies. Some vets even specialize in animal dentistry. It takes two to five more years to become a specialized veterinarian. Specialized or not, all vets must continue to learn throughout their careers. There are always new medicines and treatments to study.

### How can you get started?
If you think you might want to be a vet, you can learn from your own pets. Read about them and learn how their bodies work. You can also learn from other people's pets. You might walk your neighbor's dog or feed a friend's cat when the friend is away. Vets have to be comfortable with different types of animals. Get in touch with your local animal shelter and find out how you can help as a volunteer. Many animal shelters have homeless dogs and cats who would love some special attention.

# Art

What is the Exquisite Corpse? ➡ page 33

## ART Q&A

### HOW OLD IS ART?
Art goes back to our earliest records of human life. See the cave paintings on the next page for an example.

### IS ARTISTIC TALENT SOMETHING YOU ARE BORN WITH OR SOMETHING YOU CAN LEARN?
Learning to draw is a skill like writing or playing a sport. Some people are naturally more talented, but anyone can learn to draw. Even people with severe physical disabilities can make masterpieces.

### WHEN I SEE A PAINTING IN A MUSEUM, WHAT MIGHT I SAY ABOUT IT?

Look at the painting without thinking too hard about it. How does it make you feel? Happy, sad, confused, silly? Study the painting and try to discover the colors, shapes, and textures that create those feelings in you.

Look at the information card next to the work of art. Usually, it will tell you who painted it, when it was made, and what media (materials) were used. You can compare it to other works of art by the same artist, from the same time, or in the same medium.

### WHAT IS ART?
The answer is up for debate. People who study this question are studying aesthetics (ess-THET-ics), which is a kind of philosophy. Usually art is something that an artist interprets for an audience. Art reveals something that you can see, that then makes you think and feel.

## DIFFERENT KINDS OF ART

Throughout history, artists have painted pictures of nature (called landscapes), pictures of people (called portraits), and pictures of flowers in vases, food, and other objects (known as still lifes). Today many artists create pictures that do not look like anything in the real world. These are examples of abstract art.

▶ Photography, too, is a form of art. Photos record both the commonplace and the exotic and help us look at events in new ways.

▶ Sculpture is a three-dimensional form made from clay, stone, metal, or other material. Sculptures can be large, like the Statue of Liberty. Some are realistic. Others have no form you can recognize.

▶ Contemporary artists today often use computers and video screens to create art. Some video art uses 20 or 30 video screens that show different colors or images to create one big work of art.

# ART ALL-STARS

Check out these famous works of art.

## *Lascaux* (13,000-15,000 B.C.)

Lascaux is a cave in France. It contains some of the earliest known cave art. The cave was discovered in 1940 by four teenagers. The images found on the cave walls consist of handprints and animals such as bison, deer, horses, and cattle. It is believed that the paintings may have been part of a ritual to help make a successful hunt.

## VINCENT VAN GOGH (1853–1890)
### *Starry Night* (1889)

Van Gogh was a Dutch-born painter who lived in France for many years. With his masterpiece *Starry Night*, the Expressionist movement was born. Expressionism stresses the emotion and inner vision of the artist, instead of depicting the subject matter as it appears. This is done through distorted lines and shapes and the use of intense color. *Starry Night* shows a night sky filled with exploding stars.

## GEORGIA O'KEEFFE (1887–1986)
### *Poppy* (1927)

O'Keeffe is considered one of the great American artists of the 20th century. Her paintings and drawings of her beloved New Mexico show the stark beauty of its mesas and sun-drenched landscape. But she is perhaps best known for her lush still lifes of flowers. In *Poppy*, a single bloom fills the canvas, so that the viewer sees both a flower and the abstract colors which form its parts.

## AUGUSTE RODIN (1840-1917)
### *The Thinker* (1902)

Rodin modeled his sculptures in clay and often cast them in bronze. *The Thinker* is a sculpture of a seated man with his head propped on his fist. He appears deep in thought. *The Thinker* is believed to be based on the Italian poet Dante. It has become a symbol for philosophy and intellectual activity. As a result of its fame, the sculpture has been used as the basis for a joke many times. This began in Rodin's lifetime.

# COLOR WHEEL

This color wheel shows how colors are related to each other.

**Primary colors** The most basic colors are **RED**, **YELLOW**, and **BLUE**. They're called primary because you can't get them by mixing any other colors. In fact, the other colors are made by mixing red, blue, or yellow. Arrows on this wheel show the primary colors.

**Secondary colors** ORANGE, **GREEN**, and **VIOLET** are the secondary colors. They are made by mixing two primary colors. You make orange by mixing yellow and red, or green by mixing yellow and blue. On the color wheel, GREEN appears between **BLUE** and YELLOW.

**Tertiary colors** When you mix a primary and a secondary color, you get a tertiary, or intermediate, color. **BLUE-GREEN** and YELLOW-GREEN are intermediate colors.

## More Color Terms

**VALUES** The lightness or darkness of a color is its value. Tints are light values made by mixing a color with white. **PINK** is a tint of **RED**. Shades are dark values made by mixing a color with black. **MAROON** is a shade of **RED**.

### COMPLEMENTARY COLORS

are contrasting colors that please the eye when used together. These colors appear opposite each other on the wheel and don't have any colors in common. **RED** is a complement to **GREEN**, which is made by mixing YELLOW and **BLUE**.

### COOL COLORS

are mostly **GREEN**, **BLUE**, and **PURPLE**. They make you think of cool things like water and can even make you feel cooler.

### WARM COLORS

are mostly **RED**, **ORANGE**, and YELLOW. They suggest heat and can actually make you feel warmer.

### ANALOGOUS COLORS

The colors next to each other on the wheel are from the same "family." **BLUE**, **BLUE-GREEN**, and **GREEN** all have **BLUE** in them and are analogous colors.

# ART: PASS-AROUND PICTURE
## PROJECT

This artistic game was invented by a group called the Surrealists in 1925 and is often called Exquisite Corpse. Three artists take turns drawing on a sheet of paper, folding it to conceal their work, and then passing it to the next player for a further contribution.

**Materials:** *Paper and crayons, colored pencils, or markers*

### Step 1: Fold the paper into thirds.

Fold a blank sheet of paper into thirds, as shown at right, then unfold it.

### Step 2: Set up the order of artists.

Find two friends and assign numbers to yourselves: 1, 2, and 3. Artist #1 will draw in the top section of the paper, Artist #2 will draw in the middle section, and Artist #3 will draw in the bottom section. Each artist will draw different parts of a body:

Top section (Artist #1) - Head, neck, and shoulders

Middle section (Artist #2) - Body and arms

Bottom section (Artist #3) - Legs and feet

You can draw any kind of creature you want, as long as you draw your assigned body parts. It can be real or unreal, plant, human, monster, or animal.

### Step 3: Pass around the drawing.

Each artist should sit with his or her back to the other artists while drawing. Artist #1 begins by drawing the creature's head, neck, and shoulders in the top section of the paper. Then Artist #1 folds the top section back so that only the middle and bottom sections are visible, and passes the paper to Artist #2. After Artist #2 draws in the middle section of the paper, he or she folds the middle section back so that only the bottom section is visible, then passes the paper to Artist #3. Artist #3 finishes the picture by drawing the creature's legs and feet in the bottom section.

### Step 4: Color in the drawing.

Unfold the paper and look at your drawing. Pass your paper from artist to artist and color the section that you have drawn with colored pencils, crayons, or markers. Hang your art on the wall and enjoy!

# Birthdays

What is the birthstone for December? ➡ page 37

*Martin Luther King, Jr.*

*Cesar Chavez*

## JANUARY
**Birthstone: Garnet**

1 J.D. Salinger, author, 1919
2 Kate Bosworth, actress, 1983
3 Eli Manning, football player, 1981
4 Isaac Newton, physicist/mathematician, 1643
5 Alvin Ailey, choreographer, 1931
6 Early Wynn, baseball player, 1920
7 Liam Aiken, actor, 1990
8 Stephen Hawking, physicist, 1942
9 Dave Matthews, musician, 1967
10 Jake Delhomme, football player, 1975
11 Amanda Peet, actress, 1972
12 Christiane Amanpour, journalist, 1958
13 Orlando Bloom, actor, 1977
14 Dave Grohl, musician, 1969
15 Rev. Martin Luther King Jr., civil rights leader, 1929
16 Sade, singer, 1959
17 Jim Carrey, actor, 1962
18 Mark Messier, hockey player, 1961
19 Edgar Allan Poe, writer, 1809
20 Buzz Aldrin, astronaut, 1930
21 Geena Davis, actress, 1956
22 Sir Francis Bacon, philosopher, 1561
23 John Hancock, revolutionary leader, 1737
24 Mischa Barton, actress, 1986
25 Alicia Keys, singer, 1981
26 Wayne Gretzky, hockey player, 1961
27 Wolfgang Amadeus Mozart, composer, 1756
28 Elijah Wood, actor, 1981
29 Heather Graham, actress, 1970
30 Christian Bale, actor, 1974
31 Justin Timberlake, singer, 1981

## FEBRUARY
**Birthstone: Amethyst**

1 Langston Hughes, poet, 1902
2 Bob Marley, singer, 1945
3 Elizabeth Blackwell, first woman physician, 1821
4 Rosa Parks, civil rights activist, 1913
5 Sara Evans, singer, 1971
6 Ronald Reagan, 40th president, 1911
7 Frederick Douglass, abolitionist, 1817
8 Ted Koppel, journalist, 1940
9 Travis Tritt, singer, 1963
10 Emma Roberts, actress, 1991
11 Jennifer Aniston, actress, 1969
12 Abraham Lincoln, U.S. President, 1809
13 Grant Wood, artist, 1891
14 Drew Bledsoe, football player, 1972
15 Matt Groening, cartoonist, 1954
16 Jerome Bettis, football player, 1972
17 Chaim Potok, novelist, 1929
18 Molly Ringwald, actress, 1968
19 Haylie Duff, singer/actress, 1985
20 Ansel Adams, photographer, 1902
21 Jennifer Love Hewitt, actress, 1979
22 Edna St. Vincent Millay, poet, 1892
23 Dakota Fanning, actress, 1994
24 Steve Jobs, computer innovator, 1955
25 Sean Astin, actor, 1971
26 Marshall Faulk, football player, 1973
27 Josh Groban, singer, 1981
28 Lemony Snicket (Daniel Handler), author, 1970
29 Ja Rule, rapper, 1976

*Dakota Fanning*

## MARCH
**Birthstone: Aquamarine**

1 Frederic Chopin, composer, 1810
2 Dr. Seuss, author, 1904
3 Jessica Biel, actress, 1982
4 Landon Donovan, soccer player, 1982
5 Jake Lloyd, actor, 1989
6 D.L. Hughley, actor/comedian, 1964
7 Laura Prepon, actress, 1980
8 Marcia Newby, gymnast, 1988
9 Bow Wow, actor/rapper, 1987
10 Carrie Underwood, singer, 1983
11 Benji and Joel Madden, musicians, 1979
12 Edward Albee, playwright, 1928
13 Percival Lowell, astronomer, 1855
14 Albert Einstein, physicist/Nobel laureate, 1879
15 Ruth Bader Ginsburg, U.S. Supreme Court justice, 1933
16 Lauren Graham, actress, 1967
17 Mia Hamm, soccer player, 1972
18 Queen Latifah, rapper, actress, 1970
19 Jason LaRue, baseball player, 1974
20 Spike Lee, filmmaker, 1957
21 Matthew Broderick, actor, 1962
22 Reese Witherspoon, actress, 1976
23 Jason Kidd, basketball player, 1973
24 Peyton Manning, football player, 1976
25 Sheryl Swoopes, basketball player, 1971
26 Keira Knightley, actress, 1985
27 Mariah Carey, singer, 1970
28 Vince Vaughn, actor, 1970
29 Sam Walton, Wal-Mart founder, 1918
30 Vincent Van Gogh, artist, 1853
31 Cesar Chavez, labor leader, 1927

## APRIL
**Birthstone: Diamond**

1 Phil Niekro, baseball player, 1939
2 Hans Christian Andersen, author, 1805
3 Amanda Bynes, actress, 1986
4 Heath Ledger, actor, 1979
5 Booker T. Washington, educator, 1856
6 Zach Braff, actor, 1975
7 Jackie Chan, actor, 1954
8 Kirsten Storms, actress, 1984
9 Jesse McCartney, actor/singer, 1987
10 John Madden, sportscaster, 1936
11 Jason Varitek, baseball player, 1972
12 Beverly Cleary, author, 1916
13 Thomas Jefferson, 3rd president, 1743
14 Abigail Breslin, actress, 1996
15 Emma Watson, actress, 1990
16 Kareem Abdul-Jabbar, basketball player, 1947
17 Jennifer Garner, actress, 1972
18 Alia Shawkat, actress, 1989
19 Kate Hudson, actress, 1979
20 Tito Puente, musician, 1923
21 Queen Elizabeth II, British monarch, 1926
22 Robert J. Oppenheimer, physicist, 1904
23 Andruw Jones, baseball player, 1977
24 Kelly Clarkson, singer, 1982
25 Jason Lee, actor, 1970
26 Kane, WWE wrestler, 1967
27 Samuel Morse, inventor, 1791
28 Harper Lee, author, 1926
29 Uma Thurman, actress, 1970
30 Kirsten Dunst, actress, 1982

***Sally Ride***

## MAY
**Birthstone: Emerald**

1 Tim McGraw, musician, 1967
2 Dwayne "The Rock" Johnson, actor/wrestler, 1972
3 Sugar Ray Robinson, boxer, 1921
4 Dawn Staley, basketball player, 1970
5 Brian Williams, journalist, 1959
6 Martin Brodeur, hockey player, 1972
7 Johannes Brahms, composer, 1833
8 Enrique Iglesias, singer, 1975
9 Rosario Dawson, actress, 1979
10 Bono, musician/activist, 1960
11 Salvador Dali, artist, 1904
12 Tony Hawk, skateboarder, 1968
13 Stevie Wonder, singer, 1950
14 Miranda Cosgrove, actress, 1993
15 L. Frank Baum, author, 1856
16 Janet Jackson, singer, 1966
17 Sugar Ray Leonard, boxer, 1956
18 Tina Fey, actress/comedian, 1970
19 Malcolm X, militant civil rights activist, 1925
20 Stan Mikita, hockey player, 1940
21 John Muir, naturalist, 1838
22 Sir Arthur Conan Doyle, author, 1859
23 Margaret Wise Brown, author, 1910
24 Tracy McGrady, basketball player, 1979
25 Mike Myers, actor, 1963
26 Sally Ride, astronaut, 1951
27 André 3000, musician, 1975
28 Jim Thorpe, Olympic champion, 1888
29 Andre Agassi, tennis champion, 1970
30 Manny Ramirez, baseball player, 1972
31 Walt Whitman, poet, 1819

## JUNE
**Birthstone: Pearl**

1 Justine Henin-Hardenne, tennis player, 1982
2 Freddy Adu, soccer player, 1989
3 Carl Everett, baseball player, 1971
4 Angelina Jolie, actress, 1975
5 Richard Scarry, author/illustrator, 1919
6 Cynthia Rylant, author, 1954
7 Michael Cera, actor, 1988
8 Kanye West, musician, 1977
9 Natalie Portman, actress, 1981
10 Maurice Sendak, author/illustrator, 1928
11 Diana Taurasi, basketball player, 1982
12 Anne Frank, diary writer, 1929
13 William Butler Yeats, poet, 1865
14 Harriet Beecher Stowe, author, 1811
15 Neil Patrick Harris, actor, 1973
16 Kerry Wood, baseball player, 1977
17 Venus Williams, tennis player, 1980
18 Sir Paul McCartney, musician, 1942
19 Paula Abdul, singer/TV personality, 1962
20 Nicole Kidman, actress, 1967
21 Prince William of Great Britain, 1982
22 Donald Faison, actor, 1974
23 Clarence Thomas, U.S. Supreme Court justice, 1948
24 Solange Knowles, singer/actress, 1986
25 Sonia Sotomayor, U.S. Supreme Court justice, 1954
26 Babe Didrikson Zaharias, Olympic champion, 1914
27 Tobey Maguire, actor, 1975
28 John Elway, football player, 1960
29 Theo Fleury, hockey player, 1968
30 Michael Phelps, Olympic champion, 1985

***Michael Phelps***

***Booker T. Washington***

**Missy Elliott**

## AUGUST
**Birthstone: Peridot**

1 Francis Scott Key, composer/lawyer, 1779
2 Isabel Allende, writer, 1942
3 Tom Brady, football player, 1977
4 Barack Obama, 44th U.S. president, 1961
5 Neil Armstrong, astronaut, 1930
6 Andy Warhol, artist, 1928
7 Charlize Theron, actress, 1975
8 Roger Federer, tennis player, 1981
9 Eric Bana, actor, 1968
10 Antonio Banderas, actor, 1960
11 Stephen Wozniak, computer pioneer, 1950
12 Ann M. Martin, author, 1955
13 Alfred Hitchcock, filmmaker, 1899
14 Halle Berry, actress, 1966
15 Ben Affleck, actor, 1972
16 Steve Carell, actor, 1963
17 Robert De Niro, actor, 1943
18 Meriwether Lewis, explorer, 1774
19 Bill Clinton, 42nd president, 1946
20 Fred Durst, musician, 1970
21 Stephen Hillenburg, SpongeBob creator, 1961
22 Bill Parcells, football coach, 1941
23 Julian Casablancas, singer, 1978
24 Rupert Grint, actor, 1988
25 Marvin Harrison, football player, 1972
26 Branford Marsalis, musician, 1960
27 Alexa Vega, actress, 1988
28 Jack Black, actor, 1969
29 LeAnn Rimes, country singer, 1982
30 Andy Roddick, tennis player, 1982
31 Chris Tucker, actor, 1972

**Charlie Stewart**

## SEPTEMBER
**Birthstone: Sapphire**

1 Conway Twitty, country singer, 1933
2 Keanu Reeves, actor, 1964
3 Shaun White, Olympic snowboarder, 1986
4 Beyoncé Knowles, singer/actress, 1981
5 Michael Keaton, actor, 1951
6 Mark Chesnutt, singer, 1963
7 Shannon Elizabeth, actress, 1973
8 Latrell Sprewell, basketball player, 1970
9 Charlie Stewart, actor, 1993
10 Bill O'Reilly, TV personality, 1949
11 Ludacris, rapper, 1977
12 Benjamin McKenzie, actor, 1978
13 Roald Dahl, author, 1916
14 Nas, rapper, 1973
15 Prince Harry of Great Britain, 1984
16 Alexis Bledel, actress, 1981
17 Rasheed Wallace, basketball player, 1974
18 Lance Armstrong, cyclist, 1971
19 Ryan Dusick, musician, 1977
20 Red Auerbach, basketball coach, 1917
21 Hiram Revels, first black U.S. senator, 1822
22 Tom Felton, actor, 1987
23 Ray Charles, musician, 1930
24 Paul Hamm, gymnast, 1982
25 Will Smith, actor/rapper, 1968
26 Serena Williams, tennis player, 1981
27 Avril Lavigne, singer, 1984
28 Hilary Duff, actress/singer, 1987
29 Kevin Durant, basketball player, 1988
30 Elie Wiesel, author, 1928

## JULY
**Birthstone: Ruby**

1 Missy Elliott, rapper, 1971
2 Lindsay Lohan, actress, 1986
3 Tom Cruise, actor, 1962
4 Neil Simon, playwright, 1927
5 P.T. Barnum, showman/circus founder, 1810
6 George W. Bush, 43rd president, 1946
7 Michelle Kwan, figure skater, 1980
8 John D. Rockefeller, industrialist, 1839
9 Tom Hanks, actor, 1956
10 Jessica Simpson, singer, 1980
11 E.B. White, author, 1899
12 Topher Grace, actor, 1978
13 Harrison Ford, actor, 1942
14 Matthew Fox, actor, 1966
15 Rembrandt van Rijn, artist, 1606
16 Will Farrell, actor, 1967
17 Donald Sutherland, actor, 1935
18 Kristin Bell, actress, 1980
19 Edgar Degas, artist, 1834
20 Sir Edmund Hillary, Everest climber, 1919
21 Josh Hartnett, actor, 1978
22 Selena Gomez, actress, 1992
23 Daniel Radcliffe, actor, 1989
24 Jennifer Lopez, actress/singer, 1969
25 Ray Billingsley, cartoonist, 1957
26 Kate Beckinsale, actress, 1973
27 Alex Rodriguez, baseball player, 1975
28 Beatrix Potter, author, 1866
29 Allison Mack, actress, 1982
30 Jaime Pressley, actress, 1977
31 J.K. Rowling, author, 1965

**Francis Scott Key**

## OCTOBER
**Birthstone: Opal**

1 William Boeing, founder of Boeing Company, 1881
2 Mohandas Gandhi, activist, 1869
3 Ashlee Simpson, singer, 1984
4 Rachael Leigh Cook, actress, 1979
5 Parminder Nagra, actress, 1975
6 Elisabeth Shue, actress, 1963
7 Simon Cowell, television personality, 1959
8 R. L. Stine, author, 1943
9 Brandon Routh, actor, 1979
10 Maya Lin, sculptor and architect, 1960
11 Michelle Trachtenberg, actress, 1985
12 Hugh Jackman, actor, 1968
13 Ashanti, singer, 1980
14 Usher, singer, 1978
15 Elena Dementieva, tennis player, 1981
16 John Mayer, musician, 1977
17 Mae Jemison, astronaut, 1956
18 Wynton Marsalis, musician, 1961
19 Ty Pennington, TV personality, 1965
20 Snoop Dogg, rapper/actor, 1971
21 Dizzy Gillespie, trumpet player, 1917
22 Ichiro Suzuki, baseball player, 1973
23 Tiffeny Milbrett, soccer player, 1972
24 Kevin Kline, actor, 1947
25 Ciara, singer, 1985
26 Jon Heder, actor, 1977
27 Teddy Roosevelt, 26th president, 1858
28 Bill Gates, computer pioneer, 1955
29 Winona Ryder, actress, 1971
30 John Adams, 2nd president of the United States, 1735
31 Juliette Gordon Low, Girl Scouts' founder, 1860

*Katherine Heigl*

## NOVEMBER
**Birthstone: Topaz**

1 Bo Bice, singer, 1975
2 Nelly, rapper, 1974
3 Walker Evans, photographer, 1903
4 Sean Combs (Puff Daddy), rapper, 1969
5 Johnny Damon, baseball player, 1973
6 John Philip Sousa, composer, 1854
7 Marie Curie, scientist/Nobel laureate, 1867
8 Parker Posey, actress, 1968
9 Nick Lachey, singer, 1973
10 Brittany Murphy, actress, 1977
11 Leonardo DiCaprio, actor, 1974
12 Ryan Gosling, actor, 1980
13 Rachel Bilson, actress, 1981
14 Condoleezza Rice, American statesperson, 1954
15 Zena Grey, actress, 1988
16 Marg Helgenberger, actress, 1958
17 Reggie Wayne, football player, 1978
18 Owen Wilson, actor, 1968
19 Larry Johnson, football player, 1979
20 Dominque Dawes, Olympic gymnast, 1976
21 Jena Malone, actress, 1984
22 Jamie Lee Curtis, actress, 1958
23 Billy the Kid (William Bonney), outlaw, 1859
24 Katherine Heigl, actress, 1978
25 Christina Applegate, actress, 1971
26 Charles Schulz, cartoonist, 1912
27 Bill Nye, "The Science Guy," 1955
28 Jon Stewart, TV host, 1962
29 Louisa May Alcott, author, 1832
30 Mark Twain, author, 1835

## DECEMBER
**Birthstone: Turquoise**

1 Richard Pryor, actor, 1940
2 Lucy Liu, actress, 1967
3 Brendan Fraser, actor, 1967
4 Tyra Banks, model/TV personality, 1973
5 Cliff Floyd, baseball player, 1972
6 Otto Graham, football player/coach, 1921
7 Aaron Carter, actor/singer, 1987
8 AnnaSophia Robb, actress, 1993
9 Felicity Huffman, actress, 1962
10 Raven, actress, 1985
11 Mos Def, actor/rapper, 1973
12 Edvard Munch, artist, 1863
13 Jamie Foxx, actor, 1967
14 Vanessa Hudgens, actress and singer, 1988
15 Adam Brody, actor, 1979
16 Ludwig van Beethoven, composer, 1770
17 Sean Patrick Thomas, actor, 1970
18 Brad Pitt, actor, 1963
19 Jake Gyllenhaal, actor, 1980
20 Rich Gannon, football player, 1965
21 Ray Romano, actor/comedian, 1957
22 Diane Sawyer, journalist, 1945
23 Alge Crumpler, football player, 1977
24 Ryan Seacrest, DJ/TV personality, 1974
25 Clara Barton, American Red Cross founder, 1821
26 Marcelo Rios, tennis player, 1975
27 Carson Palmer, football player, 1979
28 Denzel Washington, actor, 1954
29 Jude Law, actor, 1972
30 LeBron James, basketball player, 1984
31 Val Kilmer, actor, 1959

*Clara Barton*

*Maya Lin*

# Talkin' 'Bout Your Generation

**D**o you ever feel like your parents don't really get your slang or the clothes and music you like? Ever feel like you don't really get the stuff they like either? Maybe it's because you're from different generations.

A generation usually spans about 20 years. Not everyone agrees on which years each generation covers, but the labels can be helpful in describing the shared experiences and popular culture of a group of the population.

## iGeneration (born about 2001 and up)

- Also known as "Generation Z" or "the Internet Generation"
- First generation to grow up with a lifelong use of communications technology such as the Internet, cell phones, and digital cameras
- First Americans to grow up with widespread equality between sexes at work and home

## Generation Y (born about 1980-2000)

- Also known as "Millennials" or "Echo Boomers"
- About 27.8% of the U.S. population, or around 82 million people in 2005
- First generation to grow up fluent in—and some say too reliant on—digital technology
- Seen as confident and cooperative, eager to "fix" the world by solving its problems

## Generation X (born about 1965-79)

- About 20.6% of the U.S. population, or around 61 million people in 2005
- Born during the so-called "Baby Bust," a drop in birthrates after the Baby Boom
- The best-educated generation in U.S. history, with women educated in equal numbers to men.
- Independent-minded and obsessed with pop culture

## Baby Boomers (born about 1946-64)

- About 27.9% of the population, or around 83 million people in 2005
- The "Baby Boom" began right after World War II, as millions of soldiers returned home
- Witnessed the civil rights and women's rights movements, as well as the Vietnam War
- Seen as idealistic and free-spirited, used to getting what they want, and denying they are aging.

## MOST POPULAR NAMES

| Boys (born 1900) | Girls (born 1900) | Boys (born 2000) | Girls (born 2000) |
|---|---|---|---|
| 1. John | 1. Mary | 1. Jacob | 1. Emily |
| 2. William | 2. Helen | 2. Michael | 2. Hannah |
| 3. James | 3. Anna | 3. Matthew | 3. Madison |
| 4. George | 4. Margaret | 4. Joshua | 4. Ashley |
| 5. Charles | 5. Ruth | 5. Christopher | 5. Sarah |

# GENEALOGY TRACING YOUR FAMILY TREE

**Genealogy is the study of one's family, tracing back through generations of relatives. The first place to start in your family genealogy is with yourself. Write down the answers to the following questions:**

- What is your full name (include middle name)?
- When and where were you born (town, city, state, country)?

**Next, write down the name, birth date, and place of birth for each of your parents (ask them or the adult who takes care of you). Then, interview your grandparents and other relatives. Get their birthdates and places of birth as well. If any of these people have died, record their date of death. You might also ask about interesting events in their lives.**

Now, you have the beginnings of a family tree. Fill out as much of this chart as you can.

**PARENT**
Name _____
Birth _____
Death _____

**ME**
Your
Name _____
Birth _____

**PARENT**
Name _____
Birth _____
Death _____

**GRANDPARENT**
Name _____
Birth _____
Death _____

**GRANDPARENT**
Name _____
Birth _____
Death _____

**GRANDPARENT**
Name _____
Birth _____
Death _____

**GRANDPARENT**
Name _____
Birth _____
Death _____

To find out where you can get official copies of "vital records" for a relative such as birth, death, and marriage certificates for a particular state, check the website of the U.S. National Center for Health Statistics (www.cdc.gov/nchs). Baptism, marriage, and burial records can often be found at family churches. Also, many libraries have U.S. Census records for 1790-1930. Make sure to keep copies of the documents you find.

## Additional Sources

A good book for children to read is *Climbing Your Family Tree: Online and Off-Line Genealogy for Kids*, by Ira Wolfman. (*www.workman.com/familytree*)

The Church of Jesus Christ of Latter Day Saints (the Mormons) has Family History Centers throughout the world. There you can access their databases and programs, and possibly find members of your family.

More than 22 million immigrants passed through Ellis Island and the Port of New York as they entered the United States. The immigrants came by ship, which recorded each one's name on the ship's **manifest**, or passenger list. Now you can search the lists online at the Ellis Island website. (*http://www.ellisisland.org/*)

▲ **Old family photos are a great way to explore your family history.**

# Books

Where were paper and printing invented? ➡ page 44

# BOOK AWARDS, 2009

## Newbery Medal
For the author of the best children's book
**2009 winner:** *The Graveyard Book* by Neil Gaiman

## Michael L. Printz Award
For excellence in literature written for young adults
**2009 winner:** *Jellicoe Road* by Melina Marchetta

## Caldecott Medal
For the artist of the best children's picture book
**2009 winner:** *The House in the Night* by Susan Marie Swanson; pictures by Beth Krommes

## Coretta Scott King Award
For artists and authors whose works encourage expression of the African American experience

**2009 winners:**
**Author Award:** *We Are the Ship: The Story of Negro League Baseball* by Kadir Nelson
**Illustrator Award:** *The Blacker the Berry* Illustrated by Floyd Cooper

# NEW BOOK SPOTLIGHT

*Bird* (2009), by Zetta Elliott, tells how a love of art helps a young boy cope with two painful losses—those of his older brother and his grandfather. An elderly friend and the boy's own strength help him find the courage to face the future.

# Famous Authors FOR KIDS

| Author | Try the Book |
|---|---|
| **E.L. Konigsburg** (1930- ), or Elaine Lobl Konigsburg, taught science before becoming an author. She has twice received the Newbery Medal, for *The View From Saturday* and *From the Mixed-Up Files of Mrs. Basil E. Frankweiler*, which she also illustrated. In fact, her drawings of that book's two main characters are based upon her daughter and younger son. | ***From the Mixed-Up Files of Mrs. Basil E. Frankweiler*** |
|  **C.S. Lewis** (1898-1963), born Clive Staples Lewis, fought in World War I and later taught at Oxford University. The British author belonged to a literary group called The Inklings, whose members included J. R. R. Tolkien, author of *The Lord of the Rings*. | ***The Lion, the Witch, and the Wardrobe*** (the first book in the Narnia series) |
| **Christopher Paolini** (1983- ) began writing *Eragon* when he was 15. He read many fantasy and science fiction books and wanted to see if he could write one himself. By the time he was 20, *Eragon* was a bestseller. He and his younger sister Angela—who inspired the character of "Angela the herbalist" in his books—were home-schooled by their parents. | ***Eragon*** (the first book in the *Inheritance* series) |
|  **Gary Paulsen** (1939- ) worked a variety of jobs—including as an engineer, construction worker, and truck driver—before realizing he wanted to be a writer. His dedication to writing has led him to produce more than 175 books for children and adults. Three of his books have received the Newbery Honor award. In addition to writing, Paulsen trains dogs for the Iditarod sled race in Alaska, rides horses, and sails. | ***The Brian Saga: Hatchet, The River, Brian's Winter,*** and ***Brian's Return*** |
| **J.K. Rowling** (1965- ), whose initials stand for Joanne Kathleen, is the British author of the world-famous Harry Potter series. The idea for Harry Potter came to her suddenly during a train trip. She spent the next five years making an outline of the story and writing it out before *Harry Potter and the Sorcerer's Stone* was published. | ***Harry Potter and the Sorcerer's Stone*** (first book in the Harry Potter series) |
| **E.B. White** (1899-1985) ("E. B." stands for Elwyn Brooks) worked as a reporter and then as an essay writer for a magazine. He created the character of Stuart Little after he had a dream about a mouse-like boy. He started telling stories about Stuart to his many nephews and nieces. Another book, *Charlotte's Web*, was inspired by the animals on his farm. | ***The Trumpet of the Swan*** |

# BOOKS TO READ

There are two major types of literature: fiction and nonfiction. A **fiction** book includes people, places, and events that might be inspired by reality but are mainly from an author's imagination. **Nonfiction** is about real things that actually happened. Nonfiction may be about a person's life, an event in history, or how something works.

Within these two groups there are smaller subgroups called genres (ZHAN-ruz).

## Fiction

### Mysteries, Thrillers, and Horror

These adventure stories will keep you up late, as you follow a main character who must uncover a secret.

**Try These** *Bunnicula*, by Deborah and James Howe; *The House With a Clock in Its Walls*, by John Bellairs

### Fantasy and Science Fiction

This genre is one of the most popular for teen readers. You've heard of the Harry Potter books, but there are thousands of books for kids and teens in this genre.

**Try These** *The Hobbit*, by J.R.R. Tolkien; *The Little Prince*, by Antoine de Saint-Exupery

### Realistic Fiction

Do you like stories that might have happened to you? Realistic fiction is about real-life situations that teens and kids deal with every day.

**Try These** *A Tree Grows in Brooklyn*, by Betty Smith; *Tales of a Fourth Grade Nothing*, by Judy Blume

### Historical Fiction

If you think history is just about facts, this is the genre for you. Authors take exciting historical events and put the most interesting fictional characters right in the middle of them.

**Try These** *My Brother Sam Is Dead*, by James Lincoln Collier and Christopher Collier; *Sounder*, by William H. Armstrong

## Myths and Legends

These made-up stories go way back. Some are from nineteenth-century America, others are from ancient Greece and Africa.

**Try These** *The People Could Fly: American Black Folktales*, told by Virginia Hamilton

## Graphic Novels, Comics, and Manga

Check out these adventure series that use drawings and text to tell complicated adventure stories.

**Try These** *Robot Dreams*, by Sara Varon; *Diary of a Wimpy Kid*, by Jeff Kinney

# Nonfiction

## Biographies, Autobiographies, and Memoirs

Do you like reading all about the details of a real person's life? This genre is for you.

**Try These** *The Many Rides of Paul Revere*, by James Cross Giblin; *Lincoln: A Photobiography*, by Russell Freedman

## History

Books in this genre can be about an event, an era, a country, or even a war.

**Try These** *Team Moon: How 400,000 People Landed Apollo 11 on the Moon*, by Catherine Thimmesh

## Reference

Books that supply facts and practical information on one topic or many, including almanacs, atlases, dictionaries, and encyclopedias

**Try This** *The World Almanac for Kids*

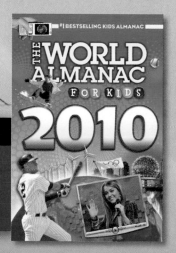

# All About...
# BOOKS

If a Roman emperor wanted to read a book, he had to unroll it. Books were written on long scrolls (kind of like a roll of paper towels) that you unrolled as you went along. This was clumsy, especially if you were looking for a certain passage. Around A.D. 100 the codex was invented. It was made up of a stack of pages stitched together at the side and protected by a cover. The codex was easier to carry around, to store, and to search through. Books we read today look something like a codex.

In the Middle Ages books were made by monks who copied them by hand onto prepared animal skins called parchment. The monks often decorated the pages with beautiful color illustrations called "illuminations." Books were scarce and very expensive, and few people who were not priests or monks could read.

A big change came with the use of paper and printing, which were first invented in China. Paper came into Europe through the Muslim world and was common by the 14th century. Johann Gutenberg of Germany perfected printing in the 1450s. Once books no longer had to be copied by hand and could be printed on paper, they became less expensive and reading became more common.

At first, books were still not easy to make and not cheap. Each letter was on a separate piece of type, and a typesetter had to put each letter into place individually. Once all the letters for the page were in place, they were covered with ink and printed, one page at a time, by hand on a press. By the 19th century, however, steam-powered presses could print out hundreds of pages at a time. Another invention was the linotype machine, which stamped out individual letters and set them up much faster than a typesetter could. Now books had become truly affordable, and the skill of reading was something that everyone was expected to learn. Today, with the use of computers, books can be easily transferred into electronic files, and read as e-books.

## WHO AM I?

I was born in Boston in 1809. My parents died while I was still young, so I was raised by John Allan, a wealthy merchant. I attended college but left after less than a year due to lack of money. I served a few years in the Army before finding work as an editor and book reviewer for various magazines. I soon began publishing short stories and poems. In 1845, I became famous with the publication of my dramatic poem "The Raven." It begins with the lines:

*Once upon a midnight dreary, while I pondered, weak and weary,*
*Over many a quaint and curious volume of forgotten lore,*
*While I nodded, nearly napping, suddenly there came a tapping,*
*As of someone gently rapping, rapping at my chamber door.*
*"'Tis some visitor," I muttered, "tapping at my chamber door;*
*Only this, and nothing more."*

Answer: Edgar Allan Poe

# ACTIVITY: MAKE YOUR OWN BOOK

> **Materials**

Paper:
- Construction paper for the cover
- Lighter paper stock for the inside pages

Stapler

Crayons/Markers

> **Pick a topic:** What are you interested in? Choose to write about something you enjoy. Remember, you're the author    you can write whatever you want, whether it's a short story, a book, or even a cookbook.

> **Choose your audience:** Before you begin to write, think about who will read the book. Are you writing an alphabet book for your 2-year-old cousin? Are you writing a biography of your grandmother? Are you writing a story for people your age?

> **Write the text:** Once you've decided on a topic, organize your thoughts. You can jot down your ideas on a piece of scrap paper. Another way of organizing is making an outline. An outline allows you to highlight your key thoughts and supporting ideas. If you're writing a short story, make a story map—write down your characters, the opening action of the story, the conflict, the climax, and the resolution. When you're done organizing, start writing.

> **Revise the text:** Once you feel done, read over what you wrote. Does it make sense? Is it interesting? Could your audience read it? Would they like it? Don't be afraid to make changes you think would be improvements. This might be a good time to show what you've written to a trusted reader, like a parent or friend. Consider any suggestions, but remember, you're the author. Then, read the text again. Look for grammar errors.

> **Make the book:** Now that you've written the text, you can decide how many words you'd like on each page, and how many pages your book will have. Remember to save the first page as a title page, where you can list your name as the author.

Once you've settled on a number of pages, assemble the book. Use the paper you want for the inside pages. Each sheet of paper will count as four book pages. For example, if you've decided to make a 12-page book, you'll need three pieces of paper.

1. Stack the paper.
2. Fold the stack of paper in half.
3. Take the heavy paper you want to use as a cover and place on the outside of the lighter paper.
4. Staple all the paper together along the crease, where the spine of the book would be.
5. You can also cut the paper to make your book smaller.

> **Fill in the pages:** Once you've bound the book, number the pages, and add your text and illustrations.

> **Start reading:** Share your book with others.

# Buildings

Why are the roofs of the Forbidden City yellow? ➡ page 49

## TALLEST BUILDINGS IN THE WORLD

**H**ere are the world's tallest buildings, with the year each was completed. Heights listed here don't include antennas or other outside structures.

◄ **Dubai Tower**
Dubai, United Arab Emirates
(2009 est.; not completed as of Sept.)
Projected height: 160 stories,
2,684 feet

**Taipei 101**
Taipei, Taiwan (2004)
Height: 101 stories, 1,667 feet

**Petronas Towers 1 & 2**
Kuala Lumpur, Malaysia (1998)
Height: each building is
88 stories, 1,483 feet

**Willis Tower**
(formerly Sears Tower)
Chicago, Illinois (1974)
Height: 110 stories, 1,450 feet

**Jin Mao Tower**
Shanghai, China (1999)
Height: 88 stories, 1,381 feet

**Two International
Finance Centre**
Hong Kong, China (2003)
Height: 88 stories, 1,362 feet

## WORLD'S TALLEST WHEN BUILT

**Great Pyramid of Giza, Egypt**
Built c. 2250 B.C. Height: 480 feet

**Cologne Cathedral, Germany**
Built 1248-1880. Height: 515 feet

**Washington Monument, Washington D.C.**
Built 1848-84. Height: 555 feet

**Eiffel Tower, Paris, France**
Built 1887-89. Height: 984 feet

**Chrysler Building, New York, NY**
Built 1930. Height: 1,046 feet

**Empire State Building, New York, NY**
Built 1931. Height: 1,250 feet ►

**Ostankino Tower, Moscow, Russia**
Built 1963-67. Height: 1,771 feet

The Willis Tower, formerly known as the Sears Tower, in Chicago, is the tallest building in the United States. In 2009, the building opened four Sky Ledges to the public. These ledges are actually four glass-enclosed boxes, with glass floors, that project out four feet from the 103rd floor of the building at a height of 1,353 feet above the ground. When you step into the box, you have the impression of floating in the air above the city. The Tower is innovating in other ways, as well. Plans have been announced to make the building nearly self-sufficient in its energy use. Possibilities include the construction of solar panels and windmills on the roof!

# A Short History of Tall Buildings

For most of history, people built tall structures to honor gods, kings, and other powerful leaders, not as places to live. Building tall required lots of wealth and workers. But the biggest challenge was gravity. Each part of a wall had to support everything above it. Building higher required thicker walls at the base. Too many windows would weaken the building. The Great Pyramid required an area equal to 10 football fields and more than 2 million massive stone blocks. The Washington Monument, the last entirely stone structure to reach a record height, has walls 15 feet thick at its base.

By the 1880s, three **key factors in the evolution of tall buildings** were in place:

**1. A NEED FOR SPACE** Crowded cities had less space for building, and land got expensive. To create more space, buildings had to go up instead of out.

**2. BETTER STEEL PRODUCTION** Mass-producing steel meant more of it was available for construction. Long vertical **columns** and horizontal girders could be joined to form a strong cube-like grid that was lighter than a similar one made of stone or brick. Weight was also directed down the columns to a solid **foundation**, usually underground, instead of to walls.

**3. THE ELEVATOR** Tall buildings need elevators! The first elevator, powered by steam, was installed in a New York store in 1857. Electric elevators came along in 1880.

As buildings got taller, a new problem sprang up—**wind**. Too much movement could damage buildings or make the people inside uncomfortable. Some tall buildings, like New York's Citicorp Center, actually have a counter-weight near the top. A computer controls a 400-ton weight, moving it back and forth to lessen the building's sway.

In California and Japan, **earthquakes** are a big problem and special techniques are needed to make tall buildings safer from quakes.

# IT'S NOT ALL ABOUT... TALL!

**W**hen it comes to buildings, the tall ones grab people's attention. But many other buildings are interesting and fun to look at. Here are a few really cool buildings.

## EL TEMPLO DE LA SAGRADA FAMILIA, Barcelona, Spain

Architect Antonio Gaudí proved he had no shortage of imagination when he designed the "Temple of the Holy Family." Work began in 1883, and it is still in progress. This very detailed project has so many carvings and towers yet to be built that it may be many years before it's ever finished.

## THE GLASS HOUSE, New Canaan, Connecticut

When architect Philip Johnson designed his own home in 1949, he created something beautiful and unique. What makes this house special is the structure: it is a steel frame with outside walls made of clear glass. This makes the house totally see-through. (Johnson did enclose the bathroom in brick!) In an interview, Johnson said, "It's the only house in the world where you can watch the sun set and the moon rise at the same time."

## NATIONAL AQUATICS CENTER, Beijing, China

The "Water Cube" was built for the 2008 Olympic Games swimming and diving competitions. It's made to look natural and random, like soap bubbles or plant cells. The walls and roof are made of thousands of steel polygons fitted with inflated Teflon (plastic) bubbles. The bubbles make a greenhouse, capturing solar energy to heat the pools. Rain cleans the bubbles while the roof catches rainwater, which is reused inside. Each bubble has skin as thin as a pen tip but each could hold the weight of a car.

## SYDNEY OPERA HOUSE, Sydney, Australia

Though it looks like a giant sea creature rising out of Sydney Harbor, architect Joern Utzon had the sections of an orange in mind when he designed this building. Finished in 1973, the shells are made of more than 2,000 concrete sections held together by 217 miles of steel cable. The roof cover—bolted on in 4,240 sections—is covered with 1.5 million ceramic tiles.

# HISTORICAL WONDERS

## DOME OF THE ROCK
### Jerusalem, Israel; 687 A.D.

The Dome of the Rock is the oldest Islamic monument still standing. A shrine, it was built over a rock sacred to both Muslims and Jews. Its 25-meter dome is covered with gold. Because the structure is considered the center of the Earth for the Arabs who built it, there are exits leading north, east, south, and west.

## ANGKOR WAT
### Angkor, Cambodia; c. 1150 A.D.

This massive temple complex covers 400 acres and is surrounded by a big moat. The towers are shaped like lotus flowers. Every surface along its winding corridors is carved with Hindu tales. It's a source of pride for Cambodians, who have placed it on their flag.

## CATHEDRAL NOTRE-DAME DE PARIS
### Paris, France; 1163-1351

"Gothic" might stir up images of ghouls. However gothic architecture was meant to be uplifting, not scary. Instead of using thicker walls to build taller, the cathedral has pointed arches and rib-like supports called flying buttresses on the outside that lean into the walls to prop them up. Those buttresses also allow more space for bigger windows, usually stained glass, including large round "rose" windows. The scary monstrous statues along the rooftop are not Gothic. They're water spouts added in the 1800s.

## FORBIDDEN CITY
### Beijing, China; 1406-1420

This was the exclusive home for emperors of the Ming and Qing dynasties for 492 years. The palace grounds are the world's largest (178 acres). It was "forbidden" because people could not enter without the emperor's permission. The palace itself contains thousands of wooden chambers and great halls that cover 37 acres. Every roof is yellow, the color of Chinese royalty.

# BRIDGES

There are four main bridge designs: beam, arch, truss, and suspension or cable-stayed.

## BEAM

The beam bridge is the most basic kind. A log across a stream is a simple style of beam bridge. Highway bridges are often beam bridges. The span of a beam bridge, or the length of the bridge without any support under it, needs to be fairly short. Long beam bridges need many supporting poles, called piers.

## ARCH

You can easily recognize an arch bridge, because it has arches holding it up from the bottom. The columns that support the arches are called abutments. Arch bridges were invented by the ancient Greeks.

## TRUSS

The truss bridge uses mainly steel beams, connected in triangles to increase strength and span greater distances.

## SUSPENSION

On suspension bridges, the roadway hangs from smaller cables attached to a pair of huge cables running over two massive towers. The ends of the giant cables are anchored firmly into solid rock or huge concrete blocks at each end of the bridge. The weight of the roadway is transferred through the cables to the anchors. On a cable-stayed bridge, the cables are attached directly from the towers (pylons) to the deck.

## FAMOUS SHAPES PUZZLE

Can you match the names of the famous structures to their silhouettes?

1. Eiffel Tower
2. The Great Sphinx
3. Transamerica Pyramid Building
4. Stonehenge
5. Space Needle

ANSWERS ON PAGES 334-336.

# PARTS OF A SUSPENSION BRIDGE

**Anchorage** Main cables are attached here, adding strength and stability

**Deck** Surface of the bridge

**Main cable** Primary load-bearing cables, secured by anchorages

**Pier** Supports for pylons

**Pylon** Tower supports that hold up cables and decks

**Suspender cable** Vertical cables that hold up the deck

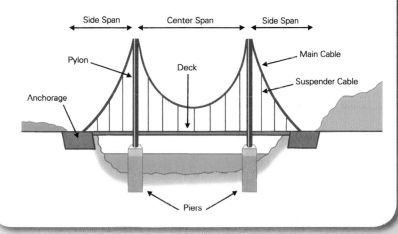

## DAM FACTS

Dams are built to control the flow of rivers. They can provide water for drinking or farming, prevent flooding, and create electricity. The first dams were embankment dams built thousands of years ago out of walls of rocks and dirt to prevent flooding or to make lakes called reservoirs for irrigation. Embankment dams are still made but require a lot of land. To save space, most dams are now made of concrete. They sometimes use the same properties as bridges, like abutments, to help hold back water. "Hydroelectric" dams are used to generate electricity by channeling the force of rivers and waterfalls into tunnels in the dam to move enormous turbines (wheel-shaped engines).

# Calendar

Whom do we honor on Presidents' Day? ➡ page 53

## CALENDAR BASICS

Holidays and calendars go hand in hand. Using a calendar, you can see what day of the week it is and look for the next special day. Calendars divide time into days, weeks, months, and years. According to our calendar, also known as the Gregorian calendar, a year is the time it takes for one revolution of Earth around the Sun: 365¼ days. To make things easier, we just add an extra day, February 29, in "leap years," which happen every 4 years.

## THE NAMES OF THE MONTHS

| | |
|---|---|
| January | named for the Roman god Janus, guardian of gates (often shown with two faces, looking backward and forward) |
| February | named for Februalia, a Roman time of sacrifice |
| March | named for Mars, the Roman god of war (the end of winter meant fighting could begin again) |
| April | "aperire," Latin for "to open," as in flower buds |
| May | named for Maia, the goddess of plant growth |
| June | "Junius," the Latin word for the goddess Juno |
| July | named after the Roman ruler Julius Caesar |
| August | named for Augustus, the first Roman emperor |
| September | "septem," Latin for seven (the Roman year began in March) |
| October | "octo," the Latin word for eight |
| November | "novem," the Latin word for nine |
| December | "decem," the Latin word for ten |

## Other Calendars

The **Gregorian calendar** is used by the U.S. and much of the rest of the world. But some nations and religions use other calendars.

**Islamic Calendar** The Islamic calendar is used by Muslim people around the world. Twelve lunar months, each beginning with the new moon, make up the year. The year is 354 days long (355 days in leap years). Al-Hijra/Muharram (Islamic New Year) in Islamic year 1432 will fall on December 7, 2010.

**Jewish Calendar** The Jewish calendar has months of 29 and 30 days, and its years are either 12 or 13 months long. It is a lunar-solar calendar, which means its months are lunar, but its years adjust to the movement of the Earth around the Sun. It is the official calendar in Israel and is used as a religious calendar by Jewish people worldwide. Rosh Hashanah (New Year) in the year 5771 begins at sundown on September 8, 2010 on the Gregorian calendar.

**Chinese Calendar** The Chinese calendar is a lunar-solar calendar that runs on a 60-year cycle. Within the cycle, years are given one of twelve animal designations: Rat, Ox, Tiger, Rabbit, Dragon, Snake, Horse, Sheep, Monkey, Rooster, Dog, and Pig. On February 14, 2010, the Year of the Tiger starts.

# FORMAL HOLIDAYS

There are no official holidays for the entire U.S. But there are federal holidays, when the offices of the federal government are closed. Many other offices and most banks and schools in the 50 states are closed on these days. There are also other holidays that may not be an occasion for a day off from school but are enthusiastically celebrated. Holidays marked with a * are federal holidays.

## JANUARY 2010

January is National Oatmeal Month and National Skating Month. Learn how to ice skate—for free—at events at participating ice rinks nationwide. Grab a bowl of oatmeal beforehand for a nutritious way to stay warm from the inside out.

### * January 1: New Year's Day
Until the year 1753, New Year's Day was celebrated on March 25 every year. When the Gregorian calendar was adopted in 1582, the date was switched to Jan. 1.

### * January 18: Martin Luther King Day
Martin Luther King Jr., one of the civil rights movement's best-known leaders, was actually born on Jan. 15. Now, Martin Luther King Day is celebrated on the third Monday of January every year, in all 50 states.

## FEBRUARY 2010

February is Black History Month and American Heart Month. Learn about the lives of some important African Americans that you may not have studied in school. See if your school is sponsoring a "Jump Rope for Heart" event, and be sure to wear red to raise heart disease awareness on National Wear Red Day, February 5.

### February 2: Groundhog Day
Groundhog Day tradition holds that if a groundhog emerges from hibernation to see his shadow on February 2, six weeks of winter will follow. If there is no shadow, spring will come early.

### February 14: Chinese New Year
The year 4708 begins on February 14 according to China's traditional lunar-solar calendar. The celebration lasts for 15 days, ending with the Lantern Festival.

### February 14: Valentine's Day
Valentine's Day is mostly a way to celebrate those you care about—people have been exchanging Valentine cards with loved ones since the 1500s.

### * February 15: Presidents' Day
Presidents' Day, on the 3rd Monday of every year, is really two holidays in one. The day does double-duty by honoring two former U.S. presidents, who were born just 10 days (and 77 years) apart: Presidents George Washington (born Feb. 22, 1732) and Abraham Lincoln (born Feb. 12, 1809).

# MARCH 2010

In March, celebrate American Red Cross month by giving your time to a Red Cross project in your community (find a list of their local projects at *www.redcross.org*).

March is also National Frozen Food month: take the time to notice how many of the foods you eat are frozen—ice cream included!

### March 17: St. Patrick's Day
This day celebrates the patron saint of Ireland. Many people, especially those with Irish heritage, consider St. Patrick's Day a time to remember their ancestors and eat traditional Irish foods.

### March 20: First Day of Spring
Today marks the first day of Spring in the Northern Hemisphere. Also known as the Vernal Equinox, the first day of Spring is observed when the center of the sun appears directly above the Earth's equator.

# APRIL 2010

April is National Humor Month and National Poetry Month. Be sure to laugh at any pranks on April Fools' Day, then try telling a new joke every day during the month. Visit the library for books of poetry (try *Where the Sidewalk Ends*, by Shel Silverstein), then try writing some of your own.

### April 1: April Fools' Day
People have been celebrating April Fools' Day with pranks and gags for over 400 years. Have fun tricking your family or friends, but make sure that none of your pranks are cruel or harmful.

### April 22: Earth Day
First celebrated on this date in 1970, Earth Day has been an occasion to bring attention to environmental issues ever since. Contact the Earth Day Network, *www.earthday.org*, for events near you if your school doesn't have anything planned. As little as making a commitment to recycle can make a difference.

# MAY 2010

May is National Bike Month and National Hamburger Month. Enjoy a few hamburgers during May, and make sure you spend some time biking, too—whether you're trying to get somewhere or stay fit.

### May 5: Cinco de Mayo
Mexicans remember May 5, 1862, when Mexico defeated the French army in the Battle of the Puebla.

### May 9: Mother's Day
Mother's Day is celebrated every year on the second Sunday in May. By 2007, over 155 million Mother's Day cards were bought and given to moms across the U.S. every year. And that doesn't even include the homemade cards that many moms love most.

### * May 31: Memorial Day
Also known as Decoration Day, this holiday falls on the last Monday in May. Originally celebrated in honor of members of the military that died during the Civil War, the day now honors all men and women who have died while serving in the U.S. military.

# JUNE 2010

June is Great Outdoors Month. Be sure to get outside and get active at special events, from National Boating and Fishing Week to the Great American Backyard Campout, to celebrate the Great Outdoors.

### June 14: Flag Day
Celebrated on June 14, this day remembers the adoption of the first version of the Stars and Stripes by the Continental Congress in 1777. Flag Day is not an official federal holiday, but many communities hold celebrations to honor the American flag.

### June 19: Juneteenth
Juneteenth, also known as Emancipation Day, celebrates a military order on June 19, 1865, that formally completed the freeing of the slaves. People all over the country—especially in Texas, where it is a state holiday—spend Juneteenth celebrating freedom.

### June 20: Father's Day
This day that celebrates fathers falls on the third Sunday in June.

### June 21: First Day of Summer
The first day of summer in the Northern Hemisphere is observed on the Summer Solstice, when the sun rises and sets the farthest north on the horizon and daylight hours are longest.

# JULY 2010

July is Cell Phone Courtesy Month and National Hot Dog Month. Cell Phone Courtesy Month reminds the 233 million cell phone users in the U.S. to be more aware of how cell phone use in public places affects other people. When your family barbecues, enjoy a hot dog—whether it's beef, pork, turkey, or tofu—it's a summertime tradition. Over 3 billion hot dogs are eaten in the U.S. every year.

### July 1: Canada Day
Canada Day (called Dominion Day until 1982) celebrates the creation of the Dominion of Canada on July 1, 1867. Like the Fourth of July in the U.S., Canada Day is celebrated with parades and fireworks.

### * July 4: Independence Day
Commonly known as the Fourth of July, this federal holiday marks the anniversary of the signing of the Declaration of Independence on July 4, 1776. Americans celebrate with picnics, parades, barbecues, and parties—and don't forget the fireworks!

### July 14: Bastille Day
This holiday commemorates the beginning of the French Revolution by the storming of the Bastille, an event that eventually led to the formation of modern France.

# AUGUST 2010

August is American Adventures Month and Happiness Happens Month. Celebrate vacations in North, South, and Central America, by going on one of your own or remembering a fun vacation you've taken in the past. Happiness Happens Month encourages people to appreciate happiness.

### August 2: Friendship Day
This special day honors friendship.

### August 26: Women's Equality Day
This holiday remembers the day that the 19th Amendment to the Constitution was ratified to grant women the right to vote.

# SEPTEMBER 2010

September is Library Card Sign-Up Month and Hispanic Heritage Month (September 15-October 15). If you don't already have a library card, get one. And take advantage of the library to learn about the 500-year-old roots of Hispanic culture in the Americas.

### * September 5: Labor Day

A federal holiday celebrated on the first Monday in September, Labor Day celebrates workers with a day off in their honor. Labor Day has its roots in the late 19th-century labor movement, when workers began to organize to demand shorter hours and fairer pay. It was made a federal holiday in 1894.

### September 12: National Grandparents' Day

Grandparents' Day, celebrated on the Sunday after Labor Day, is a day to honor your grandparents and the knowledge they pass on.

### September 17: Constitution or Citizenship Day

Citizenship Day occurs annually on the date of the signing of the U.S. Constitution in 1787, as a day to celebrate our rights and responsibilities as U.S. citizens.

### September 23: First Day of Autumn

Today is the first day of autumn, or fall, in the Northern Hemisphere. Also known as the Autumnal Equinox, the first day of fall occurs when the center of the sun appears directly above the Earth's equator.

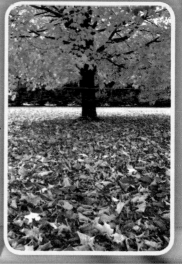

# OCTOBER 2010

October is National Dental Hygiene Month and National Popcorn Poppin' Month. Snack on plenty of popcorn this month, and experiment by adding your own flavors or spices to the wholesome treat. If you get a kernel stuck in your teeth (or just eat too much Halloween candy!), brush and floss extra carefully.

### * October 11: Columbus Day

Celebrated on the second Monday in October, Columbus Day marks Christopher Columbus's landing on an island in the Bahamas, then thought of as 'the New World,' in 1492.

### October 31: Halloween

Halloween always falls on the last day of October. A holiday similar to Halloween has been celebrated since at least the seventh century. Today, global customs vary as much as costumes do, but trick-or-treating remains the most common way to celebrate in the U.S.

# NOVEMBER 2010

November is National American Indian Heritage Month. Learn about Native Americans and their roles in American history.

### * November 2: Election Day

The first Tuesday after the first Monday in November, Election Day is a mandatory holiday in some states.

### * November 11: Veterans Day

Veterans Day honors veterans of wars for their service. It originally marked the "eleventh hour of the eleventh day of the eleventh month" in 1918. This is when World War I battles came to an end according to the conditions of an armistice (an agreement to stop fighting) signed earlier that morning.

### * November 25: Thanksgiving

Every year on the fourth Thursday in November, Americans take the day to honor the people, events, and things in their lives for which they are thankful. Tradition calls for a big meal, shared with friends and family, before or after watching football and/or the televised Thanksgiving Day parade. But make sure you spend at least a few minutes honoring the real spirit of the day, and celebrate the things you are thankful for.

# DECEMBER 2010

December is National Drunk and Drugged Driving Prevention Month. Impaired driving causes an injury every two minutes and a death every half hour. Contribute something to raise awareness of the danger of drunk and drugged driving this month.

### December 21: First Day of Winter

The first day of winter, in the Northern Hemisphere, is observed on the Winter Solstice, when the sun rises and sets the farthest south on the horizon and daylight hours are shortest. Get outside for your favorite wintertime activity. Don't worry if the days seem too short—they'll be getting longer from this day on leading up to summer.

### December 31: New Year's Eve

This day isn't technically a holiday, but you'll still find a lot of people celebrating the end of one year and the beginning of the next. Get a head start on making your New Year's resolutions before you go to bed.

# OTHER HOLIDAYS

Here are a few other holidays that you can observe in 2010. Try celebrating the end of a successful school year on National Pizza Party Day with your class on May 17.

**January 17: Kid Inventors' Day**
Lots of young people came up with ideas that seemed crazy at first—but out of those "crazy" ideas came things like water skis, earmuffs, and popsicles.

**February 7: Super Bowl XLIV**
The year's biggest game—and most-watched TV program—takes place on February 7. Over 95 million people tuned in to Super Bowl XLIII in 2009.

**March 4: Do Something Day**
The date says it all: March Forth! Do Something—ideally, something that will help you with a long term goal.

**April 22: Take Our Daughters and Sons to Work Day**
Kids (mostly between ages 8-12) have the opportunity today to go to work with an adult (not just moms and dads) and find out what their days are like.

**May 5: Cartoonists Day**
This day honors cartoonists everywhere, whether they animate your favorite TV shows and movies, or ink your favorite comic strips or books.

**June 25: National Handshake Day**
For adults in the business world, this is a day in honor of the idea that a firm handshake is an easy way to put your best foot forward.

**July 18: National Ice Cream Day**
Otherwise known as Sundae Sunday, National Ice Cream Day takes place on the third Sunday of every July.

**August 19: National Aviation Day**
Celebrated since 1939, this day honors aircraft and human flight on the anniversary of the birth date of Orville Wright, who piloted the first self-powered flight in history.

**September 12: Video Games Day**
Americans spent $18.8 billion on video games in 2007. Celebrate by playing, and thank your parents for the system, whether it's a Wii, PSP, Xbox, or other console.

**October 1: National Diversity Day**
National Diversity Day, which occurs on the first Friday in October, is a day to learn about, accept, and appreciate different cultures, religions, races, and genders.

**November: National Young Reader's Day**
Young Reader's Day encourages kids, teachers, and families to develop a love of books.

**December 21: Underdog Day**
Underdog Day celebrates past and present second bananas and unsung heroes—think Robin instead of Batman; Dr. Watson instead of Sherlock Holmes.

# Crime

## INFAMOUS CRIMINALS

**John Wilkes Booth** (1838-65) First presidential assassin. Booth was a famous actor but also a strong supporter of slavery and the South in the Civil War. On the night of April 14, 1865—five days after the South formally surrendered—President Abraham Lincoln attended a play at Ford's Theatre in Washington, DC. During the play *Our American Cousin*, Booth entered Lincoln's box seat and fired a single, fatal shot into the back of Lincoln's head. Booth shouted, "*Sic semper tyrannis*!" (Virginia's state motto, which means "Thus always to tyrants") and "The South is avenged!" He then jumped 12 feet from the box onto the stage, breaking one of his legs in the process, and escaped. He spent several days on the run before soldiers found him hiding in a barn in Virginia. When Booth refused to surrender, the soldiers set fire to the barn and shot him.

**Jesse James** (1847-1882) The James family supported the Confederate Army during the Civil War. As a teenager, Jesse joined a gang that attacked Union troops, robbed mail coaches, and terrorized and murdered those they considered to be anti-Confederate. The gang included his older brother Frank and his cousins, Cole and James Younger. After the war, Jesse and Frank became outlaws. Together with the Youngers, they formed a gang that robbed banks, trains, and stage-coaches, and sometimes killed. After the gang broke up, Jesse formed his own gang. Robert Ford, a member of Jesse's gang, killed Jesse in his own home with a single shot to the back of the head.

**Al Capone** (1899-1947) Notorious gangster. Born in Brooklyn, New York, Capone was known as "Scarface" because of a knife cut on his left cheek. He dropped out of school in the sixth grade and joined a gang. In 1925, Capone took over as leader of a Chicago criminal organization dealing in illegal liquor and gambling. This was during the era of Prohibition (1920-33), when most alcohol in the U.S. was illegal. Some of his men murdered seven members of a rival Chicago gang on February 14, 1929, in a crime dubbed the "St. Valentine's Day Massacre." Capone was never convicted of murder or other violent crimes, but in 1931 he was found guilty of not paying income taxes. He spent seven years in prison, some of that on Alcatraz Island, in San Francisco Bay.

# LEGAL PROCESS

In the U.S., the federal and state governments have their own courts. The **federal courts**, or U.S. courts, hear cases such as those involving disputes between states. **State courts** hear other types of cases. Most of the legal work in this country occurs at the state level.

Different states organize their court systems differently. Below is a description of how a typical criminal case might proceed after a judge has determined there was sufficient reason to arrest a suspect (the person accused of a crime).

**1 Grand jury.** Citizens with no connection to the case review evidence and decide if there is enough to indict, or charge, the defendant with a crime.

**2 Arraignment.** A judge tells the defendant what crimes he or she has been charged with by the grand jury. The defendant can plead guilty, not guilty, or no contest. (No contest means the person will not fight the charges but does not admit to being guilty.)

**3 Trial.** A prosecutor presents evidence of the defendant's guilt. A defense attorney represents the defendant's best interests. Witnesses may testify about what they know. A jury listens to all the evidence and arguments. The judge makes sure everyone follows the rules.

Juvenile court cases follow different procedures from those used for adults. Juveniles are usually defined as those under 18. The top age for juveniles in the justice system varies from 15 to 17, depending upon the laws of the state. Juvenile cases are determined by a juvenile court judge. Sentencing options may include a fine, community service, restitution, placement in a group or foster home, probation, or referral for treatment.

**4 Deliberations.** Jury members discuss the evidence and try to agree on a verdict, or decision about the defendant's guilt. They must agree that the defendant is not guilty or is guilty "beyond a reasonable doubt." If they cannot agree, the defendant may receive a trial before a new jury.

**5 Conviction and sentencing.** If the defendant is found guilty, the judge sentences the person, or says how he or she will be punished.

**6 Appeal.** The defendant may appeal a guilty verdict to an appellate court, which may agree or disagree with the original verdict. It may send the case back to the lower court for a new trial.

61

# Disasters

What is the Ring of Fire? ➡ page 65

## Hurricanes

Hurricanes—called typhoons or cyclones in the Pacific— are Earth's biggest storms. When conditions are right, they form over the ocean from collections of storms and clouds known as tropical disturbances. Strong winds create a wall of clouds and rain that swirl in a circle around a calm center called the **eye**.

### Hurricane Categories

**1**: 74-95 mph
**2**: 96-110 mph
**3**: 111-130 mph
**4**: 131-155 mph
**5**: over 155 mph

The eye develops as **warm, moist air** is forced upward in the storm by **denser, cooler air**. From the outer edge of the storm to the inner eye, the pressure drops and wind speeds rise sharply, creating swirling **convection currents** around the eye. If wind speeds reach 39 mph, the storm is named. If wind speeds top 74 mph, the storm is called a **hurricane**.

Convection currents    Eye    Cool dense air

Warm moist air

Hurricane winds and rain

Hurricanes can be up to 300 miles wide. On land, the storm can snap trees and tear buildings apart. Strong winds blowing toward shore can create a rise in the ocean water called a **storm surge**. It can combine with heavy rains to cause flooding and massive damage.

For the Atlantic Ocean, Caribbean Sea, and Gulf of Mexico, hurricane season runs from June 1 to November 30. Most hurricanes happen in August, September, and October, when the oceans are warmest.

## Notable U.S. Hurricanes

| Date | Location | What Happened? | Deaths |
|---|---|---|---|
| Sept. 8, 1900 | Galveston, TX | Category 4 storm flooded the island with 15-foot waves. | 8,000+ |
| Sept. 19, 1938 | NY, CT, RI, MA | "The Long Island Express," with storm surges rising 10-25 feet, caused $306 million in damages. | 600+ |
| Aug. 24-26, 1992 | FL, LA | Hurricane Andrew swept across the Gulf of Mexico, leaving 250,000 homeless. | 65 |
| Aug. 25-29, 2005 | LA, MS, AL, GA, FL | Hurricane Katrina, with 175 mph winds and a 25-foot high storm surge, caused about $125 billion in damage. | 1,833 |

## Hurricane Names

The U.S. began using women's names for hurricanes in 1953 and added men's names in 1979. When all letters (except Q, U, X, Y, and Z) are used in one season, any additional storms are named with Greek letters. Six Greek letters were needed to name 2005 storms.

**2010 Names:** Alex, Bonnie, Colin, Danielle, Earl, Fiona, Gaston, Hermine, Igor, Julia, Karl, Lisa, Matthew, Nicole, Otto, Paula, Richard, Shary, Tomas, Virginie, Walter

# Tornadoes

**T**ornadoes are rapidly spinning columns of air. They form when winds change direction, speed up, and spin around in or near a thunderstorm. They can also spin off from hurricanes.

Tornadoes can happen any time that the weather is right, but they are more common between March and July. They can happen in any state, but strong tornadoes touch down most often in the U.S. southeast or central plains.

According to the National Oceanic and Atmospheric Administration's (NOAA), an average of 1,200 tornadoes occur in the U.S. each year. They cause an average of 60 deaths and 1,500 injuries each year and over $400 million in damage.

Tornadoes are measured by how much damage they cause. In February 2007, the U.S. began using the Enhanced Fujita (EF) Scale (at left) to measure tornadoes. The EF-Scale provides an estimate of a tornado's wind speed based on the amount of damage. If a tornado doesn't hit anything, it may be hard to classify it.

Wind speeds are difficult to measure directly, because measuring instruments can be destroyed in more violent winds. The highest wind speed ever recorded—318 mph—was taken in May 1999 in an Oklahoma tornado.

**did you know?** The U.S. city hit by the most tornadoes is Oklahoma City, with more than 100 recorded tornadoes.

## Tornado Categories

**WEAK**
EF0: 65-85 mph
EF1: 86-110 mph

**STRONG**
EF2: 111-135 mph
EF3: 136-165 mph

**VIOLENT**
EF4: 166-200 mph
EF5: over 200 mph

## U.S. Tornado Records (since record keeping began in 1950)

**YEAR:** The 1,819 tornadoes reported in 2004 topped the previous record of 1,424 in 1998.

**MONTH:** In May 2003, there were a total of 543 tornadoes, easily passing the old record of 399 set in June 1992.

**TWO-DAY PERIOD:** On April 3 and 4, 1974, 147 tornadoes touched down in 13 states.

**WEB SITE** For more information on storms and weather, go to the NOAA Education page: *www.education.noaa.gov/cweather.html*

63

# EARTHQUAKES

There are thousands of earthquakes each year, but most are too small to be noticed. About 1 in 5 can be felt, and about 1 in 500 causes damage.

## WHAT CAUSES EARTHQUAKES?

To understand earthquakes, imagine the Earth as an egg with a cracked shell. The cracked outer layer (the eggshell) is called the **lithosphere,** and it is divided into huge pieces called **plates** (see map above). Underneath the lithosphere is a softer layer called the **asthenosphere**. The plates are constantly gliding over this softer layer, moving away, toward, or past one another. Earthquakes result when plates collide.

The cracks in the lithosphere are called **faults**. Many quakes occur along these fault lines.

## MAJOR EARTHQUAKES

The earthquakes listed here are among the largest and most destructive recorded in the past 50 years.

| Year | Location | Magnitude | Deaths (estimated) |
|------|----------|-----------|--------------------|
| 1960 | near Chile | 9.5 | 5,000 |
| 1970 | Northern Peru | 7.8 | 66,000 |
| 1976 | Tangshan, China | 8.0 | 255,000 |
| 1988 | Soviet Armenia | 7.0 | 55,000 |
| 1989 | United States (San Francisco area) | 7.1 | 62 |
| 1990 | Western Iran | 7.7 | 40,000 |
| 1994 | United States (Los Angeles area) | 6.8 | 61 |
| 1995 | Kobe, Japan | 6.9 | 5,502 |
| 1999 | Western Turkey | 7.4 | 17,200 |
| 2001 | Western India | 7.9 | 30,000 |
| 2004 | Sumatra | 9.0 | 225,000 |
| 2005 | Pakistan and India | 7.6 | 80,000 |
| 2008 | Sichuan, China | 7.9 | 87,652 |

# VOLCANOES

ash and gas

crater

lava

magma

A volcano is a mountain or hill **(cone)** with an opening on top known as a **crater**. Hot melted rock **(magma)**, gases, and other material from inside the Earth mix together and rise up through cracks and weak spots. When enough pressure builds up, the magma can escape, erupting through the crater. Magma is called lava when it reaches the air. Lava may be hotter than 2,000°F. The cone of a volcano is often made of layers of lava and ash that have erupted, then cooled.

Some islands, like the Hawaiian Islands, are really the tops of undersea volcanoes.

## Where is the Ring of Fire?

The hundreds of active volcanoes near the edges of the Pacific Ocean make up what is called the **Ring of Fire**. They mark the boundary between the plates under the Pacific Ocean and the plates under the surrounding continents. (Earth's plates are explained on page 64, with the help of a map.) The Ring of Fire runs from Alaska, along the west coast of South and North America, to the southern tip of Chile. The ring also runs down the east coast of Asia, starting in the far north. It continues down past Australia.

## Some Famous Volcanic Eruptions

| Year | Volcano (place) | Deaths (estimated) |
|------|-----------------|--------------------|
| 79 | Mount Vesuvius (Italy) | 16,000 |
| 1586 | Kelut (Indonesia) | 10,000 |
| 1792 | Mount Unzen (Japan) | 14,500 |
| 1815 | Tambora (Indonesia) | 10,000 |
| 1883 | Krakatau, or Krakatoa (Indonesia) | 36,000 |
| 1902 | Mount Pelée (Martinique) | 28,000 |
| 1980 | Mount St. Helens (U.S.) | 57 |
| 1982 | El Chichón (Mexico) | 1,880 |
| 1985 | Nevado del Ruiz (Colombia) | 23,000 |
| 1986 | Lake Nyos (Cameroon) | 1,700 |
| 1991 | Mount Pinatubo (Philippines) | 800 |

# TSUNAMIS

Tsunami (pronounced *tsoo-NAH-mee*) comes from two Japanese words: "tsu" (harbor) and "nami" (wave). These huge waves are sometimes called tidal waves, but they have nothing to do with the tides.

The strongest tsunamis happen when a big part of the sea floor lifts along a fault (see page 64), pushing up a huge volume of water. The resulting waves are long and low, and might not even be noticed in deep water. They move at speeds of up to 500 miles per hour. As they near shore, they slow down and the great energy forces the water upward into big waves.

On December 26, 2004, a magnitude-9.0 earthquake off the Indonesian island of Sumatra triggered a tsunami in the Indian Ocean. The tsunami hit 12 countries. An estimated 225,000 people were killed, and 1.6 million were left homeless.

# MAJOR DISASTERS

Here are some other disasters the world has faced.

Hindenburg *disaster*

## Aircraft Disasters

| Date | Location | What Happened? | Deaths |
|------|----------|----------------|--------|
| May 6, 1937 | Lakehurst, NJ | German zeppelin (blimp) *Hindenburg* caught fire as it prepared to land. | 36 |
| Aug. 12, 1985 | Japan | Boeing 747 jet collided with Mt. Osutaka. Japan's worst single-aircraft disaster in history. | 520 |
| March 27, 1977 | Tenerife, Canary Islands | Two Boeing 747s collide on the runway of Los Rodeos airport. | 582 |
| Sept. 11, 2001 | New York, NY; Arlington, VA; Shanksville, PA | Two hijacked planes crashed into the World Trade Center, one into the Pentagon, one went down in a PA field. | Nearly 3,000 |
| June 1, 2009 | Atlantic Ocean (off the coast of Brazil) | Airbus A330-200 crashed into the ocean. | 228 |

## Explosions and Fires

| Date | Location | What Happened? | Deaths |
|------|----------|----------------|--------|
| June 15, 1904 | New York City | *General Slocum,* wooden ship carrying church members up the East River, caught fire. | 1,021 |
| March 25, 1911 | New York City | Triangle Shirtwaist Factory caught fire. Workers were trapped inside. | 146 |
| Nov. 28, 1942 | Boston, MA | Fire swept through the Coconut Grove nightclub; patrons panicked. Deadliest nightclub fire in U.S. history. | 146 |
| Dec. 3, 1984 | Bhopal, India | A pesticide factory explosion spread toxic gas; worst industrial accident in history. | 15,000 |

## Rail Disasters

| Date | Location | What Happened? | Deaths |
|------|----------|----------------|--------|
| Jan. 16, 1944 | León Prov., Spain | Train crashed in the Torro Tunnel. | 500 |
| March 2, 1944 | Salerno, Italy | Passengers suffocated when train stalled in tunnel. | 521 |
| June 6, 1981 | Bihar, India | Train plunged off of a bridge into the river; India's deadliest rail disaster ever. | 800 |

*did you know?*

One of the most unusual disasters ever occurred in Boston on January 15, 1919. A giant steel vat holding 2.3 million gallons of molasses ruptured. Thirty-foot waves of the gooey substance flooded the streets, killing 21 people and injuring 150.

Lusitania *disaster*

## Ship Disasters

| Date | Location | What Happened? | Deaths |
|---|---|---|---|
| April 14, 1912 | near Newfoundland | Luxury liner *Titanic* collided with iceberg. | 1,503 |
| May 7, 1915 | Atlantic Ocean, near Ireland | British steamer *Lusitania* torpedoed and sunk by German submarine | 1,198 |
| Jan. 30, 1945 | Baltic Sea | Liner *Wilhelm Gustloff* carrying German refugees and soldiers sunk by Soviet sub. Highest death toll for a single ship. | 6,000 7,000 |
| Aug. 12, 2000 | Barents Sea | Explosions sank Russian submarine *Kursk*; multiple rescue attempts failed. | 118 |
| Sept. 26, 2002 | Atlantic Ocean near The Gambia | Senegalese ferry capsized. | 1,863 |
| Feb. 3, 2006 | Red Sea | Egyptian ferry returning from Saudi Arabia sank after fire broke out onboard. | 1,000 |

## Other Disasters

| Date | Location | What Happened? | Deaths |
|---|---|---|---|
| Aug. 1931 | China | Vast flooding on the Huang He River. Highest known death toll from a flood. | 3,700,000 |
| 1984 | Africa (chiefly Ethiopia) | Several years of severe drought caused one of the worst modern famines. | 800,000 |
| April 1986 | Chernobyl, USSR (now Ukraine) | Explosions at a nuclear power plant leaked radioactive material. 135,000 people were exposed to harmful levels of radiation. | 31 |
| Summer 2003 | Europe | A severe summer heat wave swept across Europe. More than 14,000 died in France alone. | 35,000 |
| Feb. 2006 | The Philippines | Landslide on Leyte Island buries a village. | 1,000 |

*One of the worst snowstorms in U.S. history happened March 11-14, 1888, just a week before the first day of spring. Much of the northeastern U.S. was buried in up to four feet of snow, with towering snowdrifts up to 30 feet high! At least 400 people died in the "Great White Hurricane," many of them in New York City. People were stranded by blocked streets, huge drifts, and powerless streetcars. There was no way to bring food or supplies into the city.*

# Environment

What is global warming? ➡ page 74

## HOME SWEET BIOME

A "biome" is a large natural area that is home to certain types of plants. The animals, climate, soil, and even the amount of water in the region also help distinguish a biome. There are more than 30 kinds of biomes in the world. But the following types cover most of Earth's surface.

### Forests

Forests cover about one-third of Earth's land surface. Pines, hemlocks, firs, and spruces grow in the cool **evergreen forests** farthest from the equator. These trees are called **conifers** because they produce cones.

**Temperate forests** have warm, rainy summers and cold, snowy winters. Here **deciduous trees** (which lose their leaves in the fall and grow new ones in the spring) join the evergreens. Temperate forests are home to maple, oak, beech, and poplar trees, and to wildflowers and shrubs. These forests are found in the eastern United States, southeastern Canada, northern Europe and Asia, and southern Australia.

Still closer to the equator are the **tropical rain forests**, home to the greatest variety of plants on Earth. About 60 to 100 inches of rain fall each year. Tropical trees stay green all year. They grow close together, shading the ground. There are several layers of trees. The top, **emergent layer** has trees that can reach 200 feet in height. The **canopy**, which gets lots of sun, comes next, followed by the **understory**. The **forest floor**, covered with roots, gets little sun. Many plants cannot grow there.

Tropical rain forests are found mainly in Central America, South America, Asia, and Africa. They once covered as much as 12% of Earth's land surface or more than 8 million square miles. Today, because of destruction by humans, less than 5% or fewer than 2.5 million square miles of rain forest remain. More than half the plant and animal species in the world live there. Many kinds of plants from rain forests are used to make medicines. The Amazon rain forest is the world's largest tropical rain forest. It covers about 2 million square miles—roughly two-thirds the size of the United States.

When rain forests are burned, carbon dioxide is released into the air. This adds to the **greenhouse effect** (see page 74). As forests are destroyed, the precious soil is easily washed away by the heavy rains.

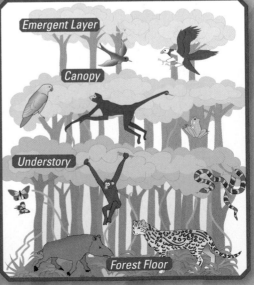

Emergent Layer

Canopy

Understory

Forest Floor

# Tundra

Tundra, the coldest biome, is a treeless plain. The temperature rarely rises above 45°F. Water in the ground freezes the soil solid (permafrost) so plant and tree roots can't dig down. Most tundra plants are mosses and lichens without roots. In some areas, the soil thaws for about two months each year. This may allow wildflowers or small shrubs to grow. Artic tundra is located in the northernmost regions of North America, Europe, and Asia surrounding the Arctic Ocean. Alpine tundra is located on top of the world's highest mountains (such as the Himalayas, Alps, Andes, and Rockies).

**What Is the Tree Line?** On mountains there is an altitude above which trees will not grow. This is the **tree line** or **timberline**. Above the tree line, you can see low shrubs and small plants.

# Deserts

The driest areas of the world are the **deserts**. Hot or cold (Antarctica has desert), they receive less than 10 inches of rain in a year. Many contain an amazing number of plants that store water in thick bodies or roots deep underground. Rain can spur fields of wildflowers to spontaneously bloom. Shrubby sagebrush and spiny cacti are native to dry regions of North and South America. Prickly pear, barrel, and saguaro cacti can be found in the southwestern United States. African and Asian deserts contain shrubs called euphorbias. Date palms grow in desert oases of the Middle East and North Africa.

*Red Rock Canyon, Nevada*

*Prairie in Indiana*

# Grasslands

Areas that are too dry to have green forests, but not dry enough to be deserts, are **grasslands**. The most common plants are grasses. Cooler grasslands are found in the Great Plains of the United States and Canada, in the steppes of Europe and Asia, and in the pampas of Argentina. Drier grasslands called steppes have short grasses and are used for grazing cattle and sheep. In **prairies**, characterized by tall grasses, there is a little more rain. Wheat, rye, oats, and barley grow there. The warmer grasslands, called **savannas**, are found in central and southern Africa, Venezuela, southern Brazil, and Australia. Most savannas have moist summers and cool, dry winters.

# Marine

Covering almost three-quarters of the earth, marine regions are the largest biome. The marine biome includes the **oceans, coastal areas, tidal zones,** and **coral reefs**. Reefs are found in relatively shallow warm waters. Like tropical rain forests, reefs are home to thousands of species of plant and animal life. Australia's Great Barrier Reef is the largest in the world.

*The Great Barrier Reef, Australia*

# WATER, WATER EVERYWHERE

**E**arth is the water planet. More than two-thirds of its surface is covered with water, and every living thing on it needs water to live. Scientists looking for life on other planets start by looking for water. Water is not only part of our daily life (drinking, cooking, cleaning, bathing); it makes up 75% of our brains and 60% of our whole bodies! Humans can survive for about a month without food, but only for about a week without water. People also use water to produce power, to irrigate farmland, and for recreation.

## HOW MUCH IS THERE TO DRINK?

Almost 97% of the world's water is salt water from the oceans and inland seas. Another 2% of the water is frozen in ice caps and glaciers. Half of the 1% left is too far underground to be reached. That leaves only 0.5% of freshwater for all the people, plants, and animals on Earth. This supply is renewable only by rainfall.

## WHERE DOES DRINKING WATER COME FROM?

Most smaller cities and towns get their freshwater from **groundwater**—melted snow and rain that seeps deep into the ground and is drawn out from wells. Larger cities usually rely on lakes or rivers (and reservoirs) for their water. Areas of the world with little fresh water sometimes use a process called desalination (removing salt from seawater) for drinking water. But this process is slow and expensive.

## THE HYDROLOGICAL CYCLE: Water's Endless Journey

Water is special. It's the only thing on Earth that exists naturally in **all three physical states**: solid (ice), liquid, and gas (water vapor). Although the water cycle has no starting or ending point, it is driven by the sun.

### HOW DOES WATER GET INTO THE AIR?

Heat from the sun causes surface water in oceans, lakes, swamps, and rivers to turn into water vapor. This is called **evaporation**. Ice and snow can also **sublimate** (go from solid to gas with no liquid stage) into water vapor. Plants release water vapor into the air as part of the process called **transpiration**. Animals release a little bit when they breathe and when they perspire.

### HOW DOES WATER COME OUT OF THE AIR?

Warm air holds more water vapor than cold air. As the air rises into the atmosphere, it cools and the water vapor **condenses**—changes back into tiny water droplets. These droplets form clouds. As the drops get bigger, gravity pulls them down as **precipitation** (rain, snow, sleet, fog, and dew are all types of precipitation). Precipitation, which falls mostly as rain, is the main route for water's return to Earth.

### WHERE DOES THE WATER GO?

Depending on where the precipitation lands, it can: **1.** evaporate back into the atmosphere, **2.** run off into streams and rivers, **3.** be absorbed by plants, **4.** soak down into the soil as groundwater, or **5.** fall as snow on a glacier and be trapped as ice for thousands of years. Snowpack from winter snow in the mountains often melts in the spring and flows into streams as snowmelt.

# WHY WE NEED WETLANDS

Wetlands are—you guessed it—wet lands. They are wet (covered with water, or with water at or near the surface) for at least part of every year. Bogs, swamps, and marshes are wet most of the year. Prairie potholes, are wet for only part of the year. Wetlands also include fens, wet meadows, vernal pools, playa lakes, and pocosins.

## Wetlands have at least three important functions:

▶ **Storing water.** They absorb water like giant sponges and hold it in, releasing it slowly. During floods an acre of wetland can hold in 1.5 million gallons of water. As a result, wetlands help to control floods.

▶ **Cleaning up water.** They slow down water flow and let harmful sediments drop to the bottom. Plant roots and tiny organisms remove human and animal waste.

▶ **Providing habitats.** They are home to huge numbers of plants, fish, and wildlife. More than one-third of all threatened and endangered species in the U.S. live only in wetlands.

There are fewer than 100 million acres of wetlands left in the lower 48 states, less than half of what there were in 1600. Wetlands are lost when people drain and fill them in for farmland, dam them up to form ponds and lakes, or pave and build up surrounding areas.

*Wetlands, Everglades National Park*

# WATER WOES

**Pollution:** Polluted water can't be used for drinking, swimming, or watering crops, nor can it provide a habitat for plants and animals. Even fish caught in polluted waters may be inedible if they contain high levels of toxins (poisons), such as mercury. Major sources of water pollutants are sewage, chemicals from factories, fertilizers and pesticides, and landfills that leak. In general, anything that anyone dumps on the ground finds its way into the water cycle. Each year, the United Nations promotes March 22 as "World Water Day" to remind people how important it is to protect precious freshwater.

**Overuse:** Using water faster than nature can pass it through the hydrological cycle can create other problems. When more water is taken out of lakes and reservoirs (for drinking, washing, watering lawns, and other uses) than is put back in, the water levels begin to drop. Combined with lower than normal precipitation, this can be devastating. In some cases, lakes become salty or dry up completely.

**The Dreaded Dripping Faucet:** Just one faucet, dripping very slowly (once a minute), can waste 38 gallons of water a year. Multiply that by several million houses and apartments, and you see a lot of water going down the drain!

# WHERE GARBAGE GOES

he disposal of garbage is a serious issue. The problem is that we now produce more garbage than our natural environment can absorb. And many modern products, such as television sets and mobile phones, have parts that may never fully break down. The piles of garbage keep growing, and we add more to them every year.

## WHAT HAPPENS TO THINGS WE THROW AWAY?

### Landfills

About half of our trash goes to places called landfills. A **landfill** (or dump) is a low area of land that is filled with garbage. Most modern landfills are lined with a layer of plastic or clay to try to keep dangerous liquids from seeping into the soil and groundwater supply. The number of landfills is one-fifth of what it was in 1988, but they're much larger.

### *The Problem with* **Landfills**

Because of the unhealthy materials many contain, landfills do not make good neighbors. But where can we dispose of waste? How can hazardous waste — material that can poison air, land, and water — be disposed of in a safe way?

### Incinerators

One way to get rid of trash is to burn it. Trash is burned in a furnace-like device called an **incinerator** to make energy. Incinerators burned a fifth of landfill-bound trash in 2005.

### *The Problem with Incinerators*

Leftover ash and smoke from burning trash like rubber tires may contain harmful chemicals, called **pollutants**, including greenhouse gases. Pollutants can make it hard for some people to breathe. They can harm plants, animals, and people.

## What We Throw Out

Metal 7%

Plastic 16%

Food and Yard Waste 25%

Rubber and Leather 3%

Other Trash 25%

Paper 24%

*2006, after recycling

**did you know?**

In 2000, humans produced 13.9 billion tons of garbage, more than 2.2 tons per person. By 2050, we will probably produce 29.4 billion tons. That's a lot of garbage.

# Reduce, Reuse, Recycle

Reducing garbage helps protect the environment. Avoid buying overly packaged goods. Reuse products. Buy durable and recyclable products or products made of recycled materials.

| | TO REDUCE WASTE | TO RECYCLE |
|---|---|---|
| **Paper** | Use both sides of the paper. Use cloth towels instead of paper towels. | Recycle newspapers, magazines, comic books, and junk mail. |
| **Plastic** | Wash food containers and store leftovers in them. Reuse plastic bags. | Return soda bottles to the store. Recycle other plastics. |
| **Glass** | Keep bottles and jars to store other things. | Recycle glass bottles and jars. |
| **Clothes** | Give clothes to younger relatives or friends. Donate clothes to thrift shops. | Cut unwearable clothing into rags to use instead of paper towels. |
| **Metal** | Keep leftovers in storage containers instead of wrapping them in foil. Use glass or stainless steel pans instead of disposable pans. | Recycle aluminum foil, pans, and trays, and steel cans and containers. Return wire hangers to the dry cleaner. |
| **Food/Yard Waste** | Cut the amount of food you throw out. Try saving leftovers for snacks or meals later on. | Make a compost heap using food scraps, leaves, grass clippings, and the like. |
| **Batteries** | Use rechargeable batteries for toys and games, radios, music players, and flashlights. | Find out about your town's rules for recycling or disposing of batteries. |

## What Is Made From RECYCLED MATERIALS?

- ▶ *From* RECYCLED PAPER we get newspapers, cereal boxes, wrapping paper, cardboard containers, and insulation.
- ▶ *From* RECYCLED PLASTIC we get soda bottles, tables, benches, bicycle racks, cameras, backpacks, carpeting, shoes, and clothes.
- ▶ *From* RECYCLED STEEL we get steel cans, cars, bicycles, nails, and refrigerators.
- ▶ *From* RECYCLED GLASS we get glass jars and tiles.
- ▶ *From* RECYCLED RUBBER we get pencil cases, computer mousepads, shoe soles, bulletin boards, floor tiles, playground equipment, and speed bumps.

Producing an aluminum can from recycled material can save enough energy to run a television for three hours.

# What is GLOBAL WARMING?

## What Causes Global Warming?

Global warming is the gradual increase in Earth's temperature. The sun's rays heat the Earth. Some energy is absorbed by Earth's surface and converted into heat. More than one-third of this energy radiates back in to space. But some is prevented from escaping by **greenhouse gases** in the atmosphere. The most common greenhouse gases are carbon dioxide, methane, nitrous oxide, water vapor, and fluorinated gases. Most greenhouse gases occur naturally, and help to make life on Earth possible.

Without the natural greenhouse effect, the Earth would be about 60° colder than it is today.

Since the mid-1800s, humans have been releasing more and more greenhouse gases into the atmosphere. Most of it comes from burning fossil fuels—like coal, natural gas, and oil—which produce carbon dioxide. Factories, farms, and landfills also add extra greenhouse gases. Deforestation adds to the problem, because trees absorb carbon dioxide.

There is more carbon dioxide and methane in the atmosphere today than has been normal for the last 650,000 years, trapping more of the sun's energy. The decade from 1998–2007 was the warmest ever recorded. Scientists now find it very likely that humans are the primary cause of this global warming. They estimate that carbon dioxide has caused up to 70% of the enhanced greenhouse effect.

**Where Greenhouse Gases Come From in the U.S. (2006)**

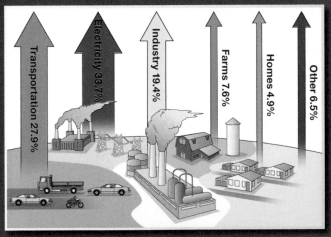

Transportation 27.9%

Electricity 33.7%

Industry 19.4%

Farms 7.6%

Homes 4.9%

Other 6.5%

## How Do We Know about Global Warming?

Worldwide records of climate have been kept since about 1850. Scientists have measured global increases in air and ocean temperatures, a rise in sea level, and melting glaciers. Today, weather balloons, ocean buoys, and satellites provide even more information.

Scientists drill thousands of feet into ice caps in Antarctica and Greenland to remove ice core samples. The layers of ice and air pockets trapped in them can be read like a timeline of climate change over the past 800,000 years.

## What Will Happen?

Scientists have created computer climate models that identify patterns and make predictions. The best current estimates predict that by the year 2100, the Earth's average temperature will increase at least 3°F and oceans will rise 7 inches. The worst-case scenarios suggest that the Earth could warm by more than 11°F and sea levels could rise nearly 3 feet.

NORTH POLE

The polar region currently has the lowest amount of sea ice ever recorded.

ARCTIC SEA ICE BOUNDARY IN 1979

PHOTO: NASA

As the Earth warms, sea levels rise:

- Water expands slightly as it warms.

- The ice sheet covering Greenland and the Arctic Sea are melting. Also, chunks of ice (icebergs) are breaking away from ice sheets in Antarctica and Greenland.

- Glaciers and permafrost are melting in non-polar regions, producing more groundwater.

- As ice melts, it exposes darker land or sea, which is less reflective and absorbs more heat.

The Arctic region may be warming up more than other places because of the albedo effect, or a surface's power to reflect light. Ice reflects the sun's rays. With less ice on Earth, more of the sun's heat will be absorbed by the oceans. Warmer water raises sea levels and melts ice faster.

Warmer air affects the water cycle (see page 70). More water evaporates, and the atmosphere can hold more water vapor. Places with plenty of water will have more rain and floods. But in places where water is scarce, evaporation will dry out the land even more. Vapor will take more time to condense, meaning less rain and more droughts.

Rising sea levels already threaten coastal villages of Alaska and Russia and many small Pacific islands.

Many scientists believe that warmer oceans will lead to more tropical cyclones (also called hurricanes and typhoons).

As environments change, animals must find new homes or they may become extinct. Warmer global climates will allow more disease-carrying creatures like mosquitoes to spread to new places.

# The World's ENERGY

Energy is all around us. You are using energy to turn the pages of this book. Energy cannot be created or destroyed, but it can change form. Heat, light, and electricity are forms of energy. The Sun's warmth is energy in the form of heat. Rubbing your hands together to keep warm is using energy to create heat. One important way we interact with our environment is by extracting energy from natural resources and putting it to use in everyday life, providing heat, electricity, and mechanical power. Some resources—like sunlight, water, and wind—will always be around. These are renewable resources. Nonrenewable resources come in limited supply, like fossil fuels and uranium. There will be no more once they're used up.

Geothermal

Coal

Wind

**Nonrenewable**   **Renewable**

Oil

Solar

Nuclear

Biomass

Natural Gas

Water

## Who Produces and Uses the MOST ENERGY?

The United States produces about 15% of the world's energy—more than any other country—but it also uses 21% of the world's supply. The table on the left lists the world's top ten energy producers and the percent of the world's production that each nation was responsible for in 2006. The table on the right lists the world's top energy users and the percent of the world's energy that each nation consumed that same year.

| TOP ENERGY PRODUCERS | | TOP ENERGY USERS | |
|---|---|---|---|
| United States | 15% | United States | 21% |
| China | 14% | China | 15% |
| Russia | 11% | Russia | 6% |
| Saudi Arabia | 5% | Japan | 4% |
| Canada | 4% | India | 3% |
| Iran | 2% | Germany | 3% |
| India | 2% | Canada | 3% |
| Australia | 2% | France | 2% |
| Mexico | 2% | United Kingdom | 2% |
| Norway | 2% | Brazil | 2% |

# SOURCES OF ENERGY

## Where Does Energy Come From?

**Non-renewable resources come in limited supply.** The "fossil fuels" coal, oil, and natural gas are the most common. Those are the decayed remains of ancient animals and plants that lived long before the dinosaurs (about 354 to 290 million years ago). They took millions of years to form and, if we run out, will take millions more for new supplies to be made. **Uranium**, the element that is split to power nuclear reactors, is more abundant than silver. However, U-235, the type of uranium used for fuel in nuclear plants, is relatively rare.

Uranium and coal are mined, either by digging huge pits or making tunnels that go deep underground. Oil and gas are pumped from wells drilled into the ground, sometimes at the bottom of the ocean. Oil fresh from the ground is called crude. It is sent to a refinery where it is separated into different types of fuel like gasoline, diesel, jet fuel, and other petroleum products. Natural gas, which consists mostly of methane, also includes propane and butane as by-products.

**Renewable sources of energy will never run out.** We can find many by just looking around. The force of moving water like a river or waterfall can create **hydropower**. It is one of the oldest sources of energy. **Ocean energy** uses the motion of the tides or the power of breaking waves to produce energy. The sun's light can be converted into **solar power**. Steady winds can be used to spin giant propellers, generating **wind power**. **Biomass**, or renewable material made from plants or animals like wood or garbage, can be burned to make energy. Heat from the Earth's mantle, called **geothermal energy**, can be collected at natural hot springs where magma boils surface water.

## How Do We Power Homes?

The most common uses of energy in the home are to control heating and cooling and provide electricity for lighting and appliances.

Most electricity is generated at power stations by wheel-shaped engines called **turbines**. Water and wind both push turbines but usually a turbine is pushed with steam. Water is heated into steam by burning biomass or fossil fuels, or by splitting uranium atoms during nuclear fission. Half of America's electricity is generated from burning coal. But two-thirds of the energy stored in coal is lost when it is burned. Natural steam from hot springs can be used to spin turbines, but natural hot springs are rare.

Some homes have solar panels that use the sun's energy to heat water. Other types of panels use solar cells to convert sunlight into electricity. Many people have natural gas, the most widely used energy source in American homes, delivered to their home through pipes. The flames on stoves burn natural gas, which can also power home furnaces and hot water heaters.

## Renewable Energy in Action:

Washington state is the nation's biggest producer of hydroelectricity and gets nearly three-quarters of its power from renewable resources. The Grand Coulee Dam that spans the Columbia River in northern Washington is the biggest hydroelectric dam in the U.S.

Iceland gets most of its heat from geothermal sources. Water is boiled in hot springs by underground volcanoes and piped into buildings like a giant radiator. Geothermal and hydropower sources provide 99% of the country's electricity.

*Nuclear Fission is a complex and carefully controlled process where atoms are "split," or broken into two smaller atoms, to release huge bursts of energy that heat water into steam. One pencil-eraser-sized pellet of uranium can produce as much energy as 1,780 pounds of coal.*

ENVIRONMENT

# Producing Electricity: Pros & Cons

## Nuclear Fission

👍 *Pros:* No greenhouse gases; big energy from a small amount of fuel; cannot explode like a nuclear bomb.

👎 *Cons:* Creates dangerous nuclear waste that takes thousands of years to become safe; meltdowns can contaminate large areas (like Chernobyl) with radiation; expensive.

## Hydroelectric

👍 *Pros:* Does not pollute or heat the water or air; no waste products, runs non-stop; very inexpensive.

👎 *Cons:* Massive dams are expensive and difficult to build; alters the environment around the dam; can affect fish migratory patterns.

## Biomass

👍 *Pros:* Reduces trash in landfills; cuts down on release of methane; plants, such as corn for ethanol, are a renewable resource.

👎 *Cons:* Burning some trash releases toxins and some greenhouse gases into the air; still leaves ash; plants require large farms and specific climate conditions; could raise food prices.

## Wind

👍 *Pros:* Clean; land for wind farms can be used for other purposes like farming; can be built offshore.

👎 *Cons:* Wind farms take up a lot of space; can kill birds if placed in migratory paths; require winds of at least 12 to 14 mph; can be noisy.

## Solar

👍 *Pros:* No pollution; little maintenance required.

👎 *Cons:* Solar panels are expensive and take up a lot of space; energy can't be gathered when the sun isn't shining; manufacturing the solar cells produces waste products.

**A solar power home**

## Fossil Fuels
### (primarily coal)

👍 *Pros:* Affordable because equipment is in wide use; needs smaller space to generate power compared to most other sources.

👎 *Cons:* Limited supply; major contributor to global warming; causes chemical reactions that create acid rain and smog; releases pollutants that cause breathing problems like asthma, can destroy land and pollute water.

# WHERE DOES **U.S. ENERGY** COME FROM?

In 2007, about 85% of the energy used in the U.S. came from fossil fuels, mainly petroleum, natural gas, or coal. The rest came mostly from nuclear power, renewable resources such as hydroelectric power, geothermal, solar, and wind energy, and from alternative fuels such as biomass (including wood, animal waste, and fuels made from plant materials).

Petroleum 40%

Natural Gas 23%

Coal 22%

Nuclear Electric Power 8%

Hydro-power 2.5%

Other Renewable and Alternative Sources 4.5%

# ENVIRONMENT
## SCRAMBLE

Unscramble these environment and energy terms and write them in the boxes at right. Then read down the light-blue boxes for the answer to the riddle!

What insulting name did the plumber call the leaky faucet?

T I C S A P L    O T L E T B

M U M L U A I N    A N C

S A S G L

R O A R D C D B A

A E P R P

E S T A I B T E R

T O M C O P S

*A nuclear power plant*

ANSWERS ON PAGES 334-336.

*An offshore oil rig*

# Fashion

What are sumptuary laws? ➡ page 82

Take a trip through fashion history over the last 100 years. What style do you like the best? It's a modern trend for the fashion-forward, especially kids, to borrow from the decades and make their own special styles.

## 1900s:
### THE EDWARDIAN ERA

**Women:** "Formal" females favored custom-made dresses, tight corsets, lots of lace, and feathered hats.
**Men:** "High society" gents wore tailored wool suits, straw "boater" hats, and narrow shoes.

## 1920s:
### THE ROARING TWENTIES

**Women:** "Flappers" had short, sleek hair and wore drop-waist sequined dresses and fancy costume jewelry.
**Men:** Distinguished men wore pastel-colored shirts, and silk ties that were secured with tie pins.

## 1940s:
### MAKE DO AND MEND

**Women:** During World War II, "Rosie the Riveter" styles (blue jeans, baggy sweaters, and "drainpipe" trousers) were practical and patriotic. Stockings were a luxury.
**Men:** Materials were scarce during the war. Pillowcases and parachutes were used to make clothing. Instead of wool, suits were made of wood pulp and had fake pockets.

## 1960s:
### FLOWER POWER

**Women:** A "groovy chick" would look mod in a bright colored miniskirt, blue eye shadow, white go-go boots, and super-long hair.
**Men:** A "hippie" guy might wear bell-bottom jeans, a paisley shirt, and a leather vest. Funky peace signs and flower patches were popular.

# 1970s:

## DISCO DAYS

**Women:** Girls were "staying alive" in "hot pants," polyester pantsuits, bell-bottoms, and platform shoes.

**Men:** "Mr. Disco" wore polyester bell-bottoms, brightly colored shirts, and gold chains on the dance floor.

# 1990s:

## ANYTHING GOES

**Women:** Dr. Martens big black boots, hooded sweatshirts, and layered T-shirts for the neo-hippie chick.

**Men:** "Grungy" guys kept themselves warm in lumberjack flannels and their money secure with trucker chain wallets. The "hip-hoppers," on the other hand, warmed up in puffy athletic jackets and sneakers.

# 2000s:

## FROM HIP-HOP TO *GOSSIP GIRL*

**Women:** Girls start the decade in low-rise jeans, tight T-shirts with bare midriffs, and bell-bottoms. As the decade continues, girls turn to fashions from teen dramas such as television's *Gossip Girl*, adopting its glamorous yet funky styles.

**Men:** Hip-hop guys keep a beat in baggy pants, gold chains, and athletic gear. The *Gossip Girl* boys bring back prep-school fashions with their blazers, striped ties, and loafers.

**did you know?**

Starting in the 1500s, fashion designers crafted doll clothes to show their designs. The dolls used were one-half to one-third the size of humans. The designers clothed the "dress dolls" in miniature samples of their fashions. Clients could then view the dolls and pick the styles they liked. The clothes were then custom-made to fit the client exactly.

# Fashion
## AROUND THE WORLD

## TOGAS

A toga is a robe that is draped and wrapped around one's body. The toga was worn by government officials in ancient Rome until about 100 A.D. Only men wore togas. Women wore a dress-like outfit called a stola. During winter, some Romans wore leggings to stay warm. There were many different styles of togas, but most were made from white wool. When Emperors passed laws requiring togas to be worn, they became a symbol of Roman citizenship. If a person was banished from the Roman Empire, he had to leave his toga behind.

## BREECHCLOTHS AND BUCKSKIN DRESSES

Early Native Americans had their own distinctive style of dress, which varied from tribe to tribe. However, in most tribes, the men wore breechcloths, a long piece of hide or cloth held in place by a belt. In colder climates, they added leather leggings for warmth. Women often wore skirts and leggings. In some tribes, they wore dresses instead, such as the Cheyenne buckskin dress. Nearly all Native Americans wore the sturdy leather shoes called *moccasins* or a boot called a *mukluk*.

## WIGS

People were wearing wigs as long ago as 3500 B.C. In ancient Egypt, people wore wigs made from vegetable matter and human hair to protect their heads from the sun. Wigs were common in Greek and Chinese theater, and were worn in ancient Roman, Assyrian, and Phoenician cultures. In Europe during the 16th and 17th centuries, wigs were associated with royalty or high fashion. Today, people wear wigs for fashion, convenience, or religious observance.

did you know?

**What Not to Wear** *A sumptuary law is a law that applies to personal habits, including dress. Laws passed in Rome in 216 B.C. limited women to wearing no more than half an ounce of gold. Later, laws were passed that forbade men to wear silk. Around 1300 A.D. these kinds of laws were made in Europe. In Florence, people were not allowed to wear anything red or made from silk. In England, only knights were allowed to wear fur and only the royal family could wear purple. During the 16th century, French and English rulers often made these laws for religious or moral reasons. Sumptuary laws passed in colonial America in 1651 forbade colonists to wear gold, silk, lace, silver, or hats made from beaver fur.*

# KIMONOS

Robes were first worn in Japan around 300 A.D. It was popular during the Heian period, around 800, for Japanese women to wear many layers of robes. Royalty wore up to 16 layers! The original Japanese word for clothing, *kimono*, stuck with the fashion. During the 15th century, warriors wore kimonos to represent their leader. Today they are worn for traditional festivals and special events, including weddings. A bridal kimono is called a *shiro-muku*.

# VEILS

The tradition of covering one's face or head with a veil was practiced more than 5,000 years ago in the ancient kingdom of Sumeria, the modern-day Middle East. Veils were worn to protect the face from desert wind. But some veils revealed the origin, tribe, or even skills of a person. In this tradition, men of the northern African Tuareg tribe wear veils today as a status symbol, even as they eat and drink!

As early as the 1st century, some Hindu women wore veils to show modesty, as many Muslim women all over the world do today. A *hijab* is the most popular form of headscarf worn by Muslim women, and is not particular to a certain color or country. The *chador* is a long black shawl that covers the entire body and head. It is typically worn in Iran. The *burqa* is a robe that covers the entire body and face, and is worn mostly in Afghanistan.

The veil has made many appearances in Western history as well. In medieval Europe, women wore chest-length veils called wimples. Today veils are worn in Western cultures for weddings, mourning, and religious ceremonies.

# MATCHING GAME

| TRADITIONAL CLOTHING | COUNTRY OF ORIGIN |
| --- | --- |
| Lederhosen (short pants with suspenders) | Uganda |
| Pien-fu (2-piece robe) | Chile |
| Kikoi (sarong-type skirt) | China |
| Chamanto (knee-length poncho) | Germany |
| Kamiks (watertight boots) | Morocco |
| Kaftan (belted shirt-dress) | Arctic Inuit people |

**ANSWERS ON PAGES 334-336.**

# Games

What is an MMORPG? ➡ page 85

## HOME CONSOLE GAMES

Home video game systems had a record-breaking year in 2008. The Nintendo Wii was by far the most popular home console, with more than 2 million units sold in December alone. Microsoft's Xbox 360 and the Sony PlayStation 3 were also big sellers. The year 2009 was another big one for gamers. Here are two of the biggest releases of 2009:

**Wii Sports Resort (Wii):** Players take a virtual trip to a resort island, where they can try 12 different sports, including sword fighting, archery, basketball, and wakeboarding. The Sports Resort package takes full advantage of the Wii MotionPlus—which allows for more accurate control of the on-screen action.

**The Beatles: Rock Band (PlayStation 3, Xbox 360, Wii):** Forty years after they split up, the Beatles remain the most popular music group in the world. Fans who never got to see the Beatles get to be the Beatles in this new version of the popular Rock Band game. Players perform 45 of the Fab Four's greatest songs during their most famous gigs—from the first to the last.

## VIDEO GAME TIME LINE

**1962** ▶ Spacewar is the first fully interactive video game.

**1974** ▶ Atari's Pong, one of the first home video games, has "paddles" to hit a white dot back and forth on-screen.

**1980** ▶ Pac-Man invades arcades.

**1985** ▶ Nintendo Entertainment System comes to the United States. Super Mario Bros. is a huge hit!

**1989** ▶ Nintendo's first handheld video game system, Game Boy, debuts.

**1996** ▶ Nintendo 64 is released.

**2000** ▶ Sony PlayStation 2 arrives.

**2001** ▶ Microsoft Xbox and Nintendo GameCube hit the shelves.

**2005** ▶ Sony PSP, a new handheld video game system, goes on sale.

**2006** ▶ Nintendo Wii, which features a wand-like controller, and PlayStation 3 are released.

**2008** ▶ Nintendo Wii Fit, a balance board that allows users to exercise as they play games, goes on sale.

# HANDHELD GAMES

**N**intendo has dominated the handheld game market since the release of the Game Boy in 1989. Today, the Nintendo DS (for dual-screen) is the leader in handheld games, followed by Sony's PlayStation Portable (PSP). Games for mobile phones—especially the Apple iPhone—continue to become more popular. Here are some of the top handheld games of 2009:

**Scribblenauts (DS):** More than any game before it, Scribblenauts lets players use their imagination to solve puzzles. Players simply write down what they need to solve a puzzle—magic carpet, mouse, night-vision goggles—and the object appears on-screen. Scribblenauts won many awards, including Best Original Game at the 2009 Electronics Entertainment Expo (E3).

**Rhythm Heaven (DS):** This challenging music game was a huge hit in Japan before being released in the United States in July 2009. Players use the DS stylus pen to tap, flick, and rub to keep the beat in Rhythm Heaven's 50 mini music games.

**Gran Turismo (PSP):** The Gran Turismo racing games have been big sellers for Sony home consoles since 1998. After years of waiting, fans finally got to play the handheld version in October 2009. Gran Turismo was part of the first batch of games for the new Sony PSP Go—a rival to the Apple iPod Touch.

# ONLINE GAMES

**O**nline games are more popular than ever, with 87 million people logging on to play in 2009. Yahoo! Games was the most popular destination, with EA Online and Nickelodeon rounding out the top three. The game choices are limitless—there's something for everyone. The biggest online game for kids is Club Penguin. Started in 2005, Club Penguin is a massively multiplayer online role-playing game (MMORPG). Players move their penguin characters through a snowy virtual world where they meet and play mini games with other players around the world.

## World of Warcraft

One of the most-awaited new online games of 2010 is **World of Warcraft: Cataclysm.** It is the third expansion of the original World of Warcraft (WoW), an MMORPG that has more than 11 million subscribers worldwide. In WoW, players create characters and join either the Alliance or the Horde. They set off on quests, interact with other players, and do battle to reach new levels. In November 2008, the last WoW expansion pack, Wrath of the Lich King, sold 2.8 million copies in one day.

# Geography

What is latitude? ➡ page 90

## SIZING UP THE EARTH

The word "geography" comes from the Greek word *geographia*, meaning "writing about the Earth." It was first used by the Greek scholar Eratosthenes, who was head of the great library of Alexandria in Egypt. Around 230 B.C., when many people believed the world was flat, he did a remarkable thing. He calculated the circumference of the Earth. His figure of about 25,000 miles was close to the modern measurement of 24,901 miles!

Actually, the Earth is not perfectly round. It's flatter at the poles and bulges out a little at the middle. This bulge around the equator is due to Earth's rotation. Although Earth seems solid to us, it is really slightly plastic, or flexible. As the Earth spins, material flows toward its middle, piling up and creating a slight bulge. The Earth's diameter is 7,926 miles at the equator, but only 7,900 miles from North Pole to South Pole. The total surface area of the Earth is 196,940,000 square miles.

## GEOGRAPHY 1 2 3

**Longest Rivers**
1. Nile (Egypt and Sudan)—4,160 miles
2. Amazon (Brazil and Peru)—4,000 miles
3. Chang (China)—3,964 miles (formerly called the Yangtze)

**Tallest Mountains**
1. Mount Everest (Tibet and Nepal)—29,035 feet
2. K2 (Kashmir)—28,250 feet
3. Kanchenjunga (India and Nepal)—28,208 feet

**Biggest Islands**
1. Greenland (Atlantic Ocean)—840,000 square miles
2. New Guinea (Pacific Ocean)—306,000 square miles
3. Borneo (Pacific Ocean)—280,100 square miles

**Biggest Desert Regions**
1. Sahara Desert (North Africa)—3.5 million square miles
2. Australian Deserts—1.3 million square miles
3. Arabian Peninsula—1 million square miles

**Biggest Lakes**
1. Caspian Sea (Europe and Asia)—143,244 square miles
2. Superior (U.S. and Canada)—31,700 square miles
3. Victoria (Kenya, Tanzania, Uganda)—26,828 square miles

**Highest Waterfalls**
1. Angel Falls (Venezuela)—3,212 feet
2. Tugela Falls (South Africa)—2,800 feet
3. Monge Falls (Norway)—2,540 feet

# READING A MAP

▶ **DIRECTION** Maps usually have a **compass rose** that shows you which way is north. On most maps, like this one, it's straight up. The compass rose on this map is in the upper left corner.

▶ **DISTANCE** As you can see, the distances on a map are much shorter than the distances in the real world. The **scale** shows you how to estimate the real distance. This map's scale is in the lower left corner.

▶ **PICTURES** Maps usually have little pictures or symbols to represent real things like roads, towns, airports, or other points of interest. The map **legend** (or **key**) tells what they mean.

▶ **FINDING PLACES** Rather than use latitude and longitude to locate features, many maps, like this one, use a grid system with numbers on one side and letters on another. An index, listing place names in alphabetical order, gives a letter and a number for each. The letter and number tell you in which square to look for a place on the map's grid. For example, Landisville can be found at A-1 on this map.

▶ **Using the map** People use maps to help them travel from one place to another. What if you lived in East Petersburgh and wanted to go to the Hands-on-House Children's Museum? First, locate the two places on the map. East Petersburgh is C1, and the Hands-on House Children's Museum is E1. Next, look at the roads that connect them and decide on the best route. (There could be several different ways to go.) One way is to travel east on Route 722, then southeast on Valley Road until you see the Children's Museum.

87

Note.
e asterisk ⬥/ between th
f S.t Helena denotes the
itherto ascertained . be

# Early Exploration

**AROUND 1000** — **Leif Ericson**, from Iceland, explored "Vinland," which may have been the coasts of northeast Canada and New England.

**1271-95** — **Marco Polo** (Italian) traveled through Central Asia, India, China, and Indonesia.

**1488** — **Bartolomeu Dias** (Portuguese) explored the Cape of Good Hope in southern Africa.

**1492-1504** — **Christopher Columbus** (Italian) sailed four times from Spain to America and started colonies there.

**1497-98** — **Vasco da Gama** (Portuguese) sailed farther than Dias, around the Cape of Good Hope to East Africa and India.

**1513** — **Juan Ponce de León** (Spanish) explored and named Florida.

**1513** — **Vasco Núñez de Balboa** (Spanish) explored Panama and reached the Pacific Ocean.

**1519-21** — **Ferdinand Magellan** (Portuguese) sailed from Spain around the tip of South America and across the Pacific Ocean to the Philippines, where he died. His expedition continued around the world.

**1519-36** — **Hernando Cortés** (Spanish) conquered Mexico, traveling as far west as Baja California.

**1527-42** — **Alvar Núñez Cabeza de Vaca** (Spanish) explored the southwestern United States, Brazil, and Paraguay.

**1532-35** — **Francisco Pizarro** (Spanish) explored the west coast of South America and conquered Peru.

**1534-36** — **Jacques Cartier** (French) sailed up the St. Lawrence River to the site of present-day Montreal.

**1539-42** — **Hernando de Soto** (Spanish) explored the southeastern United States and the lower Mississippi Valley.

**1603-13** — **Samuel de Champlain** (French) traced the course of the St. Lawrence River and explored the northeastern United States.

**1609-10** — **Henry Hudson** (English), sailing from Holland, explored the Hudson River, Hudson Bay, and Hudson Strait.

**1682** — **Robert Cavelier, sieur de La Salle** (French), traced the Mississippi River to its mouth in the Gulf of Mexico.

**1768-78** — **James Cook** (English) charted the world's major bodies of water and explored Hawaii and Antarctica.

**1804-06** — **Meriwether Lewis and William Clark** (American) traveled from St. Louis along the Missouri and Columbia rivers to the Pacific Ocean and back.

**1849-59** — **David Livingstone** (Scottish) explored Southern Africa, including the Zambezi River and Victoria Falls.

# SOME FAMOUS EXPLORERS

These explorers, and many others, risked their lives on trips to explore faraway and often unknown places. Some sought fame. Some sought fortune. Some just sought challenge. All of them increased people's knowledge of the world.

## CHRISTOPHER COLUMBUS
(1451-1506), Italian navigator who sailed for Spain. He had hoped to find a fast route to Asia by going west from Europe. Instead he became the first European (other than the Vikings) to reach America, landing in the Bahamas in October 1492.

## FERDINAND MAGELLAN (1480-1521),
Portuguese navigator and explorer who set sail from Spain in 1519, seeking a western route to the Spice Islands of Indonesia. He became the first European to cross the Pacific Ocean, but was killed by natives in the Philippines. However, because he passed the easternmost point he had reached on an earlier voyage, he is recognized as the first person to circumnavigate the Earth.

## Hernando de Soto
(about 1500–1542), Spanish explorer. Searching for riches, he and his men explored present-day Florida, Georgia, North and South Carolina, and Tennessee. Unfortunately, his party carried fatal diseases from Europe which killed thousands of Indians. Ironically, de Soto himself died on the banks of the Mississippi River of an illness contracted in America. His exploration opened up America for other explorers.

## MERIWETHER LEWIS (1774-1809) and WILLIAM CLARK
(1770-1838), American soldiers and explorers. In 1804-06 they led an expedition across the American West and back. Aided by a Shoshone woman, Sacagawea, they gained knowledge of the huge Louisiana Territory that the United States had bought from France.

## Mary Henrietta Kingsley (1862–1900),
British explorer. At a time when women were discouraged from traveling into remote regions, she made two trips to West Africa, visiting areas never seen by Europeans. She studied and wrote about the customs and natural environment.

## MATTHEW HENSON (1866-1955),
the first famous African-American explorer. As an assistant to explorer Robert Peary (1856-1920), he traveled on seven expeditions to Greenland and the Arctic region. In April 1909, Peary and Henson became the first to reach, or nearly reach, the North Pole. (Recent research suggests they may have fallen short by about 30 to 60 miles.)

## JACQUES COUSTEAU (1910-1997),
French undersea explorer and environmentalist. He helped invent the Aqualung, allowing divers to stay deep underwater for hours, and made award-winning films of what he found there.

## ANN BANCROFT
(1955- ), American educator and explorer. In 1986, she became the first woman to reach the North Pole by dogsled, and in 1992-93 was leader of the first all-woman expedition to reach the South Pole on skis.

## BENEDICT ALLEN
(1960- ), British explorer. He has published nine books about his journeys, through remote and extreme environments. While studying in New Guinea, he participated in a secret ceremony that left many scars on his body.

WEB SITE For a site about explorers with lots of useful links, try
**www.kidinfo.com/American_History/Explorers.html**

# LOOKING AT OUR WORLD

## THINKING GLOBAL

Shaped like a ball or sphere, a globe is a model of our planet. Like Earth, it's not perfectly round. It is an oblate spheroid (called a "geoid") that bulges a little in the middle.

In 1569, Gerardus Mercator found a way to project the Earth's curved surface onto a flat map. One problem with a Mercator map (like the one on page 105) is that land closer to the poles appears bigger than it is. Australia looks smaller than Greenland on this type of map, but in reality it's not.

**North Pole**

prime meridian
(0 degrees)

**North America**

40 degrees
north latitude

20 degrees
north latitude

**Africa**

**South America**

Equator

20 degrees
south latitude

40 degrees
south latitude

**South Pole**

## LATITUDE AND LONGITUDE

Imaginary lines that run east and west around Earth, parallel to the equator, are called **parallels**. They tell you the **latitude** of a place, or how far it is from the equator. The equator is at 0 degrees latitude. As you go farther north or south, the latitude increases. The North Pole is at 90 degrees **north latitude**. The South Pole is at 90 degrees **south latitude**.

Imaginary lines that run north and south around the globe, from one pole to the other, are called **meridians**. They tell you the degree of **longitude**, or how far east or west a place is from the prime meridian (0 degrees).

## Which Hemispheres Do You Live In?

Draw an imaginary line around the middle of Earth. This is the **equator**. It splits Earth into two halves called **hemispheres**. The part north of the equator, including North America, is the **northern hemisphere**. The part south of the equator is the **southern hemisphere**.

An imaginary line called the **Greenwich meridian** or **prime meridian** divides Earth into east and west. It runs north and south around the globe, passing through the city of Greenwich in England. North and South America are in the **western hemisphere**. Africa, Asia, and most of Europe are in the **eastern hemisphere**.

## THE TROPICS OF CANCER AND CAPRICORN

If you find the equator on a globe or map, you'll often see two dotted lines running parallel to it, one above and one below (see pages 139 and 148–149). The top one marks the Tropic of Cancer, an imaginary line marking the latitude (about 23°27' North) where the sun is directly overhead on June 21 or 22, the beginning of summer in the northern hemisphere.

Below the equator is the Tropic of Capricorn (about 23°27' South). This line marks the sun's path directly overhead at noon on December 21 or 22, the beginning of summer in the southern hemisphere. The area between these dotted lines is the tropics, where it is consistently hot because the sun's rays shine more directly than they do farther north or south.

# THE SEVEN CONTINENTS AND FIVE OCEANS

## ASIA
Area: 11,948,911 square miles
2010 estimated population: 4,166,741,000
Highest pt.: Mt. Everest (Nepal/Tibet) 29,035 ft
Lowest pt.: Dead Sea (Israel/Jordan) –1,348 ft

## OCEANIA (including Australia)
Area: 3,253,542 square miles
2010 estimated population: 35,838,000
Highest pt.: Jaya, New Guinea 16,500 ft
Lowest pt.: Lake Eyre, Australia –52 ft

## INDIAN OCEAN
26,469,500 square miles
13,002 feet avg. depth

## ARCTIC OCEAN
5,427,000 square miles
3,953 feet avg. depth

## EUROPE
Area: 8,815,510 square miles
2010 estimated population: 732,759,000
Highest pt.: Mt. Elbrus (Russia) 18,510 ft
Lowest pt.: Caspian Sea –92 ft

## SOUTHERN OCEAN
7,848,300 square miles
14,750 feet avg. depth

## AFRICA
Area: 11,508,043 square miles
2010 estimated population: 1,033,043,000
Highest pt.: Mt. Kilimanjaro (Tanzania) 19,340 ft
Lowest pt.: Lake Assal (Djibouti) –512 ft

## ATLANTIC OCEAN
29,637,900 square miles
12,880 feet avg. depth

## ANTARCTICA
Area: 5,405,430 square miles
2010 estimated population: no permanent residents
Highest pt.: Vinson Massif 16,864 ft
Lowest pt.: Bently Subglacial Trench –8,327 ft

## NORTH AMERICA
Area: 8,234,599 square miles
2010 estimated population: 547,086,000
Highest pt.: Mt. McKinley (AK) 20,320 ft
Lowest pt.: Death Valley (CA) –282 ft

## PACIFIC OCEAN
60,060,700 square miles
13,215 feet avg. depth

## SOUTH AMERICA
Area: 6,731,004 square miles
2010 estimated population: 393,221,000
Highest pt.: Mt. Aconcagua (Arg.) 22,834 ft
Lowest pt.: Va des Peninsula (Arg.) –131 ft

N E W S

# WHAT'S INSIDE THE EARTH?

**Starting at the Earth's surface and going down you find the lithosphere, the mantle, and then the core.**

The **lithosphere**, the rocky crust of the Earth, extends for about 60 miles.

The dense, heavy inner part of the Earth is divided into a thick shell, the **mantle**, surrounding an innermost sphere, the **core**. The mantle extends from the base of the crust to a depth of about 1,800 miles and is mostly solid.

Then there is the Earth's core. It has two parts: an inner sphere of scorchingly hot, solid iron almost as large as the moon and an outer region of molten iron. The inner core is much hotter than the outer core. The intense pressure near the center of Earth squeezes the iron in the inner core into a solid ball nearly as hot as the surface of the Sun. Scientists believe the core formed billions of years ago during the planet's fiery birth. Iron and other heavy elements sank into the planet's hot interior while the planet was still molten. As this metallic soup cooled over millions of years, crystals of iron hardened at the center.

In 1996, after nearly 30 years of research, it was found that, like the Earth itself, the inner core spins on an axis from west to east, but at its own rate, outpacing the Earth by about one degree per year.

**lithosphere**

**mantle** about 1,800 miles

**outer core** about 1,300 miles

**core** about 1,500 miles

## Homework Tip

### There are three types of rock:

**1 IGNEOUS** rocks form from underground magma (melted rock) that cools and becomes solid. Granite is an igneous rock made from quartz, feldspar, and mica.

**2 SEDIMENTARY** rocks form on low-lying land or the bottom of seas. Layers of small particles harden into rock such as limestone or shale over millions of years.

**3 METAMORPHIC** rocks are igneous or sedimentary rocks that have been changed by chemistry, heat, or pressure (or all three). Marble is a metamorphic rock formed from limestone.

# CONTINENTAL DRIFT

The Earth didn't always look the way it does now. It was only in the early 20th century that a geologist named Alfred Lothar Wegener came up with the theory of continental drift. Wegener got the idea by looking at the matching rock formations on the west coast of Africa and the east coast of South America. He named the enormous first continent Pangaea. The continents are still moving, athough most move no faster than your fingernails grow—aout 2 inches a year.

**Permian**
251 million years ago

**Triassic**
200 million years ago

**Jurassic**
145 million years ago

**Cretaceous**
65 million years ago

**Present Day**

# Health

What is a carbohydrate? ➡ page 96

## KIDS' HEALTH ISSUES

### ALLERGIES

Our immune systems protect us from harmful substances. Certain people's immune systems, however, try to fight off even harmless substances. Common **allergens**—the substances people are allergic to—include pollen and peanuts. If a person inhales, eats, or touches an allergen, he or she might have an allergic reaction. The person might look as if he or she has a cold or have trouble breathing. In severe cases, a person can die from an allergic reaction.

Some people are born more likely to have an allergy. They can control it by taking medication or staying away from whatever they're allergic to. Sometimes kids outgrow their allergies.

*Carly Roman has severe allergies. She had to drink a medicated shake as her only food for 8 weeks.*

### ASTHMA

Asthma is a condition that makes breathing difficult. Allergens, polluted air, vigorous exercise, or stress can trigger an asthma attack. When someone has an attack, his or her airways narrow and can't carry as much air to the lungs.

An asthma attack might last up to a few hours. After one attack, another might not occur until hours, days, or years later. Asthma can't be cured, but people can take medication to prevent it and to treat it. They can also avoid things that trigger an attack. About 9% of American kids, or 7 million, had asthma in 2008.

### OBESITY

When people eat more calories than they burn off through exercise, their bodies store that extra energy as fat. As many as one-third of all kids in the U.S. may be overweight or obese.

Someone is considered overweight if his or her **body mass index (BMI)** is above a certain number. If a person's BMI is even higher, he or she is considered obese. To calculate your BMI, visit **WEBSITE** *apps.nccd.cdc.gov/dnpabmi.*

### EATING DISORDERS

About 8 million teenagers in the United States have an eating disorder. Some have **anorexia nervosa**, a condition in which the person has an overwhelming desire to be thin. **Anorexics** skip meals and drastically reduce the amount of food they eat. They lose so much weight that they endanger their health. About 5 percent of anorexics die from the disorder.

Other teenagers suffer from **bulimia nervosa**, also known as bulimia. **Bulimics** alternate between bingeing, when they eat huge amounts of food, and purging, when they empty their bodies of everything they've eaten. Unlike anorexics, who are significantly underweight, most bulimics are of normal or above-normal weight.

These disorders are most common among girls between the ages of 11 and 18. However, a growing number of teenage boys are developing eating disorders, too.

# NEW FOOD PYRAMID

To stay healthy, it is important to eat the right foods and to exercise. In 2005, the U.S. government designed a new food pyramid to help people track what they should eat. The pyramid recommends different amounts of food depending on age, gender, and activity level. The colored parts of the pyramid stand for different foods. The width of each part shows you about how much of that food you should be eating. The figure on the steps reminds you to be physically active.

**GRAINS**
Make half of the grains you eat whole, such as whole-grain bread, cereal, brown rice, and pasta.

**VEGETABLES**
Try more dark green and orange vegetables. Eat more dry beans and peas.

**FRUITS**
Choose from fresh, frozen, canned, or dried fruit.

**OILS**
Not a food group but essential for good health. Get most of your fats from fish, nuts, and vegetable oils like corn and canola oil.

**MILK**
Get your calcium from low-fat or fat-free milk, yogurt, and cheese.

**MEAT & BEANS**
Eat lean meats. Don't forget to try fish, beans, peas, nuts, and seeds.

# MyPyramid.gov STEPS TO A HEALTHIER YOU

To figure out what you should be eating, based on your age, gender, and activity level, use the calculator online: **WEB SITE** www.mypyramid.gov

For example, an active girl between the ages of 9 and 13 should eat between 1,800 and 2,200 calories daily, including:

| Fruits | 1.5-2 cups | Meat & Beans | 5-6 ounces |
|---|---|---|---|
| Vegetables | 2.5-3 cups | Milk | 3 cups |
| Grains | 6-7 ounces | Oils | 5-6 teaspoons |

# YOUR BODY
## Know What Goes Into It
### NUTRITION FACTS: KNOWING HOW TO READ THE LABEL

Every food product approved by the Food and Drug Administration (FDA), whether it's a can of soup or a bag of potato chips, has a label that describes the nutrients derived from that product. For instance, the chips label on this page shows the total calories, fat, cholesterol, sodium, carbohydrate, protein, and vitamin content per serving.

A serving size is always defined (here, it is about 12 chips or 28 grams). This label shows that there are 9 servings per container. Don't be fooled by the calorie count of 140–these are calories per serving and not per container. If you ate the entire chips bag, you would have eaten 1,260 calories!

| Nutrition Facts | | |
|---|---|---|
| Serving Size 1 oz. (28g/About 12 chips) | | |
| Servings Per Container About 9 | | |
| **Amount Per Serving** | | |
| **Calories** 140 | Calories from Fat 60 | |
| | | **% Daily Value\*** |
| **Total Fat** 7g | | **11%** |
| Saturated Fat 1g | | **5%** |
| Trans Fat 0g | | |
| **Cholesterol** 0mg | | **0%** |
| **Sodium** 170mg | | **7%** |
| **Total Carbohydrate** 18g | | **6%** |
| Dietary Fiber 1g | | **4%** |
| Sugars less than 1g | | |
| **Protein** 2g | | |

| | | |
|---|---|---|
| Vitamin A 0% | • | Vitamin C 0% |
| Calcium 2% | • | Iron 2% |
| Vitamin E 4% | • | Thiamin 2% |
| Riboflavin 2% | • | Vitamin B6 4% |
| Phosphorus 6% | • | Magnesium 4% |

\* Percent Daily Values are based on a 2,000 calorie diet. Your daily values may be higher or lower depending on your calorie needs:

| | Calories: | 2,000 | 2,500 |
|---|---|---|---|
| Total Fat | Less than | 65g | 80g |
| Sat Fat | Less than | 20g | 25g |
| Cholesterol | Less than | 300mg | 300mg |
| Sodium | Less than | 2,400mg | 2,400mg |
| Total Carbohydrate | | 300g | 375g |
| Dietary Fiber | | 25g | 30g |

Calories per gram:
Fat 9    •    Carbohydrate 4    •    Protein 4

## Why You Need To Eat:

**Fats** are needed to help kids grow and to stay healthy. Fats contain nine calories per gram—the highest calorie count of any type of food. So you should limit (but not avoid) intake of fatty foods. Choose unsaturated fats, like the fat in nuts, over saturated fats and trans fats, like the fat in doughnuts.

**Carbohydrates** are a major source of energy for the body. Simple carbohydrates are found in white sugar, fruit, and milk. Complex carbohydrates, also called starches, are found in bread, pasta, and rice.

**Cholesterol** is a soft, fat-like substance produced by your body. It's also present in animal products such as meat, cheese, and eggs but not in plant products. Cholesterol helps with cell membrane and hormone production, but there are two main types. Bad cholesterol, or LDL, gets stuck easily in blood vessels, which can lead to a heart attack or stroke. Good cholesterol, or HDL, helps break down bad cholesterol.

**Proteins** help your body grow and make your immune system stronger. Lean meats and tofu are good options.

**Vitamins and Minerals** are good for all parts of your body. For example, vitamin A, found in carrots, promotes good vision; calcium, found in milk, helps build bones; and vitamin C, found in fruits, helps heal cuts.

### SOME LOW-FAT FOODS
Bananas
Oatmeal
Plain popcorn
Apples
Sunflower seeds
Lentils

### SOME FATTY FOODS
Ice cream
Cheeseburgers
Buttered popcorn
Chocolate candy
Potato chips

# HAVE FUN GETTING FIT

## Why Work Out?

As many as one in three children in America today is overweight. Overweight kids run the risk of developing serious health problems including diabetes, asthma, and high blood pressure.

Exercise is a great way to prevent obesity and improve health. Children should get at least 60 minutes of exercise every day. But keep in mind that exercise should be fun. You can play soccer, ride a bike, dance, swim, or play catch with a friend. As long as you're moving, it's exercise!

## HOW TO WORK OUT

▶ Begin with a five-minute warm-up! Warm-up exercises heat the body up, so that muscles become soft, limber, and ready for more intense activity. Warm-up exercises include jumping jacks, walking, and stretching.

▶ After warming up, do an activity that you like, such as running or playing basketball with your friends. This increases your heart rate.

▶ After working out, cool down for 5 to 10 minutes. Cooling down is like a reverse warm-up. It lets your heart rate slow gradually. Walking is an example of a cool-down activity. Afterward, do some stretching. This helps your muscles remove waste, such as lactic acid, that your muscles make while exercising. Also remember to drink plenty of water during and after your exercise.

▶ Building up strength through your workouts can be very beneficial. This doesn't mean you should lift the heaviest weights possible! It's better to do more lifts using light weights (1/2 lb or 1 lb) than fewer lifts with very heavy weights. Give your body time to recover between strength workouts.

It's becoming easier for people with all kinds of disabilities to take part in physical activities. Many groups across the U.S. help out by providing information and chances to compete. Special equipment uses the latest materials (such as light plastics) and improved design to let people with disabilities hold their own in almost any activity.

## ACTIVITY

| Activity | CALORIES PER MINUTE |
|---|---|
| Racquetball | 10 |
| Jogging (6 miles per hour) | 8 |
| Martial arts | 8 |
| Playing basketball | 7 |
| Playing soccer | 6 |
| Bicycling (10-12 miles per hour) | 5 |
| Raking the lawn | 4 |
| Skating or rollerblading (easy pace) | 4 |
| Swimming (25 yards per minute) | 3 |
| Walking (3 miles per hour) | 3 |
| Yoga | 3 |
| Playing catch | 2 |

If you're interested in running, try WEB SITE www.kidsrunning.com
There you'll find advice, activities, stories, poems, and more—all about running.

# BODY BASICS:

Your body is made up of many parts. Even though we are all individuals, our bodies share similar structures. These structures make up different systems in the body.

**CIRCULATORY SYSTEM** In the circulatory system, the **heart** pumps **blood**. Blood travels through tubes, called **arteries**, to all parts of the body. Blood carries oxygen and food that the body needs to stay alive. **Veins** carry blood back to the heart.

**DIGESTIVE SYSTEM** The digestive system moves food through the **esophagus**, **stomach**, and **intestines**. As food passes through, some of it is broken down into tiny particles called **nutrients**. Nutrients enter the bloodstream and are carried to all parts of the body. The digestive system changes whatever food isn't used into waste that is eliminated from the body.

**ENDOCRINE SYSTEM**
The endocrine system includes **glands**. There are two kinds of glands. **Exocrine** glands produce liquids such as sweat and saliva. **Endocrine** glands produce chemicals called **hormones**. Hormones control body functions like growth.

**NERVOUS SYSTEM**
The nervous system enables us to think, feel, move, hear, and see. It includes the **brain**, the **spinal cord**, and **nerves** throughout the body. Nerves in the spinal cord carry signals between the brain and the rest of the body. The brain has three major parts. The **cerebrum** controls thinking, speech, and vision. The **cerebellum** is responsible for physical coordination. The **brain stem** controls the respiratory, circulatory, and digestive systems.

**RESPIRATORY SYSTEM** The respiratory system allows us to breathe. Air enters the body through the nose and mouth. It goes through the **windpipe**, or **trachea**, to two tubes called **bronchi**, which carry air to the **lungs**. Oxygen from the air is absorbed by tiny blood vessels in the lungs. The blood then carries oxygen to the heart, from where it is sent to the body's cells.

Brain

Trachea (windpipe)

Esophagus

Lungs

Heart

Liver

Stomach

Small intestine

Large intestine

# What the Body's Systems DO

**HEALTH**

**MUSCULAR SYSTEM** Muscles are made up of elastic fibers. There are three types of muscle: **skeletal**, **smooth**, and **cardiac**. Skeletal muscles help the body move—they are the large muscles we can see. Smooth muscles are found in our digestive system, blood vessels, and air passages. Cardiac muscle is found only in the heart. Smooth and cardiac muscles are **involuntary** muscles—they work without us having to think about them.

**REPRODUCTIVE SYSTEM** Through the reproductive system, adult human beings are able to create new human beings. Reproduction begins when a man's **sperm** cell fertilizes a woman's **egg** cell.

**URINARY SYSTEM** This system, which includes the **kidneys**, cleans waste from the blood and regulates the amount of water in the body.

**IMMUNE SYSTEM** The immune system protects your body from diseases by fighting against certain outside substances, or **antigens**. This happens in different ways. For example, white blood cells called **B lymphocytes** learn to fight viruses and bacteria by producing **antibodies** to attack them. Sometimes, as with **allergies**, the immune system makes a mistake and creates antibodies to fight a substance that's really harmless.

# BRAIN DIAGRAM

The typical human brain only weighs about three pounds. But it's like the control center of the body, responsible for making sure everything functions properly. Different parts of the brain do different things.

**Right hemisphere of cerebrum**
- Controls left side of body
- Location of things relative to other things
- Recognizes faces
- Music
- Emotions

**Left hemisphere of cerebrum**
- Controls right side of body
- Ability to understand language and speech
- Ability to reason
- Numbers

**Cerebrum**

**Cerebellum**
Controls coordination, balance

**Brain stem**
Regulates vital activities like breathing and heart rate

99

# THE FIVE SENSES

Your senses gather information about the world around you. The five senses are **hearing**, **sight**, **smell**, **taste**, and **touch**. You need senses to find food, resist heat or cold, and avoid situations that might be harmful. Your ears, eyes, nose, tongue, and skin sense changes in the environment. Nerve receptors send signals about these changes to the brain, where the information is processed.

## HEARING

**1**

eardrum

inner ear

middle ear

outer ear

auditory nerve

The human ear is divided into three parts—the outer, middle, and inner. The **outer ear** is mainly the flap we can see on the outside. Its shape funnels sound waves into the **middle ear**, where the eardrum is located. The **eardrum** vibrates when sound waves hit it, causing three tiny bones behind it to vibrate as well. These vibrations are picked up in the **inner ear** by tiny filaments of the **auditory nerve**. This nerve changes the vibrations into nerve impulses and carries them to the brain.

### did you know?

*You have several thousand taste buds on your tongue. Each taste bud is actually a tiny nerve ending that allows you to perceive different tastes. Although you probably know about the taste receptors for sweet, sour, salty, and bitter tastes, scientists recently located a fifth taste receptor as well, for* **umami**. *It's the savory flavor found in meats and cheeses, due to the glutamic acid in these foods. The word* umami *means "delicious" in Japanese.*

## SIGHT

**2**

The **lens** of the eye is the first stop for light waves, which tell you the shapes and colors of things around you. The lens focuses light waves onto the **retina**, located on the back wall of the eye. The retina has light-sensitive nerve cells. These cells translate the light waves into patterns of nerve impulses that travel along the **optic nerve** to your brain, where an image is produced. So in reality, all the eye does is collect light. It is the brain that actually forms the image.

optic nerve

lens

retina

# SMELL

## 3

In our noses are nerve cells called **olfactory receptors**. Tiny mucus-covered hairs from these receptors detect chemicals in the air. These chemicals make what we call odor, or scent. This information then travels along the **olfactory nerves** to the brain. Nerves from the olfactory receptors connect with the **limbic system**, the part of the brain that deals with emotions. That's why we tend to like or dislike a smell right away. The smell can leave a strong impression on our memory, and very often a smell triggers a particular memory.

# TASTE

## 4

**Taste buds** are the primary receptors for taste. They are located on the surface and sides of the tongue, on the roof of the mouth, and at the back of the throat. These buds can detect five qualities—**sweet** (like sugar), **sour** (like lemons), **salty** (like chips), **bitter** (like coffee), and **umami** or savory flavors (like meat). Taste signals come together with smell signals in the same part of your brain. That's why you need both senses to get a food's full flavor.

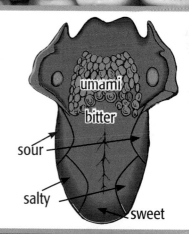

umami
bitter
sour
salty
sweet

# TOUCH

## 5

Your sense of touch allows you to feel temperature, pain, and pressure. These environmental factors are all sensed by nerve fibers located in the **epidermis**, the outer layer of skin, and the **dermis**, the second layer of skin, throughout the body. As with all the other senses, nerves send information to the brain through the nervous system.

# Homework Help

What's the difference between "its" and "it's"? ➡ page 103

## If you need to study for an exam or write a research paper, there are helpful hints in this chapter.

In other chapters, you can find lots of information on topics you may write about or study in school. **Facts About Nations,** pages 150-175, and **Facts About U.S. States,** pages 294-311, are good places to look. For math tips and formulas, look up the chapter on **Numbers**. For good books to read, and write about, see the **Books** chapter. Plus, there are many other study and learning tips throughout the book. Look for the **"Homework Tip" icon!**

# THOSE TRICKY TESTS

## GETTING READY

**Being prepared for a test can relieve some of your jitters and can make test taking a lot easier! Here are some tips to help you get ready.**

▶ Take good notes in class and keep up with assignments, so you don't have to learn material at the last minute! Just writing down the notes helps you remember the information.

▶ Make a study schedule and stick to it! Don't watch TV or listen to distracting music while studying.

▶ Start reviewing early if you can—don't wait until the night before the test.

▶ Go over the headings, summaries, and questions in each chapter to review key points. Read your notes and highlight the most important topics.

▶ Take study breaks so you can concentrate and stay alert.

▶ Get a good night's sleep and eat a good breakfast before the test.

## THE BIG EVENT

**Follow these suggestions for smooth sailing during test time:**

▶ Take a deep breath and relax! That will help calm your nerves.

▶ If you are allowed, skim through the entire exam so you know what to expect and how long it may take.

▶ As you start each part of the exam, read directions carefully.

▶ Read each question carefully before answering. For a multiple choice question, check every possible answer before you decide on one. The best answer could be the last one.

▶ Don't spend too much time on any one question. Skip hard questions and go back to them at the end.

▶ Keep track of time so you can pace yourself. Use any time left at the end to go back and review your answers. Make sure you've written the answer you meant to select.

# GRAMMAR:
## IT'S EASIER THAN YOU THINK

**Here are a few rules to remember to help your writing.**

Use a comma to show a pause—especially both before and after a group of words. This is called using paired commas. You should also use a comma after introductory words and phrases like "next" and "after a while."

**▶ RIGHT:** *My favorite aunt, Emily Jones, is an expert when it comes to using commas. The rules for good writing, I am afraid, are often hard to remember. After a while, I figured out the answer to the problem.*

Never let a sentence run on into another sentence without a period in between.

**WRONG:** *My teacher drives to school every day, she lives 12 miles away.*

**▶ RIGHT:** *My teacher drives to school every day. She lives 12 miles away.*

When a phrase at the beginning of a sentence has a verb form ending in -ing, make sure it does not refer to the wrong thing.

**WRONG:** *Walking into the cafeteria, my milk spilled onto the floor.*

**▶ RIGHT:** *Walking into the cafeteria, I spilled my milk onto the floor.* [Think about it… your milk wasn't walking into the cafeteria.]

Use the "subjective" form of personal pronouns (I, we, he, she, they) when something is the subject of a sentence. Use the "objective" [me, us, him, her, them] when it is the object of the sentence or of a preposition (like with or by).

**WRONG:** *Michael and me played basketball.* [You should use I, since it's the subject.]

**WRONG:** *Can you play with Ashley and I?* [You should use me since it's the object of the preposition with.]

**Hint:** Don't use myself in sentences like those two above. Never use myself when you could use me, or I, instead.

# It's a Common Mistake. Unlike nearly all other possessive words, its does not use an apostrophe to show possession.

**WRONG:** *Every game has it's rules.*

**▶ RIGHT:** *Every game has its rules.*

Use an apostrophe for it's only when you mean it is, as in the heading above. If you keep on the lookout, you might find this mistake before long in something an adult has written.

## IF NOTHING ELSE, REMEMBER THIS:

After you finish a writing assignment, look it over carefully. Be sure to read what is really on the paper and not what you think you wrote. Don't be surprised if you find some obvious mistakes—like a capital letter you forgot to use or a simple word that you misspelled. Even book editors have to check and re-check their work.

# HOW TO WRITE A RESEARCH PAPER

## Doing Research

**To start any research paper or project, the first thing to do is research.**

▶ **Encyclopedias are a good place to start.** They can give you a good overview of the subject.

▶ **The electronic catalog** of your school or public library will probably be your main source for finding books and articles about your subject. A librarian can help show you how this works.

▶ You can also use **the Internet** as a research tool (see opposite page).

▶ As you read each source, **write down the facts and ideas** that you may need. Include the title and author for each source and the page numbers or the web site and address for the web page where you found the particular information.

## Writing It Down

**The next step** is to organize your facts. **Develop a rough outline** of your ideas in the order in which they'll appear. Then, write a draft of your paper. It should contain three main parts:

**INTRODUCTION** The introduction, or first paragraph, explains your topic and your point of view on it. It should draw readers into the paper and let them know what to expect.

**BODY** The body of the paper develops your ideas. Use specific facts, examples, and details to make your points clear and convincing. Use separate paragraphs for each new idea and use words and phrases that link one paragraph to the next so your ideas flow smoothly.

**CONCLUSION** Summarize your main points in the final paragraph, or conclusion.

## Showing Your Sources

You may need to do a **bibliography** at the end of your paper. This is a list of all the sources you used to prepare the report.

**FOR A BOOK:** Author. *Title.* City Published: Publisher, Year.
Burgan, Michael. *The Alamo.* New York: Chelsea Clubhouse, 2010.

**FOR A MAGAZINE ARTICLE:** Author. "Article Title." *Magazine Title*, Date of Issue, Pages.
Dunn, Robert R. "Dune Buggies." *Natural History*, September 2009, 38-39.

**FOR ONLINE (INTERNET):** Author. "Entry Title." *Book Title.* City Published: Publisher, Year. *Database Name.* Database Company. URL (date accessed).
Longshore, David. "Hurricane Katrina." *Encyclopedia of Hurricanes, Typhoons, and Cyclones,* New ed. New York: Facts On File, Inc., 2008. *American History Online.* Facts On File, Inc. http://www.fofweb.com/activelink2.asp? ItemID=WE5 2&DataID=2&iPin=EAFP019&SingleRecord=True (accessed April 30, 2009).

# RESEARCH ON THE INTERNET

## Using Library Resources

Your school or public library is a great place to start. It probably has a list (catalog) of its books and periodicals (newspapers and magazines) available from computers at the library, or even from home over the Internet through your library's web site. You can search using **keywords** (words that describe your subject) in three basic ways: by **author**, by **title**, or by **subject**.

For example, doing a subject search for "Benjamin Franklin" will give you a list of books and articles about him, along with their locations in the library.

Your library may also subscribe to online reference databases that companies like Facts On File create especially for research. These are accessible over the Internet and could contain almanacs, encyclopedias, reference books, other nonfiction books, or collections of articles. You can access these databases from the library, and maybe even from home from your library's web site.

When you write your report, don't copy directly from books, articles, or the Internet—that's **plagiarism**, a form of cheating. Keep track of all your **sources**—the books, articles, and web sites you use—and list them in a **bibliography**. (See page 104 for some examples.)

## Why shouldn't I just search the Internet?

The library's list may look just like other information on the Internet. But these sources usually have been checked by experts. This is not true of all the information on the Internet. It could come from almost anybody, and may not be trustworthy.

## When can I use the Internet?

The Internet is still a great way to look things up. You can find addresses or recipes, listen to music, or find things to do. You can look up information on hobbies or musical instruments, or read a magazine or newspaper online.

If you search the Internet on your own, make sure the web site you find is reliable. A U.S. government site or a site produced by a well-known organization or publication is usually your best bet.

## Using a Search Engine

The best way to find web sites is to use a search engine. Here are some helpful ones:

**Yahooligans** (www.yahooligans.com)
**Kidsclick** (www.kidsclick.org)
**Lycos Zone** (www.lycoszone.lycos.com)
**Ask Jeeves Kids** (www.ajkids.com)

Start by typing one or two search terms—words that describe your topic. The search engine scans the Internet and gives you a list of sites that contain them. The results appear in a certain order, or **rank**. Search engines use different ways of measuring which web sites are likely to be the most helpful. One way is by counting how many times your search terms appear on each site. The site that's listed first may not have what you want. Explore as many of the sites as possible.

You might have to narrow your search by using more keywords. Or try using **directories** to help find what you need.

# Inventions

## Invention TIME LINE

| YEAR | INVENTION | INVENTOR (COUNTRY) |
|---|---|---|
| 105 | paper | Ts'ai Lun (China) |
| 1440s | printing press/movable type | Johann Gutenberg (Germany) |
| 1590 | 2-lens microscope | Zacharias Janssen (Netherlands) |
| 1608 | telescope | Hans Lippershey (Netherlands) |
| 1616 | reflecting telescope | Niccolo Zucchi |
| 1714 | mercury thermometer | Gabriel D. Fahrenheit (Germany) |
| 1752 | lightning rod | Benjamin Franklin (U.S.) |
| 1783 | parachute | Sebastien Lenormand (France) |
| 1800 | electric battery | Alessandro Volta (Italy) |
| 1804 | steam locomotive | Richard Trevithick (England) |
| 1837 | telegraph | Samuel F. B. Morse (U.S.) |
| 1842 | anesthesia (ether) | Crawford W. Long (U.S.) |
| 1846 | sewing machine | Elias Howe (U.S.) ▶ |
| 1870 | telephone* | Antonio Meucci (Italy), Alexander G. Bell (U.S.) |
| 1879 | practical light bulb | Thomas A. Edison (U.S.) |
| 1886 | automobile (gasoline) | Karl Benz (Germany) |
| 1891 | escalator | Jesse W. Reno (U.S.) |
| 1892 | moving picture viewer | Thomas A. Edison & William K. Dickson (U.S.) |
| 1895 | X-ray | Wilhelm Roentgen (Germany) |
| 1897 | diesel engine | Rudolf Diesel (Germany) |
| 1902 | air conditioning | Willis Carrier (U.S.) |
| 1922 | insulin | Sir Frederick G. Banting & Charles Best (Canada) |
| 1923 | television** | Vladimir K. Zworykin (U.S.) ▶ |
| 1926 | rocket engine | Robert H. Goddard (U.S.) |
| 1928 | tape recorder | Fritz Pfleumer (Germany) |
| 1928 | penicillin | Alexander Fleming (Scotland) |
| 1933 | FM radio | Edwin Armstrong (U.S.) |
| 1939 | jet airplane | Hans van Ohain (Germany) |
| 1941 | electronic computer | John V. Atanasoff & Clifford Berry (U.S.) |
| 1955 | Velcro® | George de Mestral (Switzerland) |
| 1957 | digital image | Russell Kirsch (U.S.) |
| 1957 | laser*** | Gordon Gould (U.S.) |
| 1971 | CAT scanner | Godfrey N. Hounsfield (England) |
| 1973 | cellular telephone | Motorola/Martin Cooper (U.S.) |
| 1975 | digital camera | Steven Sasson (U.S.) |
| 1975 | personal computer IBM | E. Roberts, W. Yates, & J. Bybee (U.S.) |
| 1990 | handheld digital camera | Dycam (U.S.) |
| 2001 | Segway® Personal Transporter (PT) | Dean Kamen (U.S.) |
| 2007 | iPhone | Steve Jobs (U.S.) ▶ |

* Meucci developed a version of the telephone (early 1870s); Bell received a patent for another version.
** Others who helped invent the television include Philo T. Farnsworth (1927) and John Baird (1925).
*** First working laser built in 1960 by Theodore Maiman.

# CURRENT Inventions

## BIOMIMETICS: DESIGNED BY NATURE

Spider web silk is stronger than steel. A beetle in Africa's Namib Desert uses its bumpy wings to collect drinking water from fog. Sharks are covered in teeth-like scales that help them swim faster. Humans have made many great inventions but sometimes nature still does things better.

Researchers who study biomimetics look to natural abilities and designs for new advances in engineering, medicine, and other sciences. Their research mimics nature to create new inventions.

Swiss engineer George de Mestral could be called the father of biomimicry. Mestral liked to hike but he was always removing sticky seeds called burrs from his clothes and his dog's fur. Curious about their sticking power, he looked at one under a microscope and saw hundreds of tiny hooks. After several years of research, he made a tape with burr-like hooks that could stick to a tape of wool-like loops: Velcro.

Geckos' feet aren't sticky but, thanks to millions of microscopic hairs, they can climb up most surfaces whether wet, dry, dirty, smooth, or bumpy. Ron Fearing and students at the University of California at Berkeley have mimicked those tiny foot hairs with plastic microfibers (42 million per square centimeter) to create an adhesive, like tape. It attaches by sliding instead of pushing. A simple pull in another direction (releasing the stress) can remove it. It leaves no sticky gunk and does not stick to itself.

Watch a fly lift off. It certainly doesn't fly like an airplane. Flies flap their wings much like the way people tread water, in twisting movements and with varying force. Robert Wood at Harvard University has created a flying microrobot that copies the basic makeup of a fly. It's the size of a penny and weighs 60 milligrams. Its wings, which flap 120 times a second, are made of carbon fiber and polymer. In the future, the robot could be used in rescues and exploration.

### did you know?

*George Washington Carver (1864–1943) was an inventor who created hundreds of new products (such as cheese, milk, flour, and soap) from peanuts and other legumes. This made the peanut one of the country's leading cash crops, and helped to revitalize farming in the American south. Carver, whose parents were slaves, went on to advise many world leaders, including Presidents Calvin Coolidge and Franklin D. Roosevelt.*

# Language

How do you say "January" in Italian? ➤ page 109

## TOP LANGUAGES

Mandarin, the principal language of China, has the most native speakers of any language. Hindi (spoken in India) ranks second as the most common native, or first, language in the world.*

*2005 estimates

| LANGUAGE | KEY PLACES WHERE SPOKEN | NATIVE SPEAKERS |
|---|---|---|
| Mandarin | China, Taiwan | 873 million |
| Hindi | India | 366 million |
| Spanish | Latin America, Spain | 329 million |
| English | U.S., Canada, Britain, Australia | 328 million |
| Bengali | Bangladesh, India | 207 million |
| Portuguese | Portugal, Brazil | 177 million |
| Russian | Russia | 145 million |
| Japanese | Japan | 122 million |

## Which LANGUAGES Are SPOKEN in the UNITED STATES?

Most Americans speak English at home. But since the beginning of American history, immigrants have come to the U.S. from all over the world. Many have brought other languages with them.

"¡Hola!" That's how 34 million Spanish-speaking Americans say "hi" at home.

The table at the right lists the most frequently spoken languages in the U.S., according to a 2006 Census Bureau report.

| | LANGUAGE USED AT HOME | SPEAKERS OVER 5 YEARS OLD |
|---|---|---|
| 1 | Speak only English | 224,154,712 |
| 2 | Spanish, Spanish Creole | 34,024,945 |
| 3 | Chinese | 2,492,871 |
| 4 | Tagalog (Philippines) | 1,415,599 |
| 5 | French | 1,395,732 |
| 6 | Vietnamese | 1,207,721 |
| 7 | German | 1,135,999 |
| 8 | Korean | 1,060,631 |
| 9 | Italian | 828,524 |
| 10 | Russian | 823,210 |
| 11 | Arabic | 732,519 |
| 12 | Portuguese | 683,405 |
| 13 | Polish | 640,265 |
| 14 | French Creole | 601,856 |
| 15 | Hindi | 504,607 |
| 16 | Japanese | 475,414 |
| 17 | Greek | 353,200 |
| 18 | Persian | 348,769 |
| 19 | Urdu | 324,578 |
| 20 | Gujarathi (India & parts of Africa) | 298,658 |

# LANGUAGE
# EXPRESS

Ciao! (Italian)
Hello! (English)
Konnichi wa! (Japanese)

Surprise your friends and family with words from other languages.

| English | Italian | French | German | Chinese |
|---|---|---|---|---|
| January | gennaio | janvier | Januar | yi-yue |
| February | febbraio | février | Februar | er-yue |
| March | marzo | mars | Marz | san-yue |
| April | aprile | avril | April | si-yue |
| May | maggio | mai | Mai | wu-yue |
| June | giugno | juin | Juni | liu-yue |
| July | luglio | juillet | Juli | qi-yue |
| August | agosto | août | August | ba-yue |
| September | settembre | septembre | September | jiu-yue |
| October | ottobre | octobre | Oktober | shi-yue |
| November | novembre | novembre | November | shi-yi-yue |
| December | dicembre | decembre | Dezember | shi-er-yue |
| blue | azzurro | bleu | blau | lan |
| red | rosso | rouge | rot | hong |
| green | verde | vert | grün | lu |
| yellow | giallo | jaune | gelb | huang |
| black | nero | noir | schwarz | hei |
| white | bianco | blanc | weiss | bai |
| happy birthday! | buon compleanno! | joyeux anniversaire! | Glückwunsch zum Geburtstag! | sheng-ri kuai le! |
| hello! | ciao! | bonjour! | hallo! | ni hao! |
| good-bye! | arrivederci! | au revoir! | auf Wiedersehen! | zai-jian! |
| fish | pesci | poisson | Fisch | yu |
| bird | uccello | oiseau | Vogel | niao |
| horse | cavallo | cheval | Pferd | ma |
| one | uno | un | eins | yi |
| two | due | deux | zwei | er |
| three | tre | trois | drei | san |
| four | quattro | quatre | vier | si |
| five | cinque | cinq | fünf | wu |

did you know?

There is only one English word with three consecutive sets of double letters:

Bookkeeper.

109

# ¡SAY IT EN ESPAÑOL!

**S**panish is the most commonly spoken language in the U.S. after English. More than 34 million people speak Spanish at home. That's more than 10 percent of all people in the U.S.

## Pronouncing **Spanish** Words

In Spanish, the vowels only make one type of sound. The sound each vowel makes in Spanish is the same sound it makes in the English words at right.

Also, if you see the letters J, G, or X followed by a vowel, pronounce them like the English "H." So, "Frijoles" sounds like "Free-hole-ace." "Ejecutivo" sounds like "Eh-he-coo-tee-vo." "Región" sounds like "Ray-hee-own."

**Try your pronunciation on the words and phrases on this page.**

| | |
|---|---|
| A | w**a**ter |
| E | b**e**t |
| I | f**ee**t (like you are saying the letter *e*) |
| O | sl**ow** |
| U | t**u**be |

## Sister Languages

There are some words that sound alike in both Spanish and English. These are called cognates. See if you can guess how each kid listed at right answered the question: **What do you want to be when you grow up?**

| | |
|---|---|
| **Julio** | Yo quiero ser *músico*. |
| **Maria** | Un dia, yo quisiera ser *autora*. |
| **Juan** | Yo quiero ser *banquero*. |
| **Olivia** | Un dia, yo quisiera ser *doctora*. |
| **Jose** | Yo quiero ser *presidente*. |

Answers: Julio—musician; Maria—author; Juan—banker; Olivia—doctor; Jose—president.

## Food

Next time you're having dinner, ask your brother to pass the *arroz*.

Salad **Ensalada**

Juice **Jugo**

Beans **Frijoles**

Rice **Arroz**

Chicken **Pollo**

## Basic Spanish Phrases

| Hello | Hola |
|---|---|
| Goodbye | Adiós |
| How are you? | ¿Cómo estás? |
| Please | Por favor |
| Thank you | Gracias |
| It's nice to meet you. | Mucho gusto en conocerte. |

# Your Body
# Es Su Cuerpo

Use your *boca* to say these parts of the body (*cuerpo*). Use your *cabeza* to remember how to say them!

| Head | Cabeza |

| Face | Cara |

| Eyes | Ojos |

| Ears | Orejas |

| Mouth | Boca |

| Neck | Cuello |

| Hair | Cabello |

| Arm | Brazo |

| Belly | Barriga |

| Hand | Mano |

| Leg | Pierna |

| Knee | Rodilla |

| Foot | Pie |

## Numbers

| 1 | uno | 6 | seis |
|---|------|----|-------|
| 2 | dos | 7 | siete |
| 3 | tres | 8 | ocho |
| 4 | cuatro | 9 | nueve |
| 5 | cinco | 10 | diez |

## Joke en Español

**Teacher** ¿Como se escribe "nariz" en inglés?
(How do you write "nose" in English?)

**Student** No sé. (I don't know.)

**Teacher** ¡Correcto! (Correct!)

# THE ENGLISH LANGUAGE

## Facts About English

▶ According to the *Oxford English Dictionary*, the English language contains between 250,000 and 750,000 words. (The number depends on whether you count different meanings of the same word as separate words and on how many obscure technical terms you count.)

▶ The most frequently used letters of the alphabet are E, T, A, and O, in that order.

▶ Here are the 30 most common English words: the, of, and, a, to, in, is, that, it, was, he, for, as, on, with, his, be, at, you, I, are, this, by, from, had, have, they, not, or, one. Try to make a sentence with just these words. Here's an example: "I had to be with it for that is not the one they have."

## New Words

**English is always changing as new words are born and old ones die out. Many new words come from the fields of electronics and computers, from the media, or from slang.**

**hoodie:** a hooded sweatshirt, usually with a zipper down the front

**manga:** a Japanese comic book or graphic novel

**ollie:** a skateboarding or snowboarding maneuver in which the board rises off the ground

**qigong:** pronounced chee-gong, this is a Chinese philosophy of exercise. *Qi*, or *chi*, is the Chinese term for "vital life energy."

**ringtone:** a sound or song programmed in or downloaded to ring from a cell phone.

**tweet:** a message sent using the Twitter social networking service

## In Other Words: SIMILES

*Similes are comparisons of two dissimilar things that use "as" or "like." Here are some to wrap your brain around:*

**graceful as a swan**—"smooth and elegant." Swans are admired for their long necks and the way they quietly glide through the water. Ballerinas are often compared to swans, with their extended, smooth movements on the stage.

**quiet as a mouse**—"almost too quiet to hear." Mice are quiet and shy, and good at hiding. Even their squeaks are practically too soft to hear.

**strong as an ox**—"stronger than most people." Oxen are cattle that are trained to pull very heavy loads.

# GETTING TO THE ROOT

**M**any English words and parts of words can be traced back to Latin or Greek. If you know the meaning of a word's parts, you can probably guess what it means. A root (also called a stem) is the part of the word that gives its basic meaning but can't be used by itself. Roots need other word parts to complete them: either a prefix at the beginning, or a suffix at the end, or sometimes both. The following tables give some examples of Greek and Latin roots, prefixes, and suffixes.

## LATIN

| root | basic meaning | example |
|---|---|---|
| -alt- | high | altitude |
| -dict- | to say | dictate |
| -port- | to carry | transport |
| -scrib-/-script- | to write | prescription |
| -vert- | turn | invert |

| prefix | basic meaning | example |
|---|---|---|
| de- | away, off | defrost |
| in-/im- | not | invisible |
| non- | not | nontoxic |
| pre- | before | prevent |
| re- | again, back | rewrite |
| trans- | across, through | trans-Atlantic |

| suffix | basic meaning | example |
|---|---|---|
| -ation | (makes verbs into nouns) | invitation |
| -fy/-ify | make or cause to become | horrify |
| -ly | like, to the extent of | highly |
| -ment | (makes verbs into nouns) | government |
| -ty/-ity | state of | purity |

## GREEK

| root | basic meaning | example |
|---|---|---|
| -anthrop- | human | anthropology |
| -biblio- | book | bible |
| -bio- | life | biology |
| -dem- | people | democracy |
| -phon- | sound | telephone |
| -psych- | soul | psychology |

| prefix | basic meaning | example |
|---|---|---|
| anti-/ant- | against | antisocial |
| auto- | self | autopilot |
| biblio-/bibl- | book | bibliography |
| micro- | small | microscope |
| tele- | far off | television |

| suffix | basic meaning | example |
|---|---|---|
| -graph | write, draw, describe, record | photograph |
| -ism | act, state, theory of | realism |
| -ist | one who believes in, practices | capitalist |
| -logue/-log | speech, to speak | dialogue |
| -scope | see | telescope |

113

# JOKES AND RIDDLES

1. Who is President if the Vice President dies?

2. A farmer combined four bales of hay with two bales of hay. How many bales does he have?

3. What keeps the beat for your head?

4. How do you make the number one disappear?

5. What do you lose when you stand up?

6. What's the last thing you take off before you go to bed?

7. Why was the chef arrested?

8. Why is the letter E like London?

9. What happens to a white hat when you throw it in the Red Sea?

10. Why do birds fly south for the winter?

11. Think of words ending in "gry." Two are "angry" and "hungry." There are three words in "the English language." What is the third word? *HINT:* Everyone uses it every day and if you've listened closely, I've already said the answer.

12. What did one traffic light say to the other?

13. Two mothers and their two daughters went shopping. They each bought something, but came home with only three new things. Why?

14. What does everyone do at the same time, all day long, every day?

15. What can you put in a wooden box so that it's lighter?

16. How does the solar system hold up its pants?

17. You can keep it only after giving it to someone else. What is it?

18. What's black and white and read all over?

19. What has wheels and flies but never leaves the ground?

20. What type of dog can jump higher than a skyscraper?

21. What comes once in a minute, twice in a moment, but never in a billion years?

22. Why did the boy put a ruler under his pillow before he went to bed?

23. What can you hold without using your limbs?

24. What did one microchip say to the other when he wouldn't give him back his toy?

25. Why do seagulls fly over the sea?

26. How many birthdays does the average person have?

27. Some months have 31 days, some months only have 30. How many have 28 days?

28. What is light as a feather but not even the strongest man can hold it for long?

29. A herder had 11 sheep. All but 9 died. How many were left?

30 Why can't a man living in Cincinnati be buried south of the Ohio River?

31 What has four eyes but cannot see?

32 What goes up when the rain comes down?

33 What do you get when you cross a rooster and a duck?

34 What kind of horses go out after dark?

35 What time is it when an elephant sits on a fence?

36 When is a car not a car?

37 What has arms but can't hug?

38 You're the driver of a bus. You stop on a corner and pick up 6 people. At the second stop, 4 people get on and 3 people get off. When you stop again, 5 people get on and 2 people get off. At the last stop, 5 people get on and 1 person gets off. How old is the bus driver?

39 You live in a one-story purple house. Everything in the house is purple. The walls are purple, the refrigerator is purple, the plates are purple, etc. What color are the stairs?

40 What do you get when you cross the world's best fairy tale with the world's biggest mammal?

# WORD-CONNECT

Synonyms are words that have the same meaning. For example, "funny" and "comic" are synonyms. The answers to this crossword puzzle are all synonyms of the clues given below. See if you can fill in all the blanks.

**ACROSS**
1 Unbelievable
5 Point
7 Accept
8 Paddle
9 Tale
11 Bill
13 Mad
15 Even [straight]

**DOWN**
2 Performer
3 Fly
4 Container
6 Toss
8 Choice
10 Journey
12 Child
14 Shout

ANSWERS ON PAGES 334-336.

# Military

What country has the largest armed forces? ➡ page 118

## American Revolution

**Why?** The British king sought to control American trade and tax the 13 colonies without their consent. The colonies wanted independence.

**Who?** British and American loyalists vs. American revolutionaries with French support

**When?** 1775-1783

**Result?** The colonies gained independence.

## War of 1812

**Why?** Britain interfered with American commerce and forced American sailors to join the British navy.

**Who?** Britain vs. United States

*U.S.S. Constitution*

**When?** 1812-1814

**Result?** There was no clear winner. The U.S. unsuccessfully invaded Canada, a British colony. The British burned Washington, D.C., and the White House but were defeated in other battles.

*The lyrics to the "The Star Spangled Banner" were written by Francis Scott Key in 1814 after seeing the British attack on Fort McHenry and the resulting American victory during the War of 1812.*

## Mexican War

**Why?** The U.S. annexed Texas. It also sought control of California, a Mexican province.

**Who?** Mexico vs. United States

**When?** 1846-1848

**Result?** Mexico gave up its claim to Texas and ceded to the U.S. California and all or part of six other Western states.

## Civil War

**Why?** Eleven Southern states seceded from the U.S. The U.S. fought to keep them.

**Who?** Confederacy vs. Union

**When?** 1861-1865

**Result?** The United States remained a unified country. Slavery was abolished.

## Spanish-American War

**Why?** The Americans supported Cuban independence from Spain.

**Who?** United States vs. Spain

**When?** 1898

*The Charge of San Juan Hill*

**Result?** Spain handed the Philippines, Guam, and Puerto Rico over to the U.S. Cuba became independent.

*Future President Theodore Roosevelt led the charge of San Juan Hill.*

## World War I

**Why?** Colonial and military competition between European powers.

**Who?** Allies (including the U.S., Britain, France, Russia, Italy, and Japan) vs. Central Powers (including Germany, Austria-Hungary, and Turkey)

**When?** 1914-1918 (The U.S. entered in 1917)

**Result?** The Allies defeated the Central Powers. An estimated 8 million soldiers and close to 10 million civilians were killed.

## World War II

**Why?** The Axis sought world domination.

**Who?** Axis (including Germany, Italy, and Japan) vs. Allies (including the U.S., Britain, France, and the Soviet Union). The U.S. did not enter the war until Japan attacked Pearl Harbor in 1941.

**When?** 1939-1945 (U.S. dropped atomic bombs on Hiroshima and Nagasaki.)

*Yalta summit in 1945 with Winston Churchill, Franklin Roosevelt and Josef Stalin*

**Result?** The Allies defeated the Axis. The Holocaust (the Nazi effort to wipe out the Jews and other minorities) was stopped. The U.S. helped rebuild Western Europe and Japan. The Soviet Union set up Communist governments in Eastern Europe.

 *The Allied invasion of Nazi-occupied France on June 6, 1944, known as D-Day, was the biggest invasion in world history. More than 150,000 American, British, and Canadian soldiers stormed the beaches of Normandy.*

## Korean War

**Why?** North Korea invaded South Korea. In many ways, the conflict was part of the Cold War between the Communist and non-Communist nations.

**Who?** North Korea with support from China and the Soviet Union vs. South Korea backed by the United States and its allies.

**When?** 1950-1953

**Result?** The war ended with a cease-fire agreement. North Korean forces retreated north of the 38th parallel. Korea remains divided.

 *Nonmetallic body armor was used for the first time during the Korean War.*

## Vietnam War

**Why?** Communists (Viet Cong) backed by North Vietnam attempted to overthrow South Vietnam's government.

**Who?** North Vietnam with support from the Soviet Union and China vs. South Vietnam with support from the U.S. and its allies

**When?** 1959-1975

**Result?** The U.S. withdrew its troops in 1973. In 1975, South Vietnam surrendered. Vietnam became a unified Communist country

 *Two thirds of the Americans who served in Vietnam were volunteers.*

## Persian Gulf War

**Why?** Iraq invaded and annexed Kuwait. It refused to withdraw despite United Nations demands.

**Who?** Iraq vs. U.S.-led coalition

**When?** 1991

**Result?** The coalition drove out Iraqi forces from Kuwait.

*A-10A Thunderbolt II ground attack plane flying during Desert Storm, 1991*

# Where Are We Now?

## Afghanistan War

**Why?** The U.S. demanded that Afghanistan's Taliban regime turn over Osama bin Laden, the man who planned the 9/11 terrorist attacks. The Taliban claimed not to know bin Laden's whereabouts.

**Who?** Taliban regime vs. Afghani Northern Alliance fighters, supported by the U.S. and its allies

**When?** 2001-

**Result?** The Taliban was driven from power but in recent years has been regaining control over large parts of the country. The U.S. and its NATO allies continue to fight the Taliban and to train Afghan security forces.

 did you know?

*Small handheld or gun-mounted cameras, powered by two AA batteries and weighing less than a pound, allow U.S. soldiers to see in total darkness or through smoke or fog.*

## Iraq War

**Why?** The U.S. accused Iraq of hiding weapons of mass destruction (WMDs) and supporting terrorists.

**Who?** Iraq vs. United States, Great Britain, and their allies

**When?** 2003-

**Result?** Saddam Hussein's government was toppled. Hussein was captured, put on trial, and hanged. No WMDs were found. The U.S. has begun withdrawing its troops and hopes to have all combat forces out of Iraq in 2010.

## TOP ⑩ NATIONS WITH LARGEST ARMED FORCES

| | | | | | | |
|---|---|---|---|---|---|---|
| 1. | China | 2,225,000 | 6. | Pakistan | 700,000 |
| 2. | United States | 1,473,000 | 7. | South Korea | 687,000 |
| 3. | India | 1,414,000 | 8. | Turkey | 515,000 |
| 4. | North Korea | 1,106,000 | 9. | Vietnam | 484,000 |
| 5. | Russia | 1,037,000 | 10. | Egypt | 450,000 |

Source: International Institute for Strategic Studies, 2006. Figures are for active troops.

# MEDALS

The **MEDAL OF HONOR** is the nation's highest medal for any branch of the military. It's awarded by the President and Congress to a person who risks his or her life by going "above and beyond the call of duty" in battle. The five-pointed star is worn around the neck. It's been awarded about 3,467 times since 1863.

The **PURPLE HEART** is given to any soldier who is wounded or killed in battle. It is the oldest American decoration for military merit, first awarded by General George Washington in 1782. Washington's face has been on the medal since 1932.

# MODERN-DAY HEROES

The heroes below were each awarded the country's highest decoration for valor in combat, the Medal of Honor, posthumously (after death). Each one died in selfless, courageous acts of bravery that saved other lives.

## WAR IN AFGHANISTAN

MICHAEL P. MURPHY (1976-2005) Lieutenant, United States Navy

## OPERATION IRAQI FREEDOM

JASON L. DUNHAM (1981-2004) ▶
Corporal, United States Marine Corps

ROSS A. McGINNIS (1987-2006)
Private First Class, United States Army

MICHAEL A. MONSOOR (1981-2006)
Master-At-Arms Second Class (Sea, Air, and Land), United States Navy

JARED C . MONTI (1975-2006)
Sergeant First Class, United States Army

PAUL R. SMITH (1969-2003) Sergeant First Class, United States Army

# Money

What presidents were honored by the U.S. Mint with a gold coin in 2009?
➡ page 121

## World's Ten Richest People*

| Name | Age | Country | Industry | Worth (in billions) |
|---|---|---|---|---|
| Bill Gates | 53 | United States | Software (Microsoft) | 40.0 |
| Warren Buffett | 78 | United States | Investments | 37.0 |
| Carlos Slim Helu | 69 | Mexico | Communications | 35.0 |
| Lawrence Ellison | 64 | United States | Data Management – Oracle | 22.5 |
| Ingvar Kamprad | 83 | Sweden | Retail – IKEA | 22.0 |
| Karl Albrecht | 89 | Germany | Retail – Aldi | 21.5 |
| Mukesh Ambani | 51 | India | Manufacturing – Oil | 19.5 |
| Lakshmi Mittal | 58 | United Kingdom | Manufacturing – Steel | 19.3 |
| Theo Albrecht | 87 | Germany | Retail – Aldi, Trader Joe's | 18.8 |
| Amancio Ortega | 73 | Spain | Retail | 18.3 |

*As of March 2009 (Source www.forbes.com)

## Youngest Billionaires*

| Name | Age | Country | Industry | Worth (in billions) |
|---|---|---|---|---|
| Sergey Brin | 35 | United States | Technology – Google | 12.0 |
| Larry Page | 36 | United States | Technology – Google | 12.0 |
| Sheikh Mansour Bin Zayet Al Nahayan | 39 | Abu Dhabi | Family, Investments | 4.9 |
| John Arnold | 35 | United States | Hedge Fund Manager | 2.7 |
| Prince Albert von Thurn und Taxis | 25 | Germany | Diversified Investments | 2.1 |
| Kenneth Griffin | 40 | United States | Hedge Fund Manager | 1.5 |
| Chu Lam Yiu | 39 | China | Industrialist | 1.5 |
| William Ding | 38 | China | Industrialist | 1.1 |
| Jerry Yang | 40 | United States | Technology – Yahoo | 1.1 |
| Andrey Melnichenko | 37 | Russia | Industrialist | 1.0 |

*As of March 2009 (Source www.forbes.com)

# PRESIDENT DOLLARS

**N**ew gold-colored dollar coins honoring the nation's presidents are now being circulated. The U.S. Mint has started making one-dollar coins that show the faces of the presidents in the order they served in office. The Mint plans to issue four presidential $1 coins per year through 2016.

The George Washington dollar coin was the first. It was released on February 15, 2007. Coins with Presidents John Adams, Thomas Jefferson, and James Madison were also released in 2007. In 2008, the coins honored Presidents James Monroe, John Quincy Adams, Andrew Jackson, and Martin Van Buren.

So far, the coins have been released mid-month in February, May, August, and November. The presidents added in 2009 were William Henry Harrison, John Tyler, James K. Polk, and Zachary Taylor.

**T**he size, weight, and metal composition of the new coins are identical to the Sacagawea Golden dollar first minted in 2000. The heads side design of each coin shows a picture and the name of the President, his term in office, and the numerical order in which he served. The tails side design has a picture of the Statue of Liberty to represent Liberty, a term that appears on all other coins in circulation. The tail side design is the same for all these Presidential coins. Inscriptions that traditionally appear on the face of other U.S. coins are located on the edge of the Presidential $1 coins.

As they are introduced into circulation, the Presidential $1 coins will be available from banks, credit unions, and thrift institutions. The program is modeled after the 50 States Quarter Program, in which state quarters were introduced into circulation over a 10-year period from 1999 through 2008. For more information and a Presidential Dollar coin release schedule, visit the U.S. Mint's website at www.usmint.gov.

# The U.S. $1 Bill: AN OWNER'S MANUAL

**Everybody knows that George Washington is on the U.S. one-dollar bill, but did you ever wonder what all that other stuff is?**

**Plate position**
Shows where on the 32-note plate this bill was printed.

**The Treasury Department seal:** The balancing scales represent justice. The pointed stripe across the middle has 13 stars for the original 13 colonies. The key represents authority.

**Serial number**
Each bill has its own.

**Plate serial number**
Shows which printing plate was used for the face of the bill.

**Federal Reserve District Number**
Shows which district issued the bill.

**Treasurer of the U.S. Signature**

**Series indicator** (year note's design was first used)

**Secretary of the Treasury signature**

**(Since 1949, every Treasurer of the U.S. has been a woman.)**

**Federal Reserve District Seal**
The name of the Federal Reserve Bank that issued the bill is printed in the seal. The letter tells you quickly where the bill is from. Here are the letter codes for the 12 Federal Reserve Districts:

**A:** Boston **G:** Chicago
**B:** New York **H:** St. Louis
**C:** Philadelphia **I:** Minneapolis
**D:** Cleveland **J:** Kansas City
**E:** Richmond **K:** Dallas
**F:** Atlanta **L:** San Francisco

**Front of the Great Seal of the United States:** The bald eagle is the national bird. The shield has 13 stripes for the 13 original colonies. The eagle holds 13 arrows (symbol of war) and an olive branch (symbol of peace). Above the eagle is the motto "E Pluribus Unum," Latin for "out of many, one," and a constellation of 13 stars.

**Plate serial number**
Shows which plate was used for the back.

**Back of the Great Seal of the United States:**
The pyramid symbolizes something that lasts for ages. It is unfinished because the U.S. is always growing. The eye, known as the "Eye of Providence," probably comes from an ancient Egyptian symbol. The pyramid has 13 levels; at its base are the Roman numerals for 1776, the year of American independence. "Annuit Coeptis" is Latin for "God has favored our undertaking." "Novus Ordo Seclorum" is Latin for "a new order of the ages." Both phrases are from the works of the Roman poet Virgil.

# WORLD CURRENCY

ost countries have their own currency. Sometimes two countries call their currency by the same name, but the money usually has different designs and may have different values. Most currency is decorated with cultural symbols and pictures of important people in the country's history. The designs are colorful and interesting, and they also make it harder to counterfeit the money.

An exchange rate is the price of a country's currency in terms of another. For example, one U.S. dollar cost, or could buy, 6.83 yuan in China in September 2009. These rates are based on a country's economy, the value of products it makes and buys, and inflation, the increase in how much money is needed to buy goods.

When people want to buy goods or services from someone in another country, they need to exchange their money for, or buy, some of the other country's currency.

## THE EURO

For most of their histories, countries in Europe, like countries around the world, all had their own currencies. France, for example, used the franc. Germany's currency was called the mark, and Italy's was called the lira. Because Europe is so small and because many European countries wanted to make it easier for companies in one country to do business with companies in other countries, an organization was formed to find ways to eliminate barriers to trade. This organization, now called the European Union (EU), decided, among other things, to create one currency that could be used by many countries.

The euro, whose symbol is €, became the official currency of 11 EU members on January 1, 2002. Today, it is used by 16 EU countries, called the Eurozone: Austria, Belgium, Cyprus, Finland, France, Germany, Greece, Ireland, Italy, Luxembourg, Malta, the Netherlands, Portugal, Slovakia, Slovenia, and Spain. The euro is also now used by agreement in five other countries as well.

## HOW MUCH IS A DOLLAR WORTH?

In September 2009, here is about how much one dollar could buy of 12 other currencies:

| | | | |
|---|---|---|---|
| 0.60 | British pounds | 91.84 | Japanese yen |
| 1.08 | Canadian dollars | 13.33 | Mexican pesos |
| 6.83 | Chinese yuan | 31.12 | Russian rubles |
| 0.69 | euros | 3.75 | Saudi Arabian riyals |
| 48.50 | Indian rupees | 1,226.84 | South Korean won |
| 3.76 | Israeli new shekels | 1.49 | Turkish lira |

$$?

# Movies & TV

When will the final Harry Potter movie hit theaters? ➡ page 127

## MOVIE & TV FACTS

**What a Night!** *The Dark Knight* holds the record for highest one-day box office sales in the U.S. It also set a record for highest opening-day sales. The movie made $66.4 million when it opened in theaters on July 18, 2008.

**Giving Credit** *The Lord of the Rings: The Return of the King* (2003) has one of the longest closing credits of any movie. Hundreds of people, including a horse makeup artist, are listed in the credits, which last for nearly 10 minutes.

**A Good Run** Before *The Simpsons, The Flintstones* held the record for TV's longest running prime-time animated series. The cartoon, about two Stone Age families, lasted six seasons, from 1960 to 1966. *The Simpsons*, which has been on air since 1989, is currently in its 21st season.

*The Simpsons* ▶

| ALL-TIME TOP ANIMATED MOVIES* | | | ALL-TIME TOP MOVIES* | | |
|---|---|---|---|---|---|
| 1 | *Shrek 2* (2004) | $436.7 | 1 | *Star Wars* (1977) | $461.0 |
| 2 | *Finding Nemo* (2003) | 339.7 | 2 | *Shrek 2* (2004) | 436.7 |
| 3 | *The Lion King* (1994) | 328.5 | 3 | *E.T. the Extra-Terrestrial* (1982) | 435.0 |
| 4 | *Shrek the Third* (2007) | 322.7 | 4 | *Star Wars: Episode I— The Phantom Menace* (1999) | 431.1 |
| 5 | *Up* (2009) | 290.9 | 5 | *Finding Nemo* (2003) | 339.7 |
| 6 | *Shrek* (2001) | 267.7 | 6 | *The Lion King* (1994) | 328.5 |
| 7 | *The Incredibles* (2004) | 261.4 | 7 | *Shrek the Third* (2007) | 322.7 |
| 8 | *Monsters, Inc.* (2001) | 255.9 | 8 | *Harry Potter and the Sorcerer's Stone* (2001) | 317.6 |
| 9 | *Toy Story 2* (1999) | 245.9 | 9 | *Star Wars: Episode II— Attack of the Clones* (2002) | 310.7 |
| 10 | *Cars* (2006) | 244.1 | 10 | *Star Wars: Episode VI—Return of the Jedi* (1983) | 309.2 |

Source: *The Nielsen Group 2009*; rankings for movies rated G or PG.
*Through September 2009. Gross in millions of dollars based on box office sales in the U.S. and Canada.

# TOP TV SHOWS IN 2008-09

## AGES 6-11

### NETWORK
1. *American Idol*
2. *FOX NFL Sunday*
3. *WWE Friday Night Smackdown*
4. *Dancing with the Stars*
5. *Wipeout*

### CABLE
1. *Wizards of Waverly Place: The Movie*
2. *Kids' Choice Awards*
3. *iCarly Movie: iFight Shelby Marx*
4. *Princess Protection Program*
5. *Sonny with A Chance*

## AGES 12-17

### NETWORK
1. *American Idol*
2. *FOX NFL Sunday*
3. *NFL on CBS*
4. *NBC Sunday Night Football*
5. *Family Guy*

### CABLE
1. *Wizards of Waverly Place: The Movie*
2. *Kids' Choice Awards*
3. *Princess Protection Program*
4. *iCarly Movie: Shelby Marx5*
5. *iCarly Movie: Date a Bad Boy*

Source: *The Nielsen Group 2009*

▲ American Idol

## did you know?

Vampires seemed be everywhere in 2009, as fans of *Twilight* attended DVD release parties for the first movie and came out to see *New Moon* in theaters. The CW network aired its first episodes of *The Vampire Diaries*, and HBO pulled in strong ratings for its series *True Blood*. The movie *Cirque du Freak: The Vampire's Assistant* was released in October, starring Salma Hayek and John C. Reilly.

# ★ HITTING THEATERS IN 2009...

 *Cloudy with a Chance of Meatballs* is about an inventor who builds a machine that can turn water into food. (September)

 Based on the beloved children's book by Maurice Sendak, *Where the Wild Things Are* follows a boy named Max as he enters a magical world. (October)

 The documentary *More Than a Game* tells the story of a young LeBron James. (October)

 In *New Moon*, the Twilight saga continues. Bella must find a way to go on when she's faced with heartbreak. (November)

 The characters from Roald Dahl's book come to life in the stop-motion animated movie *The Fantastic Mister Fox*. (November)

 *The Princess and the Frog* is a traditional ▶ animated film based on the classic fairy tale. (November)

# ...AND IN 2010

 Tim Burton's remake of *Alice in Wonderland*, starring Johnny Depp and Anne Hathaway, hits theaters in March.

 *Shrek Forever After*, the fourth movie in the animated series, comes out in July.

 Robert Downey Jr., Gwyneth Paltrow, and Scarlett Johansson suit up for *Iron Man 2*, due in May.

 The next movie in the series, *Harry Potter and the Deathly Hallows: Part I*, will be released in November.

# BOOKS TO FILM

**Movie:** *The Wizard of Oz* (1939)
**Book:** *The Wonderful Wizard of Oz* by L. Frank Baum (1900)

The making of the classic film *The Wizard of Oz* was delayed by script problems. No one knew exactly how to make L. Frank Baum's magical story come to life on screen. Another problem was that 16-year-old Judy Garland was much older than the Dorothy Gale character that Baum had written about. When filming first began, Garland was dressed in a blond wig and childish make-up to make her look younger, but that idea was quickly scrapped.

Readers of *The Wonderful Wizard of Oz* could easily spot where changes were made to adapt the movie for the big screen. In Baum's story, Dorothy's slippers were silver, but ruby slippers looked more dramatic in technicolor! Baum's book was also pretty violent for a children's book—the Wizard sends Dorothy to kill the Wicked Witch, not just to get her broomstick. The Tin Man (Tin Woodsman, in the book) uses his ax on forest creatures. In the end, the filmmakers didn't think that moviegoers would buy all of Baum's fantasy, and they changed the story so Dorothy would wake up at the end as if it were all a dream.

**Movies:** *Willy Wonka and the Chocolate Factory* (1971); *Charlie and the Chocolate Factory* (2005)
**Book:** *Charlie and the Chocolate Factory* by Roald Dahl (1964)

*Charlie and the Chocolate Factory* was first adapted to the big screen in 1971. Dahl himself wrote the original screenplay, but it was heavily changed. By the time the movie came out, much of Dahl's original story had been altered, and he was rumored to have hated the film. During Veruca Salt's downfall in the book, she is judged a "bad nut" by nut-selecting squirrels; in the first film version, she is judged a bad egg by the golden egg machine.

Fortunately, in the Hollywood movie business, there's usually a second chance! The screenwriter for the 2005 remake *Charlie and the Chocolate Factory* had never seen the original film before he began writing. He wrote a script working solely from Dahl's novel. The squirrel scene was reinstated. But other changes were made. For instance, in the book, Willy Wonka never mentions his father, but in the movie, his candy-hating dentist father becomes a big part of the story. There's much debate among Charlie fans over which movie follows the book more closely—and whether that's important.

**Movie:** *Harry Potter and the Half-Blood Prince* (2009)
**Book:** *Harry Potter and the Half-Blood Prince* (2005)

Each of the books in the tremendously popular Harry Potter series by J.K. Rowling has been or will be made into a movie. The movie stories follow the basic plots of the books closely. The movies have also been very popular.

## Harry Potter Retrospective

**1** *Harry Potter and the Sorcerer's Stone* (book: 1997; movie: 2001)

**2** *Harry Potter and the Chamber of Secrets* (book: 1998; movie: 2002)

**3** *Harry Potter and the Prisoner of Azkaban* (book: 1999; movie: 2004)

**4** *Harry Potter and the Goblet of Fire* (book: 2000; movie: 2005)

**5** *Harry Potter and the Order of the Phoenix* (book: 2003; movie: 2007)

**6** *Harry Potter and the Half-Blood Prince* (book: 2005; movie: 2009)

**7** *Harry Potter and the Deathly Hallows* (book: 2007; movies: 2010 and 2011)

*Image from Harry Potter and the Half-Blood Prince*

**Movie:** *The Chronicles of Narnia: Prince Caspian* (2008)
**Book:** *The Chronicles of Narnia: Prince Caspian* (1951)

*The Chronicles of Narnia* is a series of seven books written by C.S. Lewis. *The Lion, the Witch, and the Wardrobe* is the first book in the series and *Prince Caspian* is the second book. (A movie version of *The Voyage of the Dawn Treader*, the next book in the series, is expected to come out in 2010.)

Both the book and movie of *Prince Caspian* follow four siblings who return to the land of Narnia. It has been one year in their world but 1,300 years have passed in Narnia. The Pevensie children help the rightful heir, Prince Caspian, reclaim his throne. There are some differences between the movie and the book. Peter and Caspian have a bit of a rivalry. Susan also plays a more active role as an archer in battle in the movie version.

*Image from The Chronicles of Narnia: Prince Caspian*

# MOVIES & TV MATCH-UPS

Match these duos with the movie or TV show in which they belong.

| DUOS | MOVIE OR TV SHOW |
|------|------------------|
| Mac & Blooregard | *Wizards of Waverly Place* |
| Katara & Sokka | *Pirates of the Caribbean* |
| Will & Elizabeth | *American Idol* |
| Alex & Justin | *Iron Man* |
| Susan & Reed | *Foster's Home for Imaginary Friends* |
| Simon & Ryan | *Zoey 101* |
| Tony & Pepper | *Fantastic Four* |
| Quinn & Lola | *Avatar: The Last Airbender* |

ANSWERS ON PAGES 334–336.

# Museums

What is the largest museum complex in the world? ➡ page 128

**M**useums collect things of great interest, such as works of art or everyday objects from different times in the past, and show them off to visitors. Some museums teach you all about science and technology.

## The American Museum of Natural History, in New York City, dates back to

1869, and is the biggest natural science museum in the world. It has huge dinosaur skeletons, lifelike scenes of animals in different environments, and exhibits that show humans as they lived tens of thousands of years ago. The museum's **Rose Center for Earth and Space** (pictured at right) contains interactive exhibits about astronomy and astrophysics, as well as the world's most advanced star projector. Inside the Hayden Planetarium, the projector takes you on a journey through a virtual re-creation of the Milky Way Galaxy.
**WEB SITE** *www.amnh.org*

**Exploratorium**, in San Francisco, California, is a place to learn about everything from frogs to earthquakes to space weather. Grope through darkness in the Tactile Dome, where the sense of touch is your only guide. There are "hands-on" exhibits in all areas of science, with plenty of things to look at, pick up, and tinker with. **WEB SITE** *www.exploratorium.com*

## The Smithsonian Institution,
in Washington, DC, is not just one museum, but 18 museums, most of them located along the Mall in Washington. It's the biggest museum complex in the world, holding about 142 million objects, from First Ladies' dresses to the first airplane flown by the Wright Brothers. The Smithsonian includes the National Air and Space Museum, the National Portrait Gallery, and the National Zoo.
**WEB SITE** *www.si.edu*

# MUSEUMS OF ALL KINDS

The **Newseum** in **Washington, DC**, opened in 2008. This interactive museum allows visitors to explore how and why news is made. The exhibits blend five centuries of news history with modern technology to illustrate the importance of the news. The museum has 14 major galleries, 8 sections of the Berlin Wall, 7 levels, and 2 television studios. **WEB SITE** *www.newseum.org*

**Jamestown Settlement** in **Williamsburg, Virginia.** This "living museum" includes re-creations of an Indian village, a fort, and the first permanent English settlement in America. Museum staff wear costumes and show what life was like for colonists 400 years ago. **WEB SITE** *www.historyisfun.org*

## The International UFO Museum and Research Center
in **Roswell, New Mexico**, is dedicated to research into UFOs, or "unidentified flying objects" from outer space. Some say that a UFO crashed in the nearby desert back in 1947. **WEB SITE** *www.iufomrc.com*

The **Buffalo Bill Historical Center** in **Cody, Wyoming**, includes five museums and a research library devoted to the American west. The museums include artworks of the American West, Plains Indian art and artifacts, and a natural history museum that provides a multidisciplinary perspective on the Greater Yellowstone Ecosystem, its surrounding area, and human interactions. **WEB SITE** *www.bbhc.org*

## National Museum of Health and Medicine in **Washington, DC**. Founded
during the Civil War as the Army Medical Museum, it holds specimens for research in military medicine and surgery. One of the most popular exhibits has artifacts from President Lincoln's assassination, including the bullet. **WEB SITE** *nmhm.washingtondc.museum*

The Temple of Dendur is one of the most popular exhibits at the Metropolitan Museum of Art in NYC. It was built in 15 BC to honor the goddess Isis. The temple was a gift to the United States from Egypt in gratitude for American help in saving monuments from ancient Egypt. It had to be moved because a dam was built near its original location. The building was taken apart and shipped to the US. Engineers used detailed drawings to reconstruct the original temple inside the museum.

AMERICAN MUSEUM OF NATURAL HISTORY

# Music & Dance

Which popular singer performed the song for President and Michelle Obama's "first dance" in 2009? ➡ page 131

## TOP ALBUMS OF 2008

1. As I Am..............................Alicia Keys ▶
2. Noël................................Josh Groban
3. Tha Carter III......................Lil Wayne
4. Long Road Out of Eden...............Eagles
5. Taylor Swift........................Taylor Swift
6. Rock N Roll Jesus...................Kid Rock
7. Viva La Vida or Death and All His Friends...Coldplay
8. NOW 26..............................Various Artists
9. Carnival Ride.......................Carrie Underwood
10. The Ultimate Hits..................Garth Brooks

*Source: Billboard 200*/The Nielsen Company

## All About >> American Idol

*American Idol* is a popular television reality competition show. The program's goal is to discover the best singer in the country. Auditions are held in various cities across the United States. The show's judges select a group of semifinalists who sing each week on the program. The judges offer comments after each performance. Then the viewing public votes by phone or text message to decide who advances or who goes home. The results are announced the following night. Eventually, only two finalists are left to compete for the title of American Idol. In 2009, the winner was **Kris Allen**. Winners from previous seasons are Kelly Clarkson, Ruben Studdard, Fantasia Barrino, Carrie Underwood, Taylor Hicks, Jordin Sparks, and David Cook. Many of the runners-up and other contestants have gone on to successful musical and acting careers, including Chris Daughtry and Jennifer Hudson. In late 2009 one the original judges, Paula Abdul, announced she would not be returning to the show. Actress and talk show host Ellen DeGeneres will take her place in 2010. Ellen will join judges Simon Cowell, Randy Jackson, and Kara DioGuardi.

# WHO'S HOT NOW

## BEYONCÉ KNOWLES

**Born:** September 4, 1981, in Houston, Texas

**Albums (Solo):** *Dangerously in Love* (2003), *B'Day* (2006), *I Am . . . Sasha Fierce* (2008)

R&B star Beyoncé grew up in Houston, Texas, with her parents and younger sister, Solange. Beyoncé was a shy child, but she always loved performing. She won her first talent show at age seven, after singing John Lennon's "Imagine." The crowd gave her a standing ovation. After trying out a few different groups, Beyoncé was signed to Columbia Records in 1997 with Destiny's Child. The group became very popular and had a long list of hits with songs such as "Say My Name" and "Survivor." In 2003, Beyoncé released her first solo album, *Dangerously in Love*. The first single from the album, "Crazy in Love," featured then-boyfriend Jay-Z and spent eight straight weeks at number one on the Billboard Hot 100 list. The album went on to win five Grammy awards. "Single Ladies (Put a Ring On It)," the first single from *I Am . . . Sasha Fierce*, gave Beyoncé her fifth number-one single in the United States. Beyoncé is also a successful actress. Some of her best-known roles include Deena Jones in *Dreamgirls* and Etta James in *Cadillac Records*. Beyoncé was honored when she was asked to sing Etta James's "At Last" for President Barack Obama and First Lady Michelle Obama during their inaugural-ball first dance, on January 20, 2009 (see photo).

## BRAD PAISLEY

**Born:** October 28, 1972, in Glen Dale, West Virginia

**Albums:** *Who Needs Pictures* (1999), *Part II* (2001), *Mud on the Tires* (2003), *Time Well Wasted* (2005), *Brad Paisley Christmas* (2006), *5th Gear* (2007), *Play* (2008), *American Saturday Night* (2009)

This country music singer started learning how to play the guitar when he was just eight years old. He wrote his first song at age twelve, and by thirteen was already opening for established country acts such as the Judds and George Jones. Brad had his first hit song in December 1999, with "He Didn't Have to Be." He won the Academy of Country Music's Best New Artist award in 2000. In 2003, Brad married actress Kimberly Williams. Their first son, William, was born in 2007, and son Jasper followed in 2009. After receiving many nominations over the years, Brad won his first Grammy in 2008, for the song "Throttleneck." In July 2009, Brad performed at the White House as part of the White House Music Series. In the audience was President Barack Obama, the nation's first African-American president. After the performance Brad said, "Being able to deliver that message [singing about change in America] personally to one of the people who ushered in this new era is really one of the most completely, artistically satisfying moments I've ever had."

# MUSICAL INSTRUMENTS

There are many kinds of musical instruments. Instruments in an orchestra are divided into four groups, or sections: string, woodwind, brass, and percussion.

**PERCUSSION INSTRUMENTS** Percussion instruments make sounds when they are struck. They include drums, cymbals, triangles, gongs, bells, and xylophones. Keyboard instruments, like the piano, are sometimes included in percussion instruments.

**BRASSES** Brass instruments are hollow inside. They make sounds when air is blown into a mouthpiece. The trumpet, French horn, trombone, and tuba are brasses.

**WOODWINDS** Woodwinds are cylindrical and hollow inside. They make sounds when air is blown into them. The clarinet, flute, oboe, bassoon, and piccolo are woodwinds.

**STRINGS** Stringed instruments make sounds when the strings are either stroked with a bow or plucked with the fingers. The violin, viola, cello, bass, and harp are used in an orchestra. The guitar, banjo, and mandolin are other stringed instruments.

# UNUSUAL MUSICAL INSTRUMENTS

The Aeolian Wind Harp, also called a harmonic harp, is an ancient musical instrument that is played by the wind. It dates back to ancient Greece and is named for the Greek god of the wind, Aeolus. It is designed to play only pure harmonic tones. Changes in wind velocity create higher or lower harmonics at louder or softer volumes. Aeolian wind harps are still hand-crafted today.

The Sea Organ is a musical instrument that is played by the sea. It was created by Nikoa Basic in 2005. The Sea Organ is a pipe organ with 35 organ pipes built under concrete along the shores of Zadar, Croatia. Sea water and wind movements push air through the pipes to create a variety of random, beautiful musical sounds.

# DANCING WITH THE STARS

*Dancing with the Stars* is a television reality-competition show that pairs a celebrity with a professional ballroom dancer. The professional dancer teaches the celebrity how to perform various ballroom dances. Among these dances are the foxtrot, cha-cha-cha, quickstep, jive, tango, paso doble, rumba, samba, and waltz.

Each pair dances live on the show every week. The dancers receive scores from three professional dance judges. Program viewers may also cast their votes by calling a toll-free number, online at the ABC website, or by text messaging. The judges' scores and the viewer votes are combined to create a score. The pair with the lowest score is eliminated from the competition each week.

The winners of the 2009 season were **Shawn Johnson** (2008 Olympic Gold Medalist in gymnastics) and professional dancer **Mark Ballas**. It was the second win for Ballas, who won in 2008 with partner Kristi Yamaguchi.

## SALSA DANCING

Salsa dancing is a mix of different Latin American dance forms. Here are the basic steps in salsa dancing:

You will be the leader. Face your partner, and take their right hand with your left hand. Put your right hand around your partner and rest it in the middle of his/her back. Your partner should put his/her left hand on your right shoulder.

1. Stand with your feet together. This is the starting position. Slide your left foot forward. At the same time, your partner steps back with the right foot.
2. Shift your weight to your right foot, and slide your left foot back to starting position. At the same time, your partner shifts his/her weight to the left foot and slides the right foot forward to starting position.
3. Slide your right foot back, while your partner steps forward with the left foot.
4. Shift your weight onto your left foot, and bring your right foot back to starting position. Your partner shifts his/her weight to the right foot and slides the left foot back to starting position.

# Mythology

What is Pandora's Box? ➡ page 135

## MYTHS OF THE GREEKS

As the ancient Greeks went about their daily lives, they believed that a big family of gods and goddesses were watching over them from Mount Olympus. Farmers planting crops, sailors crossing the sea, and poets writing verses thought that these powerful beings could help or harm them. Stories of the gods and goddesses are called **myths**. Some of the oldest myths come from the *Iliad* and *Odyssey*, long poems in Greek composed around 700 B.C.

After the Romans conquered Greece in 146 B.C., they adopted Greek myths but gave Roman names to the main gods and goddesses. The planets in our solar system are named after Roman gods.

The family of Greek and Roman gods and goddesses was large. Their family tree would have more than 50 figures on it. The deities listed are the Olympian gods, the most important of the gods, who lived on Mount Olympus. Those with * are children of Zeus (Jupiter).

| Greek Name | Roman Name | Description |
|---|---|---|
| Aphrodite | Venus | Goddess of beauty and of love |
| *Apollo | Phoebus | God of prophecy, music, and medicine |
| *Ares | Mars | God of war; protector of the city |
| *Artemis | Diana | Goddess of the Moon; and of the Hunt |
| *Athena | Minerva | Goddess of wisdom and of war |
| Cronus | Saturn | Father of Zeus (Jupiter), Poseidon (Neptune), Hades (Pluto), Hera (Juno), and Demeter (Ceres) |
| Demeter | Ceres | Goddess of crops and harvest, sister of Zeus (Jupiter) |
| *Dionysus | Bacchus | God of wine, dancing, and theater |
| Hades | Pluto | Ruler of the Underworld, brother of Zeus (Jupiter) |
| Hephaestus | Vulcan | God of fire |
| Hera | Juno | Queen of the gods, wife of Zeus (Jupiter), goddess of marriage |
| *Hermes | Mercury | Messenger god, had winged helmet and sandals |
| Poseidon | Neptune | God of the sea and of earthquakes, brother of Zeus (Jupiter) |
| Zeus | Jupiter | Sky god, ruler of gods and mortals |

**Greek & Roman Gods**

# MAKING SENSE of the WORLD

Unlike folklore or fables, myths were once thought to be true. Most ancient peoples explained many things in nature by referring to gods and heroes with superhuman qualities. To the Greeks a rough sea meant that POSEIDON was angry. Lightning was THOR'S hammer in Norse mythology. Ancient Egyptians believed that the sun, as it rose and set everyday, was a lifetime for RE, the creator and ruler of the universe. In Japan, AMATERASU was the Shinto sun goddess who gave light to the land. Her brother SUSANOO was the storm god who ruled the sea.

There are even stories of gods or heroes who chose brain over brawn to get what they wanted. COYOTE was wild and cunning, a true trickster for many Native American tribes throughout the West. He was usually a loner and was never simply good or bad. ANANSI was a spider in the stories of the Akan tribes of West Africa. The tiny spider used his wits to capture the hornet, python, and leopard. In return the sky god NYAME let him own every story ever told.

Myths have remained popular long after people knew they weren't real because the stories hold important life lessons and morals for cultures around the world. Myths have also inspired countless stories and works of art.

Re

# Greek & Roman Heroes

Besides stories about the gods, Greek and Roman mythology has many stories about other heroes with amazing qualities.

• ODYSSEUS, the king of Ithaca, was a hero of the Trojan War in the *Iliad*. It was his idea to build a huge wooden horse, hide Greek soldiers inside, and smuggle them into the city of Troy to capture it. The *Odyssey* is the story of his long and magical trip home after the war.

• PANDORA was the first woman created by the Greek gods. Zeus ordered Hephaestus to create a beautiful woman out of earth. All the Olympian gods gave her gifts (her name means "gifts of all"). Hera's gift was curiosity. When Pandora was finished, she received a box which she was never to open. Her curiosity could not resist and Pandora opened the box to release all the evil spirits upon the world.

• JASON and the Argonauts set out on a quest to find the golden fleece, so Jason could reclaim his rightful throne. Among the Argonauts were Herakles and Orpheus. After many adventures and with the help of Medea, Jason slew the Minotaur and claimed the fleece. He later betrayed Medea

and eventually died when a beam from his ship, the Argo, fell off and hit him on the head.

Hercules

The most popular hero was Herakles, or **Hercules**. The most famous of his deeds were his 12 labors. They included killing the **Hydra**, a many-headed monster, and capturing the three-headed dog **Cerberus**, who guarded the gates of the Underworld. Hercules was so great a hero that the gods granted him immortality. When his body lay on his funeral pyre, Athena came and carried him off to Mount Olympus in her chariot.

# Nations

How many official languages are spoken at the United Nations?
➡ page 137

# GOVERNMENTS

Among the world's 195 independent nations there are various kinds of governments.

**Totalitarianism** In **totalitarian** countries the rulers have strong power, and the people have little freedom. North Korea currently has a totalitarian government.

**Monarchy** A country with a king or queen can be called a **monarchy**. Monarchies are almost always hereditary, meaning the throne is passed down in one family.

**Democracy** The word **democracy** comes from the Greek words *demos* ("people") and *kratos* ("rule"). In a democracy, the people rule. In most modern democracies, there are too many people to agree on everyday decisions. So people make decisions through the leaders they choose. These democracies are called **representative** democracies. If people are unhappy with their leaders, they can vote them out of office. Winston Churchill, a former British prime minister, probably had that in mind when he said, "Democracy is the worst form of government except all those other forms that have been tried from time to time."

**UN SECRETARY-GENERAL BAN KI-MOON** of South Korea became the eighth secretary-general of the United Nations January 1, 2007, succeeding Kofi Annan. So what does the secretary-general do?

The secretary-general heads the Secretariat, which has a staff of thousands from all different countries. The Secretariat oversees the UN's day-to-day operation. The secretary-general makes sure that programs and policies the UN has agreed on, such as peacekeeping operations, are running smoothly. He also functions as a diplomat. He tries to resolve disputes between countries. In addition, the secretary-general is an advocate for those who are less fortunate. He learns what social and economic problems exist around the world and prepares reports on them. As a leader, the secretary-general upholds the UN's commitment to world peace.

The secretary-general is appointed by the General Assembly on the Security Council's recommendation. The term of office is five years, which can be renewed.

Before becoming secretary-general, Ban served in the South Korean government. (Ban is his family name, Ki-moon is his personal name.) He can speak Korean, English, and French.

# A COMMUNITY OF NATIONS

The UN emblem shows the world surrounded by olive branches of peace.

The **United Nations (UN)** was started in 1945 after World War II. The first members were 51 nations, 50 of which met in San Francisco, California. They signed an agreement known as the UN Charter. The UN now has 192 members, including Montenegro, which joined in 2006. Only three independent nations—Kosovo, Taiwan, and Vatican City—are not members.

## HOW THE UN IS ORGANIZED

▶ **GENERAL ASSEMBLY** **What It Does:** Discusses world problems, admits new members, appoints the secretary-general, decides the UN budget. **Members:** All UN members; each country has one vote.

▶ **SECURITY COUNCIL** **What It Does:** Handles questions of peace and security. **Members:** Five permanent members (China, France, UK, Russia, U.S.) who must all vote the same way before certain proposals can pass; ten elected by the General Assembly to two-year terms. In 2009, the ten were Austria, Japan, Mexico, Turkey, and Uganda (terms ending December 31, 2010) and Burkina Faso, Costa Rica, Croatia, Libya, and Vietnam (terms ending December 31, 2011).

▶ **ECONOMIC AND SOCIAL COUNCIL** **What It Does:** Deals with issues related to economic development, population, education, health, and human rights. **Members:** 54 member countries elected to three-year terms.

▶ **INTERNATIONAL COURT OF JUSTICE (WORLD COURT)** located in The Hague, Netherlands. **What It Does:** UN court for disputes between countries. **Members:** 15 judges, each from a different country, elected to nine-year terms.

▶ **SECRETARIAT** **What It Does:** Carries out the UN's day-to-day operations. **Members:** UN staff, headed by the secretary-general.

*For more information, e-mail* inquiries@un.org *or write to:* Public Inquiries Unit, Dept. of Public Information, United Nations, Room GA-57, New York, NY 10017

**WEB SITE** www.un.org

The United Nations Headquarters is in New York City but the land and buildings are considered international territory. The United Nations flies its own flag and has its own post office—which sells UN postage stamps. Six official languages are spoken at the UN—Arabic, Chinese, English, French, Russian and Spanish.

## Other UN Agencies

The UN also runs a number of special agencies that perform humanitarian work. They include the Food and Agriculture Organization, the World Health Organization, and the World Bank.

# Maps showing Nations of the World

Maps showing the continents and nations of the world appear on pages 138-149. Flags of the nations appear on pages 150-175. A map of the United States appears on pages 290-291.

# AUSTRALIA

- ⊛ National Capital
- ★ State Capital
- • Other City

1:40,886,000

0       250      500 mi
0    250    500 km

Two-Point Equidistant Projection

© GeoNova

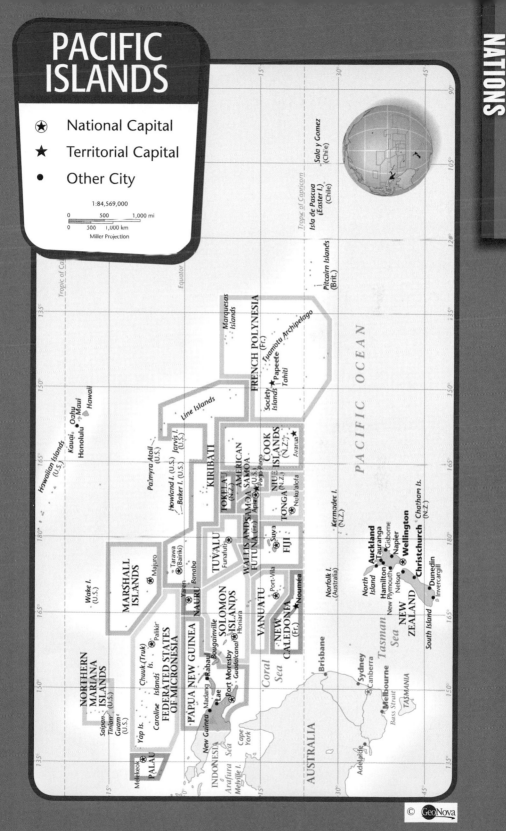

# PACIFIC ISLANDS

- ⍟ National Capital
- ★ Territorial Capital
- ● Other City

1:84,569,000

0      500      1,000 mi
0    300    1,000 km
Miller Projection

*Sala y Gomez (Chile)*

*Isla de Pascua (Easter I.) (Chile)*

*Pitcairn Islands (Brit.)*

*Marquesas Islands*

**FRENCH POLYNESIA** (Fr.)

*Tuamotu Archipelago*

Society Islands ★ Papeete · Tahiti

PACIFIC OCEAN

*Line Islands*

*Hawaiian Islands (U.S.)* · Kauai · Oahu · Maui · Hawaii · Honolulu

*Palmyra Atoll (U.S.)*

*Howland I. (U.S.)* · *Baker I. (U.S.)* · *Jarvis I. (U.S.)*

**KIRIBATI**

**COOK ISLANDS** (N.Z.) · ★ Avarua

**TOKELAU** (N.Z.)

**AMERICAN SAMOA** (U.S.) · Pago Pago

**SAMOA** ⍟ Apia

**NIUE** (N.Z.)

**TONGA** ⍟ Nuku'alofa

*Kermadec I. (N.Z.)*

Wake I. (U.S.)

**MARSHALL ISLANDS** ⍟ Majuro

· Tarawa (Bairiki) · Banaba

**TUVALU** ⍟ Funafuti

**WALLIS AND FUTUNA** (Fr.)

**FIJI** · Suva

**VANUATU** · Port-Vila

*Norfolk I. (Australia)*

Auckland · Tauranga
Hamilton · Gisborne
New Plymouth · Napier
Nelson · ⍟ Wellington
**NORTH ISLAND**
Christchurch · *Chatham Is. (N.Z.)*
**NEW ZEALAND**
**SOUTH ISLAND** · Dunedin · Invercargill

**NORTHERN MARIANA ISLANDS** (U.S.) · Saipan · Tinian (U.S.) · Guam (U.S.)

Yap Is. · Chuuk (Truk) · Palikir · Caroline Islands
**FEDERATED STATES OF MICRONESIA**

★ Yaren · **NAURU**

**SOLOMON ISLANDS** · Honiara

Bougainville · Guadalcanal

**PAPUA NEW GUINEA** · Rabaul · Madang · Lae · ⍟ Port Moresby

*New Guinea*

**NEW CALEDONIA** (Fr.) · ★ Nouméa

*Coral Sea*

*Cape York*

· Brisbane

**AUSTRALIA**

· Sydney · ⍟ Canberra

*Tasman Sea*

⍟ Melbourne · *Bass Strait* · **TASMANIA**

· Adelaide

Melekeok ⍟ **PALAU**

**INDONESIA** · *Arafura Sea* · *Melville I.*

© GeoNova

SWEDEN
NORWAY
UNITED KINGDOM
ICELAND

Greenland Sea

Spitsbergen

Denmark Strait

Cape Farewell

Tasiilaq

Arctic Circle

GREENLAND
(KALAALLIT NUNAAT)
(Den.)

Nuuk

Davis Strait

Labrador Sea

NEWFOUNDLAND
AND LABRADOR

St. Anthony
Island of
Newfoundland
Happy Valley
Goose Bay

Corner Brook

St. Pierre &
Miquelon (Fr.)
St. John's
Sydney

Anticosti I.
N.E.P.I.
BRUNS.

Hebron

Schefferville

Labrador City
Sept-Îles

QUEBEC

Chibougamau
Chicoutimi

Cape
Morris Jessup

North Pole

Arctic Ocean

Nord

Knud Rasmussen
Land

Qaanaaq
(Thule)

Alert

Ellesmere
I.

Gibse Fiord

Queen
Elizabeth
Islands

Resolute

Baffin
Bay

Pangnirtung

Baffin Island

Arctic Bay

Pond Inlet

Iqaluit

Hudson Strait

Povungnituk

Ungava
Peninsula

Belcher
Is.

James
Bay

Moosonee

ONTARIO

CANADIAN SHIELD

Holman

Banks
I.

Victoria
I.

Cambridge
Bay

Repulse-Bay

Southampton
I.

Hudson
Bay

Churchill

York
Factory

Winnipeg

Mississippi

Beaufort
Sea

Sachs
Harbour

Kugluktuk

NUNAVUT

CANADA

MANITOBA

Thompson

Flin Flon

SASK.

La Ronge

Prince
Albert

Saskatoon

Regina

Point
Barrow

Barrow

Kotzebue

Point
Hope

RUSSIA

Bering Strait

Arctic Circle

Nome

Bethel

Kenai

Seward

Kodiak

Inuvik
Fort McPherson

Fort Yukon

Yukon

Fairbanks

ALASKA RANGE

Mt. McKinley
6,194 m.
(20,320 ft.)

Anchorage

Valdez

Mt. Logan
5,959 m
(19,551 ft.)

Gulf of
Alaska

Yakutat

Bering
Sea

Great
Bear L.

Déline

Mackenzie

NORTHWEST
TERRITORIES

Yellowknife

Great
Slave

Ft.
Simpson

Hay
River

Ft.
Smith

Uranium
City

Athabasca

Ft.
McMurray

ALBERTA

Peace
River

Edmonton

Calgary

GREAT

ROCKY

Watson
Lake

Dawson

Mayo

YUKON

Whitehorse

Carmacks

Skagway

Juneau

Sitka

Ketchikan

COAST MOUNTAINS

Prince Rupert

Queen
Charlotte Is.

Kitimat

BRITISH
COLUMBIA

Prince George

Jasper

Williams Lake

Fraser

Peace

Athabasca

La Loche

RANGE

Vancouver
I.

Vancouver

Victoria

140

# NORTH AMERICA

⊛ National Capital

★ Territorial Capital

• Other City

1:39,978,000

0    350    700 mi

0    350    700 km

Azimuthal Equal Area Projection

© GeoNova

ATLANTIC OCEAN

PACIFIC OCEAN

Caribbean Sea

Gulf of Mexico

Bay of Campeche

Gulf of California

Straits of Florida

VENEZUELA

COLOMBIA

BRAZIL

UNITED STATES

MEXICO

CUBA

THE BAHAMAS

HAITI

DOMINICAN REPUBLIC

PUERTO RICO (U.S.)

JAMAICA

BELIZE

GUATEMALA

HONDURAS

EL SALVADOR

NICARAGUA

COSTA RICA

PANAMA

Bermuda (Brit.)

New York City

Washington, D.C.

Mexico City

Santo Domingo

San Juan

Havana

Port-au-Prince

Kingston

Nassau

Belmopan

Guatemala City

San Salvador

Tegucigalpa

Managua

San José

Panama City

141

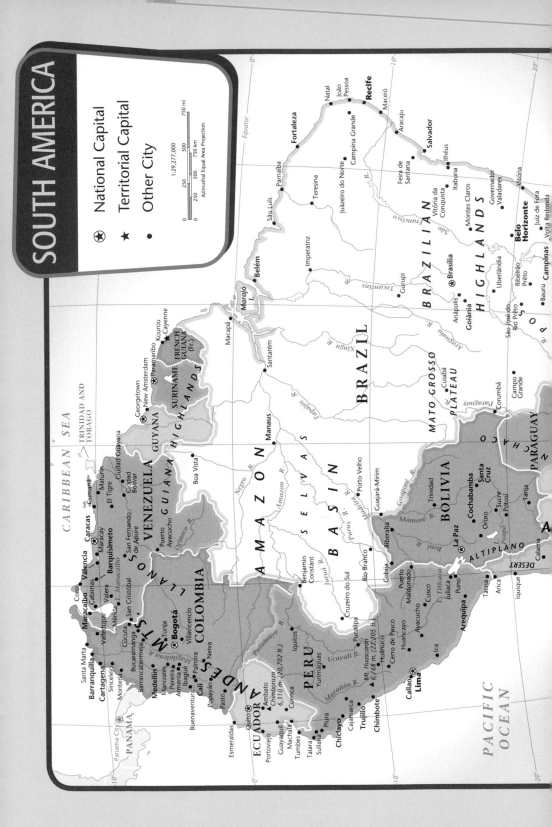

# SOUTH AMERICA

⊛ National Capital

★ Territorial Capital

• Other City

1:29,277,000

```
0    250   500   750 km
0    250   500      750 mi
```
Azimuthal Equal Area Projection

CARIBBEAN SEA

TRINIDAD AND TOBAGO

PACIFIC OCEAN

Panama City ⊛
PANAMA

Santa Marta
Barranquilla
Cartagena
Sincelejo
Montería
Coro
Maracaibo
Cabimas
L. Maracaibo
Valencia
Caracas ★
Maracay
Barquisimeto
Cumaná
Maturín
El Tigre
Ciudad Guayana
Ciudad Bolívar
VENEZUELA
San Fernando de Apure
Puerto Ayacucho
Orinoco R.
GUIANA HIGHLANDS
Georgetown
GUYANA
New Amsterdam
Paramaribo ⊛
SURINAME
Kourou
Cayenne
FRENCH GUIANA (Fr.)

Valledupar
Cúcuta
Valera
Mérida
San Cristóbal
Bucaramanga
Barrancabermeja
Medellín
Manizales
Pereira
Ibagué
Armenia
COLOMBIA
Tunja
Bogotá ⊛
Villavicencio
Palmira
Cali
Neiva
Popayán
Pasto
Buenaventura
LLANOS
ANDES MTS.

Esmeraldas
Quito ⊛
Portoviejo
Ambato
Chimborazo 6,310 m (20,702 ft.)
ECUADOR
Guayaquil
Machala
Cuenca
Tumbes
Talara
Sullana
Piura
Chiclayo
Cajamarca
Trujillo
Chimbote
Callao ⊛
Lima ⊛
PERU
Yurimaguas
Iquitos
Huánuco
Cerro de Pasco
Mt. Huascarán ▲ 6,768 m (22,205 ft.)
Pucallpa
Cruzeiro do Sul
Huancayo
Ayacucho
Ica
Cusco
Arequipa
Juliaca
Puno
Tacna
Arica
Iquique

Putumayo R.
Marañón R.
Ucayali R.
Negro R.
Japurá R.
Purus R.
Juruá R.
Madeira R.
AMAZON
SELVAS
BASIN
Benjamin Constant
Rio Branco
Boa Vista
Manaus
Santarém
Macapá
Marajó I.
Belém
Imperatriz
São Luís
Parnaíba
Fortaleza
Teresina
Natal
João Pessoa
Recife
Maceió
Aracaju
Campina Grande
Juazeiro do Norte
Feira de Santana
Salvador
Ilhéus
Itabuna
Vitória da Conquista
Montes Claros
Governador Valadares
Vitória
Belo Horizonte
Juiz de Fora
Volta Redonda
Campinas
Bauru
Ribeirão Prêto
São José do Rio Prêto
Uberlândia
Gurupi
Anápolis
Goiânia
Brasília ⊛
BRAZILIAN HIGHLANDS
B R A Z I L I A N
H I G H L A N D S

São Francisco R.
Tocantins R.
Xingu R.
Tapajós R.
Araguaia R.

BRAZIL
B R A Z I L

MATO GROSSO PLATEAU
Cuiabá
Corumbá
Campo Grande
CHACO
PARAGUAY
Paraguay R.

Porto Velho
Guajará-Mirim
Riberalta
Cobija
Guaporé R.
Mamoré R.
Beni R.
Puerto Maldonado
Trinidad
BOLIVIA
La Paz
Cochabamba
Oruro
Santa Cruz
Sucre
Potosí
Tarija
L. Titicaca
L. Poopó
ALTIPLANO
DESERT
Calama
A

Equator

South Polar Region

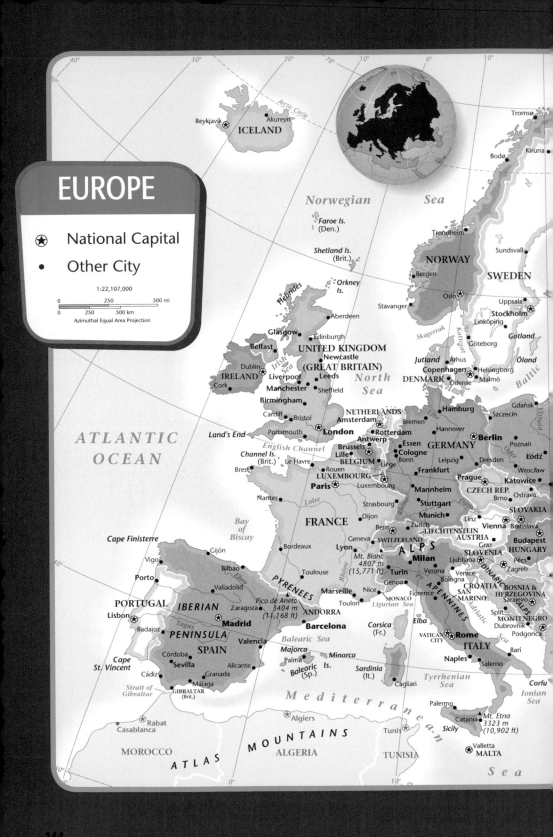

# EUROPE

★ National Capital

• Other City

1:22,107,000

0    250    500 mi
0  250  500 km
Azimuthal Equal Area Projection

40°   30°   20°   70°   10°   0°   10°

Arctic Circle

Reykjavík ★   Akureyri
ICELAND

Tromsø

Bodø
Kiruna

Norwegian    Sea

Faroe Is.
(Den.)

Trondheim
Sundsvall

Shetland Is.
(Brit.)

NORWAY
Bergen
Oslo

SWEDEN
Uppsala

Stavanger

Stockholm
Linköping

Orkney
Is.

Skagerrak
Göteborg
Gotland

Hebrides

Aberdeen

Jutland   Århus
Öland

Glasgow   Edinburgh
Copenhagen ★   Helsingborg
Malmö
Baltic

Belfast
UNITED KINGDOM
Newcastle
(GREAT BRITAIN)
DENMARK   Odense

Dublin   Liverpool   Leeds
North
Sea

Hamburg
Gdańsk
Szczecin

IRELAND
Cork
Manchester   Sheffield

Birmingham
Bremen
Hannover
★ Berlin

Cardiff   Bristol
NETHERLANDS
Amsterdam
Poznań

ATLANTIC
OCEAN

Land's End
Portsmouth ★ London
Rotterdam
Essen
GERMANY
Łódź

English Channel
Antwerp
Cologne
Leipzig
Dresden
Wrocław

Channel Is.
(Brit.)   Le Havre
Brussels
Bonn
Lille
BELGIUM   Liège
Frankfurt
Prague
Katowice

Brest
Rouen
LUXEMBOURG
Mannheim
CZECH REP.
Brno   Ostrava

Nantes
Paris ★
Luxembourg
Stuttgart
SLOVAKIA

Loire
Strasbourg
Munich
Linz   Vienna   Bratislava

Dijon
Bern   Zürich
LIECHTENSTEIN
AUSTRIA

Cape Finisterre
FRANCE
Geneva   SWITZERLAND
Graz
Budapest

Vigo
Gijón
Bordeaux
Lyon
ALPS
Ljubljana
SLOVENIA
HUNGARY
Pécs

Porto
Bilbao
Mt. Blanc
4807 m
(15,771 ft)   Turin
Milan
Verona
Venice
Zagreb

PYRENEES
Toulouse
Nice
Genoa
Po
Bologna
DINARIC
CROATIA
BOSNIA &

Valladolid
Marseille
MONACO
Florence
APENNINES
SAN
HERZEGOVINA
Sarajevo

PORTUGAL   IBERIAN
Zaragoza
Pico de Aneto
3404 m
(11,168 ft)
ANDORRA
Toulon
Ligurian Sea
MARINO
Split

Lisbon
Badajoz
Madrid
Barcelona
Corsica
(Fr.)
Elba
VATICAN
CITY ★ Rome
MONTENEGRO
Dubrovnik
Podgorica

Tagus
PENINSULA
Valencia
Balearic Sea
ITALY
Bari

Cape
St. Vincent
Córdoba
SPAIN
Majorca
Minorca

Cádiz
Sevilla
Granada
Alicante
Palma
Balearic Is.
(Sp.)
Sardinia
(It.)
Naples
Salerno
Corfu

Málaga
Cagliari
Tyrrhenian
Sea
Ionian
Sea

Strait of
Gibraltar
GIBRALTAR
(Brit.)
Mediterranean
Sea
Palermo
Catania
Mt. Etna
3323 m
(10,902 ft)

Rabat
Casablanca
Algiers
Sicily

Tunis
Valletta
MALTA

MOROCCO
ATLAS
MOUNTAINS
ALGERIA
TUNISIA
Sea

0°   10°

144

North Cape
Hammerfest
*Barents Sea*
LAPLAND
Murmansk
KOLA PENINSULA
Apatity
Nar'yan-Mar
Pechora
*Pechora*
*Ob*
*Irtysh*
Luleå
Oulu
*White Sea*
Arkhangel'sk
Ukhta
R U S S I A
U R A L
*Arctic Circle*
Petropavl
Jmeå
Belomorsk
*Dvina*
Serov
Berezniki
FINLAND
Vaasa
Tampere
Lahti
Helsinki
*Lake Onega*
Petrozavodsk
Kotlas
Syktyvkar
Kirov
Perm'
Yekaterinburg
Chelyabinsk
M O U N T A I N S
Qostanay
*Lake Ladoga*
St. Petersburg
Vologda
Cherepovets
Izhevsk
*Kama*
Ufa
Magnitogorsk
Tallinn
ESTONIA
Tartu
Velikiy Novgorod
Yaroslavl'
Naberezhnyye Chelny
Kazan
Nizhniy Novgorod
Ivanovo
Riga
LATVIA
Pskov
E U R O P E A N
Tver'
Moscow
Ryazan'
Ul'yanovsk
Saransk
Tol'yatti
Samara
Orenburg
Orsk
*Volga*
*Ural*
Aktobe
LITHUANIA
Kaunas
RUSSIA
liningrad
Vilnius
Daugavpils
Vitsyebsk
Smolensk
Mahilyow
Tula
Penza
*Ural*
Oral
KAZAKHSTAN
Atyraū
*Aral Sea*
NORTHERN
Hrodna
Minsk
BELARUS
Homyel
Bryansk
Lipetsk
Tambov
Saratov
Warsaw
Brest
Kursk
Voronezh
*PLAIN*
Aktaū
Aktaū
POLAND
aków
L'viv
Kyiv
Kharkiv
Volgograd
Astrakhan
UZBEKISTAN
*Dnieper*
Luhans'k
*Dnister*
ARPATHIAN
Chernivtsi
UKRAINE
Dnipropetrovs'k
Donets'k
*Don*
Makhachkala
TURKMENISTAN
Košice
MTS.
MOLDOVA
Zaporizhzhia
Kryvyy Rih
Rostov na Donu
Debrecen
Iaşi
Chişinău
Mykolaiv
Mariupol'
Stavropol'
Groznyy
*Caspian Sea*
Timişoara
ROMANIA
Odesa
*Sea of Azov*
Krasnodar
Mt. Elbrus 5642 m (18,510 ft)
C A U C A S U S
Türkmenbashy
vi Sad
Ploieşti
CRIMEA
Simferopol'
GEORGIA
Belgrade
Bucharest
Constanţa
Sevastopol'
Tbilisi
Baku
RBIA
*Danube*
Varna
*Black Sea*
ARMENIA
AZERBAIJAN
BULGARIA
Burgas
Trabzon
Yerevan
Pristina
Sofia
SOVO
Plovdiv
Tabriz
Tehran
Skopje
ACEDONIA
İstanbul
ANIA
ana
Thessaloniki
Ankara
TURKEY
IRAN
ALKAN
NINSULA
Larisa
İzmir
Adana
GREECE
atras
Athens
*Tigris*
Baghdad
ELOPONNESE
*Aegean Sea*
Cyclades
Rhodes
Nicosia
SYRIA
*Euphrates*
Crete
Iraklion
*Sea of Crete*
CYPRUS
LEBANON
Beirut
Damascus
IRAQ
*Persian Gulf*

© GeoNova

ATLANTIC OCEAN

IRELAND

UNITED KINGDOM

PORTUGAL

SPAIN

MOROCCO

FRANCE

BEL. NETH. DEN.

SWITZ.

GERMANY

CZECH

AUS. REP.

ITALY

POLAND LITH.

HUNG.

ALGERIA

TUNISIA

SERB.

ALB.

ROM.

BUL.

GREECE

LIBYA

NORWAY

SWEDEN

FINLAND

ESTONIA

LAT.

BELARUS

MOL.

UKRAINE

Mediterranean Sea

Black Sea

Izmir

Istanbul

Ankara

TURKEY

CYPRUS

Nicosia

LEBANON

Beirut

Tel Aviv

SYRIA

Jerusalem

Damascus

ISRAEL

Amman

JORDAN

IRAQ

ARMENIA

Yerevan

GEORGIA

Tbilisi

AZERBAIJAN

Baku

Tabriz

Caspian Sea

Aral Sea

TURKMENISTAN

Murmansk

Barents Sea

Kara Sea

Arctic Circle

St. Petersburg

Arkhangel'sk

Moscow

RUSSIA

URAL MOUNTAINS

Noril'sk

Yekaterinburg

Chelyabinsk

Irtysh

Ob

Tomsk

Magnitogorsk

Omsk

Novosibirsk

Astana

Novokuznetsk

Pavlodar

KAZAKHSTAN

Semey

Karaganda

Lake Balkhash

UZBEKISTAN

Bishkek

Almaty

Ürümqi

Tashkent

Dushanbe

KYRGYZSTAN

Kashi

TAJIKISTAN

Takla Makan Desert

CHAD

Tropic of Cancer

EGYPT

Sinai

Red Sea

Baghdad

SAUDI ARABIA

Al Basrah

KUWAIT

Kuwait City

Jeddah

Mecca

Riyadh

Manama

BAHRAIN

QATAR

Doha

UNITED ARAB EMIRATES

Abu Dhabi

Tehran

Esfahan

Mashhad

IRAN

Shiraz

Kerman

Persian Gulf

Muscat

Gulf of Oman

Ashgabat

AFGHANISTAN

Kabul

Kandahar

Islamabad

Srinagar

Lahore

Amritsar

PAKISTAN

Sukkur

Karachi

Hyderabad

XIZANG (TIBET)

HIMALAYAS

Delhi

New Delhi

NEPAL

Kathmandu

Jaipur

Kanpur

Lucknow

Ganges

AFRICA

SUDAN

ERITREA

ETHIOPIA

DJI.

Nile

Sanaa

YEMEN

Aden

Gulf of Aden

SOMALIA

Socotra (Yemen)

Arabian Sea

Ahmadabad

INDIA

Nagpur

Mumbai (Bombay)

Hyderabad

Bengaluru (Bangalore)

Kolkata (Calcutta)

Chennai (Madras)

Laccadive Islands (India)

Kochi

Madurai

SRI LANKA

Colombo

Male

MALDIVES

INDIAN OCEAN

Equator

# ASIA

⊛ National Capital

★ Territorial Capital

• Other City

1:51,084,000

0   500   1,000 mi

0   500   1,000 km

Two-Point Equidistant Projection

North Pole

ARCTIC
OCEAN

Chukchi
Sea

ALASKA

East
Siberian
Sea

Bering
Sea

Anadyr

Laptev
Sea

KAMCHATKA
PENINSULA

Magadan

Petropavlovsk-
Kamchatskly

Sea of
Okhotsk

Sakhalin

Kuril
Islands
(Russia)

Yakutsk

A

SIBERIA

Komsomolsk
na Amure

Khabarovsk

Sapporo

Krasnoyarsk

Bratsk

Lake
Baikal

Chita

Blagoveshchensk

Harbin

Vladivostok

Sea of
Japan
(East Sea)

JAPAN

Sendai

Irkutsk

Ulan-Ude

Changchun

Shenyang

Tokyo

Yokohama

Kyoto

Ulaanbaatar

Pyongyang

N. KOREA

Kobe

Osaka

MONGOLIA

Hohhot

Beijing

Dalian

Seoul

Hiroshima

GOBI DESERT

Tianjin

S. KOREA

Nagasaki

PACIFIC
OCEAN

ALTAY
MTS.

XINJIANG

Taiyuan

Jinan

Qingdao

Yellow
Sea

Lanzhou

Yellow
(Huang)

Zhengzhou

Nanjing

Shanghai

East
China
Sea

Okinawa (Japan)

CHINA

Xi'an

Wuhan

Chengdu

Changsha

Wenzhou

Fuzhou

Ryukyu
Islands

t. Everest
850 m
9,035 ft.)

Chongqing

Yangtze Chang

Xiamen

Taipei

BHUTAN
Thimphu

Lhasa

Kunming

Guangzhou

Hong Kong

TAIWAN

Philippine
Sea

ANGLADESH
Dhaka

Nanning

Macao

Mandalay

Hanoi

Gulf
of
Tonkin

LUZON

LAOS

Nay Pyi Taw

Manila

PHILIPPINES

ay of
engal

MYANMAR
(BURMA)

Vientiane

Da Nang

South
China
Sea

Cebu

Yangon
(Rangoon)

THAILAND

VIETNAM

MINDANAO

daman
Islands
(India)

Bangkok

CAMBODIA

Phnom
Penh

Ho Chi Minh City

Sulu
Sea

Davao

Manado

NEW GUINE

Gulf of
Thailand

Kota Kinabalu

Celebes
Sea

Nicobar
Islands
(India)

Bandar Seri Begawan

BRUNEI

Medan

Kuching

MALAYSIA

BORNEO

Banda
Sea

Arafura
Sea

Kuala
Lumpur

SINGAPORE

Singapore

SUMATRA

INDONESIA

Padang

Banjarmasin

Makassar

Timor
Sea

TIMOR-
LESTE

Palembang

Jakarta

Surabaya

Dili

Kupang

AUSTRALIA

Bandung

JAVA

Java
Sea

© GeoNova

**AFRICA**

⊛ National Capital

• Other City

1:39,550,000

0    250    500    750 km
0    250    500    750 mi

Azimuthal Equal Area Projection

ATLANTIC OCEAN

INDIAN OCEAN

*Equator*

KENYA

Kismaayo

Nakuru
Nairobi
⊛ Kisumu
Kampala ⊛
Kisangani •
L. Victoria
RWANDA
Kigali ⊛
BURUNDI
Bukavu
Bujumbura ⊛
L. Tanganyika
DEMOCRATIC REPUBLIC OF THE CONGO

Mombasa
Tanga
Zanzibar ⊛ Dar es Salaam
Dodoma ⊛
Arusha
TANZANIA
SERENGETI PLAIN
*Kilimanjaro* 5895 m (19,340 ft)
Tabora
Mbeya
GREAT RIFT VALLEY
L. Mweru
Lake Nyasa

COMOROS
Moroni

Mtwara
Nacala-Porto
Nampula
MOZAMBIQUE

MADAGASCAR
Antsiranana
Toamasina
Antananarivo ⊛
Fianarantsoa
Toliara

*Tropic of Capricorn*

Mozambique Channel

Quelimane
Beira

MALAWI
Lilongwe ⊛
Blantyre
Chipata
Zambezi

Inhambane

Maputo ⊛
Mbabane ⊛ SWAZILAND
Pietermaritzburg
Newcastle
Durban

Mutare
Harare ⊛
ZIMBABWE
Bulawayo
Pretoria ⊛
Johannesburg
Kimberley
Bloemfontein ⊛
LESOTHO
Maseru ⊛
East London
Port Elizabeth

Lubumbashi
Likasi
KATANGA PLATEAU
Kolwezi
Kitwe
Ndola
ZAMBIA
Lusaka ⊛
Kabwe
L. Kariba
Livingstone
Francistown
BOTSWANA
Gaborone ⊛
KALAHARI DESERT

Kananga
Mbuji-Mayi
Kinshasa ⊛
Brazzaville ⊛
GABON
REP. OF THE CONGO
Libreville ⊛
Franceville
Pointe-Noire
Cabinda (Ang.)
Luanda
Maradi

Tshikapa
Kikwit
Mbandaka

ANGOLA
Malanje
Huambo
Menongue
Lobito
Benguela
Namibe
Cunene

NAMIBIA
NAMIB DESERT
Grootfontein
Windhoek ⊛
Walvis Bay
Lüderitz
Orange
Keetmanshoop

SOUTH AFRICA
Klerksdorp
Upington
Cape Town
Cape of Good Hope
Cape Agulhas

SÃO TOMÉ AND PRÍNCIPE ⊛
São Tomé
Port-Gentil

ASCENSION (Brit.)

ST. HELENA (Brit.)

© GeoNova

149

# FACTS
## About NATIONS

**H**ere are basic facts about each of the 195 independent nations in the world. The color of the heading for each country tells you what continent it belongs in. The population is an estimate for mid-2009. The language entry gives official languages and other common languages.

### COLOR KEY
- Africa
- Asia
- Australia
- Europe
- North America
- Pacific Islands
- South America

---

### Afghanistan

- **Capital:** Kabul
- **Population:** 33,609,937
- **Area:** 250,001 sq mi (647,500 sq km)
- **Language:** Afghan Persian (Dari), Pashtu
- **Did You Know?** The national sport *buzkashi* is played on horseback and literally means "goat grabbing."

### Andorra

- **Capital:** Andorra la Vella
- **Population:** 83,888
- **Area:** 181 sq mi (468 sq km)
- **Language:** Catalan, French, Castilian
- **Did You Know?** The average life expectancy of people in Andorra in 2009 was about 83 years, the highest of any country in the world.

### Albania

- **Capital:** Tirana
- **Population:** 3,639,453
- **Area:** 11,100 sq mi (28,748 sq km)
- **Language:** Albanian, Greek
- **Did You Know?** The double-headed eagle on Albania's flag was a symbol of the Byzantine Empire, to which Albania once belonged.

### Angola

- **Capital:** Luanda
- **Population:** 12,799,293
- **Area:** 481,354 sq mi (1,246,700 sq km)
- **Language:** Portuguese, African languages
- **Did You Know?** Angola is the second largest oil-producer in sub-Saharan Africa after Nigeria.

### Algeria

- **Capital:** Algiers (El Djazair)
- **Population:** 34,178,188
- **Area:** 919,595 sq mi (2,381,740 sq km)
- **Language:** Arabic, French, Berber dialects
- **Did You Know?** Algeria's desert region contains large "sand seas" called *ergs*, which feature constantly shifting dunes up to 2,000 feet high.

### Antigua & Barbuda

- **Capital:** St. John's
- **Population:** 85,632
- **Area:** 171 sq mi (443 sq km)
- **Language:** English
- **Did You Know?** On Aug. 1, 1834, Antigua became the first of the British Caribbean colonies to free its slaves.

**BEACH IN AUSTRALIA**

## Argentina

- **Capital:** Buenos Aires
- **Population:** 40,913,584
- **Area:** 1,068,302 sq mi (2,766,890 sq km)
- **Language:** Spanish, English, Italian, German, French
- **Did You Know?** About 90% of Argentina's population is urban; one-third of the total population lives in the capital alone.

## Armenia

- **Capital:** Yerevan
- **Population:** 2,967,004
- **Area:** 11,506 sq mi (29,800 sq km)
- **Language:** Armenian, Russian
- **Did You Know?** Armenia considers itself the first country to have formally adopted Christianity as a state religion, in the year 301.

## Australia

- **Capital:** Canberra
- **Population:** 21,262,641
- **Area:** 2,967,909 sq mi (7,686,850 sq km)
- **Language:** English, Aboriginal languages
- **Did You Know?** The world's biggest rock—Uluru (also called Ayers Rock)—is located here, a monolith that stands more than 1,000 feet tall.

## Austria

- **Capital:** Vienna
- **Population:** 8,210,281
- **Area:** 32,382 sq mi (83,870 sq km)
- **Language:** German, Slovene, Croatian, Hungarian
- **Did You Know?** Austria's Hohe Tauern National Park is one of Europe's largest protected natural areas.

## Azerbaijan

- **Capital:** Baku
- **Population:** 8,238,672
- **Area:** 33,436 sq mi (86,600 sq km)
- **Language:** Azeri, Russian, Armenian
- **Did You Know?** Although Nagorno-Karabakh, a region in Azerbaijan whose population is mostly Armenian, declared its independence in 1991, Azerbaijan does not recognize its claim.

## The Bahamas

- **Capital:** Nassau
- **Population:** 309,156
- **Area:** 5,382 sq mi (13,940 sq km)
- **Language:** English, Creole
- **Did You Know?** About two-thirds of the population lives on New Providence, one of The Bahamas' nearly 700 islands.

## Bahrain

- **Capital:** Manama
- **Population:** 727,785
- **Area:** 257 sq mi (665 sq km)
- **Language:** Arabic, English, Farsi, Urdu
- **Did You Know?** Groundwater and treated seawater are the only sources of freshwater in Bahrain.

## Bangladesh

- **Capital:** Dhaka
- **Population:** 156,050,883
- **Area:** 55,599 sq mi (144,000 sq km)
- **Language:** Bangla, English
- **Did You Know?** About one-third of Bangladesh floods each year during monsoon season, between June and early October.

## Barbados

- **Capital:** Bridgetown
- **Population:** 284,589
- **Area:** 166 sq mi (431 sq km)
- **Language:** English
- **Did You Know?** Considered one of the Seven Wonders of Barbados, the grapefruit is believed to have been developed in Barbados from other fruits.

## Belarus

- **Capital:** Minsk
- **Population:** 9,648,533
- **Area:** 80,155 sq mi (207,600 sq km)
- **Language:** Belarusian, Russian
- **Did You Know?** Contamination from the 1986 Chernobyl nuclear power plant explosion, in neighboring Ukraine, continues to affect Belarus. High numbers of children have been diagnosed with cancer. Many people are unemployed because land that was contaminated could no longer be farmed.

## Belgium

- **Capital:** Brussels
- **Population:** 10,414,336
- **Area:** 11,787 sq mi (30,528 sq km)
- **Language:** Dutch, French, German
- **Did You Know?** Belgium produces about 170,000 tons of chocolate every year, supporting about 300 chocolate makers and more than 2,000 shops.

## Belize

- **Capital:** Belmopan
- **Population:** 307,899
- **Area:** 8,867 sq mi (22,966 sq km)
- **Language:** English, Spanish, Mayan, Garifuna, Creole
- **Did You Know?** Belize Barrier Reef is the second largest coral reef system (a diverse underwater habitat) in the world.

## Benin

- **Capital:** Porto-Novo (constit.); Cotonou (admin.)
- **Population:** 8,791,832
- **Area:** 43,483 sq mi (112,620 sq km)
- **Language:** French, Fon, Yoruba
- **Did You Know?** About 4 million people in Benin practice Vodun (also known as Voodoo), one of the country's official religions.

## Bhutan

- **Capital:** Thimphu
- **Population:** 691,141
- **Area:** 18,147 sq mi (47,000 sq km)
- **Language:** Dzongkha, Tibetan dialects
- **Did You Know?** Bhutan had been under the rule of an absolute monarchy since 1907 but became a democracy in 2008.

## Bolivia

- **Capital:** La Paz (admin.); Sucre (legislative/judiciary)
- **Population:** 9,775,246
- **Area:** 424,164 sq mi (1,098,580 sq km)
- **Language:** Spanish, Quechua, Aymara
- **Did You Know?** Bolivia's administrative capital, La Paz, is the highest capital city in the world, at about 13,000 feet above sea level.

## COLOR KEY

- Africa
- Asia
- Australia
- Europe
- North America
- Pacific Islands
- South America

## Bosnia and Herzegovina

- **Capital:** Sarajevo
- **Population:** 4,613,414
- **Area:** 19,741 sq mi (51,129 sq km)
- **Language:** Bosnian, Croatian, Serbian
- **Did You Know?** This country has three presidents, who serve consecutive eight-month terms.

## Botswana

- **Capital:** Gaborone
- **Population:** 1,990,876
- **Area:** 231,804 sq mi (600,370 sq km)
- **Language:** Setswana, English
- **Did You Know?** Chobe National Park is home to about 100,000 elephants, possibly the largest elephant population in the world.

## Brazil

- **Capital:** Brasília
- **Population:** 198,739,269
- **Area:** 3,286,488 sq mi (8,511,965 sq km)
- **Language:** Portuguese, Spanish, English, French
- **Did You Know?** By 2006, Brazil had won 5 men's World Cup soccer tournaments, the most of any country.

## Brunei

- **Capital:** Bandar Seri Begawan
- **Population:** 388,190
- **Area:** 2,228 sq mi (5,770 sq km)
- **Language:** Malay, English, Chinese
- **Did You Know?** The same royal family has ruled Brunei since the 1400s.

## Bulgaria

- **Capital:** Sofia
- **Population:** 7,204,687
- **Area:** 42,823 sq mi (110,910 sq km)
- **Language:** Bulgarian, Turkish
- **Did You Know?** The image of a man on horseback that appears on some Bulgarian coins is based on an 8th-century rock carving called the Madara Rider.

## Burkina Faso

- **Capital:** Uuagadougou
- **Population:** 15,746,232
- **Area:** 105,869 sq mi (274,200 sq km)
- **Language:** French, indigenous languages
- **Did You Know?** "Burkina Faso" means "land of honest people."

## Burundi

- **Capital:** Bujumbura
- **Population:** 8,988,091
- **Area:** 10,745 sq mi (27,830 sq km)
- **Language:** Kirundi, French, Swahili
- **Did You Know?** The Twa, a Pygmy group (adult males average about 5 feet tall), are thought to be Burundi's original inhabitants.

## Cambodia

- **Capital:** Phnom Penh
- **Population:** 14,494,293
- **Area:** 69,900 sq mi (181,040 sq km)
- **Language:** Khmer, French, English
- **Did You Know?** About 75% of Cambodian families are subsistence farmers, growing just enough food for themselves.

**BRUSSELS, BELGIUM**

97

## Cameroon

- **Capital:** Yaoundé
- **Population:** 18,879,301
- **Area:** 183,568 sq mi (475,440 sq km)
- **Language:** English, French, African languages
- **Did You Know?** "Cameroon" comes from the Portuguese word camarões, meaning "shrimps," which early Portuguese explorers found in abundance in Cameroon's Wouri River.

## Canada

- **Capital:** Ottawa
- **Population:** 33,487,208
- **Area:** 3,855,103 sq mi (9,984,670 sq km)
- **Language:** English, French
- **Did You Know?** The 2010 Olympic Winter Games will be held in Vancouver, British Columbia.

## Cape Verde

- **Capital:** Praia
- **Population:** 429,474
- **Area:** 1,557 sq mi (4,033 sq km)
- **Language:** Portuguese, Crioulo
- **Did You Know?** More Cape Verdeans live abroad than live on the nation's islands. Severe droughts in the late 20th century forced many to leave.

## Central African Republic

- **Capital:** Bangui
- **Population:** 4,511,488
- **Area:** 240,535 sq mi (622,984 sq km)
- **Language:** French, Sangho
- **Did You Know?** With fewer than 20 people per square mile, this is one of Africa's most thinly populated nations.

## Chad

- **Capital:** N'Djamena
- **Population:** 10,329,208
- **Area:** 495,755 sq mi (1,284,000 sq km)
- **Language:** French, Arabic, Sara
- **Did You Know?** The surface area of Lake Chad was nearly 10,000 sq mi in 1963. Forty years later, the lake had shrunk to one-twentieth of that size (about 500 sq mi) due to climate change and human use.

## Chile

- **Capital:** Santiago
- **Population:** 16,601,707
- **Area:** 292,260 sq mi (756,950 sq km)
- **Language:** Spanish
- **Did You Know?** Chile is about 2,500 miles long but only 93 miles wide.

## China

- **Capital:** Beijing
- **Population:** 1,338,612,968
- **Area:** 3,705,407 sq mi (9,596,960 sq km)
- **Language:** Mandarin, and many dialects
- **Did You Know?** China's economy is the second largest in the world, behind the United States. China produced about $8 trillion worth of goods and services in 2008.

## Colombia

- **Capital:** Bogotá
- **Population:** 45,644,023
- **Area:** 439,736 sq mi (1,138,910 sq km)
- **Language:** Spanish
- **Did You Know?** Colombia is the only South American country that touches both the Caribbean Sea and the Pacific Ocean.

**GREAT WALL OF CHINA**

## Comoros

- **Capital:** Moroni
- **Population:** 752,438
- **Area:** 838 sq mi (2,170 sq km)
- **Language:** Arabic, French, Shikomoro
- **Did You Know?** The endangered Livingstone's flying fox, a fruit bat native to the islands of Comoros, has a wing span of more than 4 feet.

## Congo, Democratic Republic of the

- **Capital:** Kinshasa
- **Population:** 68,692,542
- **Area:** 905,568 sq mi (2,345,410 sq km)
- **Language:** French, Lingala, Kingwana, Kikongo, Tshiluba
- **Did You Know?** In 2006, the Democratic Republic of the Congo held its first free, democratic multi-party elections since 1960.

## Congo, Republic of the

- **Capital:** Brazzaville
- **Population:** 4,012,809
- **Area:** 132,047 sq mi (342,000 sq km)
- **Language:** French, Lingala, Monokutuba, Kikongo
- **Did You Know?** The production and export of crude oil makes up a major part of the Congolese economy.

## Costa Rica

- **Capital:** San José
- **Population:** 4,253,877
- **Area:** 19,730 sq mi (51,100 sq km)
- **Language:** Spanish, English
- **Did You Know?** At its narrowest point, between the Pacific Ocean and Caribbean Sea, Costa Rica is only about 75 miles wide. The country's name means "rich coast" in Spanish.

## Côte d'Ivoire (Ivory Coast)

- **Capital:** Yamoussoukro
- **Population:** 20,617,068
- **Area:** 124,503 sq mi (322,460 sq km)
- **Language:** French, Dioula
- **Did You Know?** There are about 60 native ethnic groups in Côte d'Ivoire. The largest group is the Akan.

## Croatia

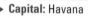

- **Capital:** Zagreb
- **Population:** 4,489,409
- **Area:** 21,831 sq mi (56,542 sq km)
- **Language:** Croatian, Serbian
- **Did You Know?** Croatia has more than 1,000 islands off its coast in the Adriatic Sea. Only about 50 are inhabited.

## Cuba

- **Capital:** Havana
- **Population:** 11,451,652
- **Area:** 42,803 sq mi (110,860 sq km)
- **Language:** Spanish
- **Did You Know?** Havana hosts one of the largest annual film festivals in Latin America.

## Cyprus

- **Capital:** Nicosia
- **Population:** 796,740
- **Area:** 3,571 sq mi (9,250 sq km)
- **Language:** Greek, Turkish, English
- **Did You Know?** Halloumi, a salty cheese made from a mixture of goat and sheep milk, is a traditional food in Cyprus.

**COLOR KEY**

- Africa
- Asia
- Australia
- Europe
- North America
- Pacific Islands
- South America

## Czech Republic

- **Capital:** Prague
- **Population:** 10,211,904
- **Area:** 30,450 sq mi (78,866 sq km)
- **Language:** Czech, Slovak
- **Did You Know?** The so-called "Velvet Revolution" brought about the end of communism in Czechoslovakia in 1989. The term "Velvet Divorce" was used to describe the 1993 division of the Czech Republic and Slovakia.

## Denmark

- **Capital:** Copenhagen
- **Population:** 5,500,510
- **Area:** 16,639 sq mi (43,094 sq km)
- **Language:** Danish, Faroese
- **Did You Know?** Each year in Copenhagen, around 1 million people visit a statue depicting the Little Mermaid from Hans Christian Andersen's famous fairy tale.

## Djibouti

- **Capital:** Djibouti
- **Population:** 516,055
- **Area:** 8,880 sq mi (23,000 sq km)
- **Language:** French, Arabic, Somali, Afar
- **Did You Know?** Most of the country is barren. It receives little rainfall, and few plants survive in Djibouti's rocky deserts.

## Dominica

- **Capital:** Roseau
- **Population:** 72,660
- **Area:** 291 sq mi (754 sq km)
- **Language:** English, French patois
- **Did You Know?** Mary Eugenia Charles, who governed from 1980 to 1995, was the first female prime minister in the Caribbean.

## Dominican Republic

- **Capital:** Santo Domingo
- **Population:** 9,650,054
- **Area:** 18,815 sq mi (48,730 sq km)
- **Language:** Spanish
- **Did You Know?** Merengue, a lively music and dance, originated here. A combination of African and European styles of dancing, the merengue is now a popular ballroom dance.

## Ecuador

- **Capital:** Quito
- **Population:** 14,573,101
- **Area:** 109,483 sq mi (283,560 sq km)
- **Language:** Spanish, Quechua
- **Did You Know?** Observations of the wildlife on Ecuador's Galapagos Islands helped scientist Charles Darwin come up with his theory of evolution.

## Egypt

- **Capital:** Cairo
- **Population:** 83,082,869
- **Area:** 386,662 sq mi (1,001,450 sq km)
- **Language:** Arabic, English, French
- **Did You Know?** In the Western Desert, the sand dunes often shift due to the wind, moving up to 300 feet and covering homes in mounds of sand.

## El Salvador

- **Capital:** San Salvador
- **Population:** 7,185,218
- **Area:** 8,124 sq mi (21,040 sq km)
- **Language:** Spanish, Nahua
- **Did You Know?** El Salvador is the most densely-populated country on the mainland of the Americas, with more than 880 people per square mile.

### COLOR KEY

- Africa
- Asia
- Australia
- Europe
- North America
- Pacific Islands
- South America

PYRAMIDS AT GIZA, EGYPT

## Fiji

- **Capital:** Suva
- **Population:** 944,720
- **Area:** 7,054 sq mi (18,270 sq km)
- **Language:** English, Fijian, Hindustani
- **Did You Know?** Wearing a hat is a sign of disrespect in Fijian culture.

## Equatorial Guinea

- **Capital:** Malabo
- **Population:** 633,441
- **Area:** 10,831 sq mi (28,051 sq km)
- **Language:** Spanish, French, Fang, Bubi
- **Did You Know?** Equatorial Guinea is the only African country in which Spanish is an official language.

## Finland

- **Capital:** Helsinki
- **Population:** 5,250,275
- **Area:** 130,559 sq mi (338,145 sq km)
- **Language:** Finnish, Swedish
- **Did You Know?** Finland is home to several odd competitions, including the Wife-Carrying World Championships and the Mobile-Phone-Throwing World Championships.

## Eritrea

- **Capital:** Asmara
- **Population:** 5,647,168
- **Area:** 46,842 sq mi (121,320 sq km)
- **Language:** Afar, Arabic, Tigre, Kunama, Tigrinya
- **Did You Know?** Eritrea was once a colony of Italy, then occupied by British forces, and finally annexed by Ethiopia before it achieved independence in 1993.

## France

- **Capital:** Paris
- **Population:** 64,057,792
- **Area:** 211,209 sq mi (547,030 sq km)
- **Language:** French
- **Did You Know?** France produces more films each year than any other European country.

## Estonia

- **Capital:** Tallinn
- **Population:** 1,299,371
- **Area:** 17,462 sq mi (45,226 sq km)
- **Language:** Estonian, Russian
- **Did You Know?** Despite its small geographic size, Estonia has more than 1,400 lakes and 1,500 islands.

## Gabon

- **Capital:** Libreville
- **Population:** 1,514,993
- **Area:** 103,347 sq mi (267,667 sq km)
- **Language:** French, Fang, Myene, Nzebi
- **Did You Know?** Omar Bongo, Gabon's president since 1967, was Africa's longest-serving leader when he died in 2009 after 41 years in power.

## Ethiopia

- **Capital:** Addis Ababa
- **Population:** 85,237,338
- **Area:** 435,186 sq mi (1,127,127 sq km)
- **Language:** Amharic, Tigrinya, Oromigna, Guaragigna, Somali, Arabic
- **Did You Know?** Ethiopian children traditionally take their father's first name as their last name.

## The Gambia

- **Capital:** Banjul
- **Population:** 1,782,893
- **Area:** 4,363 sq mi (11,300 sq km)
- **Language:** English, Mandinka, Wolof
- **Did You Know?** The Gambia is the smallest country by area on the continent of Africa.

## Georgia

- **Capital:** T'bilisi
- **Population:** 4,615,807
- **Area:** 26,911 sq mi (69,700 sq km)
- **Language:** Georgian, Russian, Armenian, Azeri, Abkhaz
- **Did You Know?** The Georgian alphabet is one of only a few alphabets still in use today. It is believed to have been created in the 5th century.

## Germany

- **Capital:** Berlin
- **Population:** 82,329,758
- **Area:** 137,847 sq mi (357,021 sq km)
- **Language:** German
- **Did You Know?** Germany is the second most populous country in Europe, after Russia.

## Ghana

- **Capital:** Accra
- **Population:** 23,832,495
- **Area:** 92,456 sq mi (239,460 sq km)
- **Language:** English, Akan, Moshi-Dagomba, Ewe, Ga
- **Did You Know?** In 1957, the British colony known as the Gold Coast was merged with another territory to form Ghana.

## Greece

- **Capital:** Athens
- **Population:** 10,737,428
- **Area:** 50,942 sq mi (131,940 sq km)
- **Language:** Greek, English, French
- **Did You Know?** Democracy was invented in Greece in the 5th century B.C.

## Grenada

- **Capital:** Saint George's
- **Population:** 90,739
- **Area:** 133 sq mi (344 sq km)
- **Language:** English, French patois
- **Did You Know?** Grenada is sometimes referred to as the "Spice of the Caribbean" because its top export is nutmeg.

## Guatemala

- **Capital:** Guatemala City
- **Population:** 13,276,517
- **Area:** 42,043 sq mi (108,890 sq km)
- **Language:** Spanish, Amerindian languages
- **Did You Know?** Before the arrival of the Spanish, the Mayan Indian empire flourished for more than 1,000 years in what is today Guatemala.

## Guinea

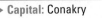

- **Capital:** Conakry
- **Population:** 10,057,975
- **Area:** 94,926 sq mi (245,857 sq km)
- **Language:** French, Susu, Pulaar, Malinke
- **Did You Know?** In its first five decades as an independent country (1958-2008), Guinea had only 2 different rulers.

**TAJ MAHAL AT AGRA, INDIA**

## Guinea-Bissau

- **Capital:** Bissau
- **Population:** 1,533,964
- **Area:** 13,946 sq mi (36,120 sq km)
- **Language:** Portuguese, Crioulo, African languages
- **Did You Know?** Most of the nation's farmers grow cashew nuts, providing a vital cash crop and accounting for 90% of Guinea-Bissau's exports.

## Guyana

- **Capital:** Georgetown
- **Population:** 772,298
- **Area:** 83,000 sq mi (214,970 sq km)
- **Language:** English, Amerindian dialects, Creole, Hindi
- **Did You Know?** Guyana is the only Latin American country whose official language is English.

## Haiti

- **Capital:** Port-au-Prince
- **Population:** 9,035,536
- **Area:** 10,714 sq mi (27,750 sq km)
- **Language:** French, Creole
- **Did You Know?** Haiti gained independence from France in 1804 and, after the U.S., is the second oldest country in the Americas.

## Honduras

- **Capital:** Tegucigalpa
- **Population:** 7,792,854
- **Area:** 43,278 sq mi (112,090 sq km)
- **Language:** Spanish, Amerindian dialects
- **Did You Know?** Christopher Columbus was the first recorded European to reach Honduras, where he landed in 1502.

## Hungary

- **Capital:** Budapest
- **Population:** 9,905,596
- **Area:** 35,919 sq mi (93,030 sq km)
- **Language:** Hungarian (Magyar)
- **Did You Know?** Budapest was originally two separate cities, Buda and Pest. The two areas are separated by the Danube River.

## Iceland

- **Capital:** Reykjavik
- **Population:** 306,694
- **Area:** 39,769 sq mi (103,000 sq km)
- **Language:** Icelandic, English
- **Did You Know?** The Althingi, Iceland's general assembly, was established in the year 930 and is the world's oldest surviving parliament.

## India

- **Capital:** New Delhi
- **Population:** 1,166,079,217
- **Area:** 1,269,346 sq mi (3,287,590 sq km)
- **Language:** Hindi, English, Bengali, Urdu
- **Did You Know?** Jammu and Kashmir—part of a region in dispute between India, Pakistan, and China—is India's only Muslim-majority state.

## Indonesia

- **Capital:** Jakarta
- **Population:** 240,271,522
- **Area:** 741,100 sq mi (1,919,440 sq km)
- **Language:** Bahasa Indonesian, English, Dutch, Javanese
- **Did You Know?** About one-seventh of the world's active volcanoes are found on this nation of islands.

## Iran

- **Capital:** Tehran
- **Population:** 66,429,284
- **Area:** 636,296 sq mi (1,648,000 sq km)
- **Language:** Farsi (Persian), Turkic, Kurdish
- **Did You Know?** Although Arabs are the majority ethnic group in some Middle East countries, they are a minority in Iran. About half of all Iranians are Persian.

## Iraq

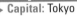

- **Capital:** Baghdad
- **Population:** 28,945,657
- **Area:** 168,754 sq mi (437,072 sq km)
- **Language:** Arabic, Kurdish
- **Did You Know?** The Sumer, one of the world's oldest known civilizations, lived in the Tigris-Euphrates Valley in the 4th millennium B.C.

## Ireland

- **Capital:** Dublin
- **Population:** 4,203,200
- **Area:** 27,135 sq mi (70,280 sq km)
- **Language:** English, Irish
- **Did You Know?** The country of Ireland occupies only 83% of the "Emerald Isle." The rest of the island is part of the United Kingdom and is called Northern Ireland.

## Israel

- **Capital:** Jerusalem
- **Population:** 7,233,701
- **Area:** 8,019 sq mi (20,770 sq km)
- **Language:** Hebrew, Arabic, English
- **Did You Know?** Hebrew, Israel's official language, was revived as a spoken language in the 19th and 20th centuries; it was last spoken widely in 3rd century B.C.

## Italy

- **Capital:** Rome
- **Population:** 58,126,212
- **Area:** 116,306 sq mi (301,230 sq km)
- **Language:** Italian, German, French, Slovenian
- **Did You Know?** Italy has one of the highest cell-phone-use rates in the world, with about 135 cell-phone subscriptions for every 100 Italians.

## Jamaica

- **Capital:** Kingston
- **Population:** 2,825,928
- **Area:** 4,244 sq mi (10,991 sq km)
- **Language:** English, Jamaican Creole
- **Did You Know?** Jamaica's name comes from the Arawak Indian word *Xaymaca*, which means "land of wood and water."

## Japan

- **Capital:** Tokyo
- **Population:** 127,078,679
- **Area:** 145,883 sq mi (377,835 sq km)
- **Language:** Japanese
- **Did You Know?** With the world's third-largest economy (after the U.S. and China), Japan is also one of the largest and most technologically advanced producers of cars and electronic equipment.

## Jordan

- **Capital:** Amman
- **Population:** 6,342,948
- **Area:** 35,637 sq mi (92,300 sq km)
- **Language:** Arabic, English
- **Did You Know?** The Dead Sea, on the Israel-Jordan border, is 6 to 10 times saltier than the ocean.

## COLOR KEY

- Africa
- Asia
- Australia
- Europe
- North America
- Pacific Islands
- South America

## Kazakhstan

- **Capital:** Astana
- **Population:** 15,399,437
- **Area:** 1,049,155 sq mi (2,717,300 sq km)
- **Language:** Kazakh, Russian
- **Did You Know?** Baikonur Cosmodrome, one of the Russian Space Agency's launch facilities, is located in Kazakhstan.

## Kenya

- **Capital:** Nairobi
- **Population:** 39,002,772
- **Area:** 224,962 sq mi (582,650 sq km)
- **Language:** Kiswahili, English
- **Did You Know?** Fossils of our human ancestors dating from more than 1 million years ago have been found in Kenya. Its National Museum is home to one of the world's best collections of human ancestral bones.

## Kiribati

- **Capital:** Tarawa
- **Population:** 112,850
- **Area:** 313 sq mi (811 sq km)
- **Language:** English, I-Kiribati
- **Did You Know?** Kiribati's islands are spread across an area of the Pacific Ocean about the same size as the continental U.S.

## Korea, North
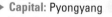
- **Capital:** Pyongyang
- **Population:** 22,665,345
- **Area:** 46,541 sq mi (120,540 sq km)
- **Language:** Korean
- **Did You Know?** North and South Korea have officially been at war for more than 50 years. A ceasefire has maintained the peace since 1953.

## Korea, South

- **Capital:** Seoul
- **Population:** 48,508,972
- **Area:** 38,023 sq mi (98,480 sq km)
- **Language:** Korean
- **Did You Know?** The martial art of tae kwon do is the national sport. It means "way of the foot and fist."

## Kosovo

- **Capital:** Pristina
- **Population:** 1,804,838 (2007 est.)
- **Area:** 4,212 sq mi (10,887 sq km)
- **Language:** Albanian, Serbian, Bosnian, Turkish, Roma
- **Did You Know?** In 2008, the Kosovo Assembly declared its independence from Serbia, making it the world's newest country.

## Kuwait

- **Capital:** Kuwait City
- **Population:** 2,691,158
- **Area:** 6,880 sq mi (17,820 sq km)
- **Language:** Arabic, English
- **Did You Know?** In 2005, women were granted full political rights, including the right to vote and run in parliamentary elections.

## Kyrgyzstan

- **Capital:** Bishkek
- **Population:** 5,431,747
- **Area:** 76,641 sq mi (198,500 sq km)
- **Language:** Kyrgyz, Russian
- **Did You Know?** The 40 "rays of light" on Kyrgyzstan's flag represent the country's various Kyrgyz tribes.

SAVANNA IN KENYA

## Laos

> **Capital:** Vientiane
> **Population:** 6,834,942
> **Area:** 91,429 sq mi (236,800 sq km)
> **Language:** Lao, French, English
> **Did You Know?** The first kingdom in what is now Laos was called *Lan Xang*, or "Kingdom of the Million Elephants."

## Latvia

> **Capital:** Riga
> **Population:** 2,231,503
> **Area:** 24,938 sq mi (64,589 sq km)
> **Language:** Latvian, Russian, Lithuanian
> **Did You Know?** Latvia calls itself the "Land that Sings." Choirs and dance groups compete each year for a place in the Nationwide Latvian Song and Dance Celebration which attracts more than 30,000 dancers, singers, and musicians.

## Lebanon

> **Capital:** Beirut
> **Population:** 4,017,095
> **Area:** 4,015 sq mi (10,400 sq km)
> **Language:** Arabic, French, English, Armenian
> **Did You Know?** The cedar of Lebanon is one of four cedar species in the world. The tree is mentioned in myths and even appears on the country's flag.

## Lesotho

> **Capital:** Maseru
> **Population:** 2,130,819
> **Area:** 11,720 sq mi (30,355 sq km)
> **Language:** English, Sesotho, Zulu, Xhosa
> **Did You Know?** The Kingdom of Lesotho is completely surrounded by South Africa.

## Liberia

> **Capital:** Monrovia
> **Population:** 3,441,790
> **Area:** 43,000 sq mi (111,370 sq km)
> **Language:** English, ethnic languages
> **Did You Know?** Liberia was founded in 1822 by freed African slaves from the U.S. It became an independent republic in 1847.

## Libya

> **Capital:** Tripoli
> **Population:** 6,310,434
> **Area:** 679,362 sq mi (1,759,540 sq km)
> **Language:** Arabic, Italian, English
> **Did You Know?** In 1922, Libya reached 136°F, the highest temperature ever recorded.

## Liechtenstein

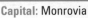

> **Capital:** Vaduz
> **Population:** 34,761
> **Area:** 62 sq mi (160 sq km)
> **Language:** German, Alemannic dialect
> **Did You Know?** Liechtenstein is one of only two countries in the world (Uzbekistan is the other) that is "doubly landlocked." It has no coastline and is surrounded by countries without coastlines.

## Lithuania

> **Capital:** Vilnius
> **Population:** 3,555,179
> **Area:** 25,174 sq mi (65,200 sq km)
> **Language:** Lithuanian, Russian, Polish
> **Did You Know?** Basketball is one of the country's most popular sports. Lithuania's men's Olympic basketball team won the bronze medal at three Summer Olympic games.

## Luxembourg

- **Capital:** Luxembourg
- **Population:** 491,775
- **Area:** 998 sq mi (2,586 sq km)
- **Language:** French, German, Luxembourgish
- **Did You Know?** Luxembourg's per capita gross national product (GDP) is more than $80,000, the highest in the world.

## Macedonia

- **Capital:** Skopje
- **Population:** 2,066,718
- **Area:** 9,781 sq mi (25,333 sq km)
- **Language:** Macedonian, Albanian, Turkish
- **Did You Know?** Macedonia's Albanian and Turkish minorities are legacies of the Ottoman Empire, which ended its rule of Macedonia in 1913 after 500 years in power.

## Madagascar

- **Capital:** Antananarivo
- **Population:** 20,653,556
- **Area:** 226,657 sq mi (587,040 sq km)
- **Language:** Malagasy, French
- **Did You Know?** Madagascar is the world's fourth largest island after Greenland, New Guinea, and Borneo. Because of its isolation from mainland Africa, most of its wildlife and plants exist nowhere else on Earth.

## Malawi

- **Capital:** Lilongwe
- **Population:** 14,268,711
- **Area:** 45,745 sq mi (118,480 sq km)
- **Language:** English, Chichewa
- **Did You Know?** Malawi means "flaming waters" and is named for the sun setting on Lake Malawi, Africa's third largest lake.

## Malaysia

- **Capital:** Kuala Lumpur
- **Population:** 25,715,819
- **Area:** 127,317 sq mi (329,750 sq km)
- **Language:** Malay, English, Chinese, Tamil
- **Did You Know?** About half of Malaysia's exports are electronics.

## Maldives

- **Capital:** Male
- **Population:** 396,334
- **Area:** 116 sq mi (300 sq km)
- **Language:** Maldivian Divehi, English
- **Did You Know?** The capital island of this 1,190-island nation is so overcrowded that Hulhumale, an artificial island, was created nearby.

## Mali

- **Capital:** Bamako
- **Population:** 12,666,987
- **Area:** 478,767 sq mi (1,240,000 sq km)
- **Language:** French, Bambara
- **Did You Know?** The Grand Mosque in Djenné is the largest mud-brick building in the world.

## Malta

- **Capital:** Valletta
- **Population:** 405,165
- **Area:** 122 sq mi (316 sq km)
- **Language:** Maltese, English
- **Did You Know?** This island nation is located midway between Europe and Africa, but it considers itself part of Europe and joined the European Union in 2004.

## COLOR KEY

- Europe
- Africa
- North America
- Asia
- Pacific Islands
- Australia
- South America

## Marshall Islands

- **Capital:** Majuro
- **Population:** 64,522
- **Area:** 4,577 sq mi (11,854 sq km)
- **Language:** English, Marshallese
- **Did You Know?** The United States occupied this island nation for several decades after World War II and the country still uses the U.S. dollar as its currency.

## Mauritania

- **Capital:** Nouakchott
- **Population:** 3,129,486
- **Area:** 397,955 sq mi (1,030,700 sq km)
- **Language:** Arabic, Wolof, Pulaar
- **Did You Know?** Since 80% of the country is covered by desert, most farming takes place on the banks of the Senegal River.

## Mauritius

- **Capital:** Port Louis
- **Population:** 1,284,264
- **Area:** 788 sq mi (2,040 sq km)
- **Language:** Creole, Bhojpuri, French, English
- **Did You Know?** About 70% of the people are descended from immigrants who came from India to work on Mauritius's sugar plantations.

## Mexico

- **Capital:** Mexico City
- **Population:** 111,211,789
- **Area:** 761,606 sq mi (1,972,550 sq km)
- **Language:** Spanish, Mayan languages
- **Did You Know?** Before 1848, Mexico included the area now covered by Arizona, California, Nevada, New Mexico, western Colorado, Texas, and Utah.

## Micronesia

- **Capital:** Palikir
- **Population:** 107,434
- **Area:** 271 sq mi (702 sq km)
- **Language:** English, Trukese, Pohnpeian, Yapese
- **Did You Know?** There are no formal political parties in Micronesia.

## Moldova

- **Capital:** Chisinau
- **Population:** 4,320,748
- **Area:** 13,067 sq mi (33,843 sq km)
- **Language:** Moldovan, Russian
- **Did You Know?** On March 1, Moldovans celebrate the beginning of spring by wearing a pin with braided threads of red (symbolizing blood) and white (symbolizing life).

## Monaco

- **Capital:** Monaco
- **Population:** 32,965
- **Area:** 1 sq mi (1.95 sq km)
- **Language:** French, English, Italian, Monegasque
- **Did You Know?** Except for a period of time when France annexed Monaco, the House of Grimaldi has been in power since 1297.

## Mongolia

- **Capital:** Ulaanbaatar
- **Population:** 3,041,142
- **Area:** 603,909 sq mi (1,564,116 sq km)
- **Language:** Khalkha Mongolian
- **Did You Know?** Mongolia was founded more than 360 years ago, but its capital has changed locations more than 20 times.

## Montenegro

- **Capital:** Cetinje; Podgorica (admin.)
- **Population:** 672,180
- **Area:** 5,415 sq mi (14,026 sq km)
- **Language:** Serbian, Bosnian, Albanian, Croatian
- **Did You Know?** Montenegro adopted its first constitution in 2007, a little more than a year after it declared its independence from Serbia. Both countries had been a part of Yugoslavia.

## Morocco

- **Capital:** Rabat
- **Population:** 34,859,364
- **Area:** 172,414 sq mi (446,550 sq km)
- **Language:** Arabic, Berber dialects, French
- **Did You Know?** One of the world's most grueling foot races is the Marathon des Sables ("Marathon of Sands"), a 7-day, 143-mile trek across the Sahara Desert in Morocco.

## Mozambique

- **Capital:** Maputo
- **Population:** 21,669,278
- **Area:** 309,496 sq mi (801,590 sq km)
- **Language:** Portuguese, Bantu languages
- **Did You Know?** Mozambique has been hurt by colonial rule, civil war and famine. But after a peace deal in 1992 ended 16 years of civil conflict, the country has enjoyed a period of rapid economic growth.

## Myanmar (Burma)

- **Capital:** Yangon (Rangoon); Nay Pyi Taw (admin.)
- **Population:** 48,137,741
- **Area:** 261,970 sq mi (678,500 sq km)
- **Language:** Burmese
- **Did You Know?** The Mogok Stone Tract is known for producing some of the world's most brilliant rubies.

## Namibia

- **Capital:** Windhoek
- **Population:** 2,108,665
- **Area:** 318,696 sq mi (825,418 sq km)
- **Language:** Afrikaans, English, German
- **Did You Know?** Until it gained independence from South Africa in 1990, Namibia was known as South-West Africa.

## Nauru

- **Capital:** Yaren district
- **Population:** 14,019
- **Area:** 8 sq mi (21 sq km)
- **Language:** Nauruan, English
- **Did You Know?** Named "Pleasant Island" by its first European visitors, this island nation is the world's smallest republic.

## Nepal

- **Capital:** Kathmandu
- **Population:** 28,563,377
- **Area:** 56,827 sq mi (147,181 sq km)
- **Language:** Nepali, Maithali, Bhojpuri, English
- **Did You Know?** In Nepali, Mt. Everest is called Sagarmatha, which translates as "Goddess of the Sky."

## Netherlands

- **Capital:** Amsterdam; The Hague (admin.)
- **Population:** 16,715,999
- **Area:** 16,033 sq mi (41,526 sq km)
- **Language:** Dutch, Frisian
- **Did You Know?** There are twice as many bikes as cars in this country.

### COLOR KEY
- Africa
- Asia
- Australia
- Europe
- North America
- Pacific Islands
- South America

CUPOLAS OF THE CHAPEL OF CHRIST IN THE KREMLIN, MOSCOW, RUSSIA

## New Zealand

- **Capital:** Wellington
- **Population:** 4,213,418
- **Area:** 103,738 sq mi (268,680 sq km)
- **Language:** English, Maori
- **Did You Know?**
  This wealthy Pacific nation has two main cultural groups: people of European descent who arrived in the last 200 years, and the Maori, whose ancestors arrived from Polynesia around 1,000 years ago.

## Nicaragua

- **Capital:** Managua
- **Population:** 5,891,199
- **Area:** 49,998 sq mi (129,494 sq km)
- **Language:** Spanish, Miskito, indigenous languages
- **Did You Know?** The islands of the Miskito Cays, once an area for pirate hideouts, are now a protected area for coral reefs and wildlife.

## Niger

- **Capital:** Niamey
- **Population:** 15,306,252
- **Area:** 489,192 sq mi (1,267,000 sq km)
- **Language:** French, Hausa, Djerma
- **Did You Know?** Niger was a crossroads of ancient trade in Africa. Caravans would stop here on their way to Timbuktu, Mali.

## Nigeria

- **Capital:** Abuja
- **Population:** 149,229,090
- **Area:** 356,669 sq mi (923,768 sq km)
- **Language:** English, Hausa, Yoruba, Ibo
- **Did You Know?** In the tradition of Nigeria's Yoruba people, the birth of twins brings good luck to their parents.

## Norway

- **Capital:** Oslo
- **Population:** 4,660,539
- **Area:** 125,021 sq mi (323,802 sq km)
- **Language:** Norwegian, Sami
- **Did You Know?** Norway's coast is known for its many fjords—narrow sea inlets surrounded by steep slopes.

## Oman

- **Capital:** Muscat
- **Population:** 3,418,085
- **Area:** 82,031 sq mi (212,460 sq km)
- **Language:** Arabic, English, Indian dialects
- **Did You Know?** As part of their traditional clothing, Omani men carry an ornate dagger called a khanjar tucked in the front of a special belt.

## Pakistan

- **Capital:** Islamabad
- **Population:** 176,242,949
- **Area:** 310,403 sq mi (803,940 sq km)
- **Language:** Urdu, English, Punjabi, Sindhi
- **Did You Know?** After gaining its independence from Britain in 1947, Pakistan was divided into two sections, nearly 1,000 miles apart on opposite sides of India. In 1971, East Pakistan declared its independence as the country of Bangladesh.

**BERGEN, NORWAY**

## Palau

- **Capital:** Melekeok
- **Population:** 20,796
- **Area:** 177 sq mi (458 sq km)
- **Language:** English, Palauan, Sonsoral, Tobi, Angaur
- **Did You Know?** Palau's marine life is among the world's most diverse—more than 1,400 species of fish and 500 species of coral can be found here.

## Panama
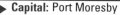
- **Capital:** Panama City
- **Population:** 3,360,474
- **Area:** 30,193 sq mi (78,200 sq km)
- **Language:** Spanish, English
- **Did You Know?** Panama is the shortest link between the Atlantic and Pacific Oceans in the Americas, making its 50-mile-long (80-km) canal of great strategic importance.

## Papua New Guinea

- **Capital:** Port Moresby
- **Population:** 6,057,263
- **Area:** 178,704 sq mi (462,840 sq km)
- **Language:** English, Motu, Melanesian pidgin
- **Did You Know?** More than 700 ethnic groups, each with its own language and customs, live in this country.

## Paraguay

- **Capital:** Asunción
- **Population:** 6,995,655
- **Area:** 157,047 sq mi (406,750 sq km)
- **Language:** Spanish, Guarani
- **Did You Know?** One of the world's largest hydroelectric power plants by capacity is Itaipu, located in Paraguay and Brazil.

## Peru

- **Capital:** Lima
- **Population:** 29,546,963
- **Area:** 496,226 sq mi (1,285,220 sq km)
- **Language:** Spanish, Quechua, Aymara
- **Did You Know?** Peru's rich heritage includes Machu Picchu, the beautiful and mysterious ruins of an Incan city high in the Andes Mountains.

## Philippines

- **Capital:** Manila
- **Population:** 97,976,603
- **Area:** 115,831 sq mi (300,000 sq km)
- **Language:** Filipino, English
- **Did You Know?** The Philippines are vulnerable to many natural hazards, including tropical cyclones (known as typhoons), landslides, earthquakes, tsunamis, and volcanic eruptions.

## Poland
- **Capital:** Warsaw
- **Population:** 38,482,919
- **Area:** 120,728 sq mi (312,685 sq km)
- **Language:** Polish, Ukrainian, German
- **Did You Know?** In 1989, the Polish people voted in eastern Europe's first post-communist government.

## Portugal

- **Capital:** Lisbon
- **Population:** 10,709,924
- **Area:** 35,672 sq mi (92,391 sq km)
- **Language:** Portuguese
- **Did You Know?** The national style of music, called *fado*, originated in Lisbon. It has a sad and longing sound.

### COLOR KEY
- Africa
- Asia
- Australia
- Europe
- North America
- Pacific Islands
- South America

## Qatar

- **Capital:** Doha
- **Population:** 833,285
- **Area:** 4,416 sq mi (11,437 sq km)
- **Language:** Arabic, English
- **Did You Know?** North Field, one of the largest natural gas reservoirs in the world, is just off the coast of Qatar.

## Romania

- **Capital:** Bucharest
- **Population:** 22,215,421
- **Area:** 91,699 sq mi (237,500 sq km)
- **Language:** Romanian, Hungarian, German
- **Did You Know?** Prince Vlad Tepes ("the Impaler"), who once ruled part of Romania, was the inspiration for the fictional Dracula.

## Russia

- **Capital:** Moscow
- **Population:** 140,041,247
- **Area:** 6,592,772 sq mi (17,075,200 sq km)
- **Language:** Russian, many minority languages
- **Did You Know?** The Trans-Siberian Railroad is the world's longest railway line, stretching 5,778 miles from Moscow east to Vladivostok.

## Rwanda

- **Capital:** Kigali
- **Population:** 10,473,282
- **Area:** 10,169 sq mi (26,338 sq km)
- **Language:** French, English, Kinyarwanda, Kiswahili
- **Did You Know?** Volcanoes National Park is home to one of only two remaining mountain gorilla populations in the world.

## Saint Kitts and Nevis

- **Capital:** Basseterre
- **Population:** 40,131
- **Area:** 101 sq mi (261 sq km)
- **Language:** English
- **Did You Know?** The islands of St. Kitts and Nevis declared independence from Britain in 1983. They are inhabited mainly by descendants of enslaved West Africans.

## Saint Lucia

- **Capital:** Castries
- **Population:** 160,267
- **Area:** 238 sq mi (616 sq km)
- **Language:** English, French patois
- **Did You Know?** The Caribbean island is a popular spot to visit because of its beautiful beaches, unusual plants and the Qualibou volcano with its boiling sulphur springs.

## Saint Vincent and the Grenadines

- **Capital:** Kingstown
- **Population:** 104,574
- **Area:** 150 sq mi (389 sq km)
- **Language:** English, French patois
- **Did You Know?** The deadly Soufrière volcano on St. Vincent island last erupted in 1979.

## Samoa (formerly Western Samoa)

- **Capital:** Apia
- **Population:** 219,998
- **Area:** 1,137 sq mi (2,944 sq km)
- **Language:** English, Samoan
- **Did You Know?** In 1962, Samoa (then known as Western Samoa) became the first South Pacific island nation to achieve independence.

## San Marino

- **Capital:** San Marino
- **Population:** 30,324
- **Area:** 24 sq mi (61 sq km)
- **Language:** Italian
- **Did You Know?** According to legend, San Marino was founded in 301 A.D. by a Christian stonemason, Marinus, for whom the country was named.

## São Tomé and Príncipe

- **Capital:** São Tomé
- **Population:** 212,679
- **Area:** 386 sq mi (1,001 sq km)
- **Language:** Portuguese, Creole
- **Did You Know?** Cocoa makes up 80% of all the country's exports.

## Saudi Arabia

- **Capital:** Riyadh
- **Population:** 28,686,633
- **Area:** 756,985 sq mi (1,960,582 sq km)
- **Language:** Arabic
- **Did You Know?** Saudi Arabia is the world's leading exporter of oil.

## Senegal

- **Capital:** Dakar
- **Population:** 13,711,597
- **Area:** 75,749 sq mi (196,190 sq km)
- **Language:** French, Wolof, Pulaar
- **Did You Know?** Dakar is the westernmost point on the continent of Africa.

## Serbia

- **Capital:** Belgrade
- **Population:** 7,379,339
- **Area:** 34,116 sq mi (88,361 sq km)
- **Language:** Serbian, Albanian, Romanian
- **Did You Know?** The Roma (Gypsies), one of Serbia's largest minority groups, have helped to maintain the country's folk music tradition.

## COLOR KEY

- Africa
- Asia
- Australia
- Europe
- North America
- Pacific Islands
- South America

**TOWER BRIDGE IN LONDON, ENGLAND**

## Seychelles

- **Capital:** Victoria
- **Population:** 87,476
- **Area:** 176 sq mi (455 sq km)
- **Language:** Creole, English, French
- **Did You Know?** The colors of Seychelles' flag represent the sky and sea (blue), the sun (yellow), the people and their work (red), social justice and harmony (white), and the environment (green).

## Sierra Leone

- **Capital:** Freetown
- **Population:** 6,440,053
- **Area:** 27,699 sq mi (71,740 sq km)
- **Language:** English, Mende, Temne, Krio
- **Did You Know?** Diamonds are one of this country's major exports.

## Singapore
- **Capital:** Singapore
- **Population:** 4,657,542
- **Area:** 267 sq mi (693 sq km)
- **Language:** Chinese, Malay, Tamil, English
- **Did You Know?** The Port of Singapore is the world's second busiest in tons of cargo shipped. The Port of Shanghai, China, is the busiest.

## Slovakia

- **Capital:** Bratislava
- **Population:** 5,463,046
- **Area:** 18,859 sq mi (48,845 sq km)
- **Language:** Slovak, Hungarian
- **Did You Know?** Bryndzové halušky, or potato dumplings with sheep's milk cheese, is considered Slovakia's national dish.

## Slovenia

- **Capital:** Ljubljana
- **Population:** 2,005,692
- **Area:** 7,827 sq mi (20,273 sq km)
- **Language:** Slovenian, Serbo-Croatian
- **Did You Know?** Slovenia has more than a thousand underground caves. The famous Postojna Cave system has about 13 miles of known passageways.

## Solomon Islands
- **Capital:** Honiara
- **Population:** 595,613
- **Area:** 10,985 sq mi (28,450 sq km)
- **Language:** English, Melanesian pidgin
- **Did You Know?** Because so many different languages are spoken in the Solomon Islands, many people communicate using a simplified English called Melanesian pidgin.

## Somalia
- **Capital:** Mogadishu
- **Population:** 9,832,017
- **Area:** 246,201 sq mi (637,657 sq km)
- **Language:** Somali, Arabic, Italian, English
- **Did You Know?** Iman, a supermodel from Somalia, speaks five languages and studied political science in college.

## South Africa

- **Capital:** Pretoria (admin.); Cape Town (legis.); Bloemfontein (judicial)
- **Population:** 49,052,489
- **Area:** 471,011 sq mi (1,219,912 sq km)
- **Language:** Afrikaans, English, Ndebele, Sotho, Zulu, Xhosa
- **Did You Know?** Racial segregation was law between 1948 and 1994. In the era of apartheid (Afrikaans for "apartness"), only whites could vote or run for public office. The rest of the population held limited political rights.

## Spain

- **Capital:** Madrid
- **Population:** 40,525,002
- **Area:** 194,897 sq mi (504,782 sq km)
- **Language:** Castilian Spanish, Catalan, Galician
- **Did You Know?** Spain produces and exports the most olives and olive oil in the world.

## Sri Lanka

- **Capital:** Colombo
- **Population:** 21,324,791
- **Area:** 25,332 sq mi (65,610 sq km)
- **Language:** Sinhala, Tamil, English
- **Did You Know?** Ceylon tea takes its name from this country, which used to be called Ceylon while under European rule.

## Sudan

- **Capital:** Khartoum
- **Population:** 41,087,825
- **Area:** 967,499 sq mi (2,505,810 sq km)
- **Language:** Arabic, Nubian, Ta Bedawie
- **Did You Know?** The ancient kingdom of Kush, whose civilization reflected Egyptian and African influences, once thrived in Sudan.

## Suriname

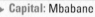

- **Capital:** Paramaribo
- **Population:** 481,267
- **Area:** 63,039 sq mi (163,270 sq km)
- **Language:** Dutch, English, Sranang Tongo
- **Did You Know?** Many Surinamers are descended from escaped West African slaves, who were brought to Suriname when it was still a Dutch colony.

## Swaziland

- **Capital:** Mbabane
- **Population:** 1,123,913
- **Area:** 6,704 sq mi (17,363 sq km)
- **Language:** English, siSwati
- **Did You Know?** Swaziland's king is one of the few remaining absolute monarchs in the world. Although a new constitution was adopted in 2006, political parties are still officially banned.

## Sweden

- **Capital:** Stockholm
- **Population:** 9,059,651
- **Area:** 173,732 sq mi (449,964 sq km)
- **Language:** Swedish, Sami, Finnish
- **Did You Know?** Sweden has not participated in any wars since 1814, when it ceased fighting in the Napoleonic Wars.

SKYLINE OF SINGAPORE

## Switzerland

- **Capital:** Bern (admin.); Lausanne (judicial)
- **Population:** 7,604,467
- **Area:** 15,942 sq mi (41,290 sq km)
- **Language:** German, French, Italian, Romansch
- **Did You Know?** Switzerland has long remained neutral during wars, giving it a political stability that has helped it become one of the world's wealthiest countries. Banking is one of its most important industries.

## Syria

- **Capital:** Damascus
- **Population:** 20,178,485
- **Area:** 71,498 sq mi (185,180 sq km)
- **Language:** Arabic, Kurdish, Armenian
- **Did You Know?** Tablets found in the ancient city of Ugarit contain one of the world's oldest alphabets, dating back to around 1400 B.C.

## Taiwan

- **Capital:** Taipei
- **Population:** 22,974,347
- **Area:** 13,892 sq mi (35,980 sq km)
- **Language:** Mandarin Chinese, Taiwanese
- **Did You Know?** Although Taiwan set up its own government in 1949, China considers Taiwan to be one of its provinces and still under its control.

## Tajikistan

- **Capital:** Dushanbe
- **Population:** 7,349,145
- **Area:** 55,251 sq mi (143,100 sq km)
- **Language:** Tajik, Russian
- **Did You Know?** Tajikistan's main source of energy is hydroelectricity. Its Nurek Dam is the highest dam in the world.

## Tanzania

- **Capital:** Dar es Salaam Dodoma (legislative)
- **Population:** 41,048,532
- **Area:** 364,900 sq mi (945,087 sq km)
- **Language:** Kiswahili (Swahili), English, Arabic
- **Did You Know?** Tanzania's Mt. Kilimanjaro, which peaks at 19,340 feet, is the highest point in Africa.

## Thailand

- **Capital:** Bangkok
- **Population:** 65,905,410
- **Area:** 198,457 sq mi (514,000 sq km)
- **Language:** Thai, English
- **Did You Know?** Formerly known as Siam, after a 19th-century king, Thailand is the only country in Southeast Asia to have never been colonized. Thailand means "land of the free."

**COLOR KEY**
- Africa
- Asia
- Australia
- Europe
- North America
- Pacific Islands
- South America

## Timor-Leste (East Timor)

- **Capital:** Dili
- **Population:** 1,131,612
- **Area:** 5,794 sq mi (15,007 sq km)
- **Language:** Tetum, Portuguese, Indonesian, English
- **Did You Know?** This country occupies the eastern half of Timor island; the island's western half (except for an area on the coast) belongs to Indonesia.

## Togo

- **Capital:** Lomé
- **Population:** 6,019,877
- **Area:** 21,925 sq mi (56,785 sq km)
- **Language:** French, Ewe, Mina, Kabye, Dagomba
- **Did You Know?** In October 2007, a record 85% of registered voters turned out for Togo's first free and fair parliamentary elections since 2002.

## Tonga

- **Capital:** Nuku'alofa
- **Population:** 120,898
- **Area:** 289 sq mi (748 sq km)
- **Language:** Tongan, English
- **Did You Know?** Tonga is ruled by the only surviving monarchy in Polynesia, though it does have a parliament in which most of the members are elected.

## Trinidad and Tobago

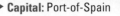

- **Capital:** Port-of-Spain
- **Population:** 1,229,953
- **Area:** 1,980 sq mi (5,128 sq km)
- **Language:** English, Hindi, French, Spanish
- **Did You Know?** Steel drums were invented on the island of Trinidad around the time of World War II, using recycled metal containers such as oil drums.

## Tunisia

- **Capital:** Tunis
- **Population:** 10,486,339
- **Area:** 63,170 sq mi (163,610 sq km)
- **Language:** Arabic, French
- **Did You Know?** Lamb is the basis of most meat dishes in Tunisia. Long, social meals frequently begin with lamb soup.

## Turkey

- **Capital:** Ankara
- **Population:** 76,805,524
- **Area:** 301,384 sq mi (780,580 sq km)
- **Language:** Turkish, Kurdish, Arabic
- **Did You Know?** Hisarlik, an archaeological site in northwest Turkey, contains the ancient city of Troy, site of the legendary Trojan War.

**VIEW OF THE SWISS ALPS FROM JUNGFRAU, SWITZERLAND**

## Turkmenistan

- **Capital:** Ashgabat
- **Population:** 4,884,887
- **Area:** 188,456 sq mi (488,100 sq km)
- **Language:** Turkmen, Russian, Uzbek
- **Did You Know?** This desert nation has the smallest population of the five former Soviet republics in Central Asia, but possesses the world's fifth largest reserves of natural gas as well as large deposits of oil.

## Tuvalu

- **Capital:** Funafuti
- **Population:** 12,373
- **Area:** 10 sq mi (26 sq km)
- **Language:** Tuvaluan, English
- **Did You Know?** One of Tuvalu's main exports is copra, the dried coconut meat from which coconut oil is made.

## Uganda

- **Capital:** Kampala
- **Population:** 32,369,558
- **Area:** 91,136 sq mi (236,040 sq km)
- **Language:** English, Ganda, Swahili
- **Did You Know?** The crested crane is a national symbol and appears on Uganda's flag.

## Ukraine

- **Capital:** Kiev
- **Population:** 45,700,395
- **Area:** 233,090 sq mi (603,700 sq km)
- **Language:** Ukrainian, Russian
- **Did You Know?** Ukraine was once known as the "bread basket of the Soviet Union" for its exports of wheat. It is still one of the world's top wheat producers.

## United Arab Emirates

- **Capital:** Abu Dhabi
- **Population:** 4,798,491
- **Area:** 32,000 sq mi (82,880 sq km)
- **Language:** Arabic, Persian, English, Hindi, Urdu
- **Did You Know?** More than 2,600 feet tall, the Dubai Tower (Burj Dubai in Arabic) will be the tallest building in the world upon its completion, scheduled for the end of 2009.

## United Kingdom (Great Britain)

- **Capital:** London
- **Population:** 61,113,205
- **Area:** 94,526 sq mi (244,820 sq km)
- **Language:** English, Welsh, Scottish Gaelic
- **Did You Know?** At the height of its power during the 19th century, the British Empire controlled one-fourth of all the land in the world and more than one-fourth of the world's population.

## United States

- **Capital:** Washington, DC
- **Population:** 307,524,279*
- **Area:** 3,718,712 sq mi (9,631,420 sq km)
- **Language:** English, Spanish
- **Did You Know?** The U.S. is the world's leading economic and military power. It is also a major source of entertainment: American TV, films, and music are all popular around the globe.

*Sept. 2009

## Uruguay

- **Capital:** Montevideo
- **Population:** 3,494,382
- **Area:** 68,039 sq mi (176,220 sq km)
- **Language:** Spanish, Portunol
- **Did You Know?** The leaves of the *yerba maté* shrub are used to brew a popular drink in Uruguay. The tea is often drunk from a gourd using a metal straw.

## COLOR KEY

- Africa
- Asia
- Australia
- Europe
- North America
- Pacific Islands
- South America

## Uzbekistan

- **Capital:** Tashkent
- **Population:** 27,606,007
- **Area:** 172,742 sq mi (447,400 sq km)
- **Language:** Uzbek, Russian, Tajik
- **Did You Know?** Samarkand, in east-central Uzbekistan, is one of Central Asia's oldest cities. It was once an important trading center on the Silk Road between Asia and the West.

## Vanuatu

- **Capital:** Port-Vila
- **Population:** 218,519
- **Area:** 4,710 sq mi (12,200 sq km)
- **Language:** French, English, Bislama, local languages
- **Did You Know?** More than 100 local languages and dialects are spoken on the 80-plus islands that make up this Pacific nation.

## Vatican City

- **Population:** 826
- **Area:** 0.17 sq mi (0.44 sq km)
- **Language:** Italian, Latin, French
- **Did You Know?** Not only is Vatican City the world's smallest country, it also has the smallest population of any country—826 people.

## Venezuela

- **Capital:** Caracas
- **Population:** 26,814,843
- **Area:** 352,144 sq mi (912,050 sq km)
- **Language:** Spanish, indigenous dialects
- **Did You Know?** The highest waterfall on Earth, Angel Falls, is in Venezuela, dropping 3,212 feet over the side of a mountain.

## Vietnam

- **Capital:** Hanoi
- **Population:** 86,967,524
- **Area:** 127,244 sq mi (329,560 sq km)
- **Language:** Vietnamese, English, French, Chinese
- **Did You Know?** Vietnam endured a long civil war that drew in first France, then the U.S. before ending in 1976. But the nation now has one of Asia's fastest-growing economies.

## Yemen

- **Capital:** Sana'a
- **Population:** 23,822,783
- **Area:** 203,850 sq mi (527,970 sq km)
- **Language:** Arabic
- **Did You Know?** One of Yemen's chief crops is coffee. "Mocha" coffee beans take their name from the Yemeni port city of Mocha.

## Zambia

- **Capital:** Lusaka
- **Population:** 11,862,740
- **Area:** 290,586 sq mi (752,614 sq km)
- **Language:** English, indigenous languages
- **Did You Know?** Victoria Falls, one of the world's largest waterfalls, provides Zambia with a source of hydroelectric power.

## Zimbabwe

- **Capital:** Harare
- **Population:** 11,392,629
- **Area:** 150,804 sq mi (390,580 sq km)
- **Language:** English, Shona, Sindebele
- **Did You Know?** The nation takes its name from the famous stone ruins of Great Zimbabwe, a city built by wealthy Shona-speaking cattlemen between the 13th and 14th centuries.

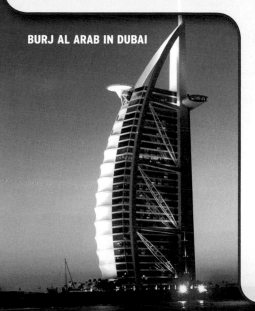

**BURJ AL ARAB IN DUBAI**

# Native Americans

**Where do most Seneca live?** ➡ page 179

**n**ative Americans are thought to have arrived in the Americas 18,000 years ago, most likely from northeast Asia. Although their population decreased significantly through the 17th, 18th, and 19th centuries from disease and war, there are still hundreds of tribes or nations, each with its own unique language and traditions. From the names of states and towns to foods like corn and squash, the influence of Native American cultures can be found everywhere in America.

## TIME LINE NORTH AMERICAN INDIANS

| | |
|---|---|
| **1492** | Christopher Columbus made contact with Taino tribes on the island he named Hispaniola. |
| **c.1600** | Five tribes—Mohawk, Oneida, Onondaga, Cayuga, and Seneca—formed the Iroquois Confederacy in the Northeast. |
| **1754-63** | Many Native Americans fought with both French and British troops in the French and Indian War. |
| **1804-06** | Sacagawea served as an interpreter and guide for Lewis and Clark. It's doubtful that the expedition could have succeeded without her. |
| **1821** | Sequoyah completed an alphabet for the Cherokee language. |
| **1827** | Cherokee tribes in what is now Georgia formed the Cherokee Nation with a constitution and elected governing officials. |
| **1830** | Congress passed the Indian Removal Act, the first law that forced tribes to move so that U.S. citizens could settle certain areas of land. |
| **1834** | Congress created the Indian Territory for tribes removed from their lands. It covered the present-day states of Oklahoma, Kansas, and Nebraska. |
| **1912** | Jim Thorpe, a Native American, wins the decathalon and the pentathalon in the 1912 Olympic Games. |
| **1924** | Congress granted all Native Americans U.S. citizenship. |
| **1929** | Charles Curtis, a member of the Kaw nation, became the first American of Indian ancestry elected vice president. |
| **1985** | Wilma Mankiller became the first female chief of the Cherokee Nation. |

# MAJOR CULTURAL AREAS OF NATIVE NORTH AMERICANS

**C**limate and geography influenced the culture of the people who lived in these regions. On the plains, for example, people depended on the great herds of buffalo for food. For Aleuts and Eskimos in the far north, seals and whales were an important food source. There are more than 560 tribes officially recognized by the U.S. government today and more than 56 million acres of tribal lands. Below are just a few well-known tribal groups that have lived in these areas.

## NORTHEAST WOODLANDS
The Illinois, Iroquois (Mohawk, Onondaga, Cayuga, Oneida, Seneca, and Tuscarora), Lenape, Menominee, Micmac, Narragansett, Potawatomi, Shawnee

## SOUTHEAST WOODLANDS
The Cherokee, Chickasaw, Choctaw, Creek, Seminole

## PLAINS & PRAIRIE
The Arapaho, Blackfoot, Cheyenne, Comanche, Hidatsa, Kaw, Mandan, Sioux

## SOUTHWEST
The Apache, Navajo, Havasupai, Mojave, Pima, Pueblo (Hopi, Isleta, Laguna, Zuñi)

## GREAT BASIN
The Paiute, Shoshoni, Ute

## CALIFORNIA
The Klamath, Maidu, Miwok, Modoc, Patwin, Pomo, Wintun, Yurok

## PLATEAU
The Cayuse, Nez Percé, Okanagon, Salish, Spokan, Umatilla, Walla Walla, Yakima

## NORTHWEST COAST
The Chinook, Haida, Kwakiutl, Makah, Nootka, Salish, Tillamook, Tlingit, Tsimshian

## SUBARCTIC
The Beaver, Chipewyan, Chippewa, Cree, Ingalik, Kaska, Kutchin, Montagnais, Naskapi, Tanana

## ARCTIC
The Aleut, Eskimo (Inuit and Yipuk)

# MAJOR NATIVE AMERICAN GROUPS*

1. Cherokee, 279,123
2. Navajo, 281,135
3. Apache, 131,360
4. Alaska Native, 110,637
5. Sioux, 109,213
6. Chippewa, 105,028
7. Iroquois, 90,173
8. Choctaw, 85,647
9. Lumbee, 72,943
10. Pueblo, 72,880

*2007 U.S. Census Bureau estimates. Figures for all groups except Apache, Lumbee, Alaska Native, and Iroquois are for people reporting only one tribal grouping. Other figures include those reporting one or more tribal groupings.

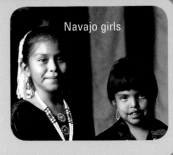

Navajo girls

## Native American Populations by State*

| State | Population | State | Population |
|---|---|---|---|
| Alabama | 23,799 | Nebraska | 17,103 |
| Alaska | 103,497 | Nevada | 34,813 |
| Arizona | 294,118 | New Hampshire | 3,458 |
| Arkansas | 21,635 | New Jersey | 27,970 |
| California | 421,346 | New Mexico | 190,826 |
| Colorado | 54,626 | New York | 104,936 |
| Connecticut | 12,497 | North Carolina | 111,148 |
| Delaware | 3,454 | North Dakota | 34,190 |
| Florida | 80,369 | Ohio | 27,546 |
| Georgia | 30,893 | Oklahoma | 287,728 |
| Hawaii | 6,378 | Oregon | 51,209 |
| Idaho | 20,897 | Pennsylvania | 24,077 |
| Illinois | 41,231 | Rhode Island | 6,574 |
| Indiana | 18,603 | South Carolina | 16,849 |
| Iowa | 11,145 | South Dakota | 66,665 |
| Kansas | 27,374 | Tennessee | 18,733 |
| Kentucky | 9,988 | Texas | 163,455 |
| Louisiana | 27,042 | Utah | 33,663 |
| Maine | 7,582 | Vermont | 2,386 |
| Maryland | 18,584 | Virginia | 26,020 |
| Massachusetts | 19,044 | Washington | 104,405 |
| Michigan | 60,820 | West Virginia | 4,045 |
| Minnesota | 60,491 | Wisconsin | 51,937 |
| Mississippi | 13,816 | Wyoming | 12,668 |
| Missouri | 28,332 | Wash., DC | 2,161 |
| Montana | 60,725 | U.S. total | 2,902,851 |

*2006 U.S. Census Bureau estimates. Figures do not include people who reported belonging to other ethnic groups in addition to Native American.

# TOTEM POLES

Northwest Coast Indians carve totem poles with painted images of animals and human faces. The carvings represent animals and spirits and may also tell stories about specific people or events. The poles are carved from tree trunks or smaller pieces of wood and may be used as memorials, gravemarkers, and as welcome signs in front of homes. The tallest totem pole, erected in 1994 and dismantled in 1997, was located in Victoria, British Columbia, Canada. It was 180 feet, 3 inches tall.

# NATIVE AMERICAN GROUPS

## THE SIOUX NATION

The Sioux Nation is comprised of the Lakota or Titonwan, the Dakota or Santee, and the Nakota or Yankton. The Sioux were nomadic (moved often), lived in teepees, and many of the tribes roamed the Great Plains. Their lands included the Black Hills (in western South Dakota). When gold was discovered in the Black Hills, the U.S. government wanted to buy or rent the land from the Lakota Sioux. These lands were sacred to the Sioux and they refused to sell. General George Custer was supposed to remove the Sioux to reservations. On June 15, 1876, the Battle of the Little Big Horn between Custer's cavalry and the Lakota and their allies was fought. The Sioux Nation won a victory in this battle. The last conflict between the Lakota Sioux and the U.S. government was the Massacre at Wounded Knee on December 29, 1890.

Great Sioux leaders include Chief Red Cloud, Sitting Bull, Crazy Horse, and Black Elk.

Chief Sitting Bull

## NAVAJO NATION (DINE)

The Navajo Nation spans 27,000 square miles across Arizona, New Mexico, and Utah and is America's most populated reservation with about 175,000 residents. Many Dine (dee-NAY), as they call themselves, still speak a highly descriptive and unique language called Athapaskan. It was used as a code in World War II and never cracked. Local radio still broadcasts sports in Athapaskan, including New Mexico State University's football games. High school sports, especially basketball and cross country, are important to the Navajo. The Dine belong to clans within their nation, which are passed down from a mother to her children.

## SENECA

The Seneca are one of the nations that formed the Iroquois Confederacy. There are about 7,200 people who make up the Seneca Nation today. Most live on one of two reservations in western New York. People inherit their Seneca clan status through their mothers. Women have always been important in their society. When clan families used to share wooden longhouses, which could extend more than 100 feet, the oldest woman was always the leader. Corn, beans, and squash are traditional foods. Lacrosse is a traditional sport popular today. A lesser known sport is snowsnake, a game where a polished staff is thrown down an iced snow track.

# Numbers

What is a googol? ➡ page 180

# From 0 to Infinity

**T**he set of numbers includes whole numbers like 8, negative numbers like –23, fractions like 2/27, decimals like 46.9 and even "irrational" numbers that cannot be expressed as a fraction. Zero and infinity are two particularly interesting numbers.

## Zero

In Roman Numerals, I stands for 1 and X stands for 10. Do you know the Roman numeral for "0"? Probably not, because there isn't one. The Babylonians in Asia, Hindus in India, and Mayans in the Americas were among the first to use the idea of zero as a "placeholder." In our number system "10" means 1 "ten" and 0 "ones." The 0 in 10 is a "placeholder" in the ones column.

A "numeral" is a symbol that represents a number. The Babylonians used place value and the idea of zero. But at first they didn't have a numeral for zero, so they just left a blank space where a zero should be, like writing 10,301 as 1 3 1. That was confusing because there was no numeral "to hold the place." Later they used two wedges to stand for zero. The Mayans used a symbol that looks like an eye.

Zero has some cool properties. Any number multiplied by 0 equals zero. Any number added to 0 equals the original number.

**Babylonian Zero**

**Mayan Zero**

## Infinity

∞ This symbol, which looks like an 8 lying on its side, represents infinity. Infinity can be very hard to picture, because it never ends. For example, infinity is just as far from the number 1 as it is from 1 million, or even from a 1 with 100 zeroes after it (known as a googol).

In math, numbers are thought of as infinite because you can always imagine a larger number. For example, what's the biggest number you know? Add 1 to that number; you have a bigger number. Negative numbers are infinite too.

Here's a puzzler: which is larger, the set of all counting numbers (1, 2, 3, 4…) or the set of all even numbers (2, 4, 6, 8…)? According to mathematicians' concept of infinity, they are the same size, infinite. For every counting number (for example, 1), there is a corresponding even number (for example, 2).

# NUMERALS
## in Ancient Civilizations

People have been counting since the earliest of times.
This is what some numerals look like in different cultures.

| Modern | 1 | 2 | 3 | 4 | 5 | 6 | 7 | 8 | 9 | 10 | 20 | 50 | 100 |
|---|---|---|---|---|---|---|---|---|---|---|---|---|---|
| Egyptian | I | II | III | IIII | IIIII | IIIIII | IIIIIII | IIIIIIII | IIIIIIIII | ∩ | ∩∩ | ∩∩∩∩∩ | ϟ |
| Babylonian | | | | | | | | | | < | ≪ | ≪≪ | <≪ |
| Greek | A | B | Γ | Δ | E | F | Z | H | θ | I | K | N | P |
| Mayan | • | •• | ••• | •••• | — | — • | — •• | — ••• | — •••• | = | ☉ | ≐ | ⊙ |
| Chinese | 一 | 二 | 三 | 四 | 五 | 六 | 七 | 八 | 九 | 十 | 二十 | 五十 | 百 |
| Hindu | 1 | 2 | 3 | 8 | Y | ६ | ) | < | ६ | 10 | 20 | 40 | 100 |
| Arabic | 1 | 2 | 3 | ٣ | ٤ | ٤ | ٧ | ٨ | 9 | 10 | 20 | 80 | 100 |

## ROMAN *NUMERALS*

Roman numerals are still used today.
They are built up from different letters.

I stands for 1     V stands for 5
X stands for 10    L stands for 50
C stands for 100   D stands for 500
M stands for 1,000

If one Roman numeral is followed by one with a greater value, the first is subtracted from the second. For example, IX means 10 – 1 = 9. Think of it as "one less than ten." On the other hand, if a Roman numeral is followed by one or more others that are equal or of lesser value, add them together. Thus, LXI means 50 + 10 + 1 = 61.

What year is it now? Write the number in Roman numerals.

The Colosseum in Rome probably fit about 50,000 people. Write that number in Roman numerals. This will probably give you a clue as to why Roman numerals lost popularity.

| | | | | | | |
|---|---|---|---|---|---|---|
| 1 | I | 14 | XIV | 90 | XC |
| 2 | II | 15 | XV | 100 | C |
| 3 | III | 16 | XVI | 200 | CC |
| 4 | IV | 17 | XVII | 300 | CCC |
| 5 | V | 18 | XVIII | 400 | CD |
| 6 | VI | 19 | XIX | 500 | D |
| 7 | VII | 20 | XX | 600 | DC |
| 8 | VIII | 30 | XXX | 700 | DCC |
| 9 | IX | 40 | XL | 800 | DCCC |
| 10 | X | 50 | L | 900 | CM |
| 11 | XI | 60 | LX | 1,000 | M |
| 12 | XII | 70 | LXX | 2,000 | MM |
| 13 | XIII | 80 | LXXX | 3,000 | MMM |

ANSWERS ON PAGES 334-336.

# Pascal's Triangle

Row 0
Row 1
Row 2
Row 3
Row 4
Row 5
Row 6
Row 7
Row 8

**m**athematicians spend a lot of time looking for patterns. Sometimes, they find a pattern of numbers that can be useful for all sorts of things. Pascal's Triangle is just that kind of pattern.

## How Is the Triangle Constructed?

Notice that all of the numbers on the sides of the triangle are the number 1. The top row is called row 0, the second, row 1, the third, row 2. Look at row 2. The number 2 in the middle of the row comes from adding the two numbers directly above it (1 + 1). This is the way the triangle works—as you go down the rows, each number is the sum of the two numbers directly above it. Look for yourself and check to see if it's true. Can you figure out what the numbers in row 8 will be?

## What Can This Triangle Do?

This triangle can help you with probability and combinations. All of the numbers in the triangle have a place. To name the place, count in from the left, starting at 0. So, the first "2", closest to the top would be in row 2 (remember, rows start at 0, too), place 1.

## Who Was Pascal?

Blaise Pascal was a mathematician from the seventeenth century. He wrote his first book on mathematics when he was only 16 years old, in 1639. He spent his life trying to solve problems in math and science.

## Here's a Question This Triangle Can Help You Solve

You are taking a special trip for your birthday and you can only invite two friends. But you have five friends you would enjoy taking along with you. How many choices do you have for the combination of friends on your birthday trip? Or, simply—how many different ways can you pick two things from a set of five things?

The answer is the number in row 5, place 2. There are ten different combinations of friends you could bring.

That's just the start. You can use this triangle for many other mathematical problems. Look up Pascal's Triangle at **WEB SITE** **mathforum.org**

# PRIME TIME

**A** prime number is a number that can only be divided by itself and the number 1. So, prime numbers include: 2, 3, 5, 7, 11, 13, 17, and so on. All other positive numbers (other than 1) are called composite numbers, because they have at least two factors (numbers they can be divided by) other than 1. For example, 6 is a composite number: its factors are 1, 2, 3, and 6.

Mathematicians around the world participate in the Great Internet Mersenne Prime Search (GIMPS) project. These mathematicians use powerful computers to search for the biggest prime number.

In September 2008, mathematicians at UCLA found the largest prime number yet discovered. It's expressed as a power. Powers work by multiplying the base number by as many times as the raised exponent number shows.

$$So, 2^3 = 2 \times 2 \times 2 = 8.$$

The prime number they found is $2^{43,112,609}$ minus 1. The number has 12,978,189 digits, enough to fill more than 10 *World Almanacs for Kids*.

# SUDOKU

A Sudoku puzzle is usually made up of nine rows and nine columns of numbers. The rows and columns make up mini-grids within the boundary of the puzzle. Each row, column, and region (mini-grid) can only have the numbers 1 through 9. Duplicate numbers are not permitted in any row, column, or region. Solving Sudoku is a great way to practice logical and deductive reasoning skills.

The basic rule for Sudoku is: complete the puzzle so that each row, column, and region contains the numbers 1 through 9 only once.

|   |   | 7 |   | 5 |   | 3 |   |   |
|---|---|---|---|---|---|---|---|---|
| 6 | 8 | 1 | 4 | 7 | 3 | 5 | 9 | 2 |
|   |   | 3 | 2 |   | 6 |   |   |   |
| 7 |   | 5 |   | 3 |   | 4 |   | 8 |
|   |   | 8 |   | 4 |   | 2 |   |   |
| 2 |   | 4 |   | 1 |   | 6 |   | 7 |
|   |   | 2 | 3 |   | 7 |   |   |   |
|   | 5 | 9 | 1 |   | 4 | 8 | 7 |   |
|   |   | 6 |   | 8 |   | 1 |   |   |

ANSWERS ON PAGES 334-336.

# Population

In the year 2030, what country in the world will have the most people? ➡ page 185

# WHERE DO PEOPLE LIVE?

In 1959, there were 3 billion people in the world. In 1999, there were 6 billion. According to United Nations (UN) estimates, the world population reached 6.8 billion in 2009 and will grow to 7 billion by 2011 and more than 9 billion by 2050.

It's a big world out there! Our planet has about 196.9 million square miles of surface area, but about 70% of that is water. The total land area, 57.5 million square miles, is about 16 times the land area of the U.S.

Russia is the largest nation with over 6.5 million square miles of land. China is a distant second with 3.6 million square miles. The smallest countries are Vatican City and Monaco.

## Populations

### Largest (2009)

1 **China***
1,338,612,968

2 **India**
1,116,079,217

3 **United States**
307,524,279

4 **Indonesia**
240,271,522

5 **Brazil**
198,739,269

### Smallest (2009)

| | COUNTRY | POPULATION |
|---|---|---|
| 1. | Vatican City | 826 |
| 2. | Tuvalu | 12,373 |
| 3. | Nauru | 14,019 |
| 4. | Palau | 20,796 |
| 5. | San Marino | 30,324 |

\* Excluding Taiwan, pop. 22,974,397; Hong Kong, pop. 7,055,071; and Macau, pop. 559,846.

Source: U.S. Census Bureau, CIA *The World Factbook 2009*

## MOST SPARSELY POPULATED

| | COUNTRY | PERSONS PER SQ MI |
|---|---|---|
| 1. | Mongolia | 5.1 |
| 2. | Namibia | 6.6 |
| 3. | Australia | 7.2 |
| 4. | Suriname | 7.7 |
| 5. | Iceland | 7.9 |

To get the population density, divide the population by the area. Density is calculated here according to land area, and is based on 2009 population.

## MOST DENSELY POPULATED

| | COUNTRY | PERSONS PER SQ MI* |
|---|---|---|
| 1. | Monaco | 43,400 |
| 2. | Singapore | 17,600 |
| 3. | Vatican City | 4,850 |
| 4. | Maldives | 3,400 |
| 5. | Malta | 3,300 |

\* For comparison, New Jersey is the most densely populated state, with about 1,170 people per square mile in 2008.

# FIVE LARGEST CITIES IN THE WORLD

Here are the five cities that had the most people, according to revised UN estimates for 2007. Numbers include people from the built-up area around each city (metropolitan area), not just the city. (See page 186 for the 10 biggest U.S. cities.)

| CITY, COUNTRY | POPULATION | CITY, COUNTRY | POPULATION |
|---|---|---|---|
| 1. Tokyo, Japan | 35,676,000 | 4. Mumbai, India | 18,978,000 |
| 2. New York, NY, U.S. | 19,040,000 | 5. Sao Paulo, Brazil | 18,845,000 |
| 3. Mexico City, Mexico | 19,028,000 | | |

## All About >>
# POPULATION GROWTH

There are more people in the world now than before. About four in every 10 people on Earth live in China or India. Historically, population growth rates were low but started to increase in the 17th and 18th centuries. The world grew very fast in the 20th century. While growth is expected to slow down, the United Nations estimates the world population will still increase by about 2.3 billion people between now and 2050.

Almost all this growth will be in poorer countries. In developed countries more people are elderly and families also have fewer children. In some of these countries, the population is falling. Japan's population is projected to decline about 20% between 2010 and 2050. People aged 65 or older will then make up almost 40% of the population.

India is expected to overtake China to become the world's most populous country by 2030. Its population is projected to climb an estimated 33% between 2010 and 2050, to over 1.6 billion. Over two-thirds of the people will be between 15 and 64.

What does all that mean? For Japan, there will be fewer workers and fewer people to take care of the elderly. Having more workers may help India develop its economy. But high population growth puts a strain on land and resources, especially in developing countries, where many people are poor.

185

# POPULATION OF THE UNITED STATES, 2008

as of July 1, 2008

| RANK & STATE NAME | POPULATION | RANK & STATE NAME | POPULATION |
|---|---|---|---|
| 1. California (CA) | 36,756,666 | 27. Oregon (OR) | 3,790,060 |
| 2. Texas (TX) | 24,326,974 | 28. Oklahoma (OK) | 3,642,361 |
| 3. New York (NY) | 19,490,297 | 29. Connecticut (CT) | 3,501,252 |
| 4. Florida (FL) | 18,328,340 | 30. Iowa (IA) | 3,002,555 |
| 5. Illinois (IL) | 12,901,563 | 31. Mississippi (MS) | 2,938,618 |
| 6. Pennsylvania (PA) | 12,448,279 | 32. Arkansas (AR) | 2,855,390 |
| 7. Ohio (OH) | 11,485,910 | 33. Kansas (KS) | 2,802,134 |
| 8. Michigan (MI) | 10,003,422 | 34. Utah (UT) | 2,736,424 |
| 9. Georgia (GA) | 9,685,744 | 35. Nevada (NV) | 2,600,167 |
| 10. North Carolina (NC) | 9,222,414 | 36. New Mexico (NM) | 1,984,356 |
| 11. New Jersey (NJ) | 8,682,661 | 37. West Virginia (WV) | 1,814,468 |
| 12. Virginia (VA) | 7,769,089 | 38. Nebraska (NE) | 1,783,432 |
| 13. Washington (WA) | 6,549,224 | 39. Idaho (ID) | 1,523,816 |
| 14. Arizona (AZ) | 6,500,180 | 40. Maine (ME) | 1,316,456 |
| 15. Massachusetts (MA) | 6,497,967 | 41. New Hampshire (NH) | 1,315,809 |
| 16. Indiana (IN) | 6,376,792 | 42. Hawaii (HI) | 1,288,198 |
| 17. Tennessee (TN) | 6,214,888 | 43. Rhode Island (RI) | 1,050,788 |
| 18. Missouri (MO) | 5,911,605 | 44. Montana (MT) | 967,440 |
| 19. Maryland (MD) | 5,633,597 | 45. Delaware (DE) | 873,092 |
| 20. Wisconsin (WI) | 5,627,967 | 46. South Dakota (SD) | 804,194 |
| 21. Minnesota (MN) | 5,220,393 | 47. Alaska (AK) | 686,293 |
| 22. Colorado (CO) | 4,939,456 | 48. North Dakota (ND) | 641,481 |
| 23. Alabama (AL) | 4,661,900 | 49. Vermont (VT) | 621,270 |
| 24. South Carolina (SC) | 4,479,800 | 50. District of Columbia (DC) | 591,833 |
| 25. Louisiana (LA) | 4,410,796 | 51. Wyoming (WY) | 532,668 |
| 26. Kentucky (KY) | 4,269,245 | **TOTAL U.S. POPULATION** | **304,059,724** |

## Largest Cities in the United States

Cities grow and shrink in population. Below is a list of the largest cities in the United States in 2008 compared with their populations in 1950. Populations are for people living within the city limits only.

| RANK & CITY | 2008 | 1950 |
|---|---|---|
| 1. New York, NY | 8,363,710 | 7,891,957 |
| 2. Los Angeles, CA | 3,833,995 | 1,970,358 |
| 3. Chicago, IL | 2,853,114 | 3,620,962 |
| 4. Houston, TX | 2,242,193 | 596,163 |
| 5. Phoenix, AZ | 1,567,924 | 106,818 |
| 6. Philadelphia, PA | 1,447,395 | 2,071,605 |
| 7. San Antonio, TX | 1,353,105 | 408,442 |
| 8. Dallas, TX | 1,279,910 | 334,387 |
| 9. San Diego, CA | 1,279,329 | 434,462 |
| 10. San Jose, CA | 948,279 | 95,280 |

2008 Population Estimates, US Census Bureau

# The Growing U.S. Population

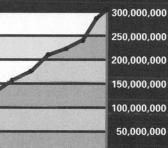

| | |
|---|---|
| 1790: 3,929,214 | 1970: 203,211,926 |
| 1850: 23,191,876 | 1990: 248,709,873 |
| 1900: 76,212,168 | 2000: 281,421,906 |
| 1930: 123,202,660 | 2007: 300,912,947 |
| 1950: 151,325,798 | 2009: 307,524,279 |

300,000,000
250,000,000
200,000,000
150,000,000
100,000,000
50,000,000

1790   1820   1850   1880   1910   1940   1970   2009

## POPULATION TIME LINE

**1790** Most populous state: Virginia, 692,000

**1850** Most populous state: New York, 3.1 million

**1900** Life expectancy at birth: 47.3 years
Population of Florida, 33rd most populous state: 529,000
Top country of birth of foreign-born population: Germany, 2.7 million
Percent of women participating in labor force: 20.6%
Number of cars registered in the U.S.: 8,000

**1910** 14.7% of U.S. population is foreign-born, highest percentage on record.
Population of Phoenix, Arizona: 11,134

**1915** U.S. population reaches 100 million.

**1930** Life expectancy at birth: 59.7 years
Top country of birth of foreign-born population: Italy, 1.8 million
Number of cars and trucks registered in the U.S.: 26.7 million

**1950** Life expectancy at birth: 68.2 years
Population of Florida, 20th most populous state: 2.8 million
Percent of women participating in labor force: 29%
Number of cars and trucks registered in the U.S.: 48.9 million

**1960** Population of Phoenix, Arizona, 29th most populous city: 439,170

**1967** U.S. population reaches 200 million.

**1970** 4.7% of U.S. population is foreign-born, lowest percentage on record.

**2000** Life expectancy at birth: 77 years
Population of Florida, 4th most populous state: 16 million
Top country of birth of foreign-born population: Mexico, 9.2 million
Percent of women participating in labor force: 59.9%
Number of cars and trucks registered in the U.S.: 220.7 million

**2006** U.S. population reaches an estimated 300 million on October 17.
Population of Phoenix, Arizona, 6th most populous U.S. city: 1.5 million

**2039** U.S. population projected to reach 400 million

# The Many Faces of America:
# IMMIGRATION

The number of people in the U.S. who were born in another country (foreign-born) reached 38 million in 2007, or almost 13% of the population. This percentage has been rising since 1970, when it was at a low of 4.7%, and is at its highest since 1930. In the early 1900s, most immigrants came from Europe. In 2007, 34% of the foreign-born came originally from Latin America, and 27% from Asia; only about 13% were born in Europe.

Immigrants come for various reasons, such as to escape poverty or oppression and to make better lives for themselves and their children. The figures below, from the Department of Homeland Security, cover legal immigrants only. Each year hundreds of thousands of people come across the border illegally or overstay a temporary visa. (Visas are official government documents that grant permission for a person to visit, work, or attend school in another country.) Many of these people are workers who come by themselves to earn money for their families back home. The Pew Hispanic Center estimated there were about 12 million unauthorized immigrants in the U.S. in 2008, with the majority having come from Mexico.

## What Countries Do Immigrants Come From?

A record total of 1,046,539 immigrants were naturalized—that is, were sworn in—as U.S. citizens in 2008. The table below shows the countries where the largest numbers of these immigrants came from.

| COUNTRY | Number | Percent of total |
|---|---|---|
| Mexico | 231,815 | 22.2 |
| India | 65,971 | 6.3 |
| Philippines | 58,792 | 5.6 |
| China, People's Republic | 40,017 | 3.8 |
| Cuba | 39,871 | 3.8 |
| Vietnam | 39,584 | 3.8 |
| El Salvador | 35,796 | 3.4 |
| Dominican Republic | 35,251 | 3.4 |
| Colombia | 22,926 | 2.2 |
| North and South Korea | 22,759 | 2.2 |
| Jamaica | 21,324 | 2.0 |
| Haiti | 21,229 | 2.0 |
| Nicaragua | 17,954 | 1.7 |
| Guatemala | 17,087 | 1.6 |

## Where Do Immigrants Settle?

In 2007, 1,052,415 people from foreign countries became "permanent legal residents" of the U.S. About 63% of them settled in the states below. California received roughly one-third of the immigrants born in Vietnam, Mexico, and the Philippines. Florida received 85% of immigrants born in Cuba and over half of those born in Haiti. Nearly half of those born in the Dominican Republic settled in New York.

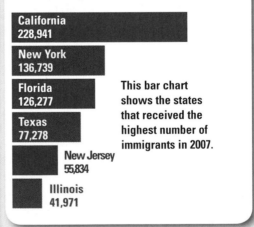

California 228,941

New York 136,739

Florida 126,277

Texas 77,278

New Jersey 55,834

Illinois 41,971

This bar chart shows the states that received the highest number of immigrants in 2007.

◄ Immigrants entering the U.S. at Ellis Island in New York, early 1900s

# All About >> Hispanic AMERICANS

Hispanics, or Latinos, are people of any race who trace their heritage back to Mexico, Puerto Rico, Cuba, the Dominican Republic, or any Central American, South American, or other Spanish-speaking culture. In 2008, there were more than 47 million Hispanics in the U.S., making up about 15% of the population. About 60% were born in the U.S.

Hispanics are already the largest minority group in the U.S., and their numbers are growing rapidly. By 2050, they are expected to make up close to 30% of the population.

As of mid-2008, there were an estimated 13.5 million Hispanics living in California, more than in any other state. Texas ranked second, with a Hispanic population of 8.9 million. Florida followed, with about 3.8 million Hispanics.

New Mexico had the highest percentage of Hispanics in its population. In 2008, about 45% of New Mexico's residents were Hispanic. California and Texas had the second- and third-highest percentage of Hispanics in their populations, with about 37% each.

## U.S. Hispanic Population by Place of Origin, 2007

| Place | Number | Percent of All Hispanics |
|---|---|---|
| Mexico | 29,189,334 | 64.3 |
| Puerto Rico | 4,114,701 | 9.1 |
| Cuba | 1,608,835 | 3.5 |
| El Salvador | 1,473,482 | 3.2 |
| Dominican Rep. | 1,198,849 | 2.6 |
| Guatemala | 859,815 | 1.9 |
| Colombia | 797,195 | 1.8 |
| Honduras | 527,154 | 1.2 |
| Ecuador | 523,108 | 1.2 |
| Peru | 470,519 | 1.0 |
| All other countries | 4,615,604 | 10.2 |
| Total U.S. Hispanic Population (2007) | 45,378,596 | 100.0 |

Source: Pew Hispanic Center; American Community Survey, U.S. Census Bureau

189

# Prizes and Contests

Can a kid win a prize for a pair of smelly sneakers? ➡ page 193

# NOBEL PRIZES

The Nobel Prizes are named after Alfred B. Nobel (1833–1896), a Swedish scientist who invented dynamite and who left money for most of the prizes. They are given every year for promoting peace, as well as for physics, chemistry, physiology or medicine, literature, and economics.

In 2009, U.S. President **Barack Obama** was awarded the Nobel Peace Prize "for his extraordinary efforts to strengthen international diplomacy and cooperation between peoples.... Obama [has] captured the world's attention and given its people hope for a better future."

## Past winners of the Nobel Peace Prize include:

**2007 Albert Arnold (Al) Gore Jr. (former U.S. vice president)** and the **International Panel on Climate Change (IPCC)**, for their efforts in educating the world about human-caused climate change

**2004 Wangari Maathai**, activist; her Green Belt Movement in Kenya planted more than 30 million trees and promoted education, nutrition, and family planning.

**2002 Jimmy Carter**, former U.S. president and peace negotiator

**1997 Jody Williams** and the International Campaign to Ban Landmines

**1993 Nelson Mandela**, leader of South African blacks; **F.W. de Klerk** president of South Africa

**1989 Dalai Lama**, Tibetan Buddhist leader, forced into exile in 1959

**1986 Elie Wiesel**, holocaust survivor and author

**1979 Mother Teresa**, leader of the order of the Missionaries of Charity, who care for the sick and dying in India

**1964 Martin Luther King Jr.**, civil rights leader

**1954 Albert Schweitzer**, missionary, surgeon

**1919 Woodrow Wilson**, U.S. president who played a key role in founding the League of Nations

**1905 Baroness Bertha von Suttner**, early advocate of peace through international cooperation; first woman to win the prize. ▼

# ENTERTAINMENT
## *Awards*

## 2009 KIDS' CHOICE AWARDS

**The 2009 Kids' Choice Awards** were held Saturday, March 28, 2009, and hosted by ◀Dwayne Johnson. For more information, go to:

**WEB SITE** www.nick.com

## KIDS' CHOICE AWARDS

More than 88 million votes were cast by kids in the 2009 Nickelodeon's Kids' Choice Awards. Winners included:

- Music Group . . . . . . . . . The Jonas Brothers
- Movie . . . . . . . . . . . . . . *High School Musical 3*
- Book . . . . . . . . . . . . . . . *Twilight*
- Video Game . . . . . . . . . . *Guitar Hero World Tour*
- Reality TV Show . . . . . . *American Idol*
- TV Show . . . . . . . . . . . . . *iCarly*
- Cartoon . . . . . . . . . . . . . *SpongeBob SquarePants*
- TV Actor . . . . . . . . . . . . . Dylan Sprouse
- TV Actress . . . . . . . . . . . Selena Gomez
- Movie Actor . . . . . . . . . . Will Smith
- Movie Actress . . . . . . . Vanessa Hudgens ▶
- Animated Movie . . . . . . *Madagascar 2: Escape 2 Africa*
- Voice from an Animated Movie . . . . . . Jack Black (*Kung Fu Panda*)
- Male Singer . . . . . . . . . . Jesse McCartney
- Female Singer . . . . . . . Miley Cyrus
- Song . . . . . . . . . . . . . . . "Single Ladies (Put a Ring On It)," Beyoncé
- Male Athlete . . . . . . . . . Peyton Manning
- Female Athlete . . . . . . . Candace Parker
- The Big Green Help Award . . . . . . . . . Leonardo DiCaprio

# BEE INVOLVED

If you have a knack for spelling or an interest in world geography, then these two national contests may be for you.

## National Spelling Bee

The **National Spelling Bee** was started in Louisville, Kentucky, by the *Courier-Journal* in 1925. Today, newspapers across the U.S. run spelling bees for kids 15 and under. Winners may qualify for the Scripps National Spelling Bee held in Washington, D.C., in late May or early June. If interested, ask your school principal to contact your local newspaper. (For a behind-the-scenes look at the National Spelling Bee, try the 2002 film *Spellbound*.)

**Kavya Shivashankar,** 13, from Olathe, Kansas won the 82nd annual Scripps National Spelling Bee contest on May 28, 2009. After 15 rounds, she won the bee by correctly spelling the word "Laodicean," which means "lukewarm or indifferent, particularly in matters of politics or religion." This is the fourth time Shivashankar has competed in the National Spelling Bee.

**WEB SITE** www.spellingbee.com

Here are some of the words used in the 2009 spelling bee. Some of them are just a little bit difficult!

phoresy
menhir
Maecenas
sophrosyne
isagoge
guayabera

ophelimity
oriflamme
bouquiniste
antonomasia
diacoele
reredos

## National Geographic Bee

### The 2009 winner is...

**Eric Yang**, a 13-year-old from The Colony, Texas. After Yang and two other contestants answered every question correctly, all three advanced to a tie-breaking round. Yang won by answering this question: Timis County shares its name with a tributary of the Danube and is located in the western part of which European country? (The answer: Romania. The dictionary definition of a tributary is "a stream or river that flows into a larger one.") Yang won a $25,000 scholarship for college and a lifetime membership in the National Geographic Society. "I just made an educated guess," Yang said after his win. He has always liked studying maps. "I just wanted to figure out why did they build those roads and how did these places get here?" he said. For the third year in a row, the National Geographic Bee champion did not miss one question. At 13, Erik has already scored 2200 on the SATs, a test usually taken by high school juniors and seniors. The highest possible score is 2400.

The National Geographic Bee draws 5 million contestants from nearly 15,000 schools in all parts of the United States. To enter, you must be in grades 4-8. School-level bees are followed by state-level bees and then the nationals (which are moderated by *Jeopardy!* host Alex Trebek).

For more information: **WEB SITE** www.nationalgeographic.com/geobee

# Odd Contests

It just seems to be part of human nature to find out who is the best at something, no matter what it is! There are state, national, and international competitions in a wide variety of events. Most of them are normal ones such as foot races, trivia contests, and such. But then there are others that are just plain weird. Here are a few contests that are not very ordinary.

## ROTTEN SNEAKER CONTEST

Held annually in Montpelier, Vermont, the Odor-Eaters Rotten Sneaker Contest was won in March 2009 by seven-year-old Joshua Boothe from American Fork, Utah. The panel of judges included NASA "Master Sniffer" George Aldrich, Chemical Specialist for NASA space missions. Joshua's sneakers joined the other winners' in the Odor-Eaters "Hall of Fumes." Joshua won $2,500, the Golden Sneaker Award trophy, a lifetime supply of Odor-Eaters®, and a trip to see the play *The Lion King* on Broadway in New York City. Joshua says he is saving his prize money for college.

For more information, visit **WEB SITE** www.odoreaters.com

## DUCT TAPE PROM OUTFITS

Couples entering the Duck® Brand Duct Tape Stuck on Prom Contest must attend a high school prom wearing complete outfits and accessories made from duct tape. The winning couple is chosen based on originality, workmanship, quantity of Duck Tape used, use of colors, and creative use of accessories. The first place couple each receives a $3,000 scholarship and a $3,000 cash prize is awarded to the school that hosted the prom. **WEB SITE** www.stuckatprom.com

## NATHAN'S FAMOUS FOURTH OF JULY HOT DOG EATING CONTEST

Joey Chestnut of San Jose, California, won the Nathan's Famous hot dog eating contest for the third year in a row in 2009. He beat his rival Takeru Kobayashi of Nagano, Japan, who has won the title six times. Chestnut set a new world record in the contest, polishing off 68 hot dogs (with buns) in just 10 minutes.

# Religion

Where do most Hindus live? ➡ page 195

How did the universe begin? Why are we here on Earth? What happens to us after we die? For most people, religion provides answers to questions like these. Believing in a God or gods, or in a higher power, is one way people make sense of the world around them. Religion can also help guide people's lives.

Different religions have different beliefs. For example, Christians, Jews, and Muslims are monotheists, meaning they believe in only one God. Hindus are polytheists, meaning they believe in many gods. On this page and the next are some facts about the world's major religions.

## Christianity

WHO STARTED CHRISTIANITY? Christianity is based on the teachings of Jesus Christ. He was born in Bethlehem between 8 B.C. and 4 B.C. and died about A.D. 29.

WHAT WRITINGS ARE THERE? The **Bible**, consisting of the Old Testament and New Testament, is the main spiritual text in Christianity.

WHAT DO CHRISTIANS BELIEVE? There is only one God. God sent his Son, Jesus Christ, to Earth. Jesus died to save humankind but later rose from the dead.

HOW MANY ARE THERE? Christianity is the world's biggest religion. In 2005, there were more than 2.1 billion Christians worldwide.

WHAT KINDS ARE THERE? More than one billion Christians are **Roman Catholics**, who follow the Pope's leadership. **Orthodox Christians** accept similar teachings but follow different leadership. **Protestants** disagree with many Catholic teachings. They believe in the Bible's authority.

## Buddhism

WHO STARTED BUDDHISM? Siddhartha Gautama (the Buddha), around 525 B.C.

WHAT WRITINGS ARE THERE? The **Tripitaka**, or "Three Baskets," contains three collections of teachings, rules, and commentaries. There are also other texts, many of which are called **sutras**.

WHAT DO BUDDHISTS BELIEVE? Buddha taught that life is filled with suffering. Through meditation and deeds, one can end the cycle of endless birth and rebirth and achieve a state of perfect peace known as **nirvana**.

HOW MANY ARE THERE? In 2005, there were about 376 million Buddhists in the world, 98% of them in Asia.

WHAT KINDS ARE THERE? There are two main kinds: **Theravada** ("Way of the Elders") Buddhism, the older kind, is more common in countries such as Sri Lanka, Myanmar, and Thailand. **Mahayana** ("Great Vehicle") Buddhism is more common in China, Korea, Japan, and Tibet.

# Hinduism

**WHO STARTED HINDUISM?** The beliefs of Aryans, who migrated to India around 1500 B.C., intermixed with the beliefs of the people who already lived there.

**WHAT WRITINGS ARE THERE?** The **Vedas** ("Knowledge") collect the most important writings in Hinduism, including the ancient hymns in the **Samhita** and the teachings in the **Upanishads**. Also important are the stories the **Bhagavad-Gita** and the **Ramayana**.

**WHAT DO HINDUS BELIEVE?** There is one divine principle, known as **brahman**; the various gods are only aspects of it. Life is an aspect of, yet separate from the divine. To escape a meaningless cycle of birth and rebirth (**samsara**), one must improve one's **karma** (the purity or impurity of one's past deeds).

**HOW MANY ARE THERE?** In 2005, there were about 900 million Hindus, mainly in India and places where people from India have immigrated to.

**WHAT KINDS ARE THERE?** Most Hindus are primarily devoted to a single deity, the most common being the gods **Vishnu** and **Shiva** and the goddess **Shakti**.

# Islam

**WHO STARTED ISLAM?** Muhammad, the Prophet, about A.D. 622.

**WHAT WRITINGS ARE THERE?** The **Koran** (*al-Qur'an* in Arabic), regarded as the word of God. The **Sunna**, or example of the Prophet, is recorded in the **Hadith**.

**WHAT DO MUSLIMS BELIEVE?** People who practice Islam are known as Muslims. There is only one God. God revealed the Koran to Muhammad so he could teach humankind truth and justice. Those who "submit" (literal meaning of "Islam") to God will attain salvation.

**HOW MANY ARE THERE?** In 2005, there were approximately 1.5 billion Muslims, mostly in parts of Africa and Asia.

# Judaism

**WHO STARTED JUDAISM?** Abraham is thought to be the founder of Judaism, one of the first monotheistic religions. He probably lived between 2000 B.C. and 1500 B.C.

**WHAT WRITINGS ARE THERE?** The most important is the **Torah** ("Law"), comprising the five books of Moses. The **Nevi'im** ("Prophets") and **Ketuvim** ("Writings") are also part of the Hebrew Bible.

**WHAT DO JEWS BELIEVE?** There is one God who created and rules the universe. One should be faithful to God and observe God's laws.

**HOW MANY ARE THERE?** In 2005, there were close to 14 million Jews around the world. Many live in Israel and the United States.

**WHAT KINDS ARE THERE?** In the U.S. there are three main forms: **Orthodox**, **Conservative**, and **Reform**. Orthodox Jews are the most traditional, following strict laws about dress and diet. Reform Jews are the least traditional. Conservative Jews are somewhere in-between.

# Major Holy Days

## FOR CHRISTIANS, JEWS, MUSLIMS, BUDDHISTS, AND HINDUS

### CHRISTIAN HOLY DAYS

|  | 2010 | 2011 | 2012 |
|---|---|---|---|
| Ash Wednesday | February 17 | March 9 | February 22 |
| Good Friday | April 2 | April 22 | April 6 |
| Easter Sunday | April 4 | April 24 | April 8 |
| Easter for Orthodox Churches | April 4 | April 24 | April 15 |
| Christmas* | December 25 | December 25 | December 25 |

*Russian and some other Orthodox churches celebrate Christmas in January.

### JEWISH HOLY DAYS

The Jewish holy days begin at sundown the night before the first full day of the observance. The dates of first full days are listed below.

|  | 2010-11 (5771) | 2011-12 (5772) | 2012-13 (5773) |
|---|---|---|---|
| Rosh Hashanah (New Year) | September 9, 2010 | September 29, 2011 | September 17, 2012 |
| Yom Kippur (Day of Atonement) | September 18, 2010 | October 8, 2011 | September 26, 2012 |
| Hanukkah (Festival of Lights) | December 2, 2010 | December 21, 2011 | December 9, 2012 |
| Passover | April 19, 2011 | April 7, 2012 | March 26, 2013 |

### ISLAMIC (MUSLIM) HOLY DAYS

The Islamic holy days begin at sundown the night before the first full day of the observance. The dates of first full days are listed below.

|  | 2009-2010 (1431) | 2010-2011 (1432) | 2011-2012 (1433) |
|---|---|---|---|
| Muharram 1 (New Year) | December 18, 2009 | December 7, 2010 | November 26, 2011 |
| Mawlid (Birthday of Muhammad) | February 26, 2010 | February 15, 2011 | February 4, 2012 |
| Ramadan (Month of Fasting) | August 11, 2010 | August 1, 2011 | July 20, 2012 |
| Eid al-Fitr (End of Ramadan) | September 10, 2010 | August 30, 2011 | August 19, 2012 |
| Eid al-Adha | November 16, 2010 | November 6, 2011 | October 26, 2012 |

# BUDDHIST HOLY DAYS

Not all Buddhists use the same calendar to determine holidays and festivals. A few well-known Buddhist observances and the months in which they may fall are listed below.

NIRVANA DAY, **February:** Marks the death of Siddhartha Gautama (the Buddha).

VESAK OR VISAKAH PUJA (BUDDHA DAY), **April/May:** Celebrates the birth, enlightenment, and death of the Buddha.

ASALHA PUJA (DHARMA DAY), **July:** Commemorates the Buddha's first teaching

MAGHA PUJA OR SANGHA DAY, **February:** Commemorates the day when 1,250 of Buddha's followers (**sangha**) visited him without his calling them.

VASSA (RAINS RETREAT), **July-October:** A three-month period during Asia's rainy season when monks travel little and spend more time on meditation and study. Sometimes called Buddhist Lent

# HINDU HOLY DAYS

Different Hindu groups use different calendars. A few of the many Hindu festivals and the months in which they may fall are listed below.

MAHA SHIVARATRI, **February/March:** Festival dedicated to Shiva, creator and destroyer.

HOLI, **February/March:** Festival of spring

RAMANAVAMI, **March/April:** Celebrates the birth of Rama, the seventh incarnation of Vishnu.

DIWALI, **October/November:** Festival of Lights

## All About >> Islam: Sunni and Shiite

There are two major groups of Muslims, the Sunnis and the Shiites. About 83% of the world's 1.3 billion Muslims are Sunni. They live all over the world but mostly in the Middle East, Africa, and Asia. Shiites make up the majority of Muslims in several countries, including Iran, Iraq, and Lebanon. The differences between these groups go back to the early years of Islam. The Sunnis accept an early follower of Muhammad, Abu Bakr, as Muhammad's successor. The Shiites believe that Ali ibn Abi Talib, the son-in-law and cousin of Muhammad, was Muhammad's rightful successor. Today, Sunnis and Shiites still follow different religious leaders and celebrate some different holidays. Historically, the Sunnis and Shiites have been opposed to each other, and even today, there is conflict in some areas between the two groups. The country of Iraq is an example of this. Minority Sunnis ruled and persecuted Shiites under the government of Saddam Hussein. Now Shiites represent the majority in government, and conflicts between the two groups have become violent.

*Grand Ayatollah Ali al-Sistani, Iraqi Shiite religious leader* ▶

# Science

What is a genome? ➡ page 204

## THE WORLD OF Science

The Latin root of the word "science" is *scire*, meaning "to know." There are many kinds of knowledge, but when people use the word *science* they usually mean a kind of knowledge that can be discovered and backed up by observation or experiments.

The branches of scientific study can be loosely grouped into four main branches: Physical Science, Life Science (Biology), Earth Science, and Social Science. Each branch has more specific areas of study. For example, zoology includes entomology (study of insects), which in turn includes lepidopterology (the study of butterflies and moths)!

In answering questions about our lives, our world, and our universe, scientists must often draw from more than one discipline. Biochemists, for example, deal with the chemistry that happens inside living things. Paleontologists study fossil remains of ancient plants and animals. Astrophysicists study matter and energy in outer space. And mathematics, considered by many to be both an art and a science, is used by all scientists.

### Physical Science

**ASTRONOMY**—stars, planets, outer space

**CHEMISTRY**—properties and behavior of substances

**PHYSICS**—matter and energy

### Life Science (Biology)

**ANATOMY**—structure of the human body

**BOTANY**—plants

**ECOLOGY**—living things in relation to their environment

**GENETICS**—heredity

**PATHOLOGY**—diseases and their effects on the human body

**PHYSIOLOGY**—the body's biological processes

**ZOOLOGY**—animals

### Earth Science

**GEOGRAPHY**—Earth's surface and its relationship to humans

**GEOLOGY**—Earth's structure

**HYDROLOGY**—water

**METEOROLOGY**—Earth's atmosphere and weather

**MINERALOGY**—minerals

**OCEANOGRAPHY**—the sea, including currents and tides

**PETROLOGY**—rocks

**SEISMOLOGY**—earthquakes

**VOLCANOLOGY**—volcanoes

### Social Science

**ANTHROPOLOGY**—human cultures and physical characteristics

**ECONOMICS**—production and distribution of goods and services

**POLITICAL SCIENCE**—governments

**PSYCHOLOGY**—mental processes and behavior

**SOCIOLOGY**—human society and community life

# HOW DO SCIENTISTS MAKE DISCOVERIES? *THE SCIENTIFIC METHOD*

**T**he scientific method was developed over many centuries. You can think of it as having five steps:

1. Ask a question.
2. Gather information through observation.
3. Based on that information, make an educated guess (hypothesis) about the answer to your question.
4. Design an experiment to test that hypothesis.
5. Evaluate the results.

If the experiment shows that your hypothesis is wrong, make up a new hypothesis. If the experiment supports your hypothesis, then your hypothesis may be correct! However, it is usually necessary to test a hypothesis with many different experiments before it can be accepted as a scientific law—something that is generally accepted as true.

You can **apply the scientific method** to problems in everyday life. For example, suppose you plant some seeds and they fail to sprout. You would probably **ask** yourself, "Why didn't they sprout?"—and that would be step one of the scientific method. The next step would be to make **observations**; for example, you might take note of how deep the seeds were

planted, how often they were watered, and what kind of soil was used. Then, you would make an **educated guess** about what went wrong—for example, you might hypothesize that the seeds didn't sprout because you didn't water them enough. After that, you would **test** your hypothesis—perhaps by trying to grow the seeds again, under the exact same conditions as before, except that this time you would water them more frequently.

Finally, you would wait and **evaluate** the results of your experiment. If the seeds sprouted, then you could conclude that your hypothesis may be correct. If they didn't sprout, you'd continue to use the method to find a scientific answer to your original question.

## did you know?

More than 6,000 people die everyday because they don't have safe drinking water. A lot of those people are kids. In some countries, even water that looks clean can be full of bacteria. These bacteria cause serious illnesses like typhoid, dysentery, and cholera. That's why LifeStraw, a drinking straw that filters out harmful bacteria, was invented in 2005. The LifeStraw, which is about the size of a fat pencil, uses a combination of mesh filters, iodine beads, and active carbon to make water drinkable and taste better. It is designed for both adults and children older than 3 years. They dip the Lifestraw into a water source and suck on it to drink the purified water. There is also a larger version of the device that can be used by a family to purify water for all family members.

# WHAT EVERYTHING *IS* MADE OF

**E**verything we see and use is made of basic ingredients called elements. There are more than 100 elements. They are found in nature or made by scientists.

### Elements in Earth's Crust
(percent by weight)

- Oxygen 47%
- Silicon 28%
- Aluminum 8%
- Iron, Calcium, Sodium, Potassium, Others 17%

### Elements in the Atmosphere
(percent by volume)

- Nitrogen 78%
- Oxygen 21%
- 1% Argon, Carbon Dioxide, Others

# How Elements Are Named

**E**lements are named after places, scientists, figures in mythology, or properties of the element. But no element gets a name until the International Union of Pure and Applied Chemistry (IUPAC) accepts it. In November 2004, the 111th element was approved and named. Roentgenium, with symbol Rg, was discovered by German scientists in 1995. As of 2009, claims for other new elements were being studied.

| NAME | SYMBOL | WHAT IT IS | WHEN FOUND | NAMED FOR |
|------|--------|------------|------------|-----------|
| Argon | Ar | gas | 1894 | the Greek word *argos* which means inactive or lazy; it is one of the least reactive of all elements |
| Californium | Cf | radioactive metal | 1950 | state of California, and the University of California |
| Hydrogen | H | non-metal | 1766 | the Greek words *hydro* and *genes* which mean water and forming |
| Iodine | I | nonmetallic solid | 1811 | the Greek word *iodes*, meaning violet |
| Iridium | Ir | transitional metal | 1804 | the Latin word *iridis*, meaning rainbow |
| Lutetium | Lu | metal | 1907 | an ancient name for the city of Paris, *Lutetia* |
| Nickel | Ni | transitional metal | 1774 | the German word *kupfernickel*, meaning devil's copper |
| Selenium | Se | non-metal | 1817 | the Greek word for the moon, *selene* |
| Tungsten | W | transitional metal | 1783 | the Swedish words *tung sten,* meaning heavy stone. |
| Vanadium | V | metal | 1801 | Vandis, the Scandinavian Goddess of Beauty; its salts have beautiful colors |

# ALL ABOUT...
# Compounds

SCIENCE

Carbon, hydrogen, nitrogen, and oxygen are the most common chemical elements in the human body. Many other elements may be found in small amounts. These include calcium, iron, phosphorus, potassium, and sodium.

When elements join together, they form compounds. Water is a compound made up of hydrogen and oxygen. Salt is a compound made up of sodium and chlorine.

| Common Name | Contains the Compound | Contains the Elements |
|---|---|---|
| Chalk | calcium carbonate | calcium, carbon, oxygen |
| Fool's Gold | iron disulfide | iron, sulfur |
| Marble | calcium carbonate | calcium, carbon, oxygen |
| Rust | iron oxide | iron, oxygen |
| Sugar | sucrose | carbon, hydrogen, oxygen |
| Toothpaste | sodium fluoride | sodium, fluorine |
| Vinegar | acetic acid | carbon, hydrogen, oxygen |

## CHEMICAL SYMBOLS ARE SCIENTIFIC SHORTHAND

When scientists write the names of elements, they often use a symbol instead of spelling out the full name. The symbol for each element is one or two letters. Scientists write O for oxygen and He for helium. The symbols usually come from the English name for the element (C for carbon). The symbols for some of the elements come from the element's Latin name. For example, the symbol for gold is Au, which is short for *aurum*, the Latin word for gold.

# TURNING BASE METALS INTO GOLD?

Hundreds of years ago, during the Middle Ages, some people believed that they could change base metals like lead into gold. These people, called alchemists, believed that something called a philosopher's stone and intense faith could combine to cause the change. This belief persisted for centuries; even Sir Isaac Newton, the great scientist, believed in alchemy!

*Medieval physician and alchemist Philippus Aureolus Paracelsus*

# Physical Science

## SOUND and LIGHT

## What Is Sound?

Sound is a form of energy that is made up of waves traveling through mass. When you "hear" a sound, it is actually your ear detecting the vibrations of molecules as the sound wave passes through. To understand sound, you first have to understand waves. Take a bowl full of water and drop a penny into the middle of it. You'll see little circular waves move away from the area where the penny hit, spread out toward the bowl's edges, and bounce back. Sound moves in the same way. The waves must travel through a gas, liquid, or a solid. In the vacuum of space, there is no sound because there are no molecules to vibrate. When you talk, your vocal chords vibrate to produce sound waves.

## What Is Light?

Light is a little tricky. It is a form of energy known as electromagnetic radiation that is emitted from a source. It travels as waves in straight lines and spreads out over a larger area the farther it goes. Scientists also think it goes along as particles known as photons. Light is produced in many ways, but mostly it comes from electrons that vibrate at high frequencies when heated to a high enough temperature.

Regular white light is made up of all the colors of the spectrum from red to violet. Each color has its own frequency. When you see a color on something, such as a red apple, that means that the apple absorbed all other colors of the spectrum and only reflected the red light. Things that are white reflect almost all the light that hits them. Things that are black, on the other hand, absorb all the light that hits them.

## Light vs. Sound

Sound travels fast but light travels a whole lot faster. You've probably noticed that when you see lightning, you don't hear thunder until several seconds later. That's because the light reaches you before the sound. The speed of sound varies depending on temperature and air pressure (it also travels faster through liquids and solids). A jet traveling at about 761 miles per hour is considered to be flying at the "speed of sound." But this is nothing compared to light. It goes 186,000 miles per *second*! It goes the same speed no matter what. Scientists don't think anything in the universe can travel faster.

# How Simple Machines Work

Simple machines are devices that make our lives easier. Cars could not run, skyscrapers couldn't be built, and elevators couldn't carry people up—if it weren't for simple machines.

**Inclined Plane** When trying to get a refrigerator onto the back of a truck, a worker will use a ramp, or inclined plane. Instead of lifting something heavy a short distance, we can more easily push it over a longer distance, but to the same height.
*Examples:* escalators, staircases, slides

**Lever** Any kind of arm, bar, or plank that can pivot on something (known as a fulcrum), is a lever. Depending on where the fulcrum is located on the lever, it can be used for different things.
*Examples:* shovel, bottle opener, "claw" part of a hammer used for prying out nails, seesaw

**Wedge** These machines are two inclined planes fastened onto each other to make a point. Wedges are used to pull things apart and even cut.
*Examples:* axes, knives

**Wheel and Axle** This is another kind of lever, but instead of going up and down, it goes around. The wheel is the lever and the axle on which it turns is the fulcrum.
*Examples:* cars, bicycles, wagons

**Pulley** A pulley is similar to a wheel and axle, except that there's no axle. It can be used to change both the direction and level force needed to move an object. The best example is a crane. An object is tied to a cable, which goes up and around the pulley, and down to the crane engine which is pulling it.
*Examples:* a block and tackle, a flag pole, tow trucks

**Screw** A screw is an inclined plane wrapped around a cylinder. In the case of a wood screw, as it is turned it travels deeper into the piece of wood. Another use of a screw is to hold things in place such as the lid on a jar.
*Examples:* drills, corkscrews

# Biological Science

Plant cell

## WHAT ARE LIVING THINGS MADE OF?

Cells are sometimes called the "building blocks" of all living things. Complex life forms have many cells. There are trillions of them in the human body.

There are two main kinds of cells: **eukaryotic** and **prokaryotic**. All the cells in your body—along with the cells of other animals, plants, and fungi—are eukaryotic. These contain several different structures, called **organelles**. Like tools in a toolbox, each kind of organelle has its own function. The **nucleus**, for example, contains most of the cell's DNA, while the **mitochondria** provide energy for the cell. The **ribosomes** are involved in making proteins.

Though both plant and animal cells are eukaryotic, they are different in a few ways. Animal cells rely only on mitochondria for energy, but plant cells also make use of another kind of organelle called a **chloroplast**. Chloroplasts contain chlorophyll, a green chemical plants use to make oxygen and energy from sunlight and water. This process is called **photosynthesis**. Unlike animal cells, plant cells are surrounded by a nonliving, rigid cell wall made of **cellulose**.

**Prokaryotes** (organisms with prokaryotic instead of eukaryotic cells) are all around you—and even inside of you. Most prokaryotes, such as bacteria, are single-celled. They don't have the variety of organelles that eukaryotic cells do.

## WHAT IS DNA?

**E**very cell in every living thing (or organism) has **DNA**, a molecule that holds all the information about that organism. The structure of DNA was discovered in 1953 by the British scientist Francis Crick and the American scientist James Watson. James Watson was a *World Almanac* reader as a kid.

Lengths of connected DNA molecules, called **genes**, are tiny pieces of code. They determine what each organism is like. Almost all the DNA and genes come packaged in thread-like structures called **chromosomes**.

Humans have 46. There are 22 almost identical pairs, plus the X and Y chromosomes, which determine whether a human is male (one X chromosome and one Y chromosome) or female (two X chromosomes).

Genes are passed on from parents to children, and no two organisms (except clones or identical twins) have the same DNA.

Many things—the color of our eyes or hair, whether we're tall or short, our chances of getting certain diseases—depend on our genes.

## What Is the Human Genome?

The human genome contains 20,000 to 25,000 genes. A genome is all the DNA in an organism, including its genes. That's fewer than the 50,000-plus genes of a rice plant! Human genes can produce more than one kind of protein. Proteins perform most life functions and make up a large part of cellular structures.

By studying human genes, scientists can learn more about hereditary diseases and get a better idea of how humans evolved.

# Tiny Creatures

**Microbes** Anton van Leeuwenhoek (pronounced Lay-wen-ook) made the first practical microscope in 1674. When he looked through it, he saw tiny bacteria, plant cells, and fungi, among other things. When he wrote about his findings, Leeuwenhoek called the creatures "wee beasties." We call them **microorganisms** ("micro" means *little*), or microbes. Before the microscope, people had no idea that there were millions of tiny living things crawling all over them.

**Amoebas** Amoebas (uh-ME-buhz) are eukaryotic jelly-like blobs of protoplasm that ooze through their microscopic world. They eat by engulfing their food and slowly digesting it. To move around, the cell extends a part of its goo to create something called a **pseudopod** (SOO-doh-pod), which means "false foot." The amoeba uses this to pull the rest of its "body" along. Amoebas normally live in water or on moist surfaces. In humans, most kinds of amoebas are harmless, but some cause diseases.

**Diatoms** Diatoms are one-celled algae that make glass shells to protect themselves. When they die, their shells collect at the bottom of the ocean in great numbers and form something called **diatomaceous earth**. It's gritty like sandpaper. Diatomaceous earth was once used in toothpaste to help scrape plaque off teeth. Nowadays, among other things, it is used as a pesticide—when sprayed in the air, it gets caught in the lungs of insects and slowly suffocates them.

# USING DNA TO SOLVE CRIMES

DNA evidence can be used to prove that someone did or did not commit a crime. Investigators at crime scenes carefully gather any bits of evidence that the criminal may have left behind, such as hair, skin, or fingernails. Scientists then create a DNA profile from the evidence and compare it to the profile of anyone suspected in the crime or to other profiles stored in data banks. This can help them identify the criminal.

*Scientist extracting DNA from crime scene evidence*

# SCIENCE Q&A

**HOW STRONG IS GRAVITY?** Compared to other forces, gravity is weak. It may feel powerful on Earth, where it takes lots of energy for airplanes and rockets to leave the ground. But this is only because the planet is so massive that it pulls everything toward its center. Magnets use a force stronger than gravity when they stick on metal. Static electricity defies gravity when it makes your hair stand on end.

**WHY CAN'T SCUBA DIVERS GO TO THE BOTTOM OF THE OCEAN?** Pressure, that's why. On dry land at sea level, there is about 14.7 pounds per square inch (psi) of atmospheric pressure pressing down on you. That's like having a 14.7 pound weight placed on top of you. We don't feel it because we've adapted to it. In water, the pressure increases the deeper you go. For every 33 feet a person dives, it goes up by 14.7 psi. The pressure can get to be so great that it literally crushes people. Scuba divers don't normally go deeper than 100 feet without specialized equipment. Even then, it's hard to go lower than 300 feet because of the effects of pressure on the human body. Instead, people use specially-built submarines to reach the deepest parts of the oceans.

**WHY DON'T OIL AND WATER MIX?** Water and oil don't mix because they are made up of different kinds of molecules. Water molecules are polar, meaning that their negatively charged particles (electrons) are bunched up on one side, and their positively charged particles (protons in the atoms' nuclei) are bunched on the other. In oil molecules, on the other hand, positive and negative particles are spread out evenly, with no bunching. These molecules are nonpolar. Opposite charges attract each other, so water molecules cling to each other and not to oil molecules. Scientists actually call nonpolar molecules "hydrophobic," which means "fearful of water."

**IS QUICKSAND FOR REAL?** Yes, but it's not as deadly as it is in the movies. Quicksand forms when sand gets mixed with too much water and becomes loosened and soupy. It may look like normal sand, but if you were to step on it, the pressure from your foot would cause the sand to act more like a liquid, and you'd sink right in. In quicksand, the more you struggle, the more you'll sink. But if you remain still, you'll start to float. So if you ever do fall into quicksand, remember to stay calm, and don't move until you've stopped sinking. Then very slowly try to get flat on your stomach and crawl out. Quicksand isn't very common, but if you were to step in some, you're not likely to sink deeper than up to your waist.

# SOME FAMOUS SCIENTISTS

**NICOLAUS COPERNICUS** (1473-1543), Polish scientist who is known as the founder of modern astronomy. He came up with the theory that Earth and other planets revolve around the Sun. But most thinkers continued to believe that Earth was the center of the universe.

**JOHANNES KEPLER** (1571-1630), German astronomer who developed three laws of planetary motion. He was the first to propose a force (later named gravity) that governs planets' orbits around the Sun.

**BENJAMIN BANNEKER** (1731-1806), African-American astronomer, mathematician, and writer. Banneker taught himself astronomy at the age of 58 and began publishing daily star and planet positions in his own almanac in 1792. He correctly predicted a 1789 solar eclipse that more famous astronomers missed. Banneker used his renown to argue against slavery, and exchanged letters with Thomas Jefferson on the topic.

**CHARLES DARWIN** (1809-1882), British scientist who is best known for his theory of **evolution by natural selection**. According to this theory, living creatures, by gradually changing so as to have the best chances of survival, slowly developed over millions of years into the forms they have today.

**SVANTE ARRHENIUS** (1859-1927), Swedish scientist who was the first person to investigate the effect that heat-absorbing gases, such as carbon dioxide, would have on global climate. In 1903, he was awarded the Nobel Prize for Chemistry.

**ALBERT EINSTEIN** (1879-1955), German-American physicist who developed revolutionary theories about the relationships between time, space, matter, and energy. Probably the most famous and influential scientist of the 20th century, he won a Nobel Prize in 1921.

**NIELS BOHR** (1885-1962), Danish physicist who studied the structure of properties of atoms. His work led to the development of quantum mechanics. In 1922, he won the Nobel Prize for Physics for his work on atomic structure.

**RACHEL CARSON** (1907-1964), U.S. biologist and leading environmentalist whose 1962 book *Silent Spring* warned that chemicals used to kill pests were killing harmless wildlife. Eventually, DDT and certain other pesticides were banned in the U.S.

**JANE GOODALL** (1934- ), British scientist who is a leading authority on chimpanzee behavior. Goodall discovered that chimpanzees use tools, such as twigs to "fish" for ants. She also found that chimpanzees have complex family structures and personalities. She has written widely and is an advocate for the preservation of wild habitats.

**STEPHEN HAWKING** (1942- ), British physicist and leading authority on **black holes**—dense objects in space whose gravity is so strong that not even light can escape them. Hawking has also written best-selling books, including *A Brief History of Time* (1988) and *The Universe in a Nutshell* (2001).

# Space

What is a black hole? ➡ p. 217

## The Solar System

Mercury  Venus  Earth  Mars  Jupiter  Saturn  Uranus  Neptune

—— Planets

—— Dwarf Planet

Ceres  Pluto  Eris

## The SUN Is a STAR

Did you know that the Sun is a star, like the other stars you see at night? It is a typical, medium-size star. But because the Sun is much closer to our planet than any other star, we can study it in great detail. The diameter of the Sun is 865,000 miles—more than 100 times Earth's diameter. The gravity of the Sun is nearly 28 times the gravity of Earth.

**How hot is the Sun?** The surface temperature of the sun is close to 10,000° F, and it is believed that the Sun's inner core may reach temperatures around 28 million degrees! The Sun provides enough light and heat energy to support all forms of life on our planet.

## Homework Tip

Here's a useful way to remember the names of planets in order of their distance from the Sun. Think of this sentence: My Very Excellent Mother Just Sent Us Nachos.

**M** = Mercury, **V** = Venus, **E** = Earth, **M** = Mars, **J** = Jupiter, **S** = Saturn, **U** = Uranus,
**N** = Neptune

# The Planets Are in Motion

The planets move around the Sun along elliptical paths called **orbits**. One complete path around the Sun is called a **revolution**. Earth takes one year, or 365¼ days, to make one revolution around the Sun. Planets that are farther away from the Sun take longer. Most planets have one or more moons. A moon orbits a planet in much the same way that the planets orbit the Sun. Each planet also spins or rotates on its axis. An axis is an imaginary line running through the center of a planet. The time it takes Earth to rotate on its axis equals one day.

Saturn

## Planet Champions

Largest planet:
   Jupiter (88,732 miles diameter)

Smallest planet:
   Mercury (3,032 miles diameter)

Shortest orbit:
   Mercury (88 days)

Longest orbit:
   Neptune (164.8 years)

Tallest mountain:
   Mars (Olympus Mons, 15 miles high)

Hottest planet:
   Venus (867° F)

Coldest planet:
   Neptune (−330° F)

Shortest day:
   Jupiter (9 hours, 55 minutes, 30 seconds)

Longest day:
   Mercury (175.94 days)

No moons:
   Mercury, Venus

Most moons:
   Jupiter (63 known satellites)

## WHAT IS AN ECLIPSE?

During a solar eclipse, the Moon casts a shadow on Earth. A total solar eclipse is when the Sun is completely blocked out. When this happens, the halo of gas around the Sun, called the **corona**, can be seen.

The most recent total solar eclipse took place on July 22, 2009. It was seen in South and East Asia. Solar eclipses will take place on January 15, 2010 (visible in parts of Asia and Africa), and July 11, 2010 (visible in the Pacific and parts of Asia and South America).

Sometimes Earth casts a shadow on the Moon. During a total lunar eclipse, the Moon remains visible, but it looks dark.

In 2009, there were four lunar eclipses. All of them were partial eclipses. The next total lunar eclipse will not happen until December 21, 2010. It will be seen throughout North America.

# THE PLANETS

## ① MERCURY

**Average distance from the Sun:** 36 million miles
**Diameter:** 3,032 miles
**Average temp.:** 333° F
**Surface:** silicate rock
**Time to revolve around the Sun:** 88 days
**Day (synodic—midday to midday):** 175.94 d
**Number of moons:** 0

 *Until recently, we had photos of less than half of Mercury's surface, taken in 1975. But in 2008 the Messenger probe took photos of another 30 percent of the planet. The photos showed signs that Mercury is shrinking.*

## ② VENUS

**Average distance from the Sun:** 67 million miles
**Diameter:** 7,521 miles
**Average temp.:** 867° F
**Surface:** silicate rock
**Time to revolve around the Sun:** 224.7 days
**Day (synodic):** 116.75 d
**Number of moons:** 0

 *From Earth, Venus usually appears brighter than any other planet or star. At certain times, Venus can even be seen in daylight.*

## ③ EARTH

**Average distance from the Sun:** 93 million miles
**Diameter:** 7,926 miles
**Average temp.:** 59° F
**Surface:** water, basalt, and granite rock
**Time to revolve around the Sun:** 365 ¼ days
**Day (synodic):** 24 h
**Number of moons:** 1

 *Earth is a "water planet", with about 71 percent of its surface covered by water. However, most of the water is in oceans— too salty for drinking. Only about 3 percent of Earth's water is fresh and suitable for drinking.*

## ④ MARS

**Average distance from the Sun:** 142 million miles
**Diameter:** 4,213 miles
**Average temp.:** −81° F
**Surface:** iron-rich basaltic rock
**Time to revolve around the Sun:** 687 days
**Day (synodic):** 24 h 39 min 35 s
**Number of moons:** 2

 *Phobos ('fear') and Deimos ('panic') are the names of the two moons orbiting Mars. They were named for the horses that pulled a chariot for the Greek god Ares, the counterpart of the Roman god of war, Mars.*

## ⑤ JUPITER

**Average distance from the Sun:** 484 million miles
**Diameter:** 88,732 miles
**Average temp.:** −162° F
**Surface:** liquid hydrogen
**Time to revolve around the Sun:** 11.9 years
**Day (synodic):** 9 h 55 min 30 s
**Number of moons:** 63

*Giant fragments of a comet struck Jupiter in 1994, leaving impact 'bruises' the size of Earth. One of the largest fragments collided with a force that was estimated as 100,000 times greater than the force released by the largest nuclear device ever exploded.*

## ⑥ SATURN

**Average distance from the Sun:** 887 million miles
**Diameter:** 74,975 miles
**Average temp.:** −218° F
**Surface:** liquid hydrogen
**Time to revolve around the Sun:** 29.5 years
**Day (synodic):** 10 h 20 min 28 s
**Number of moons:** 56

 *Saturn may be famous for its rings, but it is not the only planet with that feature. Jupiter, Uranus, and Neptune are all circled by less dramatic rings.*

SPACE

## ⑦ URANUS

**Average distance from the Sun:** 1.8 billion miles
**Diameter:** 31,763 miles
**Average temp.:** –323° F
**Surface:** liquid hydrogen and helium
**Time to revolve around the Sun:** 84 years
**Day (synodic):** 17 h 14 min 23 s
**Number of moons:** 27

 *William Herschel, who discovered Uranus in 1781, worked as a music teacher and organist until a stipend from King George III allowed him to study astronomy full-time in 1782. He went on to make several other important discoveries.*

## ⑧ NEPTUNE

**Average distance from the Sun:** 2.8 billion miles
**Diameter:** 30,603 miles
**Average temp.:** –330° F
**Surface:** liquid hydrogen and helium
**Time to revolve around the Sun:** 164.8 years
**Day (synodic):** 16 d 6 h 37 min
**Number of moons:** 13

 *Triton, the largest of Neptune's moons, is considered the coldest object yet measured in the solar system, with an average temperature of –391° F.*

# Dwarf Planets and Plutoids

As of August 24, 2006, Pluto was no longer a planet. Pluto was reclassified a "dwarf planet" by the International Astronomical Union (IAU) when the organization changed the definition of "planet." The definition now says that a planet must "clear the neighborhood" around its orbit (have strong enough gravity that other bodies nearby either merge with it or orbit around it), which Pluto does not do. But Pluto is in good company. Four other bodies now meet the new dwarf planet standards. Eris, the largest, and Ceres, the smallest, were recognized by the IAU as dwarf planets in 2006. The two newest bodies, called Haumea and Makemake, were recognized in 2008. Both are beyond Neptune.

## PLUTO

**Average distance from the Sun:** 3.6 billion miles
**Diameter:** 1,485 miles
**Average temp.:** –369° F
**Surface:** rock and frozen gases
**Time to revolve around the Sun:** 247.7 years
**Day (synodic):** 6 d 9 h 17 min
**Number of moons:** 3

 *Pluto is a special kind of dwarf planet called a plutoid. The IAU created the term "plutoid" for a dwarf planet beyond the orbit of Neptune. There are three plutoids other than Pluto: Eris, Haumea, and Makemake.*

**CERES**, which orbits the sun in the asteroid belt between Mars and Jupiter, was also considered a planet for a short time after its discovery in the 1800s. It was then called an asteroid until it was named a dwarf planet in August 2006.

**ERIS** is the largest dwarf planet. Eris was discovered only in 2005, so scientists are still learning a lot about its features. It is believed to have a rocky, speckled landscape similar to Pluto's and is the most distant object ever found to orbit the sun.

# PLANET EARTH
# SEASONS

T he Earth spins on its axis of rotation. That's how we get day and night. But the Earth's axis isn't straight up and down. It is tilted about 23½ degrees. Because of this tilt, different parts of the globe get different amounts of sunlight during the year as the Earth orbits the Sun. This is why we have seasons.

**WINTER** Winter begins at the winter solstice (around December 21) in the Northern Hemisphere (north of the equator, where we live). Our hemisphere is tilted away from the Sun, so the Sun's rays reach us less directly. While days get longer during winter, they are still shorter than in spring and summer, so it's cold. Everything is reversed in the Southern Hemisphere, where it's summer!

**SPRING** At the vernal equinox (around March 21), daylight is 12 hours long throughout the world because Earth is not tilted toward or away from the sun. Days continue to get longer and the sunlight gets more direct in the Northern Hemisphere during spring.

Vernal Equinox

Summer Solstice

Winter Solstice

Autumnal Equinox

**SUMMER** The summer solstice (around June 21) marks the longest day of year in the Northern Hemisphere and the beginning of summer. The build-up of heat caused by more-direct sunlight during the long late spring and early summer days in the Northern Hemisphere makes summer our warmest season.

**FALL** After the autumnal equinox (around September 21) the Northern Hemisphere tilts away from the sun; sunlight is less direct and lasts less than 12 hours. The hemisphere cools off approaching winter.

Axis

23.5°

# THE MOON

The Moon is about 238,900 miles from Earth. It is 2,160 miles in diameter and has no atmosphere. The dusty surface is covered with deep craters. It takes the same time for the Moon to rotate on its axis as it does to orbit Earth (27 days, 7 hours, 43 minutes). This is why one side of the Moon is always facing Earth. The Moon has no light of its own but reflects light from the Sun. The lighted part of the Moon that we see changes in a regular cycle, waxing (growing) and waning (shrinking). It takes the Moon about 29½ days to go through all the "phases" in this cycle. This is called a lunar month.

## PHASES OF THE MOON

| New Moon | Waxing Crescent | First Quarter | Waxing Gibbous | Full Moon | Waning Gibbous | Last Quarter | Waning Crescent | New Moon |

# MOON Q&A

**Why are there dark spots on the face of the Moon?**

The dark spots you see on the face of the Moon are called *maria*. Maria are low plains made out of basalt, a fine, dark volcanic rock. The paler areas are mountains on the Moon's surface.

**Does the Moon really cause the ocean tides?**

Yes. Because the Moon is so big, its gravity causes the water in our seas and oceans to rise and fall as the Moon revolves around Earth. The Sun's gravitational pull also has an effect on ocean tides, but it is much weaker than the Moon's. That's because the Moon is so much closer to Earth than the Sun.

**Are there any plans to go back to the Moon?**

Right now, NASA is planning for another manned mission to the Moon by 2020. Other future Moon plans include a permanent lunar space station on the surface, probably on one of the Moon's poles. To prepare for this, an unmanned spacecraft was launched in July 2009 to map the moon's terrain so that NASA scientists can pick the best landing areas. There are also plans to launch unmanned spacecraft in 2012 to further study the lunar atmosphere and the effects of dust particles in the atmosphere on lunar exploration.

# EXPLORING SPACE

## SOME UNMANNED MISSIONS
### in the Solar System

| LAUNCH DATE | Mission |
|---|---|
| 1962 | **Mariner 2** First successful flyby of Venus |
| 1964 | **Mariner 4** First probe to reach Mars, 1965 |
| 1972 | **Pioneer 10** First probe to reach Jupiter, 1973 |
| 1973 | **Mariner 10** Only U.S. probe to reach Mercury, 1974 |
| 1975 | **Viking 1 and 2** Landed on Mars in 1976 |
| 1977 | **Voyager 1** Reached Jupiter in 1979 and Saturn in 1980 |
| 1977 | **Voyager 2** Reached Jupiter in 1979, Saturn in 1981, Uranus in 1986, Neptune in 1989 |
| 1989 | **Magellan** Orbited Venus and mapped its surface |
| 1989 | **Galileo** Reached Jupiter, 1995 |
| 1996 | **Mars Global Surveyor** Began mapping surface in 1999 |
| 1996 | **Mars Pathfinder** Landed on Mars. Carried a roving vehicle (Sojourner) |
| 1997 | **Cassini** Reached Saturn in June 2004 |
| 2001 | **Mars Odyssey** Began mapping and studying Mars in early 2002 |
| 2003 | **Mars rovers Spirit and Opportunity** Landed on Mars in early 2004 |
| 2004 | **Messenger** Flew past Mercury in 2008. Sent back first up-close data since 1975 |
| 2005 | **Deep Impact** Reached comet Tempel 1 July 4, 2005 |
| 2006 | **New Horizons** Launched January 19. Due to reach Pluto in 2015 |
| 2007 | **Phoenix** Landed in 2008 to search for signs that Mars once held life |
| 2009 | **Lunar Reconnaissance Orbiter** Currently orbiting the Moon, studying its atmosphere and evaluating possible landing sites |

*Phoenix Mars Lander*

*Artist's concept of the New Horizons spacecraft as it approaches Pluto and its three moons*

# Milestones
## in Human Spaceflight

The U.S. formed NASA in 1958. It was in response to the Soviet Union's launching of the first artificial satellite *Sputnik I* on October 4, 1957. Since then, more than 400 astronauts have made trips into space to conduct research, visit orbiting space stations, and explore the Moon. Below are some of the biggest moments in human space flight.

**1961** — On April 12, Soviet cosmonaut Yuri Gagarin, in *Vostok 1*, became the first person to orbit Earth. On May 5, U.S. astronaut Alan B. Shepard Jr. during the *Mercury 3* mission became the first American in space.

**1962** — On February 20, U.S. astronaut John H. Glenn Jr. during the *Mercury 6* mission became the first American to orbit Earth.

**1963** — From June 16 to 19, the Soviet spacecraft *Vostok 6* carried the first woman into space, Valentina V. Tereshkova.

**1965** — On March 18, Soviet cosmonaut Aleksei A. Leonov became the first person to "walk" in space.

**1966** — On March 16, U.S. *Gemini 8* became the first craft to dock with (become attached to) another vehicle (an unmanned Agena rocket).

**1969** — On July 20, U.S. *Apollo 11's* lunar module *Eagle* landed on the Moon's surface in the area known as the Sea of Tranquility. Neil Armstrong was the first person ever to walk on the Moon.

**1970** — In April, *Apollo 13* astronauts returned safely to Earth after an explosion damaged their spacecraft and prevented them from landing on the moon.

**1973** — On May 14, the U.S. put its first space station, *Skylab*, into orbit. The last *Skylab* crew left in January 1974.

**1975** — American and Soviet spacecraft docked, and for several days their crews worked and spent time together in space.

**1981** — *Columbia* was launched and became the first space shuttle to reach space.

**1986** — On January 28, space shuttle *Challenger* exploded 73 seconds after takeoff. All seven astronauts, including teacher Christa McAuliffe, died. In February, the Soviet space station *Mir* was launched into orbit.

**1998** — In December, *Endeavour* was launched with *Unity*, a U.S.-built part of the International Space Station (ISS). The crew attached it to the Russian-built *Zarya* control module. The first ISS crew arrived in November 2000.

**2001** — The 15-year Russian *Mir* program ended.

**2003** — On February 1, space shuttle *Columbia* disintegrated during its reentry into the Earth's atmosphere, killing the seven-member crew. China launched its first manned spacecraft on October 15.

**2004** — On June 21, Mike Melvill piloted *SpaceShipOne*, the first privately funded spacecraft, into space.

**2007** — Construction begins on projects which will send people to the Moon, where they will build a permanent outpost.

**2010** — Last flights for space shuttles *Atlantis*, *Endeavour*, and *Discovery* are planned. They will be replaced by a new vehicle as part of a project called Project Constellation, which hopes to send humans to the Moon and to Mars.

# SPACE NEWS 2010
## The Age of Space Tourism Blasts Off

NASA selected its first astronauts in 1959, but none of them made it into space until 1961. Now, less than 50 years later, space tourism is taking off. Five "space tourists" have already made the voyage to space.

## The VSS *Enterprise:* SpaceShipTwo

Virgin Galactic is working on plans to offer space tourism sometime in the next few years. The company hoped to unveil its newest space vehicle, SpaceShip Two, at the end of 2009. The flights, which will launch from desert spaceports in the American Southwest, will last about 2.5 hours and will cost each passenger $200,000!

The spaceliner, based on the prize-winning SpaceShipOne (2004) design, is actually several different crafts. The WhiteKnightTwo "mothership" will carry two SpaceShipTwo rockets (each with room for six passengers and two pilots) to launch position at about 50,000 feet (around 9.5 miles) above Earth's surface. Then, the SpaceShipTwo crafts will detach from the mothership and fire up hybrid rocket engines to actually reach outer space. Passengers will travel about 68 miles above Earth's surface, experiencing weightlessness in a zero-gravity environment.

Going to outer space isn't just a matter of buying a ticket and heading to the airport. Passengers will have to pass rigorous health exams and training—similar to what astronauts are put through. There will also be three days of pre-flight training.

## Mars Rover Redux

In 2011, NASA plans to launch the Mars Science Laboratory (MSL) rover, which is expected to touch down on Mars in 2012. The mission aims to investigate if Mars ever was—or is today— able to support microbial life (tiny organisms such as bacteria). MSL will follow in the footsteps (or tire tracks!) of Spirit and Opportunity, the twin rovers that touched down on Mars in 2004. The MSL mission should be active for at least a full Martian year (687 Earth days), but expectations are high. The Spirit and Opportunity missions were only supposed to last for 90 days, but both continue to operate. Spirit got stuck in some soft soil on Mars in March 2009, and NASA scientists continue to try to figure out how to free it.

At about 9 feet long and 6 feet tall, the Mars Science Laboratory rover is roughly three times larger than Spirit and Opportunity. But the improvements between the generations of rovers aren't just on the surface. Spirit and Opportunity were cushioned for landing with airbags. But MSL will be lowered via "sky crane" from its traveling vessel after entering Mars's atmosphere. MSL can perform on-board chemical analysis on the rock and soil samples it collects. Another new feature is a laser that can vaporize a thin surface layer from a rock in order to analyze what makes up the material underneath.

*M100, a spiral galaxy similar in shape to our home galaxy, the Milky Way*

# WHAT'S OUT THERE?

## What else is in space besides planets?

A GALAXY is a group of billions of stars held close together by gravity. The universe may have as many as 100 billion galaxies! The one we live in is called the Milky Way. Our Sun and planets are only a small part of it. Scientists think there are as many as 200 billion stars in the Milky Way!

NEBULA is the name astronomers give to any fuzzy patch in the sky, even galaxies and star clusters. Planetary nebulas come from the late stages of some stars, while star clusters and galaxies are groups of stars. Emission nebulas, reflection nebulas, and dark dust clouds are regions of gas and dust that may be hundreds of light-years wide and are often birthplaces of stars. Emission nebulas often give off a reddish glow, caused when their hydrogen gas is heated by hot, newly formed stars nearby. Dust particles in some areas reflect hot blue starlight and appear as reflection nebulas. Dark dust clouds, though still mainly gas, contain enough dust to absorb starlight and appear as dark nebulas.

BLACK HOLE is the name given to a region in space with gravity so strong that nothing can get out—not even light. Many black holes are probably formed when giant stars at least 20 times as massive as our Sun burn up their fuel and collapse, creating very dense cores. Scientists think bigger, "supermassive" black holes may form from the collapse of many stars in the centers of galaxies. Astronomers can't see black holes, because they do not give off light. They watch for signs, such as effects on the orbits of nearby stars, or X-ray bursts from matter being sucked into the black hole.

SATELLITES are objects that move in an orbit around a planet. Moons are natural satellites. Artificial satellites, launched into orbit by humans, are used as space stations and observatories. They are also used to take pictures of Earth's surface and to transmit communications signals.

ASTEROIDS are solid chunks of rock or metal that range in size from small boulders to hundreds of miles across. Some asteroids orbit other asteroids. Hundreds of thousands of asteroids orbit the Sun in the main asteroid belt between Mars and Jupiter.

COMETS are moving chunks of ice, dust, and rock that form huge gaseous heads and tails as they move nearer to the Sun. One of the most well-known is Halley's Comet. It can be seen about every 76 years and will appear again in the year 2061.

METEOROIDS are small pieces of stone or metal traveling in space. Most meteoroids are fragments from comets or asteroids that broke off from crashes in space with other objects. A few are actually chunks that blew off the Moon or Mars after an asteroid hit. When a meteoroid enters the Earth's atmosphere, it usually burns up completely. This streak of light is called a **meteor**, or **shooting star**. If a piece of a meteoroid survives its trip through our atmosphere and lands on Earth, it is called a **meteorite**.

*Comet Hale-Bopp, discovered in 1995*

# Sports

What baseball legend was known as the Iron Horse? ➡ page 228

**C**an you drive to the hoop like LeBron? Hit a backhand smash like Venus and Serena? Flip and twist on a board like Shaun White? It doesn't matter whether you play like a pro or just play for fun. Baseball or biking, hockey or hiking—there are plenty of awesome ways to stay fit, have fun, and get your game on.

## FAVORITE SPORTS

Here are the most popular sports and activities among kids in the United States in 2008.

| Boys (ages 6–17) | | Girls (ages 6–17) | |
|---|---|---|---|
| 1. Bicycling | 8.2 million | 1. Bowling | 5.3 million |
| 2. Bowling | 7.7 million | 2. Bicycling | 5.2 million |
| 3. Basketball | 7.4 million | 3. Walking | 5.1 million |
| 4. Freshwater Fishing | 6.6 million | 4. Running/Jogging | 3.9 million |
| 5. Baseball | 6.6 million | 5. Outdoor Soccer | 3.3 million |
| 6. Running/Jogging | 5.5 million | 6. Freshwater Fishing | 3.3 million |
| 7. Outdoor Soccer | 5.0 million | 7. Basketball | 3.2 million |
| 8. Walking | 4.3 million | 8. Inline Skating | 2.6 million |
| 9. Skateboarding | 4.3 million | 9. Slow-Pitch Softball | 1.4 million |
| 10. Billiards/Pool | 3.9 million | 10. Skateboarding | 1.2 million |

Source: Sporting Goods Manufacturers Association's Sports & Participation Report, 2009

## LITTLE LEAGUE

Little League Baseball is the largest youth sports program in the world. It began in 1939 in Williamsport, Pennsylvania, with 45 boys playing on three teams. Today, more than 2.6 million boys and girls ages 5 to 18 play on more than 176,000 Little League baseball and softball teams in more than 75 countries.

**WEB SITE** www.littleleague.org

# STRANGE SPORTS

You've probably seen—or played—soccer, basketball, tennis, and other popular sports. But what about volleyball played with your feet? Or hockey played at the bottom of a pool? There are plenty of sports that you probably won't find on local fields or courts. Here are some of the most unusual.

## FOOTVOLLEY

Footvolley is a game that combines soccer and beach volleyball. People started playing it on Brazilian beaches in the 1960s, but it has become popular in other countries, too. The net is the same as the one used in beach volleyball, but players use a soccer ball instead of a volleyball. Unlike volleyball, players cannot use their hands. They may use only their feet, head, and chest to get the ball over the net. Otherwise, the rules are the same as those in beach volleyball. Tournaments are held all over the world.

## BICYCLE POLO

Bicycle polo is a combination of polo (a hockey-like game that is played on horseback) and bicycle riding. There are two teams in bicycle polo. Each player has a mallet, which is slightly shorter than the ones used in traditional polo. They use these mallets to hit the ball. The object of the game is to maneuver the ball down the field and hit it into the opponent's goal. Players are not allowed to hit each other with their mallets, and their feet must stay on the bike's pedals at all times. If a player's feet touch the ground, he or she has to ride out of bounds and back in before hitting the ball again.

**WEB SITE** *bicyclepolo.org*

## UNDERWATER HOCKEY

Underwater hockey, also known as "octopush," was invented by four English scuba divers in 1954. The game is played at the bottom of a swimming pool between two teams of six. Players wear fins, a diving mask, and a snorkel to play. They use a short stick that is about 12 inches long to slide a 3-pound puck into the opposing team's underwater goal. Everyone on a team has to work together to score, since no one can go too long without coming up for air! World championships are held every two years. The 2008 tournament took place in Durban, South Africa. The next tournament will be held in Medellin, Colombia, in July 2010.

## WHO AM I ?

I was born in Bellevue, Washington, in 1984. I was a star pitcher for the University of Washington before being selected by the San Francisco Giants as the 10th pick of the 2006 draft. I reached the major leagues the following year and won seven games as a rookie. In 2008, I led the majors with 265 strikeouts and won the Cy Young Award as the top pitcher in the National League (NL). I was the starting pitcher for the NL in the 2009 All-Star Game. I am short and skinny for a pitcher, but my fastball has been clocked at 98 mph. My teammates call me the Freak. I have long black hair that I always keep covered with a baseball cap or wool cap.

Answer: Tim Lincecum

# The OLYMPIC Games

The first Olympics were held in Greece more than 2,500 years ago. In 776 B.C. they featured one event — a footrace. For more than 1,000 years, the Olympic Games were held every four years, a period the Greeks called an olympiad. In 393 A.D. the Roman emperor Theodosius put an end to the Olympics. The first modern Games were held in Athens in 1896. Since then, the Summer Olympic Games have taken place every four years at a different location. (The Games were canceled due to world wars in 1916, 1940, and 1944.) The next Summer Olympics will be held in London in 2012.

## 2008 SUMMER OLYMPICS:

Beijing, China, hosted the 29th Summer Olympic Games from August 8 to 24, 2008. About 10,500 athletes from around the world—including more than 600 Americans—competed in 302 events in more than two dozen sports.

## BEIJING, CHINA

Beijing's National Stadium hosted the opening and closing ceremonies of the 2008 Games. The stadium is nicknamed the Bird's Nest.

## 2008 SUMMER OLYMPIC SPORTS

Archery
Badminton
Baseball
Basketball
Boxing
Canoe/Kayak
Cycling
 (road, mountain
 bike, track, BMX)
Diving

Equestrian
 (dressage, jumping,
 3-day event)
Fencing
Field Hockey
Gymnastics
 (artistic, rhythmic,
 trampoline)
Handball
Judo

Modern Pentathlon
Rowing
Sailing
Shooting
Soccer
Softball
Swimming
Synchronized
 Swimming
Table Tennis
 (ping-pong)

Tae Kwon Do
Tennis
Track and Field
Triathlon
Volleyball
 (beach, indoor)
Water Polo
Weightlifting
Wrestling

# EIGHT IS ENOUGH

For Americans—and much of the world—the big story at the 2008 Summer Olympics was the astounding performance by swimmer Michael Phelps. The 23-year-old from Maryland won eight gold medals, breaking the record for a single Olympics set by fellow U.S. swimmer Mark Spitz in 1972.

Phelps has won 14 gold medals in his career so far, the most of any Olympian in any sport. His total of 16 medals (14 gold and two bronze) is second to the 18 won by Soviet gymnast Larissa Latynina in the 1950s and 1960s.

## Most Gold Medals, Single Games

| Name, Country | Medals Won | Year | Sport |
|---|---|---|---|
| Michael Phelps, U.S. | 8 | 2008 | Swimming |
| Mark Spitz, U.S. | 7 | 1972 | Swimming |
| Kristin Otto, East Germany | 6 | 1988 | Swimming |
| Vitaly Scherbo, Unified Team | 6 | 1992 | Gymnastics |
| Michael Phelps, U.S. | 6 | 2004 | Swimming |

## Medal Count

A record 87 countries won at least one medal in Beijing. The United States won the most, with 110, but China won the most gold medals—51. Here are the top 10 medal winners.

| COUNTRY | Gold | Silver | Bronze | TOTAL |
|---|---|---|---|---|
| UNITED STATES | 36 | 38 | 36 | 110 |
| CHINA | 51 | 21 | 28 | 100 |
| RUSSIA | 23 | 21 | 28 | 72 |
| GREAT BRITAIN | 19 | 13 | 15 | 47 |
| AUSTRALIA | 14 | 15 | 17 | 46 |
| GERMANY | 16 | 10 | 15 | 41 |
| FRANCE | 7 | 16 | 17 | 40 |
| SOUTH KOREA | 13 | 10 | 8 | 31 |
| ITALY | 8 | 10 | 10 | 28 |
| UKRAINE | 7 | 5 | 15 | 27 |

*The Olympics bring together athletes young and old. The youngest competitor in 2008 was 12-year-old swimmer Antoinette Joyce Guedia Mouafo from Cameroon. The oldest was 67-year-old Japanese equestrian Hiroshi Hoketsu. He competed in his first Olympics in his hometown of Tokyo—way back in 1964!*

SPORTS

# Odd Olympic Events

Whether it's platform diving, the 400-meter relay (on land or in the pool), or the gymnastics floor exercises, many people look forward to watching their favorite Summer Olympic event every four years. Though some events are timeless, others are eliminated from the program during planning, and new events take their place. For example, in 2006 the International Olympic Committee voted to discontinue baseball and softball as of the 2012 Games. Baseball and softball could possibly be reinstated as Olympic events, as early as the 2016 Games. However, dozens of other events have been discontinued and never seen at the Olympics again.

## Tug-of-War (1900–1920)

Teams of eight went head-to-head in this battle of brute strength in the first few modern Olympic Games. Countries often fielded more than one team, since the teams came from champion athletic clubs. The United States won the tug-of-war in 1904, represented by a team from the Milwaukee Athletic Club. But in 1908, a British team made up of London policemen defeated the United States in just a few seconds. The U.S. team challenged the win, noting that all of the officers were wearing spiked boots. Great Britain won a stocking-feet rematch and took home the gold medal.

## Motorboating (1908)

The Games were supposed to have been held in Rome, Italy, in 1908. However, a 1906 eruption at Mount Vesuvius forced a move to London, where heavy winds and foggy weather canceled six out of nine scheduled motorboat races. The motorboating events at the 1908 Games weren't exactly high-speed thrill fests—the top speeds were only about 19 mph!

did you know?

There are 195 countries in the world, but 205 states/territories are eligible to participate in the Olympic Games. This includes all 192 United Nations member states, Taiwan, and 12 territories. The 12 are: Palestine, American Samoa, Guam, Puerto Rico, U.S. Virgin Islands, Bermuda, British Virgin Islands, Cayman Islands, Aruba, Netherlands Antilles, Hong Kong, and the Cook Islands. At the 2008 Beijing Olympic Games, 204 states/territories participated. The only one missing was Brunei, which intended to have two athletes take part but failed to register them in time.

**m**ichael Phelps may have gotten most of the attention as he raced for his eight gold medals, but plenty of other swimmers made a splash in Beijing. One of them was Maarten van der Weijden of the Netherlands, who won gold in a new Olympic event, the 10-kilometer open water marathon. His promising career appeared to be over in 2001 when he was diagnosed with leukemia. Van der Weijden won his battle against the disease and was back in 2003, swimming faster than ever before. The 6 foot 9 inch Dutchman retired from swimming after the Olympics but still raises money and works to increase awareness about leukemia.

**U**.S. gymnast Nastia Liukin had her own Olympic ▶ triumph in 2008. First, she helped Team USA win a silver medal in the team competition. Then she won the gold medal in the individual all-around competition, edging out teammate Shawn Johnson by just six-tenths of a point. Liukin also won two silvers and one bronze in other individual events, giving her a total of five Olympic medals. Gymnastics is the Liukin family business. Nastia's father, Valeri, who is also her coach, won two gold medals and two silvers for the Soviet Union in 1988.

◀ *Maarten van der Weijden*

# SOME MODERN OLYMPIC FIRSTS

| 1896 | The first modern Olympic Games were held in Athens, Greece. A total of 312 athletes from 13 nations participated in nine sports. |
|---|---|
| 1900 | Women competed in the Olympic Games for the first time. |
| 1908 | For the first time, medals were awarded to the top three competitors in each event—a gold for first, a silver for second, and a bronze for third. |
| 1920 | The Olympic flag was raised for the first time, and the Olympic oath was introduced. The five interlaced rings of the flag represent Africa, America (North and South), Europe, Asia, and Australia. |
| 1924 | The first Winter Olympic events, featuring skiing and skating, were held. The Olympic flame was introduced at the Olympic Games. A relay of runners carries a torch with the flame from Olympia, Greece, to the site of each Olympics. |
| 1994 | Starting with the 1994 Winter Olympics, the winter and summer Games have alternated every two years, instead of being held in the same year, every fourth year. |

223

# The Winter

The first Winter Olympics were held in Chamonix, France, in 1924. The competition was originally called "the Winter Sports Week." The event wasn't officially recognized as the first Winter Olympics until after the Games were completed. Sixteen countries were represented by 258 athletes—only 11 were women. About 10,000 people paid to watch the 16 events.

The Winter Games have changed quite a bit since then. Vancouver, Canada, will host about 2,500 athletes and more than 1.5 million spectators at the 21st Winter Games in 2010. From February 12 to 28, athletes from about 80 countries will compete for 86 gold medals in the sports listed below. Some 3 billion viewers worldwide are expected to watch the Games on television.

## 2010 Winter Olympic Sports

Alpine Skiing

Biathlon

Bobsleigh (bobsled)

Cross-Country Skiing

Curling

Figure Skating

Freestyle Skiing

Ice Hockey

Luge

Nordic Combined

Short Track Speed Skating

Skeleton

Ski Jumping

Snowboarding

Speed Skating

**NEW for 2010**

Skicross will make its Olympic debut in Vancouver. Skicross, also known as skiercross, is a freestyle skiing event that is a lot like a motocross race on a snowy slope. Four to six skiers race against a clock—and each other—over a course that has jumps, twisting turns, and other obstacles.

# Olympics

## Olympic Flashback: 1980

February 22, 2010, will mark the 30th anniversary of the most famous performance in U.S. Olympic history. In 1980, the Soviet hockey team was generally considered the best in the world. Team USA, on the other hand, was made up of inexperienced college students. Before the Winter Olympics, the Soviets embarrassed the U.S. team in a warm-up game, 10–3.

But the Americans played with confidence when they met the Soviets again in the Olympic semifinals in Lake Placid, New York. The teams traded goals before U.S. captain Mike Eruzione scored the go-ahead goal with about 10 minutes to play. Team USA held off a furious attack by the Soviets to win 4–3. As the last seconds ticked off the clock, TV announcer Al Michaels asked millions of stunned viewers around the U.S., "Do you believe in miracles? Yes!" Today, many fans consider "the Miracle on Ice" to be the greatest sports moment of all time. Team USA went on to beat Finland to win the gold medal.

# Going for the Gold

**Here are some of the stars who may shine for Team USA at the Vancouver Games.**

• Snowboarder Shaun White became a worldwide superstar at the 2006 Games in Turin, Italy. Fans hope "the Flying Tomato" will repeat his gold-medal-winning performance in the half-pipe. White showed he can still shred with the best by winning gold in the superpipe at the 2009 Winter X Games.

• Another "old-timer" to watch is 27-year-old Apolo Anton Ohno. The short track speed skater already owns five medals, including two golds. (Ohno also used his fancy footwork to win the reality series *Dancing with the Stars* in 2007.) In Vancouver, his biggest threat may be his 19-year-old teammate J.R. Celski.

*Lindsey Vonn*

• The best hope on the slopes is Lindsey Vonn, the most successful female American skier in history. In 2009, she won her second straight World Cup championship. Vonn plans to make up for her disappointing showing in 2006, when an injury during a training run wiped out her chances of winning a medal.

• The U.S. women's hockey team won the silver medal in 2002 and bronze in 2006. To win gold, they may have to beat their main rival, Canada, on its home ice. Team USA will look to captain Natalie Darwitz and twin sisters Jocelyne and Monique Lamoureux for scoring. U.S. coach Mark Johnson was one of the stars of the 1980 men's hockey team (see box above).

# PARALYMPICS

**T**he Paralympic Games are the official Olympic Games for athletes with physical, mental, or sensory disabilities. The Games got their start in 1948, when Sir Ludwig Guttman organized a competition in England for World War II veterans with spinal-cord injuries. When athletes from the Netherlands joined in 1952, the movement went international.

Olympic-style competition began in Rome in 1960, and the first Winter Paralympics were held in Sweden in 1976. Since 1992, the Paralympics have been held just after the Winter and Summer Olympic competitions. Following the 2008 Summer Olympics in Beijing, nearly 4,000 athletes from 146 countries took part in the Paralympic Games at the Beijing Olympic venues. Athletes from around the world will compete in the 2010 Winter Paralympic Games in Vancouver in March.

## OFFICIAL PARALYMPIC SPORTS

**Six Competitive Levels:** wheelchair, intellectual disabilities, amputees, visual disabilities, cerebral palsy, and other mobility disabilities

**Winter:** alpine skiing, biathlon, cross-country skiing, ice sledge hockey, wheelchair curling

**Summer:** archery, boccia, cycling, equestrian, goalball, judo, powerlifting, rowing, sailing, shooting, soccer, swimming, table tennis, track and field, volleyball, wheelchair basketball, wheelchair fencing, wheelchair rugby, wheelchair tennis

**WEB SITE** *www.paralympic.org*

# SPECIAL OLYMPICS

**T**he Special Olympics is the world's largest program of sports training and athletic competition for children and adults with intellectual disabilities. Founded in 1968, Special Olympics has offices in all 50 states, Washington, D.C., and throughout the world. The organization offers training and competition to more than 2.5 million athletes in more than 180 countries. In 2006, the U.S. held the first-ever National Special Olympics. The Games took place in Ames, Iowa. More than 3,000 athletes from all 50 states competed.

Special Olympics holds World Games every two years. These alternate between summer and winter sports. The last Special Olympics Winter Games were held in Boise, Idaho, in February 2009. The next World Summer Games are scheduled for June 2011 in Athens, Greece.

# Auto Racing

**SPORTS**

**NASCAR** **B**ill France founded the National Association for Stock Car Auto Racing (NASCAR) in 1947. Stock cars look a lot like the cars that are "in stock" at a car dealership. In 1949, Red Byron won the first **NASCAR** championship as the top driver of the season. Since 2008, the championship has been known as the Sprint Cup. Races in the Sprint Cup series include the Daytona 500 and the Brickyard 400.

## PAST NASCAR CHAMPIONS

| | | | | | |
|---|---|---|---|---|---|
| 1982 | Darrell Waltrip | 1991 | Dale Earnhardt | 2000 | Bobby Labonte |
| 1983 | Bobby Allison | 1992 | Alan Kulwicki | 2001 | Jeff Gordon |
| 1984 | Terry Labonte | 1993 | Dale Earnhardt | 2002 | Tony Stewart |
| 1985 | Darrell Waltrip | 1994 | Dale Earnhardt | 2003 | Matt Kenseth |
| 1986 | Dale Earnhardt | 1995 | Jeff Gordon | 2004 | Kurt Busch |
| 1987 | Dale Earnhardt | 1996 | Terry Labonte | 2005 | Tony Stewart |
| 1988 | Bill Elliott | 1997 | Jeff Gordon | 2006 | Jimmie Johnson |
| 1989 | Rusty Wallace | 1998 | Jeff Gordon | 2007 | Jimmie Johnson |
| 1990 | Dale Earnhardt | 1999 | Dale Jarrett | 2008 | Jimmie Johnson |

*Jimmie Johnson*

## INDIANAPOLIS 500

**T**he Indianapolis 500 is the biggest event in open-wheel racing. Open-wheel cars have narrow bodies and big uncovered tires. The first Indianapolis 500 was held at the world-famous Indianapolis Motor Speedway in 1911. Ray Harroun won the first Indy 500 with an average speed of only 74.602 mph.

### PAST INDY WINNERS

| | | | |
|---|---|---|---|
| 1911 | Ray Harroun . . . . . . . . . 74.602 mph | 2006 | Sam Hornish Jr. . . . . . . 157.085 mph |
| 1920 | Gaston Chevrolet . . . . . 88.618 mph | 2007 | Dario Franchitti . . . . . . 151.774 mph |
| 1930 | Billy Arnold . . . . . . . . . . 100.448 mph | 2008 | Scott Dixon . . . . . . . . . . 143.567 mph |
| 1940 | Wilbur Shaw . . . . . . . . . 114.277 mph | 2009 | Helio Castroneves . . . . 150.318 mph |
| 1950 | Johnnie Parsons . . . . . 124.002 mph | | |
| 1960 | Jim Rathmann . . . . . . . . 138.767 mph | | |
| 1970 | Al Unser . . . . . . . . . . . . . 155.749 mph | | |
| 1980 | Johnny Rutherford . . . . 142.862 mph | | |
| 1990 | Arie Luyendyk . . . . . . . . 185.981 mph* | | |
| 2000 | Juan Montoya . . . . . . . 167.607 mph | | |
| 2001 | Helio Castroneves . . . . 131.294 mph | | |
| 2002 | Helio Castroneves . . . . 166.499 mph | | |
| 2003 | Gil de Ferran . . . . . . . . 156.291 mph | | |
| 2004 | Buddy Rice . . . . . . . . . . 138.518 mph | | |
| 2005 | Dan Wheldon . . . . . . . . 157.603 mph | | |

*Helio Castroneves*

*Race record for average lap speed.

# BASEBALL

The 2009 baseball season got underway on April 5, with the Atlanta Braves beating the 2008 World Series champion Philadelphia Phillies. For only the second time ever, the season didn't end until November. (The first was in 2001, when the season was interrupted by the terrorist attacks on September 11.) On July 14, the top players from the American League (AL) and the National League (NL) met in the 80th All-Star Game, in St. Louis. The AL won 4–3 and has not lost to the NL since 1996. Carl Crawford of the Tampa Bay Rays earned the game's MVP award for his game-saving catch in the seventh inning (left). Here are some other highlights of the 2009 season:

• On July 23, pitcher Mark Buerhle of the Chicago White Sox threw only the 16th perfect game since 1900. He retired all 27 Tampa Bay batters he faced in a 5–0 win.

• On September 11, Derek Jeter became the New York Yankees' all-time leader in hits. Babe Ruth, Joe DiMaggio, Mickey Mantle, Lou Gehrig (see box below), and other legends have played for the team, but none had more hits in a Yankee uniform than Jeter.

## 2009 MAJOR LEAGUE LEADERS

### HITTERS

**BATTING**
AL: Joe Mauer, Twins, .365
NL: Hanley Ramirez, Marlins, .342

**HOME RUNS**
AL: Carlos Pena, Rays; Mark Teixeira, Yankees, 39
NL: Albert Pujols, Cardinals, 47

**RUNS BATTED IN**
AL: Mark Teixeira, Yankees, 122
NL: Prince Fielder, Brewers; Ryan Howard, Phillies, 141

### PITCHERS

**WINS**
AL: Felix Hernandez, Mariners; C.C. Sabathia, Yankees; Justin Verlander, Tigers, 19
NL: Adam Wainwright, Cardinals, 19

**STRIKEOUTS**
AL: Justin Verlander, Tigers, 269
NL: Tim Lincecum, Giants, 261

**EARNED RUN AVERAGE**
AL: Zack Greinke, Royals, 2.16
NL: Chris Carpenter, Cardinals, 2.24

## THE LUCKIEST MAN

From 1925 to 1939, Yankees slugger Lou Gehrig played in 2,130 straight games, earning the nickname "the Iron Horse." He batted .340 for his career and led the Yankees to six World Series titles. The team honored Gehrig with a special day on July 4, 1939. In his speech that day (right), Gehrig said he was "the luckiest man on the face of the earth." Fans didn't know that he was suffering from ALS, a severe nerve disease that took his life less than two years later. On July 4, 2009, all 32 major league teams honored the 70th anniversary of his famous speech to help raise awareness of ALS, which today is often called Lou Gehrig's disease.

# SOME MAJOR LEAGUE RECORDS*

**BATTERS**

## Most Home Runs

Career: 762, Barry Bonds (1986-2007)
Season: 73, Barry Bonds (2001)
Game: 4, by 12 different players

## Most Hits

Career: 4,256, Pete Rose (1963-86)
Season: 262, **Ichiro Suzuki** (2004)
Game: 7, Rennie Stennett (1975)

## Most Stolen Bases

Career: 1,406, Rickey Henderson (1979-2003)
Season: 130, Rickey Henderson (1982)
Game: 6, Eddie Collins (1912);
       **Carl Crawford** (2009)

**PITCHERS**

## Most Strikeouts

Career: 5,714, Nolan Ryan (1966-93)
Season: 383, Nolan Ryan (1973)
Game: 20, Roger Clemens (1986, 1996);
       **Kerry Wood** (1998)

## Most Wins

Career: 511, Cy Young (1890-1911)
Season: 41, Jack Chesbro (1904)

## Most Saves

Career: 591, **Trevor Hoffman** (1993-2009)
Season: 62, **Francisco Rodriguez** (2008)

*Through the 2009 season. Players in bold played in 2009. Game stats are for nine-inning games only.

# THE FALL CLASSIC

No championship in American sports can match the rich history of the World Series. It all began in 1903, when the well-established National League (NL) and the upstart American League (AL) decided to hold a championship to determine which league was best. The owners of the NL champion Pittsburgh Pirates and the AL champion Boston Pilgrims scheduled the best-of-nine "World's Championship Series." Legendary pitcher Cy Young helped Boston upset Pittsburgh and win the series five games to three. The Fall Classic was born.

*Jackie Robinson of the Brooklyn Dodgers steals home in the 1955 World Series.*

There was no series held the following year, because the NL champion New York Giants refused to play Boston. But the Giants agreed to play the AL's Philadelphia Athletics in 1905 and won the best-of-seven series. Since then, the World Series has followed the best-of-seven format (except from 1919 to 1921, when it again was a best-of-nine series).

Over the years, the Fall Classic has seen many amazing performances—from pitchers Grover Cleveland Alexander and Sandy Koufax to hitters Babe Ruth and Reggie Jackson. Through 2008, the New York Yankees held the record for most World Series championships with 26, followed by the St. Louis Cardinals with 10.

# BASEBALL Hall of Fame

The National Baseball Hall of Fame and Museum opened in 1939, in Cooperstown, New York. To be eligible for membership, players usually have to be retired from baseball for five years. Three new members were inducted in 2009, which brought the total number of members to 289. Topping the list of 2009 inductees was Rickey Henderson, baseball's all-time leader in stolen bases and runs scored. Joining him was Jim Rice, who clubbed 382 home runs in 16 seasons with the Boston Red Sox. The third new member was Joe Gordon, a nine-time All-Star with the Yankees and Cleveland Indians. **WEB SITE** www.baseballhalloffame.org

# BASKETBALL

Dr. James Naismith invented basketball in Springfield, Massachusetts, in 1891. He used peach baskets as hoops. At first, each team had nine players instead of five. Big-time pro basketball started in the late 1940s, when the National Basketball Association (NBA) was formed. The Women's National Basketball Association (WNBA) began play in 1997.

## BACK ON TOP

The Los Angeles Lakers returned to the top of the basketball world by defeating the Orlando Magic, four games to one, in the 2009 NBA Finals. Kobe Bryant, the Finals MVP, cemented his place among the greatest players of all time. The championship was Bryant's fourth with L.A.—but his first without superstar center and former teammate Shaquille O'Neal.

*Kobe Bryant and Phil Jackson*

The Lakers' victory was also the record 10th championship for coach Phil Jackson, who had won six titles as coach of the Chicago Bulls in the 1990s.

Before the playoffs began, many fans were hoping for a showdown between Bryant's Lakers and LeBron James's Cleveland Cavaliers. But the Magic, led by center Dwight Howard, had other ideas. In the Eastern Conference Finals, Orlando knocked out Cleveland in a tough six-game series to set up their match-up with the Lakers. The season wasn't a total disappointment for LeBron James, however. He won his first regular-season MVP award.

## Hall of Fame

The Naismith Memorial Hall of Fame in Springfield, Massachusetts, honors great players, coaches, and others who have had a big impact on the game. The 2009 class was one of the best ever. Topping the list was Michael Jordan, who led the NBA in scoring 10 times and won six titles with the Bulls. He was joined by 10-time All-Star David Robinson and all-time assist leader John Stockton. Two coaches were also inducted: Jerry Sloan of the Utah Jazz and Vivian Stringer of Rutgers University.

**WEB SITE** *www.hoophall.com*

# Some **All-Time** NBA Records*

## POINTS

**Career:** 38,387, Kareem Abdul-Jabbar (1969-89)

**Season:** 4,029, Wilt Chamberlain (1961-62)

**Game:** 100, Wilt Chamberlain (1962)

## ASSISTS

**Career:** 15,806, John Stockton (1984-2003)

**Season:** 1,164, John Stockton (1990-91)

**Game:** 30, Scott Skiles (1990)

## REBOUNDS

**Career:** 23,924, Wilt Chamberlain (1959-73)

**Season:** 2,149, Wilt Chamberlain (1960-61)

**Game:** 55, Wilt Chamberlain (1960)

## 3-POINTERS

**Career:** 2,560, Reggie Miller (1987-2005)

**Season:** 269, Ray Allen (2005–2006)

**Game:** 12, Kobe Bryant (2003); Donyell Marshall (2005)

*Through the 2008–2009 season

# *Highlights* of the 2009 WNBA Season

Diana Taurasi

The 2009 WNBA season was filled with good-byes. The Houston Comets, who had won four league championships, folded after the 2008 season. Two of the league's biggest stars, Lisa Leslie and Yolanda Griffith, announced their retirement. On the court in 2009, regular-season MVP Diana Taurasi led the Phoenix Mercury to a showdown with the Indiana Fever in the WNBA Finals.

**Scoring Leader**
• Diana Taurasi
  Phoenix Mercury
  Points: 631
  Average: 20.4

**Rebounding Leader**
• Candace Parker
  Los Angeles Sparks
  Rebounds: 244
  Average: 9.8

**Assists Leader**
• Sue Bird
  Seattle Storm
  Assists: 179
  Average: 5.8

# COLLEGE BASKETBALL

The men's National Collegiate Athletic Association (NCAA) Tournament began in 1939. Today, it is a spectacular 65-team extravaganza that is part of March Madness. Games on the Final Four weekend, when the semifinals and finals are played, are watched by millions of viewers. The Women's NCAA Tournament began in 1982 and has soared in popularity.

## THE 2009 NCAA TOURNAMENT RESULTS

**MEN'S FINAL FOUR**
**Semifinals:**
Michigan State 82, Connecticut 73
North Carolina 83, Villanova 69
**Final:**
North Carolina 89, Michigan State 72
**Most Outstanding Player:**
Wayne Ellington, North Carolina

**WOMEN'S FINAL FOUR**
**Semifinals:**
Louisville 61, Oklahoma 59
Connecticut 83, Stanford 64
**Final:**
Connecticut 76, Louisville 54
**Most Outstanding Player:**
Tina Charles, Connecticut

# FOOTBALL

**F**ootball began as a college sport in the 1800s. The professional league that became the modern National Football League (NFL) started in 1920. The rival American Football League began in 1960. The two leagues played the first Super Bowl in 1967. In 1970, the leagues merged to become the NFL as we know it today, with an American Football Conference (AFC) and a National Football Conference (NFC).

## The Steelers Topple the Cards

On February 1, 2009, the Pittsburgh Steelers defeated the Arizona Cardinals in one of the most exciting Super Bowls in history. Late in the fourth quarter, Arizona quarterback Kurt Warner connected with Larry Fitzgerald for a long touchdown. The Cards held a 23–20 lead, but Steelers quarterback Ben Roethlisberger didn't panic. He calmly led his team more than 70 yards in less than two minutes. With just 35 seconds left on the clock, Big Ben found Santonio Holmes in the corner of the end zone for the game-winning score (right). The 27–23 win was Pittsburgh's record sixth Super Bowl championship.

- **RUSHING YARDS:** Adrian Peterson, Minnesota Vikings, 1,760
- **RECEPTIONS:** Andre Johnson, Houston Texans, 115
- **RECEIVING YARDS:** Andre Johnson, Houston Texans, 1,575
- **TOTAL TDS (RUSHING AND RECEIVING):** DeAngelo Williams, Carolina Panthers, 20
- **PASSING YARDS:** Drew Brees, New Orleans Saints, 5,069
- **PASSING TDS:** Drew Brees, New Orleans Saints; Philip Rivers, San Diego Chargers, 34
- **POINTS:** Stephen Gostkowski, New England Patriots, 148
- **INTERCEPTIONS:** Ed Reed, Baltimore Ravens, 9
- **SACKS:** DeMarcus Ware, Dallas Cowboys, 20.0

## 2008 NFL LEADERS

## Pro Football Hall of Fame

The Pro Football Hall of Fame in Canton, Ohio, was founded in 1963 to honor outstanding players, coaches, and contributors to the NFL.

Six new members were inducted on August 8, 2009: wide receiver Bob Hayes, guard Randall McDaniel, defensive end Bruce Smith, linebacker Derrick Thomas, defensive back Rod Woodson, and Buffalo Bills owner Ralph Wilson.

**WEB SITE** www.profootballhof.com

# Famous Pro Football Firsts

## FIRST INDOOR GAME

**December 28, 1902, World Series of Pro Football Tournament, Madison Square Garden, New York City, New York.**
**New York vs. Syracuse Athletic Club**

Today, nine NFL teams have indoor stadiums. Many people think that indoor football is a relatively new development, but the first indoor pro football game was actually played in 1902. The team called "New York" was actually made up of players from two teams from Philadelphia. They lost to Syracuse Athletic Club, 6-0, in front of a crowd of 3,000. Syracuse went on to win the tournament.

*Old Madison Square Garden*

## THE FIRST FORWARD PASS

**October 27, 1906, Massillon, Ohio.**
**Massillon Tigers vs. Benwood-Moundsville**

In the old days of football, the forward pass was not allowed. Teams could only run the ball or toss it backward as a lateral. To open up the game, the National Collegiate Athletic Association (NCAA) in 1906 voted to allow the forward pass. The same rule was adopted by the pros. The first forward pass in a college game took place in a game between St. Louis University and Carroll College on Sept. 5, 1906, when Bradbury Robinson of St. Louis threw a pass to Jack Schneider. The first known forward pass in a pro game took place in a game between the Massillon Tigers and Benwood-Moundsville. George Parratt of Massillon threw a pass to Dan "Bullet" Riley. Massillon won 61-0.

## FIRST GAME PLAYED UNDER THE LIGHTS

**November 6, 1929, Kinsley Park Stadium, Providence, Rhode Island. Providence Steam Roller vs. Chicago Cardinals**

Providence used to have an NFL team from 1925 to 1931 called the Steam Roller. Their home stadium was called the Cyclodrome. In 1925, the Steam Roller played four games in six days. The second game was against the Chicago Cardinals (today's Arizona Cardinals). Heavy rains made the Cyclodrome unplayable. So the game was moved to nearby Kinsley Park Stadium where floodlights had recently been installed. The night game was played in front of a crowd of 6,000. The Cardinals stopped the Steam Roller, 16-0.

# NFL All-Time Record Holders*

## RUSHING YARDS
- Career: 18,355, Emmitt Smith (1990-2004)
- Season: 2,105, Eric Dickerson (1984)
- Game: 296, Adrian Peterson (2007)

## RECEIVING YARDS
- Career: 22,895, Jerry Rice (1985-2004)
- Season: 1,848, Jerry Rice (1995)
- Game: 336, Willie Anderson (1989)

## PASSING YARDS
- Career: 65,127, Brett Favre (1991-2008)
- Season: 5,084, Dan Marino (1984)
- Game: 554, Norm Van Brocklin (1951)

## POINTS SCORED
- Career: 2,544, Morten Andersen (1982-2004, 2006-2007)
- Season: 186, LaDainian Tomlinson (2006)
- Game: 40, Ernie Nevers (1929)

*Through the 2008 season.

# COLLEGE FOOTBALL

The 2008 college football season was one of the wildest in memory. Five different teams were ranked number 1 in the major polls but could not hang on to the top spot.

On January 8, 2009, the top-ranked Oklahoma Sooners faced the Florida Gators in the BCS National Championship Game in Miami. The Florida defense kept the high-powered Oklahoma offense in check for most of the game. Gators quarterback Tim Tebow (left) threw for two touchdowns, and Percy Harvin ran for 122 yards and a touchdown. Florida won 24–14 and earned its second national championship in three years.

## Bowled Over!

Here are the results of other major bowl games played in January 2009.

| Rose Bowl | Pasadena, CA | Southern Cal 38, Penn State 24 |
| --- | --- | --- |
| Orange Bowl | Miami, FL | Cincinnati 20, Virginia Tech 7 |
| Sugar Bowl | New Orleans, LA | Utah 31, Alabama 17 |
| Fiesta Bowl | Glendale, AZ | Texas 24, Ohio State 21 |

## HEISMAN TROPHY

Oklahoma quarterback Sam Bradford won the 2008 Heisman Trophy as the top college player. He became just the second sophomore to receive the award. (Tim Tebow, who won the Heisman the previous year, was the first.) Bradford threw for 4,464 yards, 48 touchdowns, and only six interceptions. With Bradford leading the way, the Sooners scored 702 points, the most in NCAA history. They also became the first team to ever score at least 60 points in five straight games. Bradford's stellar play helped Oklahoma to a 12–1 record and a spot in the BCS National Championship Game.

## ALL-TIME DIVISION I NCAA LEADERS *

### RUSHING YARDS

1. 6,397, Ron Dayne, Wisconsin
2. 6,279, Ricky Williams, Texas
3. 6,082, Tony Dorsett, Pittsburgh
4. 6,026, DeAngelo Williams, Memphis
5. 5,598, Charles White, USC

### PASSING YARDS

1. 17,072, Timmy Chang, Hawaii
2. 15,793, Graham Harrell, Texas Tech
3. 15,031, Ty Detmer, Brigham Young
4. 14,193, Colt Brennan, Hawaii
5. 13,484, Philip Rivers, North Carolina State

*Through the 2008 season.

# GOLF

**G**olf began in Scotland as early as the 1400s. The first golf course in the United States opened in 1888 in Yonkers, New York. The sport has grown to include both men's and women's professional tours. And millions play just for fun.

The men's tour in the U.S. is run by the Professional Golf Association (PGA). The four major championships (with the year first played) are:
- British Open (1860)
- United States Open (1895)
- PGA Championship (1916)
- Masters Tournament (1934)

The women's tour in the U.S. is guided by the Ladies Professional Golf Association (LPGA). The four major championships are:
- United States Women's Open (1946)
- McDonald's LPGA Championship (1955)
- Kraft Nabisco Championship (1972)
- Women's British Open (1976)

## The All-Time "Major" Players

These pro golfers have won the most major championships through 2009.

**MEN**
1. Jack Nicklaus, 18
2. Tiger Woods, 14
3. Walter Hagan, 11
4. Ben Hogan, 9
   Gary Player, 9

**WOMEN**
1. Patty Berg, 15
2. Mickey Wright, 13
3. Louise Suggs, 11
4. Babe Didrikson Zaharias, 10
   Annika Sorenstam, 10

*Tiger Woods*

# GYMNASTICS

Although the sport dates back to ancient Egypt, modern-day gymnastics began in Europe in the early 1800s. It has been part of the Olympics since 1896. The first World Gymnastic Championships were held in the city of Antwerp, Belgium, in 1903.

Artistic gymnastics is the most popular form of gymnastics. Men compete in the high bar, parallel bars, rings, vault, pommel horse, floor exercise, individual all-around, and team events. The women's events are the uneven parallel bars, vault, balance beam, floor exercise, individual all-around, and team competition. Only women compete in rhythmic gymnastics, which includes the rope, hoop, ball, clubs, ribbon, and all-around events.

The two biggest stars of the 2008 Olympics, Shawn Johnson and Nastia Liukin, took time off from gymnastics in 2009. That gave other U.S. artistic gymnasts a chance to shine. In August, 17-year-old Bridget Sloan from Pittsboro, Indiana, won the all-around competition at the Visa National Championships.

*Bridget Sloan*

# ICE HOCKEY

Ice hockey began in Canada in the mid-1800s. The National Hockey League (NHL) was formed in 1917. Today the NHL has 30 teams—24 in the U.S. and six in Canada.

## HIGHLIGHTS

The Pittsburgh Penguins capped a thrilling 2008–2009 NHL season by defeating the Detroit Red Wings in the Stanley Cup Finals. The series was a rematch of the 2008 Finals, which Detroit won in six games. The Pens got their payback in 2009, but it wasn't easy. The series wasn't decided until the final seconds of Game 7, when Pittsburgh goalie Marc-Andre Fleury made a diving save to preserve a 2–1 victory. Pittsburgh center Evgeni Malkin won the Conn Smythe Trophy as the MVP of the playoffs.

In November 2009, the Hockey Hall of Fame in Toronto inducted five new members: former NHL stars Brett Hull, Brian Leetch, Luc Robitaille, and Steve Yzerman and New Jersey Devils team president Lou Lamoriello.

| SEASON | WINNER | RUNNER-UP |
|---|---|---|
| 1991-92 | Pittsburgh Penguins | Chicago Black Hawks |
| 1992-93 | Montreal Canadiens | Los Angeles Kings |
| 1993-94 | New York Rangers | Vancouver Canucks |
| 1994-95 | New Jersey Devils | Detroit Red Wings |
| 1995-96 | Colorado Avalanche | Florida Panthers |
| 1996-97 | Detroit Red Wings | Philadelphia Flyers |
| 1997-98 | Detroit Red Wings | Washington Capitals |
| 1998-99 | Dallas Stars | Buffalo Sabres |
| 1999-2000 | New Jersey Devils | Dallas Stars |
| 2000-01 | Colorado Avalanche | New Jersey Devils |
| 2001-02 | Detroit Red Wings | Carolina Hurricanes |
| 2002-03 | New Jersey Devils | Anaheim Mighty Ducks |
| 2003-04 | Tampa Bay Lightning | Calgary Flames |
| 2004-05 | Season canceled | |
| 2005-06 | Carolina Hurricanes | Edmonton Oilers |
| 2006-07 | Anaheim Ducks | Ottawa Senators |
| 2007-08 | Detroit Red Wings | Pittsburgh Penguins |
| 2008-09 | Pittsburgh Penguins | Detroit Red Wings |

Alex Ovechkin

## 2008–2009 NHL Award Winners

Hart Trophy (regular-season MVP): Alex Ovechkin, Washington Capitals

Vezina Trophy (top goaltender): Tim Thomas, Boston Bruins

Norris Trophy (top defenseman): Zdeno Chara, Boston Bruins

Art Ross Trophy (top scorer): Evgeni Malkin, Pittsburgh Penguins

Calder Trophy (rookie of the year): Steve Mason, Columbus Blue Jackets

Conn Smythe Trophy (playoff MVP): Evgeni Malkin, Pittsburgh Penguins

## Some All-Time NHL Records*

### GOALS SCORED
**Career:** 894, Wayne Gretzky (1979-99)
**Season:** 92, Wayne Gretzky (1981-82)
**Game:** 7, Joe Malone (1920)

### GOALIE WINS
**Career:** 557, Martin Brodeur (1992–2009)
**Season:** 48, Martin Brodeur (2006-07)

### POINTS
**Career:** 2,857, Wayne Gretzky (1979-99)
**Season:** 215, Wayne Gretzky (1985-86)
**Game:** 10, Darryl Sittler (1976)

### GOALIE SHUTOUTS
**Career:** 103, Terry Sawchuk (1949-70)
**Season:** 22, George Hainsworth (1928-29)

*Through the 2008-2009 season.

# SOCCER

In 2009, the U.S. men's soccer team scored one of its biggest victories ever. The Americans stunned Spain, the top-ranked team in the world, in the semifinals of the FIFA Confederations Cup in South Africa. The loss was the Spanish team's first in more than two years. Jozy Altidore and Clint Dempsey scored goals, and goalie Tim Howard made eight saves in the shocking 2–0 win. The U.S. team's championship dreams died in the final, however, as Brazil came back from 2–0 down to win the Confederations Cup, 3–2. The next big test for the American team will be in the FIFA 2010 World Cup, which begins in South Africa in June.

*Jozy Altidore*

## Major League Soccer

The 13th season of Major League Soccer (MLS) ended with the Columbus Crew beating the New York Red Bulls for the 2008 MLS Cup. Guillermo Barros Schelotto assisted on all three goals in the 3–1 victory. The midfielder from Argentina was named MVP of the MLS Cup, as well as regular-season MVP. Landon Donovan of the Los Angeles Galaxy won the Golden Boot as the league's top goal scorer.

## Women's Professional Soccer

Women's Professional Soccer (WPS) kicked off its first season in 2009. The United States had been without a top pro women's league since the Women's United Soccer Association (WUSA) folded after the 2003 season. The WPS season began at the end of March and ended with the WPS Championship in August. Sky Blue FC, who play in New Jersey, beat the Los Angeles Sol 1–0 to win the first league title. Brazilian striker Marta of the Sol was named the league MVP. The seven-team league plans to expand to nine teams for the 2010 season.

*Marta of the Los Angeles Sol*

# TENNIS

**M**odern tennis began in 1873. The first championships were held in Wimbledon, near London, four years later. In 1881, the first official U.S. men's championships were held at Newport, Rhode Island. Six years later, the first U.S. women's championships took place in Philadelphia. Today, the four most important tournaments, or Grand Slams, are the Australian Open, the French Open, the All-England (Wimbledon) Championships, and the U.S. Open.

## Grand Slam Tournaments

### ALL-TIME GRAND SLAM SINGLES WINS

| MEN | Australian | French | Wimbledon | U.S. | Total |
|---|---|---|---|---|---|
| Roger Federer (b. 1981)** | 3 | 1 | 6 | 5 | 15 |
| Pete Sampras (b. 1971) | 2 | 0 | 7 | 5 | 14 |
| Roy Emerson (b. 1936) | 6 | 2 | 2 | 2 | 12 |
| Bjorn Borg (b. 1956) | 0 | 6 | 5 | 0 | 11 |
| Rod Laver (b. 1938) | 3 | 2 | 4 | 2 | 11 |
| Bill Tilden (1893-1953) | * | 0 | 3 | 7 | 10 |
| **WOMEN** | | | | | |
| Margaret Smith-Court (b. 1942) | 11 | 5 | 3 | 5 | 24 |
| Steffi Graf (b. 1969) | 4 | 6 | 7 | 5 | 22 |
| Helen Wills Moody (1905-1998) | * | 4 | 8 | 7 | 19 |
| Chris Evert (b. 1954) | 2 | 7 | 3 | 6 | 18 |
| Martina Navratilova (b. 1956) | 3 | 2 | 9 | 4 | 18 |

*Never played in tournament. **Player active in 2009. Wins through 2009.*

## SPORTS SCRAMBLE

Unscramble the team name and match it with the athlete from that team.

A P M A T   B Y A   A Y R S
☐☐☐☐☐  ☐☐☐  ☐☐☐☐

Candace Parker

D O R N A L O   A M C I G
☐☐☐☐☐☐☐  ☐☐☐☐☐

Larry Fitzgerald

N E S O N A T I M   G N I I K S V
☐☐☐☐☐☐☐☐☐  ☐☐☐☐☐☐

Carl Crawford

Z A R O I N A   S L A D R A C I N
☐☐☐☐☐☐☐  ☐☐☐☐☐☐☐☐

Adrian Peterson

S O L   L E N G A S E   R A P S K S
☐☐☐  ☐☐☐☐☐☐☐  ☐☐☐☐☐☐

Dwight Howard

ANSWERS ON PAGES 334-336.

# X GAMES

The Summer X Games were first held in June 1995 in Newport, Rhode Island. The first Winter X Games followed two years later, in Big Bear Lake, California. Considered the Olympics of extreme sports, the X Games showcase fearless athletes who are always looking for new ways to go higher and faster and invent more outrageous tricks.

## Winter X Games
From January 21 to 25, 2009, athletes from all over the world competed in the 13th Winter X Games, in Aspen, Colorado. American Tyler Walker won his second gold medal in mono-skier X (a race for disabled sit-skiers). In the snowboard superpipe, Australian Torah Bright won the women's gold. Shaun White won both the men's superpipe and slopestyle events. The most surprising gold medalist may have been France's Xavier Bertoni. He won the ski superpipe over Tanner Hall, who was going for his fourth straight gold medal in the event.

▶ A mono-skier X athlete gets some air.

## Summer X Games
The 15th Summer X Games were held in Los Angeles from July 30 to August 2, 2009. Skateboarding icon Danny Way won the gold medal in a new event, the Big Air Rail Jam, and Paul Rodriguez won the Skateboard Street. Freestyle motocross rider Kyle Loza won his record third straight gold medal in the Men's Moto X Best Trick competition. In the BMX Big Air competition, Anthony Napolitan landed the first-ever double front flip on a bicycle—but didn't win a medal. On the women's side, Ashley Fiolek, who has been deaf since birth, won the Moto X Super X. **WEB SITE** *http://cxpn.go.com*

### did you know?
Speedboarder Gary Hardwick holds the record for the fastest speed reached on a skateboard, standing up without the aid of other vehicles or engines. Hardwick was clocked at 62.55 mph during a competition in Fountain Hills, Arizona, on September 26, 1998.

◀ Travis Pastrana

# X-FACT-ORS

✗ Perhaps the greatest moment in X Games history occurred in 1999, when skateboarding legend Tony Hawk landed the first-ever 900 (two and a half spins in the air) in history.

✗ During the 2006 X Games, Travis Pastrana performed the first double back flip on a motorcycle in competition in the Men's Freestyle Motocross. Pastrana won gold in the event.

✗ Through 2009, Shaun White had a record nine Winter X Games gold medals. In 2007, he won the Skateboard Vert at the Summer X Games—making him the first athlete to win gold medals in the Summer and Winter X Games.

# Technology & Computers

**What is a cookie?** ➡ **page 241**

## COMPUTER HIGHLIGHTS TIME LINE

**1623** — Wilhelm Schickard built the first machine that could automatically add, subtract, multiply, and divide. He called it a "calculating clock."

**1946** — The first electronic, programmable, general-purpose computer was invented. It was called ENIAC, for "Electronic Numerical Integrator and Computer."

**1967** — The Advanced Research Projects Agency (ARPA) allotted money toward creating a computer network. It became ARPAnet, which evolved into the Internet.

**1968** — The first hypertext system was built by Douglas Engelbart of Stanford Research Institute. Called NLS (oN Line System), the system's design allowed users to move text and data with a mouse (which Engelbart invented in 1963).

**1971** — The "floppy disk" was introduced by IBM as a means of affordable portable storage.

**1975** — The Altair 8800 entered the market. It was the first widely sold personal microcomputer.

**1975** — Bill Gates and Paul Allen founded Microsoft. Later came the first version of Windows.

**1977** — The Apple II, Apple's first fully packaged system with a keyboard, was introduced.

**1990** — The World Wide Web was first launched with one server by British physicist Tim Berners-Lee. He also created Uniform Resource Locators (URLs), the Hypertext Transfer Protocol (HTTP), and Hypertext Markup Language (HTML).

**1996** — Google, one of the Internet's most popular search engines, was founded.

**2001** — Apple introduced the iPod, a popular portable MP3/Media player.

**2003** — MySpace, the popular online community that allows Internet users to connect and share interests and pictures, was founded.

**2005** — YouTube, the popular video sharing service, was founded.

**2006** — The social networking site Facebook opened membership to anyone over the age of 13 who has a valid e-mail address.

**2007** — Apple released the Apple iPhone to the public. Amazon released its first Kindle, a device for downloading and reading electronic books and other digital media.

### Twitter
*Since it began in 2006, Twitter has quickly become indispensable to its 55 million monthly users. People can leave short messages called Tweets that are read by their followers. Twitter is even used by politicians, who use it to send news to their supporters.*

# COMPUTER TALK

**BIT**  The smallest unit of data

**BYTE**  An amount of data equal to 8 bits

**COOKIE**  Some websites store information like your password on your computer's hard drive. When you go back to that site later, your browser sends the information (the "cookie") to the website.

**DOWNLOAD**  To transfer information from a host computer to a personal computer through a network connection or modem

**ENCRYPTION**  The process of changing information into a code to keep others from reading it

**FLASH MEMORY**  Rewriteable ROM memory that saves information without power. Popular in handheld devices like memory cards or MP3 players.

**HTTP**  Hypertext Transfer Protocol is the method of file exchange used on the World Wide Web.

**MEGABYTE (MB)**  An amount of information equal to 1,048,516 bytes, or (in some situations) 1 million bytes

**NETWORK**  A group of computers linked together so that they can share information

**RAM OR RANDOM ACCESS MEMORY**  Memory your computer uses to open programs and store your work until you save it to a hard drive or disk. Information in RAM disappears when the computer is turned off.

**ROM OR READ ONLY MEMORY**  Memory that contains permanent instructions for the computer and cannot be changed. The information in ROM stays after the computer is turned off.

**SPYWARE**  Software that observes computer activity without the user's knowledge. May record key strokes or fill the screen with ads.

**URL OR UNIFORM RESOURCE LOCATOR**  The technical name for a website address

**VIRUS**  A program that damages other programs and data. It gets into a computer through the Internet or shared disks.

**WI-FI OR WIRELESS FIDELITY**  Technology that allows people to link to other computers and the Internet from their computers without wires.

# IM (INSTANT MESSAGE) DICTIONARY

**ATM**  At the moment

**B4N**  Bye for now

**BBS**  Be back soon

**BCNU**  Be seein' you

**BRB**  Be right back

**BTW**  By the way

**CSL**  Can't stop laughing

**GTG**  Got to go

**IDK**  I don't know

**IMHO**  In my humble opinion

**JK**  Just kidding

**K or KK**  OK

**LOL**  Laughing out loud

**NM**  Nothing much or Nevermind

**NP**  No problem

**OMG**  Oh my God

**OTP**  On the phone

**PPL**  People

**ROTFL**  Rolling on the floor laughing

**SRY**  Sorry

**THX**  Thanks

**TLDR**  Too long, didn't read

**TTFN**  Ta ta for now

**TTYL**  Talk to you later

**W00t**  (expression of joy)

**WTG**  Way to go

**WU?**  What's up?

## Using a Search Engine

A search engine is a tool that locates web pages according to keywords. Here are some of the most popular search engines and their addresses.

**Google**

http://www.google.com

**Yahoo**

http://www.yahoo.com

**Ask (Ask Jeeves)**

http://www.ask.com

**AltaVista**

http://www.altavista.com

**Bing**

http://www.bing.com

**HotBot**

http://www.hotbot.com

## Limit the Keyword Search

Before you start researching a topic, decide exactly what you need. Being as specific as possible makes it easier to find sites that have information about your topic. It can also help you evaluate the source.

As you search the internet, keep the following tips in mind.

> Be as specific as possible with the terms you use in your search. Suppose you have an assignment that asks you to describe three famous inventions of Thomas Edison. Search for: famous inventions Thomas Edison.

> Put words in quotes when you are searching for a specific phrase. Some search engines also have an "Advanced Search" tool that allows you to search for an exact wording or phrase.
To find out which president said, "I cannot live without books," type the exact phrase in quotation marks (as shown) to search.

> When you want two or more terms to appear in the search results, use the word AND (in caps) to connect the terms. You can also use the plus sign (+) to connect terms.
For example, to search for information on Davy Crockett and the Alamo, type: Davy Crockett AND Alamo, or Davy Crockett + Alamo.

> Try using a synonym if you are having trouble with your search. Suppose you are searching for the different ways in which moisture, or water, reaches the earth. Try searching for "forms of precipitation."

> Try different search engines if one isn't producing results. For example, if you are searching for information on popular culture, HotBot may be a better choice than Yahoo.

# Identify the Website

Huge amounts of information are on the Internet. While this makes the Internet great for research, not all sources are reliable. Recognize that a wide variety of information is available, from facts and data to stories and opinions.

The url ending in web addresses may offer clues to the type of web page. Government sites end in **.gov**. These sites are reliable sources for data and objective reports. Non-profit organizations end in **.org**. Educational institutions end in **.edu**. Business sites usually end in **.com** or **.net**. Official U.S. sites end in **.us** (for example, official state sites).

# Assessing the Website

Unlike published books, many web sources are not checked for accuracy. For this reason, it is very important to review the content and purpose of a website. It can be difficult to distinguish informative sites from those that try to sell products or have a special interest.

Examine the site carefully to make sure it appears reliable. Check that data and sources have references. Look for links to other sites with additional information. Also look for the date of creation of the web page.

Try to select sources that offer the following:
> author's name,
> date of page creation or version,
> and a list of sources.

# Citing a Website

To cite a website, include the **title of the web page**, the **name of the entire website, the organization that posted it** (this may be the same as the name of the website). Also include the full **date the page was created or last updated** (day, month, year if available), the **date you looked at it**, and the URL address (in < > brackets).

Example for the web page that identifies Thomas Jefferson as the president who said, "I cannot live without books."

Jefferson Library: Famous Jefferson Quotations. Th. Jefferson Monticello. September 2, 2008. <www.monticello.org/library/reference/famquote.html>

# Transportation

When did the Erie Canal open? ➡ page 245

## Getting from There to Here:
### A SHORT HISTORY OF TRANSPORTATION

**5000 B.C.**
People harness animal-muscle power. Oxen and donkeys carry heavy loads.

**3500 B.C.**
Egyptians create the first sailboat. Before this, people made rafts or canoes and paddled them with poles or their hands.

**983**
First locks to raise water level are built on China's Grand Canal. By 1400, a 1,500-mile water highway system was developed.

**1450s**
Portuguese build fast ships with three masts. These plus the compass usher in an age of exploration.

**1681**
France's 150-mile Canal du Midi connects the Atlantic Ocean with the Mediterranean Sea.

**5000 B.C.**

**3500 B.C.**
In Mesopotamia (modern-day Iraq), vehicles with wheels are invented. But the first wheels are made of heavy wood, and the roads are terrible.

**800**
Fast, shallow-draft longships make Vikings a powerful force in Europe from 800 to 1100.

**Around 1000**
Using magnetic compasses, Chinese are able to sail long distances in flat-bottomed ships called junks.

**1660s**
Horse-drawn stagecoaches begin running in France. They stop at "stages" to switch horses and passengers—the first mass transit system.

244

**1730s** Stagecoach service begins in the U.S.

**1783** In Paris, the Montgolfier brothers fly the first hot air balloon.

**1825** The 363-mile Erie Canal connects the Hudson River with Lake Erie, opening up the U.S. frontier and making New York City the nation's top port.

**1832** The first U.S. horse-drawn streetcar is driven up and down the Bowery in New York City.

**1769** James Watt patents the first successful steam engine.

**1807** Robert Fulton patents a highly efficient steamboat.

**1830** Inter-city passenger rail service begins in England with a steam engine built by George Stephenson. It goes about 24 miles per hour.

**1839** Kirkpatrick Macmillan of Scotland invents the first pedaled bicycle.

**1862** — Etienne Lenoir of Belgium builds the first car with an internal-combustion engine.

**1869** — Transcontinental railroad is completed at Promontory Point, Utah. The Suez Canal in Egypt opens, saving ships a long trip around Africa.

**1887** — First practical electric street railway system opens in the U.S. in Richmond, Virginia. Suburbs soon grow around cities as trolley systems let people live farther away from the workplace.

**1908** — Henry Ford builds the first Model T, a practical car for the general public.

**1860s** — Paddle-wheel steamboats dominate U.S. river travel.

**1863** — Using steam locomotives, the London subway (known as the "tube") opens.

**1873** — San Francisco's cable car system begins service.

**1897** — The first U.S. subway service begins in Boston. New York City follows in 1904.

**1903** — At Kitty Hawk, North Carolina, the Wright brothers fly the first powered heavier-than-air machine.

The first practical helicopter and first jet plane are invented. The jet flies up to 434 mph. Jet passenger service began in 1952.

**1939**

U.S. astronauts aboard *Apollo 11* land on the Moon.

**1969**

Trains cross under the English Channel in the new Channel Tunnel or "Chunnel."

**1994**

Now

**1914**

The 50-mile Panama Canal opens, saving ships a nearly 6,000-mile trip around South America.

**1964**

Shinkansen "bullet train" service (124 mph) begins in Japan.

**1981**

The first space shuttle was launched on April 12, 1981.

**2007**

Hybrid cars, which run on gasoline and batteries, are widely available.

**2009**

General Motors says its planned hybrid-electric car, the Chevy Volt, will get more than 200 miles per gallon of gasoline.

247

# Travel

Where is the world's largest tire? ➡ page 250

In the late 13th century, famed Italian adventurer Marco Polo took a winding 5,600-mile journey overland from Venice, Italy, to Beijing, China. When he returned to Venice, Polo published a chronicle of his travels. The stories were so fantastic that many people didn't believe his tales.

You may not be taking a journey of thousands of miles on your next trip, but the excitement of traveling is the same. People travel for all kinds of reasons—business, fun, or to see distant friends and relatives. But whatever the reason, people have always had the desire to stretch their legs, explore new places, and have adventures that others may—or may not—believe.

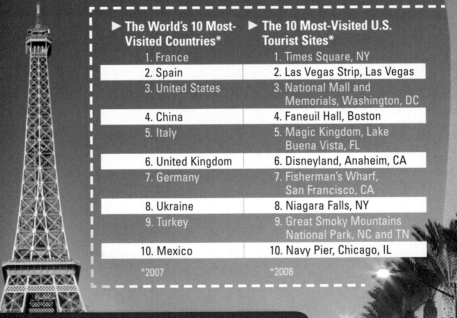

| ► The World's 10 Most-Visited Countries* | ► The 10 Most-Visited U.S. Tourist Sites* |
|---|---|
| 1. France | 1. Times Square, NY |
| 2. Spain | 2. Las Vegas Strip, Las Vegas |
| 3. United States | 3. National Mall and Memorials, Washington, DC |
| 4. China | 4. Faneuil Hall, Boston |
| 5. Italy | 5. Magic Kingdom, Lake Buena Vista, FL |
| 6. United Kingdom | 6. Disneyland, Anaheim, CA |
| 7. Germany | 7. Fisherman's Wharf, San Francisco, CA |
| 8. Ukraine | 8. Niagara Falls, NY |
| 9. Turkey | 9. Great Smoky Mountains National Park, NC and TN |
| 10. Mexico | 10. Navy Pier, Chicago, IL |
| *2007 | *2008 |

## World's Five Most-Visited Amusement Parks*

1. Magic Kingdom (Lake Buena Vista, Florida), 17.0 million
2. Disneyland (Anaheim, California), 14.7 million
3. Tokyo Disneyland (Japan), 14.3 million
4. Disneyland Paris (Marne-La-Vallee, France), 12.7 million
5. Universal Studios (Osaka, Japan), 8.3 million

*2008

# AMUSEMENT PARKS

The first amusement parks appeared in Europe more than 400 years ago. Attractions included flower gardens, bowling, music, and a few simple rides.

Today's amusement parks are much more impressive. With super-fast roller coasters, parades, shows, and other attractions, amusement parks now have something to amuse just about anyone. Here's a look at some of the most popular amusement parks in the U.S.

## FABULOUS FACTS

**Biggest Park:** Walt Disney World, Lake Buena Vista, Florida, 28,000 acres

**Most Rides:** 74, Cedar Point, Sandusky, Ohio

**Most Roller Coasters:** 17, Cedar Point, Sandusky, Ohio

**Fastest Roller Coaster:** 128 mph, Kingda Ka, Six Flags Great Adventure, Jackson, New Jersey

**Tallest Roller Coaster:** 456 feet, Kingda Ka, Six Flags Great Adventure, Jackson, New Jersey

Maverick roller coaster at Cedar Point.

▶ **Cedar Point (Sandusky, Ohio)** One of the oldest amusement parks in the U.S., Cedar Point (on Lake Erie) opened in 1870. Its first roller coaster, the Switchback Railway, opened in 1892. It had a then-dizzying 25-foot-high hill, on which riders traveled at about 10 mph. Today at Cedar Point, the Top Thrill Dragster roller coaster reaches a height of 420 feet, and the cars zip along at a top speed of 120 mph! There are also plenty of other attractions, including Soak City, which features water rides and a wave pool.

▶ **Water World (Denver, Colorado)** One of the largest water parks in the United States, Water World opened in 1982. There are 46 rides on its 64 acres. Among a wide variety of attractions are more family tube rides than any other water park in the U.S. and Wally World for young children. Voyage to the Center of the Earth is an enclosed tube ride that spans more than $\frac{1}{4}$-mile. The park also includes some of the highest water slides in the world (Flatline, Redline, and Pipeline), where riders can reach speeds of up to 40 miles per hour.

▶ **Universal Studios Florida/Islands of Adventure (Orlando, Florida)** Universal Studios opened in 1990 and visitors have been "riding the movies" there ever since. Rides, shows, and other attractions feature favorite movie and TV characters, like Shrek, and take visitors behind the scenes. Islands of Adventure has been open since 1999. The rides and attractions there pay tribute to favorite characters from books and comic books, like Spiderman, the Incredible Hulk, and Dr. Doom.

# ROAD TRIP

**W**herever you are, there is likely to be a festival, amusement park, historic site, or national park just a short drive away. A road trip—short or long—can be lots of fun, with plenty of interesting sights along the way.

The first cross-country drive was made in 1903. H. Nelson Jackson and Sewall K. Crocker (and a bulldog named Bud) drove from San Francisco to New York City in an early car known as a Winton. There were few roads or bridges in the West, and lots of mud everywhere. The whole trip took 63 days and cost $8,000, including the price of the car. In 1909, Alice Huyler Ramsey became the first woman to drive across the U.S. Her trip from New York to San Francisco took 59 days.

By 1930, there were 23 million cars on the road. More than half of American families owned one. (Today in the U.S. there are more vehicles than licensed drivers.) People wanted to see things and go places—especially west. The first coast-to-coast highway was the Lincoln Highway, which was finished by 1930. The most famous highway was Route 66, completed in 1926, connecting Chicago to Los Angeles. Now called "Historic Route 66," it still has billboards and giant statues advertising its famous hotels, attractions, and restaurants.

**H. Nelson Jackson**

# A ROADSIDE SAMPLER:

**Lunch Box Museum** Located in Columbus, Georgia, the Lunch Box Museum has more than 3,500 lunchboxes on display. Even though the boxes are old, you may recognize some of the cartoon and TV heroes on them. ▶

**Corn Palace** This huge concrete building in Mitchell, South Dakota, is covered with murals made of corn and other types of grains and grasses. No corny jokes please--they've heard them all here.

**World's Largest Tire** Located in Allen Park, Michigan, the Uniroyal Tire stands 80 feet tall. It was built for the 1964-65 World's Fair in New York. After the fair, it was moved to where it is now. In 1998, Uniroyal stabbed the tire with an 11-foot-long, 250-lb nail (the largest nail in the world) to show the toughness of Uniroyal tires. The nail was removed and sold. But the tire is as sturdy as ever.

**World's Largest Solar System Scale Model** This solar system model follows about 40 miles of highway U.S. 1 in northern Maine—from the sun, 50 feet in diameter, at the University of Maine at Presque Isle to tiny Pluto, 1 inch in diameter, mounted on a visitor center wall in Houlton. Area volunteers are planning to add the new dwarf planets, Ceres and Eris.

# THE NEW 7 WONDERS OF THE WORLD

The New Seven Wonders of the World were announced on July 7, 2007 (07/07/07). The winners were based on an online poll with over 100 million people voting from 200 countries.

The New 7 Wonders, all equal in rank, are:

**The Great Wall of China** (220 B.C.. and 1368-1644 A.D.), China

**Petra** (9 B.C.- 40 A.D.), Jordan

**The Roman Colosseum** (70-82 A.D.), Rome, Italy

**The Pyramid at Chichén Itzá** (before 800 A.D.), Yucatan Peninsula, Mexico

**Machu Picchu** (1460-1470), Peru

**Christ the Redeemer** (1931), Rio de Janiero, Brazil

**The Taj Mahal** (1630 A.D.), Agra, India

Other popular sites that were considered include the Great Pyramid of Giza in Egypt (the only remaining wonder of the ancient world), the Acropolis in Athens, the Eiffel Tower in Paris, Angkor in Cambodia, and the Moai statues of Easter Island.

# NATIONAL PARKS

The world's first national park was Yellowstone, established in 1872. Today in the U.S., there are 58 national parks, including parks in the Virgin Islands, Guam, Puerto Rico, and American Samoa. The National Park Service manages 391 units in all, including national monuments, memorials, battlefields, military parks, historic parks, historic sites, lakeshores, seashores, recreation areas, scenic rivers and trails, wilderness areas, and the White House—almost 85 million acres in all! For more information, you can write the National Park Service, Department of the Interior, 1849 C Street NW, Washington, D.C. 20240.

**WEB SITE** *www.nps.gov/parks.html*

**YOSEMITE NATIONAL PARK** This park, established in 1890, covers 761,266 acres in east-central California. It has the world's largest concentration of granite domes—mountain-like rocks that were created by glaciers millions of years ago. You can see many of them rising thousands of feet above the valley floor. Two of the most famous are Half Dome, which looks smooth and rounded, and El Capitan, which is the biggest single granite rock on Earth. Skilled climbers come from all over the world to scale this 3,000-foot-high wall of rock. Yosemite Falls, which drops 2,425 feet, is the highest waterfall in North America. It is actually two waterfalls, called the upper and lower falls, connected by a series of smaller waterfalls. Yosemite also features lakes, meadows, and giant sequoia trees, and is home to bighorn sheep and bears.

**GRAND CANYON NATIONAL PARK**
This national park, established in 1919, has one of the world's most spectacular landscapes, covering more than a million acres in northwestern Arizona. The canyon is 6,000 feet deep at its deepest point and 15 miles wide at its widest. Most of the 40 identified rock layers that form the canyon's 277-mile-long wall are exposed, offering a detailed look at the Earth's geologic history. The walls display a cross section of the Earth's crust from as far back as two billion years ago. The Colorado River—which carved out the giant canyon—still runs through the park, which is a valuable wildlife preserve with many rare, endangered animals. The pine and fir forests, painted deserts, plateaus, caves, and sandstone canyons offer a wide range of habitats.

**DENALI NATIONAL PARK** Located in the southern part of the Alaska Mountain Range in the south central part of Alaska, Denali is home to North America's highest mountain, 20,320-foot Mt. McKinley. The park was originally established in 1917 as Mount McKinley National Park, but it was expanded in 1980 and renamed Denali National Park and Preserve. Denali covers more than 6 million acres and is almost as big as the state of Massachusetts. The park is also teeming with wildlife. Among many other animals, it's possible to see what are known in Denali as the "Denali Big Five": caribou, Dall sheep, grizzly bears, moose, and wolves. Denali is the only national park that is patrolled mostly by staff riding on dog sleds.

**OLYMPIC NATIONAL PARK** This park was established in 1938 to preserve some of Washington's old growth forests. The park, located in the northwestern part of Washington state, covers 922,651 acres. Three distinctly different ecosystems lie within Olympic National Park. It includes coastal beaches, temperate rain forest valleys, and glacier capped mountains. There are 73 miles of wilderness coast along the Pacific Ocean. Less than 33 miles east of the ocean lies Mount Olympus, the highest peak in the Olympus range. With 60 named glaciers, Mount Olympus has the third largest glacial system in the lower 48 states. Forest communities include subalpine, montane, lowland, temperate rain forest, and coastal. The lush temperate rain forest, one of the few remaining in the world, has moderate temperatures and gets from 140 to 167 inches of rain each year.

**YELLOWSTONE NATIONAL PARK** Located mostly in northwestern Wyoming and partly in eastern Idaho and southwestern Montana, Yellowstone is known for its 10,000 hot springs and geysers—more than anyplace else in the world. Old Faithful, the most famous geyser, erupts for about four minutes every one to two hours, shooting 3,700-8,400 gallons of hot water as high as 185 feet. Other geysers include the Giant, which shoots a column of hot water 200 feet high, and the Giantess, which erupts for over four hours at a time, but only about two times per year. There are grizzly bears, wolves, elk, moose, buffalo, deer, beavers, coyotes, antelopes, and 300 species of birds. The use of snowmobiles in the park has been a big controversy. Some people want to ban them because of noise and air pollution; others disagree. They are allowed now, but their use is somewhat limited.

# United States

What is the Bill of Rights? ➡ page 257

## FACTS &FIGURES

| | | |
|---|---|---|
| AREA | 50 states and Washington, D.C. | |
| LAND | 3,537,437 square miles | |
| WATER | 181,272 square miles | |
| TOTAL | 3,718,709 square miles | |

POPULATION (Sept. 2009):
307,524,279

CAPITAL:
WASHINGTON, D.C.

*Willis Tower*

## LARGEST, HIGHEST, and OTHER STATISTICS

| | |
|---|---|
| Largest state: | Alaska (663,267 square miles) |
| Smallest state: | Rhode Island (1,545 square miles) |
| Northernmost city: | Barrow, Alaska (71°17′ north latitude) |
| Southernmost city: | Hilo, Hawaii (19°44′ north latitude) |
| Easternmost city: | Eastport, Maine (66°59′ west longitude) |
| Westernmost city: | Atka, Alaska (174°12′ west longitude) |
| Highest settlement: | Climax, Colorado (11,360 feet) |
| Lowest settlement: | Calipatria, California (184 feet below sea level) |
| Oldest national park: | Yellowstone National Park (Idaho, Montana, Wyoming), 2,219,791 acres, established 1872 |
| Largest national park: | Wrangell-St. Elias, Alaska (8,323,148 acres) |
| Longest river system: | Mississippi-Missouri-Red Rock (3,710 miles) |
| Deepest lake: | Crater Lake, Oregon (1,932 feet) |
| Highest mountain: | Mount McKinley, Alaska (20,320 feet) |
| Lowest point: | Death Valley, California (282 feet below sea level) |
| Tallest building: | Willis Tower, Chicago, Illinois (1,450 feet) |
| Tallest structure: | TV tower, Blanchard, North Dakota (2,063 feet) |
| Longest bridge span: | Verrazano-Narrows Bridge, New York (4,260 feet) |
| Highest bridge: | Royal Gorge, Colorado (1,053 feet above water) |

did you know?

Although the bald eagle was chosen as the national bird as early as 1782, the congressional committee named to choose the national symbol also considered the phoenix, the rooster, and the dove. Ben Franklin had his own idea for the honor—the turkey.

# SYMBOLS OF THE UNITED STATES

## The Great Seal

The Great Seal of the United States shows an American bald eagle with a ribbon in its mouth bearing the Latin words *e pluribus unum* (out of many, one). In its talons are the arrows of war and an olive branch of peace. On the back of the Great Seal is an unfinished pyramid with an eye (the eye of Providence) above it. The seal was approved by Congress on June 20, 1782.

## The Flag

The flag of the United States has 50 stars (one for each state) and 13 stripes (one for each of the original 13 states). It is unofficially called the "Stars and Stripes."

The first U.S. flag was commissioned by the Second Continental Congress in 1777 but did not exist until 1783, after the American Revolution. Historians are not certain who designed the Stars and Stripes. Many different flags are believed to have been used during the American Revolution.

**1777**

The flag of 1777 was used until 1795. In that year, Congress passed an act ordering that a new flag have 15 stripes, alternate red and white, and 15 stars on a blue field. In 1818, Congress directed that the flag have 13 stripes and that a new star be added for each new state of the Union. The last star was added in 1960 for the state of Hawaii.

**1795**

There are many customs for flying the flag and treating it with respect. For example, it should not touch the floor and no other flag should be flown above it, except for the UN flag at UN headquarters. When the flag is raised or lowered, or passes in a parade, or during the Pledge of Allegiance, people should face it and stand at attention. Those in military uniform should salute. Others should put their right hand over their heart. The flag is flown at half-staff as a sign of mourning.

**1818**

## Pledge of Allegiance to the Flag

"I pledge allegiance to the flag of the United States of America and to the republic for which it stands, one nation under God, indivisible, with liberty and justice for all."

## The National Anthem

"The Star-Spangled Banner" was a poem written in 1814 by Francis Scott Key as he watched British ships bombard Fort McHenry, Maryland, during the War of 1812. It became the National Anthem by an act of Congress in 1931. The music to "The Star-Spangled Banner" was originally a tune called "Anacreon in Heaven."

# THE U.S. CONSTITUTION

## The Foundation of American Government

The Constitution is the document that created the present government of the United States. It was written in 1787 and went into effect in 1789. It establishes the three branches of the U.S. government — the executive (headed by the president), the legislative (Congress), and the judicial (the Supreme Court and other federal courts). The first 10 amendments to the Constitution (the **Bill of Rights**) explain the basic rights of all American citizens.

**You can find the constitution on-line at:**
**WEB SITE** *www.archives.gov/exhibits/ charters/constitution.html.*

## THE PREAMBLE TO THE CONSTITUTION

**The Constitution begins with a short statement called the Preamble. The Preamble states that the government of the United States was established by the people.**

"We the people of the United States, in order to form a more perfect union, establish justice, insure domestic tranquility, provide for the common defense, promote the general welfare, and secure the blessings of liberty to ourselves and our posterity, do ordain and establish this Constitution for the United States of America."

## THE ARTICLES

The original Constitution contained seven articles. The first three articles of the Constitution establish the three branches of the U.S. government.

**Article 1, Legislative Branch** Creates the Senate and House of Representatives and describes their functions and powers.

**Article 2, Executive Branch** Creates the office of the President and the Electoral College and lists their powers and responsibilities.

**Article 3, Judicial Branch** Creates the Supreme Court and gives Congress the power to create lower courts. The powers of the courts and certain crimes are defined.

**Article 4, The States** Discusses the relationship of the states to one another and to the citizens. Defines the states' powers.

**Article 5, Amending the Constitution** Describes how the Constitution can be amended (changed).

**Article 6, Federal Law** Makes the Constitution the supreme law of the land over state laws and constitutions.

**Article 7, Ratifying the Constitution** Establishes how to ratify (approve) the Constitution.

# Amendments to the Constitution

The writers of the Constitution understood that it might need to be amended, or changed, in the future, but they wanted to be careful and made it hard to change. Article 5 describes how the Constitution can be amended.

In order to take effect, an amendment must be approved by a two-thirds majority in both the House of Representatives and the Senate. It must then be approved (ratified) by three-fourths of the states (38 states). So far, there have been 27 amendments. One of them (the 18th, ratified in 1919) banned the manufacture or sale of liquor. It was canceled by the 21st Amendment, in 1933.

## The Bill of Rights: The First Ten Amendments

The first ten amendments were adopted in 1791 and contain the basic freedoms Americans enjoy as a people. These amendments are known as the Bill of Rights.

1. Guarantees freedom of religion, speech, and the press.
2. Guarantees the right to have firearms.
3. Guarantees that soldiers cannot be lodged in private homes unless the owner agrees.
4. Protects people from being searched or having property searched or taken away by the government without reason.
5. Protects rights of people on trial for crimes.
6. Guarantees people accused of crimes the right to a speedy public trial by jury.
7. Guarantees the right to a trial by jury for other kinds of cases.
8. Prohibits "cruel and unusual punishments."
9. Says specific rights listed in the Constitution do not take away rights that may not be listed.
10. Establishes that any powers not given specifically to the federal government belong to states or the people.

## Other Important Amendments

13 (1865): Ends slavery in the United States.

14 (1868): Bars states from denying rights to citizens; guarantees equal protection under the law for all citizens.

15 (1870): Guarantees that a person cannot be denied the right to vote because of race or color.

19 (1920): Gives women the right to vote.

22 (1951): Limits the president to two four-year terms of office.

24 (1964): Outlaws the poll tax (a tax people had to pay before they could vote) in federal elections. (The poll tax had been used to keep African Americans in the South from voting.)

25 (1967): Specifies presidential succession; also gives the president the power to appoint a new vice president, if one dies or leaves office in the middle of a term.

26 (1971): Lowers the voting age to 18 from 21.

# THE EXECUTIVE BRANCH

The **executive branch** of the federal government is headed by the president, who enforces the laws passed by Congress and is commander in chief of the U.S. armed forces. It also includes the vice president, people who work for the president or vice president, the major departments of the government, and special agencies. The **cabinet** is made up of the vice president, heads of major departments, and other officials. It meets when the president chooses. The chart at right shows cabinet departments in the order in which they were created. The Department of Homeland Security was created by a law signed in November 2002.

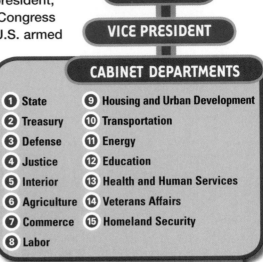

**PRESIDENT**

**VICE PRESIDENT**

### CABINET DEPARTMENTS

1. State
2. Treasury
3. Defense
4. Justice
5. Interior
6. Agriculture
7. Commerce
8. Labor
9. Housing and Urban Development
10. Transportation
11. Energy
12. Education
13. Health and Human Services
14. Veterans Affairs
15. Homeland Security

## How Long Does the President Serve?

The president serves a four-year term, starting on January 20. No president can be elected more than twice, or more than once if he or she had served two years as president filling out the term of a president who left office.

## What Happens If the President Dies?

If the president dies in office or cannot complete the term, the vice president becomes president. If the president is unable to perform his or her duties, the vice president can become acting president. The next person to become president after the vice president would be the Speaker of the House of Representatives.

**The White House has an address on the World Wide Web. It is:**

**WEB SITE** *www.whitehouse.gov*

**You can send e-mail to the president at:**

**EMAIL** *president@whitehouse.gov*

*The White House, home of the U.S. president*

## Voter Turnout in Presidential Elections, 1968-2008

(Percent of voting age, 18 and over in 1972 and afterwards, 21 and over in 1968.)

| Year | Turnout | Year | Turnout |
|------|---------|------|---------|
| 1968 | 60.7% | 1992 | 55.2% |
| 1972 | 55.1% | 1996 | 49.0% |
| 1976 | 53.6% | 2000 | 50.3% |
| 1980 | 52.8% | 2004 | 55.5% |
| 1984 | 53.3% | 2008 | 58.2% |
| 1988 | 50.3% | | |

Source: U.S. Census Bureau

# THE LEGISLATIVE BRANCH

## CONGRESS

The Congress of the United States is the legislative branch of the federal government. Congress's major responsibility is to pass the laws that govern the country and determine how money collected in taxes is spent. It is the president's responsibility to enforce the laws. Congress consists of two parts—the Senate and the House of Representatives. ▶

## THE SENATE

The Senate has 100 members, two from each state. The Constitution says that the Senate will have equal representation (the same number of representatives) from each state. Thus, small states have the same number of senators as large states. Senators are elected for six-year terms. There is no limit on the number of terms a senator can serve.

The Senate also has the responsibility of approving people the president appoints for certain jobs: for example, cabinet members and Supreme Court justices. The Senate must approve all treaties by at least a two-thirds vote. It also has the responsibility under the Constitution of putting on trial high-ranking federal officials who have been impeached by the House of Representatives.

**WEB SITE** *www.senate.gov*

*The Capitol, where Congress meets*

## THE HOUSE OF REPRESENTATIVES

The number of members of the House of Representatives for each state depends on its population according to a recent census. But each state has at least one representative, no matter how small its population. A term lasts two years.

The first House of Representatives in 1789 had 65 members. As the country's population grew, the number of representatives increased. Since 1911, however, the total membership has been kept at 435. After the results of Census 2000 were added up, 8 states gained seats and 10 states lost seats.

**WEB SITE** *www.house.gov*

# The House of Representatives, by State

Here are the numbers of representatives each state had in 2010, compared with earlier times:

| | 2010 | 1995 | 1975 | | 2010 | 1995 | 1975 |
|---|---|---|---|---|---|---|---|
| Alabama | 7 | 7 | 7 | Montana | 1 | 1 | 2 |
| Alaska | 1 | 1 | 1 | Nebraska | 3 | 3 | 3 |
| Arizona | 8 | 6 | 4 | Nevada | 3 | 2 | 1 |
| Arkansas | 4 | 4 | 4 | New Hampshire | 2 | 2 | 2 |
| California | 53 | 52 | 43 | New Jersey | 13 | 13 | 15 |
| Colorado | 7 | 6 | 5 | New Mexico | 3 | 3 | 2 |
| Connecticut | 5 | 6 | 6 | New York | 29 | 31 | 39 |
| Delaware | 1 | 1 | 1 | North Carolina | 13 | 12 | 11 |
| Florida | 25 | 23 | 15 | North Dakota | 1 | 1 | 1 |
| Georgia | 13 | 11 | 10 | Ohio | 18 | 19 | 23 |
| Hawaii | 2 | 2 | 2 | Oklahoma | 5 | 6 | 6 |
| Idaho | 2 | 2 | 2 | Oregon | 5 | 5 | 4 |
| Illinois | 19 | 20 | 24 | Pennsylvania | 19 | 21 | 25 |
| Indiana | 9 | 10 | 11 | Rhode Island | 2 | 2 | 2 |
| Iowa | 5 | 5 | 6 | South Carolina | 6 | 6 | 6 |
| Kansas | 4 | 4 | 5 | South Dakota | 1 | 1 | 2 |
| Kentucky | 6 | 6 | 7 | Tennessee | 9 | 9 | 9 |
| Louisiana | 7 | 7 | 8 | Texas | 32 | 30 | 24 |
| Maine | 2 | 2 | 2 | Utah | 3 | 3 | 2 |
| Maryland | 8 | 8 | 8 | Vermont | 1 | 1 | 1 |
| Massachusetts | 10 | 10 | 12 | Virginia | 11 | 11 | 10 |
| Michigan | 15 | 16 | 19 | Washington | 9 | 9 | 7 |
| Minnesota | 8 | 8 | 8 | West Virginia | 3 | 3 | 4 |
| Mississippi | 4 | 5 | 5 | Wisconsin | 8 | 9 | 9 |
| Missouri | 9 | 9 | 10 | Wyoming | 1 | 1 | 1 |

Washington, D.C., Puerto Rico, American Samoa, Guam, and the Virgin Islands each have one nonvoting member of the House of Representatives.

## HOUSE COMMITTEES

The House creates committees for a variety of reasons. The members of a committee work together to study national problems and suggest solutions. They propose laws that are debated and then voted on by the whole House.

In committee hearings and meetings, members are presented with information about the issues related to the proposed law. They may question experts, review documents and exhibits, and discuss the material presented. Committees then draft a bill, rewrite a bill, or revise a bill. Next, the committee can vote to send the bill to the House Chamber for debate or to another committee. If not passed on, the bill usually "dies" in committee.

The U.S. House of Representatives has twenty standing (permanent) committees.

- Agriculture
- Appropriations
- Armed Services
- Budget
- Education and Labor
- Energy and Commerce
- Financial Services
- Foreign Affairs
- Homeland Security
- House Administration
- Judiciary
- Natural Resources
- Oversight and Government Reform
- Rules
- Science and Technology
- Small Business
- Standards of Official Conduct
- Transportation and Infrastructure
- Veterans' Affairs
- Ways and Means

# THE JUDICIAL BRANCH

## The Supreme Court

The highest court in the United States is the Supreme Court. It has nine justices who are appointed for life by the president with the approval of the Senate. Eight of the nine members are called associate justices. The ninth is the Chief Justice, who presides over the Court's meetings.

## What Does the Supreme Court Do?

The Supreme Court's major responsibilities are to judge cases that involve reviewing federal laws, actions of the president, treaties of the United States, and laws passed by state governments to be sure they do not conflict with the U.S. Constitution. If the Supreme Court finds that a law or action violates the Constitution, the law is struck down.

## The Supreme Court's Decision Is Final.

Most cases must go through other state courts or federal courts before they reach the Supreme Court. The Supreme Court is the final court for a case, and the justices decide which cases they will review. After the Supreme Court hears a case, it may agree or disagree with the decision by a lower court. Each justice has one vote, and the majority rules. When the Supreme Court makes a ruling, its decision is final, so each of the justices has a very important job.

Below are the nine justices who were on the Supreme Court in October 2009, with President Obama and Vice President Biden. The justices are (from left to right) Samuel Alito, Ruth Bader Ginsburg, Arthur Kennedy, John Paul Stevens, Chief Justice John Roberts, Sonia Sotomayor, Antonin Scalia, Clarence Thomas, and Stephen Breyer.

# 2008 ELECTION

What state has the most electoral votes? ➡ page 269

## The Winning Team

**A**fter a wild and crazy primary season and then a hard-fought fall campaign, Barack Obama was elected in November 2008 as the 44th President of the United States. He and Vice President Joe Biden took office on January 20, 2009.

### President Barack Obama

Born in Honolulu, Hawaii, in 1961, Barack Obama graduated from Columbia University in 1983. He became a community organizer in Chicago, helping poor residents cope with a wave of unemployment. He then attended Harvard Law School, where he became the first African-American editor of the *Harvard Law Review*. After graduating, Obama practiced civil-rights law, taught in law school, and served in the Illinois state senate. He gained national attention by giving a rousing keynote speech at the Democratic National Convention in 2004, and he was elected to the U.S. Senate later that year. In 2007, he began his campaign for president, promising to bring change to Washington.

He and his wife, Michelle, have two children, Malia and Sasha.

### Vice President Joe Biden

Joe Biden was born in 1942, in Scranton, Pennsylvania. He is a lawyer by profession. In 1972, he was elected to the U.S. Senate, representing the state of Delaware. He served in the Senate for 35 years and became known as an expert on foreign policy. In the summer of 2008, Obama chose him to be his running mate.

## What Does the President Do?

According to the U.S. Constitution, the president is the chief executive, or head, of the executive branch of the government. The president has a role in all parts of government. Following are some of the president's jobs:

★ Suggest laws to Congress;

★ Send Congress a budget which recommends how the government should raise and spend money;

★ Approve or veto (reject) bills passed by Congress;

★ Is commander-in-chief of the U.S. armed forces;

★ Make treaties, or agreements, with other countries;

★ Appoint justices to the Supreme Court and judges to other federal courts.

The president must share power with the other two branches of government. They are the legislative branch, or Congress, and the judicial branch, headed by the U.S. Supreme Court.

The U.S. Constitution tells how each of the three branches of government checks, or limits, the powers of the other two. This system of checks and balances is intended to prevent any branch from becoming too powerful.

☆ ☆ ☆ ☆ ☆

## What Does the Vice President Do?

John Adams, the first vice president, found the job very frustrating. He described it as "the most insignificant office that ever the invention of man contrived or his imagination conceived." But the vice president is just a heartbeat away from the presidency.

According to our Constitution, the vice president has two major duties. First, the vice president must be ready to become president if the president dies, resigns, or is removed from office. Second, the vice president presides over the Senate and casts the deciding vote in case of a tie.

# Popular and Electoral Votes*

| | John McCain | | Barack Obama | |
|---|---|---|---|---|
| | Popular Votes | Electoral Votes | Popular Votes | Electoral Votes |
| Alabama | 1,266,546 | 9 | 813,479 | |
| Alaska | 193,841 | 3 | 123,594 | |
| Arizona | 1,230,111 | 10 | 1,034,707 | |
| Arkansas | 638,017 | 6 | 422,310 | |
| California | 5,011,781 | | 8;274,473 | 55 |
| Colorado | 1,073,589 | | 1,288,576 | 9 |
| Connecticut | 629,428 | | 997,772 | 7 |
| Delaware | 152,374 | | 255,394 | 3 |
| District of Columbia | 17,367 | | 245,200 | 3 |
| Florida | 4,045,624 | | 4,282,074 | 27 |
| Georgia | 2,048,744 | 15 | 1,844,137 | |
| Hawaii | 120,566 | | 325,871 | 4 |
| Idaho | 403,012 | 4 | 236,440 | |
| Illinois | 2,031,527 | | 3,419,673 | 21 |
| Indiana | 1,345,648 | | 1,374,039 | 11 |
| Iowa | 682,379 | | 828,940 | 7 |
| Kansas | 699,655 | 6 | 514,765 | |
| Kentucky | 1,048,462 | 8 | 751,985 | |
| Louisiana | 1,148,275 | 9 | 782,989 | |
| Maine | 295,273 | | 421,923 | 4 |
| Maryland | 959,862 | | 1,629,467 | 10 |
| Massachusetts | 1,108,854 | | 1,904,097 | 12 |
| Michigan | 2,048,639 | | 2,872,579 | 17 |
| Minnesota | 1,275,409 | | 1,573,354 | 10 |
| Mississippi | 724,597 | 6 | 554,662 | |
| Missouri | 1,445,814 | 11 | 1,441,991 | |

* Official results from the Federal Election Commission

| | John McCain | | Barack Obama | |
|---|---|---|---|---|
| | Popular Votes | Electoral Votes | Popular Votes | Electoral Votes |
| **Montana** | 242,763 | 3 | 231,667 | |
| **Nebraska** | 452,979 | 4 | 333,319 | 1 |
| **Nevada** | 412,827 | | 533,736 | 5 |
| **New Hampshire** | 316,534 | | 384,826 | 4 |
| **New Jersey** | 1,613,207 | | 2,215,422 | 15 |
| **New Mexico** | 346,832 | | 472,422 | 5 |
| **New York** | 2,742,298 | | 4,769,700 | 31 |
| **North Carolina** | 2,128,474 | | 2,142,651 | 15 |
| **North Dakota** | 168,601 | 3 | 141,278 | |
| **Ohio** | 2,674,491 | | 2,933,388 | 20 |
| **Oklahoma** | 960,165 | 7 | 502,496 | |
| **Oregon** | 738,475 | | 1,037,291 | 7 |
| **Pennsylvania** | 2,655,885 | | 3,276,363 | 21 |
| **Rhode Island** | 165,391 | | 296,571 | 4 |
| **South Carolina** | 1,034,896 | 8 | 862,449 | |
| **South Dakota** | 203,054 | 3 | 170,924 | |
| **Tennessee** | 1,479,178 | 11 | 1,087,437 | |
| **Texas** | 4,479,328 | 34 | 3,528,633 | |
| **Utah** | 596,030 | 5 | 327,670 | |
| **Vermont** | 98,974 | | 219,262 | 3 |
| **Virginia** | 1,725,005 | | 1,959,532 | 13 |
| **Washington** | 1,229,216 | | 1,750,848 | 11 |
| **West Virginia** | 397,466 | 5 | 303,857 | |
| **Wisconsin** | 1,262,393 | | 1,677,211 | 10 |
| **Wyoming** | 164,958 | 3 | 82,868 | |
| **TOTALS** | 59,934,814 | 173 | 69,456,897 | 365 |

# How Candidates Are Chosen

**Democratic candidates for president held their first debate in April 2007.**

The candidates for president in each of the major political parties – the Democratic Party and the Republican Party – face one another in a series of primaries and caucuses. A primary gives a state's voters a chance to help choose their party's candidate. In a caucus, party members and leaders meet in small groups to vote for a candidate.

The primary season begins in January of the election year and ends in June. During that time, every state holds either a primary or a caucus. Some hold both! In 2008 the first caucus, traditionally held in Iowa, took place on January 3. The first primary, always held in New Hampshire, was on January 8.

All the candidates took part in many television debates. They traveled from state to state to campaign. Most of the candidates began to drop out of the race early in 2008 because they had done poorly in the primaries and caucuses. Lack of money made it hard for those candidates to continue running.

By March, Arizona Senator John McCain had won enough votes to be certain that he would become the Republican **nominee**, or official candidate. On the Democratic side, New York Senator Hillary Clinton, the former First Lady, had been expected to wrap up the nomination; instead she fell behind Barack Obama. The race was very tight, but by early June, Obama had enough votes to win the Democratic nomination.

The nominees of the Democratic and Republican parties are officially chosen at each party's **national convention**. The people who vote at conventions are called **delegates**.

The candidates of the Democratic and Republican parties are not the only ones running for president. Several so-called third parties also have presidential candidates. Third-party candidates usually suggest different solutions to problems than the Republican and Democratic party candidates.

**Republican presidential candidates held their first debate in May 2007.**

## Who Can Be President?

The qualifications for being president are set by the U.S. Constitution. To become president a person must:

▶ be a native-born citizen of the United States
▶ be at least 35 years old, and
▶ have been a resident of the United States for at least 14 years.

# THE ELECTION PROCESS

## The Road to the White House

**P**ennsylvania Avenue may look flat, but the road candidates take to the White House is anything but smooth! Presidential hopefuls campaign for up to two years, facing off in debates and meeting with voters. Here's a look at key steps in the process for the 2008 election, starting at the beginning of the election year.

**January–June 2008**

**1**

**Primaries/Caucuses**
Candidates in a party compete in **primaries** and **caucuses**. In a typical primary, party members cast ballots for a candidate. In a typical caucus, party members and leaders meet to choose a candidate. For each state a candidate wins, he or she secures **delegates**, or representatives.

**Aug. 25–28 (Democrats)**
**Sept. 1–4 (Republicans)**

**2**

**Nominating Conventions**
Delegates vote on a party **platform**, which says how the party wants to solve the nation's problems. Then delegates select the official presidential and vice presidential nominees. Delegates tend to vote based on their states' primary or caucus results.

**Nov. 4, 2008**

**3**

**Election Day**
Election Day is the first Tuesday after the first Monday in November. Every four years on that day, Americans head to the polls to vote for the next president. Voters don't choose the president directly. Their votes go toward **electors**, special delegates who make up the Electoral College.

**4**

**Electoral College Vote**
The Electoral College is made up of electors from every state. The candidate who wins the most votes in a state on Election Day almost always receives that state's electoral votes. A candidate must win at least 270 electoral votes to become the president.

**Dec. 15, 2008**

**5**

**Congress Declares Winner**
Members of Congress officially count the electoral votes. The president of the Senate, a position held by the vice president, announces the results.

**Jan. 6, 2009**

**6**

**Inauguration Day**
The new president takes the oath of office and gives an inaugural address outlining his or her goals. Later, the president celebrates at festive parties called **inaugural balls** in Washington, D.C.

**Jan. 20, 2009**

# Who Can Vote?

**V**oting rules vary from state to state. However, rules in each state must agree with the Constitution, its amendments, and federal laws. States allow voters who must be away or who are serving in the military on Election Day to vote by mail using an absentee ballot. A growing number of states allow anyone to vote before Election Day.

Some states require voters to have an I.D. that was issued by the state, such as a driver's license. In some states, people convicted of a felony lose the right to vote for the rest of their lives.

### These are the qualifications for voting in the United States:

- ☑ U.S. citizenship
- ☑ At least 18 years old
- ☑ Registration: citizens must register, or sign up, before voting *(required except in North Dakota)*

## Who Does Vote?

Everyone has heard the statement, "Every vote counts." Well, it's true. A remarkably small number of votes can be the margin between victory and defeat. In 2000, for example, George W. Bush defeated Al Gore in Florida by only 537 votes and became president!

The 2008 election stirred a lot of interest. Increased numbers of young people and members of minority groups went to the polls in November. But many people still did not vote, and in the end the level of voter turnout was only slightly higher than it had been four years earlier.

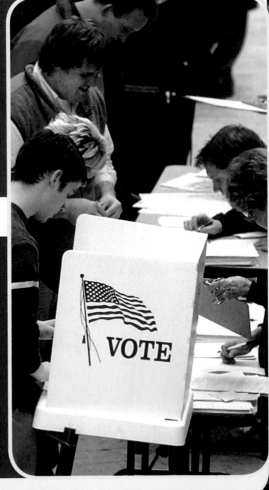

# Electing a President

## Who elects the president?

The president is actually elected by a group of "electors" known as the Electoral College. Members of this group from each state meet in December in their state capitals to cast their votes.

## But I thought Election Day was in November!

It is, but on Election Day voters don't directly vote for president. Instead, they vote for a group of presidential electors who have pledged to support whichever candidate wins that state's popular vote.

## What's the total number of electoral votes?

There are 538 total votes. A presidential candidate must win at least 270 of those.

## How many electoral votes does each state get?

Each state gets one vote for each of its senators (2) and one for each of its members in the House of Representatives. Also Washington, D.C., has 3 electoral votes.

## What if there's a tie in the end?

Then the election is in the hands of the U.S. House of Representatives. That's what happened in 1801, after Thomas Jefferson and Aaron Burr each received an equal number of electoral votes in the 1800 election. The House then voted to make Jefferson president.

Electoral College MAP

WA 11
AK 3
OR 7
ID 4
MT 3
WY 3
ND 3
SD 3
MN 10
WI 10
MI 17
NY 31
VT 3
NH 4
ME 4
MA 12
RI 4
CT 7
NJ 15
DE 3
MD 10
DC 3
NV 5
UT 5
CO 9
NE 5
IA 7
IL 21
IN 11
OH 20
PA 21
WV 5
VA 13
HI 4
CA 55
AZ 10
NM 5
KS 6
MO 11
KY 8
TN 11
NC 15
SC 8
OK 7
AR 6
MS 6
AL 9
GA 15
TX 34
LA 9
FL 27

**2008 Election**
■ Won by McCain
■ Won by Obama

Note: Of Nebraska's 5 electoral votes, John McCain received four electoral votes; Barack Obama received one.

On November 4, 2008, Barack Obama won about 53 percent of the popular vote. But what really counted was the electoral votes. He picked up 365 of them, from 29 states and the District of Columbia, more than enough for a majority.

*Can a candidate who didn't win the most popular votes still win a majority of electoral votes?*
Yes. That's what happened in 1876, 1888, and again in 2000, when George W. Bush was elected to a first term.

# ★ ★ Inauguration ★ ★
# Scramble Speech

## Scrambled Speech

"I do _____ swear (or affirm) that
*lmnloyse*

I will faithfully _____ the Office
*teuceex*

of _____ of the United States,
*snetpidre*

and will to the best of my _____,
*iyliatb*

_____, protect and _____
*pevreers*                                *nedfed*

the Constitution of the United States."

## Word Bank

**ability** *(noun):* skill or power

**defend** *(verb):* to guard or stand up for

**execute** *(verb):* to carry out or perform

**preserve** *(verb):* to care for or maintain

**president** *(noun):* chief elected official of a republic

**solemnly** *(adverb):* thoughtfully or seriously

★ ★ ★

After taking the oath, the new president gives an inaugural address. The speech explains how the president plans to solve the country's problems.

★ ★ ★

# Trivia About Inaugurations

**1793** ▶ George Washington's was the shortest inaugural address at 135 words.

**1801** ▶ Thomas Jefferson was the only president to walk to and from his inaugural. He was also the first to be inaugurated at the Capitol.

**1809** ▶ The first inaugural ball was held for James Madison.

**1825** ▶ John Quincy Adams was the first president sworn in wearing long trousers.

**1841** ▶ William H. Harrison's was the longest inaugural address at 8,445 words. Despite a snowstorm, Harrison did not wear an overcoat, hat, or gloves during his nearly two-hour Inaugural Address. He died of pneumonia one month later.

**1857** ▶ The first inauguration to be photographed was James Buchanan's.

**1865** ▶ Abraham Lincoln was the first to include African-Americans in his parade.

**1897** ▶ William McKinley's inauguration was the first ceremony to be recorded by a motion picture camera.

**1909** ▶ William Taft's wife was the first one to accompany her husband in the procession from the Capitol to the White House.

**1917** ▶ Women were included for the first time in Woodrow Wilson's second inaugural parade.

**1921** ▶ Warren G. Harding was the first president to ride to and from his inaugural in an automobile.

**1925** ▶ Calvin Coolidge's oath was the first inaugural address broadcast on the radio.

**1949** ▶ Harry Truman's was the first to be televised.

**1963** ▶ Lyndon Johnson was the first (and so far the only) president to be sworn in by a woman, U.S. District Judge Sarah T. Hughes.

**1977** ▶ Jimmy Carter's inaugural parade featured solar heat for the reviewing stand and handicap-accessible viewing.

**1985** ▶ Ronald Reagan's second inaugural had to compete with Super Bowl Sunday.

**1997** ▶ The first ceremony broadcast on the Internet was Bill Clinton's second inauguration.

**did you know?** Retracing part of the journey of Abraham Lincoln in 1861, Barack Obama arrived in Washington, D.C., by train in January 2009 to take his oath of office as the first African-American president of the U.S. About a million people attended the inauguration ceremony in front of the Capitol building. Among those sitting behind Obama was his 86-year-old step grandmother from the African nation of Kenya.

# THE ★ ★ ★ ★ ★ ★ ★
# PRESIDENTS
## OF THE UNITED STATES

**1** **GEORGE WASHINGTON** Federalist Party **1789–1797**
Born: Feb. 22, 1732, at Wakefield, Westmoreland County, Virginia
Married: Martha Dandridge Custis (1731-1802); no children
Died: Dec. 14, 1799; buried at Mount Vernon, Fairfax County, Virginia
Vice President: John Adams (1789-1797)

**2** **JOHN ADAMS** Federalist Party **1797–1801**
Born: Oct. 30, 1735, in Braintree (now Quincy), Massachusetts
Married: Abigail Smith (1744-1818); 3 sons, 2 daughters
Died: July 4, 1826; buried in Quincy, Massachusetts
Vice President: Thomas Jefferson (1797-1801)

**3** **THOMAS JEFFERSON** Democratic-Republican Party **1801–1809**
Born: Apr. 13, 1743, at Shadwell, Albemarle County, Virginia
Married: Martha Wayles Skelton (1748-1782); 1 son, 5 daughters
Died: July 4, 1826; buried at Monticello, Albemarle County, Virginia
Vice President: Aaron Burr (1801-1805), George Clinton (1805-1809)

**4** **JAMES MADISON** Democratic-Republican Party **1809-1817**
Born: Mar. 16, 1751, at Port Conway, King George County, Virginia
Married: Dolley Payne Todd (1768-1849); no children
Died: June 28, 1836; buried at Montpelier Station, Virginia
Vice President: George Clinton (1809-1813), Elbridge Gerry (1813-1817)

**5** **JAMES MONROE** Democratic-Republican Party **1817–1825**
Born: Apr. 28, 1758, in Westmoreland County, Virginia
Married: Elizabeth Kortright (1768-1830); 1 son, 2 daughters
Died: July 4, 1831; buried in Richmond, Virginia
Vice President: Daniel D. Tompkins (1817-1825)

**6** **JOHN QUINCY ADAMS** Democratic-Republican Party **1825–1829**
Born: July 11, 1767, in Braintree (now Quincy), Massachusetts
Married: Louisa Catherine Johnson (1775-1852); 3 sons, 1 daughter
Died: Feb. 23, 1848; buried in Quincy, Massachusetts
Vice President: John C. Calhoun (1825-1829)

**7** **ANDREW JACKSON** Democratic Party      1829–1837
Born: Mar. 15, 1767, in Waxhaw, South Carolina
Married: Rachel Donelson Robards (1767-1828); 1 son (adopted)
Died: June 8, 1845; buried in Nashville, Tennessee
Vice President: John C. Calhoun (1829-1833),
                   Martin Van Buren (1833-1837)

**8** **MARTIN VAN BUREN** Democratic Party      1837–1841
Born: Dec. 5, 1782, at Kinderhook, New York
Married: Hannah Hoes (1783-1819); 4 sons
Died: July 24, 1862; buried at Kinderhook, New York
Vice President: Richard M. Johnson (1837-1841)

**9** **WILLIAM HENRY HARRISON** Whig Party      1841
Born: Feb. 9, 1773, at Berkeley, Charles City County, Virginia
Married: Anna Symmes (1775-1864); 6 sons, 4 daughters
Died: Apr. 4, 1841; buried in North Bend, Ohio
Vice President: John Tyler (1841-1845)

**10** **JOHN TYLER** Whig Party      1841–1845
Born: Mar. 29, 1790, in Greenway, Charles City County, Virginia
Married: Letitia Christian (1790-1842); 3 sons, 5 daughters
     Julia Gardiner (1820-1889); 5 sons, 2 daughters
Died: Jan. 18, 1862; buried in Richmond, Virginia
Vice President: none

**11** **JAMES KNOX POLK** Democratic Party      1845–1849
Born: Nov. 2, 1795, in Mecklenburg County, North Carolina
Married: Sarah Childress (1803-1891); no children
Died: June 15, 1849; buried in Nashville, Tennessee
Vice President: George M. Dallas (1845-1849)

**12** **ZACHARY TAYLOR** Whig Party      1849–1850
Born: Nov. 24, 1784, in Orange County, Virginia
Married: Margaret Smith (1788-1852); 1 son, 5 daughters
Died: July 9, 1850; buried in Louisville, Kentucky
Vice President: Millard Fillmore (1849-1850)

**13** **MILLARD FILLMORE** Whig Party      1850–1853
Born: Jan. 7, 1800, in Cayuga County, New York
Married: Abigail Powers (1798-1853); 1 son, 1 daughter
     Caroline Carmichael McIntosh (1813-1881); no children
Died: Mar. 8, 1874; buried in Buffalo, New York
Vice President: none

**14** FRANKLIN PIERCE Democratic Party 1853–1857
Born: Nov. 23, 1804, in Hillsboro, New Hampshire
Married: Jane Means Appleton (1806-1863); 3 sons
Died: Oct. 8, 1869; buried in Concord, New Hampshire
Vice President: William R. King (1853-1857)

**15** JAMES BUCHANAN Democratic Party 1857–1861
Born: Apr. 23, 1791, Cove Gap, near Mercersburg, Pennsylvania
Married: Never
Died: June 1, 1868, buried in Lancaster, Pennsylvania
Vice President: John C. Breckinridge (1857-1861)

**16** ABRAHAM LINCOLN Republican Party 1861-1865
Born: Feb. 12, 1809, in Hardin County, Kentucky
Married: Mary Todd (1818-1882); 4 sons
Died: Apr. 15, 1865; buried in Springfield, Illinois
Vice President: Hannibal Hamlin (1861-1864),
                Andrew Johnson (1865)

**17** ANDREW JOHNSON Democratic Party 1865–1869
Born: Dec. 29, 1808, in Raleigh, North Carolina
Married: Eliza McCardle (1810-1876); 3 sons, 2 daughters
Died: July 31, 1875; buried in Greeneville, Tennessee
Vice President: none

**18** ULYSSES S. GRANT Republican Party 1869–1877
Born: Apr. 27, 1822, in Point Pleasant, Ohio
Married: Julia Dent (1826-1902); 3 sons, 1 daughter
Died: July 23, 1885; buried in New York City
Vice President: Schuyler Colfax (1869-1873),
                Henry Wilson (1873-1877)

**19** RUTHERFORD B. HAYES Republican Party 1877–1881
Born: Oct. 4, 1822, in Delaware, Ohio
Married: Lucy Ware Webb (1831-1889); 7 sons, 1 daughter
Died: Jan. 17, 1893; buried in Fremont, Ohio
Vice President: William A. Wheeler (1877-1881)

**20** **JAMES A. GARFIELD** Republican Party          1881
Born: Nov. 19, 1831, in Orange, Cuyahoga County, Ohio
Married: Lucretia Rudolph (1832-1918); 5 sons, 2 daughters
Died: Sept. 19, 1881; buried in Cleveland, Ohio
Vice President: Chester A. Arthur (1881-1881)

**21** **CHESTER A. ARTHUR** Republican Party          1881–1885
Born: Oct. 5, 1829, in Fairfield, Vermont
Married: Ellen Lewis Herndon (1837-1880); 2 sons, 1 daughter
Died: Nov. 18, 1886; buried in Albany, New York
Vice President: none

**22** **GROVER CLEVELAND** Democratic Party          1885–1889
Born: Mar. 18, 1837, in Caldwell, New Jersey
Married: Frances Folsom (1864-1947); 2 sons, 3 daughters
Died: June 24, 1908; buried in Princeton, New Jersey
Vice President: Thomas A. Hendricks (1885-1889)

**23** **BENJAMIN HARRISON** Republican Party          1889-1893
Born: Aug. 20, 1833, in North Bend, Ohio
Married: Caroline Lavinia Scott (1832-1892); 1 son, 1 daughter
     Mary Scott Lord Dimmick (1858-1948); 1 daughter
Died: Mar. 13, 1901; buried in Indianapolis, Indiana
Vice President: Levi Morton (1889-1893)

**24** **GROVER CLEVELAND**          1893–1897
See 22, above
Vice President: Adlai E. Stevenson (1893-1897)

**25** **WILLIAM MCKINLEY** Republican Party          1897–1901
Born: Jan. 29, 1843, in Niles, Ohio
Married: Ida Saxton (1847-1907); 2 daughters
Died: Sept. 14, 1901; buried in Canton, Ohio
Vice President: Garret A. Hobart (1897-1901),
          Theodore Roosevelt (1901)

**26** **THEODORE ROOSEVELT** Republican Party          1901–1909
Born: Oct. 27, 1858, in New York City
Married: Alice Hathaway Lee (1861-1884); 1 daughter
     Edith Kermit Carow (1861-1948); 4 sons, 1 daughter
Died: Jan. 6, 1919; buried in Oyster Bay, New York
Vice President: none from 1901-1905, Charles W. Fairbanks (1905-1909)

### 27 WILLIAM HOWARD TAFT Republican Party        1909–1913

Born: Sept. 15, 1857, in Cincinnati, Ohio
Married: Helen Herron (1861-1943); 2 sons, 1 daughter
Died: Mar. 8, 1930; buried in Arlington National Cemetery, Virginia
Vice President: James S. Sherman (1909-1913)

### 28 WOODROW WILSON Democratic Party        1913–1921

Born: Dec. 28, 1856, in Staunton, Virginia
Married: Ellen Louise Axson (1860-1914); 3 daughters
    Edith Bolling Galt (1872-1961); no children
Died: Feb. 3, 1924; buried in Washington, D.C.
Vice President: Thomas R. Marshall (1913-1921)

### 29 WARREN G. HARDING Republican Party        1921–1923

Born: Nov. 2, 1865, near Corsica (now Blooming Grove), Ohio
Married: Florence Kling De Wolfe (1860-1924)
Died: Aug. 2, 1923; buried in Marion, Ohio
Vice President: Calvin Coolidge (1921-1923)

### 30 CALVIN COOLIDGE Republican Party        1923–1929

Born: July 4, 1872, in Plymouth, Vermont
Married: Grace Anna Goodhue (1879-1957); 2 sons
Died: Jan. 5, 1933; buried in Plymouth, Vermont
Vice President: none from 1923-1925, Charles G. Dawes (1925-1929)

### 31 HERBERT C. HOOVER Republican Party        1929-1933

Born: Aug. 10, 1874, in West Branch, Iowa
Married: Lou Henry (1875-1944); 2 sons
Died: Oct. 20, 1964; buried in West Branch, Iowa
Vice President:  Charles Curtis (1929-1933)

### 32 FRANKLIN DELANO ROOSEVELT Democratic Party 1933–1945

Born: Jan. 30, 1882, in Hyde Park, New York
Married: Anna Eleanor Roosevelt (1884-1962); 4 sons, 1 daughter
Died: Apr. 12, 1945; buried in Hyde Park, New York
Vice President: John N. Garner (1933-1941),
                Henry A. Wallace (1941-1945),
                Harry S. Truman (1945)

### 33  HARRY S. TRUMAN  Democratic Party    1945–1953
Born: May 8, 1884, in Lamar, Missouri
Married: Elizabeth Virginia "Bess" Wallace (1885-1982); 1 daughter
Died: Dec. 26, 1972; buried in Independence, Missouri
Vice President: none from 1945-1949, Alben W. Barkley (1949-1953)

### 34  DWIGHT D. EISENHOWER  Republican Party    1953–1961
Born: Oct. 14, 1890, in Denison, Texas
Married: Mary "Mamie" Geneva Doud (1896-1979); 2 sons
Died: Mar. 28, 1969; buried in Abilene, Kansas
Vice President: Richard M. Nixon (1953-1961)

### 35  JOHN FITZGERALD KENNEDY  Democratic Party  1961–1963
Born: May 29, 1917, in Brookline, Massachusetts
Married: Jacqueline Lee Bouvier (1929-1994); 2 sons, 1 daughter
Died: Nov. 22, 1963; buried in Arlington National Cemetery, Virginia
Vice President: Lyndon B. Johnson (1961-1963)

### 36  LYNDON BAINES JOHNSON  Democratic Party    1963–1969
Born: Aug. 27, 1908, near Stonewall, Texas
Married: Claudia "Lady Bird" Alta Taylor (b. 1912); 2 daughters
Died: Jan. 22, 1973; buried in Johnson City, Texas
Vice President: none from 1963-1965, Hubert H. Humphrey (1965-1969)

### 37  RICHARD MILHOUS NIXON  Republican Party    1969–1974
Born: Jan. 9, 1913, in Yorba Linda, California
Married: Thelma "Pat" Ryan (1912-1993); 2 daughters
Died: Apr. 22, 1994; buried in Yorba Linda, California
Vice President: Spiro T. Agnew (1969-1973),
              Gerald R. Ford (1973-1974)

### 38  GERALD R. FORD  Republican Party    1974-1977
Born: July 14, 1913, in Omaha, Nebraska
Married: Elizabeth "Betty" Bloomer (b. 1918); 3 sons, 1 daughter
Died: Dec. 26, 2006; buried in Grand Rapids, Michigan
Vice President: Nelson A. Rockefeller (1974-1977)

### 39  JIMMY (JAMES EARL) CARTER  Democratic Party  1977-1981
Born: Oct. 1, 1924, in Plains, Georgia
Married: Rosalynn Smith (b. 1927); 3 sons, 1 daughter
Vice President: Walter F. Mondale (1977-1981)

**40** RONALD REAGAN  Republican Party          1981–1989
Born: Feb. 6, 1911, in Tampico, Illinois
Married: Jane Wyman (b. 1914); 1 son, 1 daughter
    Nancy Davis (b. 1923); 1 son, 1 daughter
Died: June 5, 2004; buried in Simi Valley, California
Vice President: George H. W. Bush (1981-1989)

**41** GEORGE H.W. BUSH  Republican Party          1989–1993
Born: June 12, 1924, in Milton, Massachusetts
Married: Barbara Pierce (b. 1925); 4 sons, 2 daughters
Vice President: Dan Quayle (1989-1993)

**42** BILL (WILLIAM JEFFERSON) CLINTON          1993–2001
Democratic Party
Born: Aug. 19, 1946, in Hope, Arkansas
Married: Hillary Rodham (b. 1947); 1 daughter
Vice President: Al Gore (1993-2001)

**43** GEORGE W. BUSH  Republican Party          2001-2008
Born: July 6, 1946, in New Haven, Connecticut
Married: Laura Welch (b. 1946); 2 daughters
Vice President: Dick Cheney (2001-2008)

**44** BARACK OBAMA  Democratic Party          2009–
Born: August 4, 1961, in Honolulu, Hawaii
Married: Michelle LaVaughn Robinson (b. 1964); 2 daughters
Vice President: Joe Biden

# ★ ★ *The New* ★ ★ ★ ★ ★ ★
# First Lady

In the early days of the United States, there was no title for the wife of the president. Many early first ladies expressed their own preference for how they were addressed, including the use of such titles as "Lady," "Mrs. President," "Mrs. Presidentress," and "Queen." The term "First Lady" is used to refer to the wife of an elected male head of state. Creation of the title is credited to the United States, where it was first used in 1849. U. S. President Zachary Taylor called Dolley Madison "First Lady" at her state funeral while reciting a eulogy.

Michelle Obama, wife of Barack Obama, is the new first lady. She was born Michelle LaVaughn Robinson on January 17, 1964 in Chicago, Illinois. She graduated from Princeton University and Harvard Law School. For three years after law school, Michelle worked as an associate in the area of marketing and intellectual property at the Chicago law firm Sidley and Austin, where she met Barack Obama.

She left the corporate law world in 1991 to pursue a career in public service, serving as an assistant to the mayor and then as the assistant commissioner of planning and development for the city of Chicago.

In May 2007, three months after her husband declared his presidential candidacy, she reduced her professional responsibilities by eighty percent to support his presidential campaign.

Michelle married Barack Obama on October 18, 1992. They have two daughters, Malia Ann, born in 1998, and Natasha (known as Sasha), born in 2001.

# Meet the *First Ladies*

**DOLLEY MADISON**, wife of James Madison, was famous as a hostess and for saving a portrait of George Washington during the War of 1812, when the British were about to burn the White House.

**MARY TODD LINCOLN**, wife of Abraham Lincoln, was a well-educated Southerner who strongly opposed slavery. Sadly, her husband was assassinated and three of her four children died young.

**LOU HENRY HOOVER**, wife of Herbert Hoover, spoke several languages, including Chinese, and had a degree in geology. As First Lady she worked to involve all children in sports.

**Eleanor Roosevelt**, wife of Franklin D. Roosevelt, was First Lady from 1933 to 1945. She supported the New Deal policies of her husband and assumed a role as an advocate for civil rights. After her husband's death in 1945, she continued to be an internationally prominent author and speaker and was active in politics for the rest of her life.

**JACQUELINE KENNEDY**, wife of John Kennedy, met her husband while she was working as a photographer and reporter. As First Lady, she redecorated the White House, filling it with historic furnishings and artwork. "Jackie" was also a fashion icon whose clothes and hairstyles were copied by millions of women.

**BETTY FORD,** wife of Gerald Ford, studied modern dance as a young woman and was part of the Martha Graham troupe. As First Lady, she fought for women's rights and supported the Equal Rights Amendment. In 1982 she established the Betty Ford Center for the treatment of drug and alcohol dependency.

**LAURA BUSH**, wife of George W. Bush, was a librarian and teacher. She is interested in books, history, art, and the well-being of children. She and her husband have twin daughters, Jenna and Barbara. Both girls graduated from college in 2004.

# United States History

**14,000 B.C.– 11,000 B.C.**
Paleo-Indians use stone points attached to spears to hunt big **mammoths** in northern parts of North America.

**11,000 B.C.**
Big mammoths disappear and Paleo-Indians begin to gather **plants** for food.

**After A.D. 500**
Anasazi peoples in the Southwestern United States live in homes on cliffs, called **cliff dwellings**. Anasazi pottery and dishes are well known for their beautiful patterns.

**After A.D. 700**
Mississippian Indian people in the Southeastern United States **develop farms** and build burial mounds.

**30,000 B.C.– 11,000 B.C.**
First people (called **Paleo-Indians**) cross from Siberia to Alaska and begin to move into North America.

**9500 B.C.– 1000 B.C.**
North American Indians begin using **stone** to grind food and to hunt bison and smaller animals.

**1000 B.C.– A.D. 500**
Woodland Indians, who lived east of the Mississippi River, bury their dead under large **mounds** of earth (which can still be seen today).

**700–1492**
Many **different Indian cultures** develop throughout North America.

# Colonial America
## and the
## American Revolution:
## 1492-1783

### 1492
Christopher **Columbus** sails across the Atlantic Ocean and reaches an island in the Bahamas in the Caribbean Sea.

### 1513
Juan **Ponce de León** explores the Florida coast.

### 1524
Giovanni da **Verrazano** explores the coast from Carolina north to Nova Scotia, enters New York harbor.

### 1540
Francisco Vásquez de **Coronado** explores the Southwest.

### 1565
St. Augustine, Florida, the *first town* established by Europeans in the United States, is founded by the Spanish. Later burned by the English in 1586.

**BENJAMIN FRANKLIN (1706-1790)**
was a great American leader, printer, scientist, and writer. In 1732, he began publishing a magazine called *Poor Richard's Almanack*. Poor Richard was a make-believe person who gave advice about common sense and honesty. Many of Poor Richard's sayings are still known today. Among the most famous are "God helps them that help themselves" and "Early to bed, early to rise, makes a man healthy, wealthy, and wise."

### 1634
**Maryland** is founded as a Catholic colony, with religious freedom for all granted in 1649.

### 1664
The English seize **New Amsterdam** from the Dutch. The city is renamed New York.

### 1699
**French settlers** move into Mississippi and Louisiana.

### 1732
Benjamin Franklin begins publishing *Poor Richard's Almanack*.

### 1754-1763
**French and Indian War** between England and France. The French are defeated and lose their lands in Canada and the American Midwest.

### 1764-1766
England places taxes on sugar that comes from their North American colonies. England also requires colonists to buy stamps to help pay for royal troops. Colonists protest, and the **Stamp Act** is repealed in 1766.

**1607**

**Jamestown,** Virginia, the first permanent English settlement in North America, is founded by Captain John Smith.

**1609**

Henry Hudson sails into **New York Harbor**, explores the Hudson River. Spaniards settle Santa Fe, New Mexico.

**1619**

The first African **slaves** are brought to Jamestown. (Slavery is made legal in 1650.)

**1620**

**Pilgrims** from England arrive at Plymouth, Massachusetts, on the *Mayflower*.

**1626**

Peter Minuit buys **Manhattan** island for the Dutch from Manahata Indians for goods worth $24. The island is renamed New Amsterdam.

**1630**

**Boston** is founded by Massachusetts colonists led by John Winthrop.

**FAMOUS WORDS FROM THE DECLARATION OF INDEPENDENCE, JULY 4, 1776**

"We hold these truths to be self-evident, that all men are created equal, that they are endowed by their Creator with certain unalienable rights, that among these are life, liberty, and the pursuit of happiness."

**1770**

**Boston Massacre:** During a demonstration against English taxes, protestors begin throwing rocks at English troops. The troops open fire, killing 7 .

**1773**

**Boston Tea Party:** English tea is thrown into the harbor to protest a tax on tea.

**1775**

Fighting at **Lexington and Concord**, Massachusetts, marks the beginning of the American Revolution.

**1776**

**The Declaration of Independence** is approved July 4 by the Continental Congress (made up of representatives from the American colonies).

**1781**

British General **Charles Cornwallis** surrenders to the Americans at Yorktown, Virginia, ending the fighting in the Revolutionary War.

# The New Nation
## 1784-1900

**1784**
The first successful daily **newspaper** in the U.S., the *Pennsylvania Packet & General Advertiser*, is published.

**1787**
The **Constitutional Convention** meets to write a Constitution for the U.S.

**1789**
The new **Constitution** is approved by the states. George Washington is chosen as the first president.

**1800**
The federal government moves from Philadelphia to a new capital, **Washington, D.C.**

**1803**
The U.S. makes the **Louisiana Purchase** from France. The Purchase doubles the area of the U.S.

### WHO ATTENDED THE CONVENTION?
The **Constitutional Convention** met in Philadelphia in the hot summer of 1787. Most of the great founders of America attended. Among those present were George Washington, James Madison, and John Adams. They met to form a new government that would be strong and, at the same time, protect the liberties that were fought for in the American Revolution. The Constitution they created is still the law of the United States.

**1836**
Texans fighting for independence from Mexico are defeated at the **Alamo**.

**1838**
Cherokee Indians are forced to move to Oklahoma, along "The **Trail of Tears**." On the long march, thousands die because of disease and the cold weather.

**1844**
The **first telegraph** line connects Washington, D.C., and Baltimore.

**1846-1848**
**U.S. war with Mexico:** Mexico is defeated, and the United States takes control of the Republic of Texas and of Mexican territories in the West.

**1848**
The discovery of **gold** in California leads to a "rush" of 80,000 people to the West in search of gold.

**1852**
*Uncle Tom's Cabin* Harriet Beecher Stowe's novel about the suffering of slaves, is published.

**1804**

**Lewis and Clark**, with their guide Sacagawea, explore what is now the northwestern United States.

**1812–1814**

**War of 1812** with Great Britain: British forces burn the Capitol and White House. Francis Scott Key writes the words to "The Star-Spangled Banner."

**1820**

The **Missouri Compromise** bans slavery west of the Mississippi River and north of 36°30' latitude, except in Missouri.

**1823**

The **Monroe Doctrine** warns European countries not to interfere in the Americas.

**1825**

The **Erie Canal** opens, linking New York City with the Great Lakes.

**1831**

*The Liberator*, a newspaper opposing slavery, is published in Boston.

**1869**

The **first railroad** connecting the East and West coasts is completed.

**1898**

**Spanish-American War:** The U.S. defeats Spain, gains control of the Philippines, Puerto Rico, and Guam.

**1858**

Abraham Lincoln and Stephen Douglas **debate about slavery** during their Senate campaign in Illinois.

**1860**

Abraham **Lincoln** is elected president.

**1861**

The **Civil War** begins.

**1863**

President Lincoln issues the **Emancipation Proclamation**, freeing most slaves.

**1865**

The **Civil War** ends as the South surrenders. President Lincoln is assassinated.

**1890**

**Battle of Wounded Knee** is fought in South Dakota—the last major battle between Indians and U.S. troops.

### CIVIL WAR DEAD AND WOUNDED

The U.S. **Civil War** between the North and South lasted four years (1861-1865) and resulted in the death or wounding of more than 600,000 people. Little was known at the time about the infections and spread of diseases. As a result, many soldiers died from illnesses such as influenza and measles. Many also died from infections from battle wounds.

# United States Since 1900

**WORLD WAR I**
In **World War I** the United States fought with Great Britain, France, and Russia (the Allies) against Germany and Austria-Hungary. The Allies won the war in 1918.

## 1903
The United States begins digging the **Panama Canal**. The canal opens in 1914, connecting the Atlantic and Pacific oceans.

## 1908
Henry Ford introduces the **Model T** car, priced at $850.

## 1916
**Jeannette Rankin** of Montana becomes the first woman elected to Congress.

## 1917–1918
The United States joins **World War I** on the side of the Allies against Germany.

## 1927
Charles A. **Lindbergh** becomes the first person to fly alone nonstop across the Atlantic Ocean.

## 1929
A stock market crash marks the beginning of the **Great Depression**.

## 1954
The U.S. Supreme Court **forbids racial segregation** in public schools.

**SCHOOL SEGREGATION**
The U.S. Supreme Court ruled that **separate schools** for black students and white students were **not equal**. The Court said such schools were against the U.S. Constitution. The ruling also applied to other forms of segregation (separation of the races supported by some states.)

## 1963
President John **Kennedy** is assassinated.

## 1964
Congress passes the **Civil Rights Act**, which outlaws discrimination in voting and jobs.

## 1965
The United States sends first soldiers to fight in the **Vietnam War**.

## 1968
Civil rights leader **Martin Luther King Jr.** is assassinated in Memphis. Senator **Robert F. Kennedy** is assassinated in Los Angeles.

## 1969
U.S. astronaut Neil Armstrong becomes the **first person** to walk **on the moon**.

## 1973
U.S. participation in the **Vietnam War ends**.

286

## THE GREAT DEPRESSION

The stock market crash of October 1929 led to a period of severe hardship for the American people—the **Great Depression**. As many as 25 percent of all workers could not find jobs. The Depression lasted until the early 1940s. The Depression also led to a great change in politics. In 1932, Franklin D. Roosevelt, a Democrat, was elected president. He served as president for 12 years, longer than any other president.

### 1933
President Franklin D. Roosevelt's **New Deal** increases government help to people hurt by the Depression.

### 1941
Japan attacks **Pearl Harbor**, Hawaii. The United States enters World War II.

### 1945
Germany and Japan surrender, **ending World War II**. Japan surrenders after the U.S. drops atomic bombs on Hiroshima and Nagasaki.

### 1947
Jackie Robinson becomes the **first black baseball player** in the major leagues when he joins the Brooklyn Dodgers.

### 1950–1953
U.S. armed forces fight in the **Korean War**.

## WATERGATE

In June 1972, five men were arrested in the **Watergate** building in Washington, D.C., for trying to bug telephones in the offices of the Democratic National Committee. Some of those arrested worked for the committee to re-elect President Richard Nixon. Later it was discovered that Nixon was helping to hide information about the break-in.

### 1991
**The Persian Gulf War**: The United States and its allies defeat Iraq.

### 2008
**Barack Obama** defeats **John McCain** in the U.S. election to become the first African-American president.

### 2009
**Sonia Sotomayor** becomes the first Hispanic to be named to the U.S. Supreme Court.

### 1974
President Richard **Nixon resigns** because of the Watergate scandal.

### 1979
U.S. **hostages are taken in Iran**, beginning a 444-day crisis that ends with their release in 1981.

### 1981
Sandra Day O'Connor becomes the **first woman** on the U.S. Supreme Court.

### 1985
U.S. President Ronald Reagan and Soviet leader Mikhail Gorbachev begin working together to **improve relations** between their countries.

### 1999
After an **impeachment** trial, the Senate finds President Bill Clinton not guilty.

### 2001
Hijacked jets crash into the World Trade Center and the **Pentagon**, September 11, killing about 3,000 people.

### 2003
U.S.-led forces invade Iraq and remove dictator **Saddam Hussein**.

287

# African Americans:
## A Time Line

Would you like to learn more about the history of African Americans from the era of slavery to the present? These events and personalities can be a starting point. Can you add some more?

*Barack Obama* ▶

| | |
|---|---|
| **1619** | First Africans are brought to Virginia as slaves. |
| **1831** | Nat Turner starts a **slave revolt** in Virginia that is unsuccessful. |
| **1856-57** | **Dred Scott**, a slave, sues to be freed because he had left slave territory, but the Supreme Court denies his claim. |
| **1861-65** | The North defeats the South in the brutal Civil War; the **13th Amendment** ends nearly 250 years of slavery. The Ku Klux Klan is founded. |
| **1865-77** | Southern blacks play leadership roles in government under **Reconstruction**; the 15th Amendment (1870) gives black men the right to vote. |
| **1896** | Supreme Court rules in a case called *Plessy versus Ferguson* that segregation is legal when facilities are "**separate but equal.**" Discrimination and violence against blacks increase. |
| **1910** | W. E. B. Du Bois (1868–1963) founds National Association for the Advancement of Colored People (NAACP), fighting for equality for blacks. |
| **1920s** | African-American culture (jazz music, dance, literature) flourishes during the **Harlem Renaissance**. |
| **1954** | Supreme Court rules in a case called ***Brown versus Board of Education*** of *Topeka* that school segregation is unconstitutional. |
| **1957** | Black students, backed by federal troops, enter recently desegregated Central High School in **Little Rock**, Arkansas. |
| **1955-65** | **Malcolm X** (1925–65) emerges as key spokesman for black nationalism. |
| **1963** | **Rev. Dr. Martin Luther King, Jr.** (1929–68) gives his "I Have a Dream" speech at a march that inspires more than 200,000 people in Washington, D.C.—and many others throughout the nation. |
| **1964** | Sweeping **civil rights bill** banning racial discrimination is signed by President Lyndon Johnson. |
| **1965** | King leads protest march in **Selma**, Alabama; blacks riot in **Watts** section of Los Angeles. |
| **1967** | Gary, Indiana, and Cleveland, Ohio, are first major U.S. cities to elect black mayors; Thurgood Marshall (1908–93) becomes first African American on the Supreme Court. |
| **2001** | Colin Powell becomes first African-American secretary of state. |
| **2005** | **Condoleezza Rice** becomes first African American woman secretary of state. |
| **2008** | Barack Obama becomes the first African-American elected president of the United States. |

# THEY MADE HISTORY

These people of color made big contributions to the growth of the United States as a free country.

**HARRIET TUBMAN** (1821-1913) escaped slavery when she was in her twenties. Before the Civil War, she repeatedly risked her life to lead hundreds of slaves to freedom by way of a network of homes and churches called the "Underground Railroad."

**LEWIS LATIMER** (1848-1928), American inventor and son of runaway slaves who patented a more durable version of Thomas Edison's light bulb by using a carbon filament instead of paper. He worked on the patent for the telephone and oversaw the installation of public lights throughout New York, Philadelphia, London, and Montreal. He also invented the first railroad-car toilet.

**DALIP SINGH SAUND** (1899–1973) was the first Asian elected to Congress. Born in India, Saund immigrated to the U.S., where he became a mathematician, farmer, and judge. In 1956 he was elected to the House of Representatives, opening the door for Asian Americans to enter U.S. politics.

**THURGOOD MARSHALL** (1908–1993) was one of the key lawyers in the fight to end legal segregation in the United States, winning many important cases. In 1967 he became the first African American to serve on the U.S. Supreme Court, the highest court in the nation.

**ROSA PARKS** (1913–2005) is called the mother of America's civil rights movement. When she refused to give up her bus seat to a white man in 1955, blacks in Montgomery, Alabama, started a boycott of the bus system, which led to desegregation of the city's buses. After her death she became the first woman (and 31st person) in history to lie in honor in the Capitol Rotunda in Washington, D.C.

**CESAR CHAVEZ** (1927-1993), a Mexican American who was raised in migrant worker camps, started a national farm workers union, the United Farm Workers of America, in 1966. Along with UFW cofounder **DOLORES HUERTA** (1930), he organized boycotts that eventually made growers agree to better conditions for field workers.

**REV. DR. MARTIN LUTHER KING, JR.** (1929–1968) was the most influential leader of the U.S. civil rights movement from the mid-1950s to his assassination in 1968. In 1964 he received the Nobel Peace Prize. His wife, **CORETTA SCOTT KING** (1927-2006), helped carry on his work.

**ELLISON S. ONIZUKA** (1946-1986) was the first Asian American astronaut. He flew as a mission specialist in 1985. Sadly, he died in 1986 during another mission when the *Challenger* exploded just after launch.

**ANTONIO VILLARAIGOSA** (born 1953), a Mexican American, in 2005 became the first Latino mayor of Los Angeles since the 1870s. He is a former labor leader and speaker of the California State Assembly.

**SONIA SOTOMAYOR** (born 1954), who grew up in a housing project in New York City and went on to Princeton University and Yale Law School, was confirmed in 2009 as the first Hispanic justice on the U.S. Supreme Court.

**BARACK OBAMA** (born 1961), is the son of an American mother and a Kenyan father. After serving in the Illinois Senate for eight years, he was elected to the U.S. Senate in 2004. From there he launched a successful campaign to be elected President of the United States in November 2008.

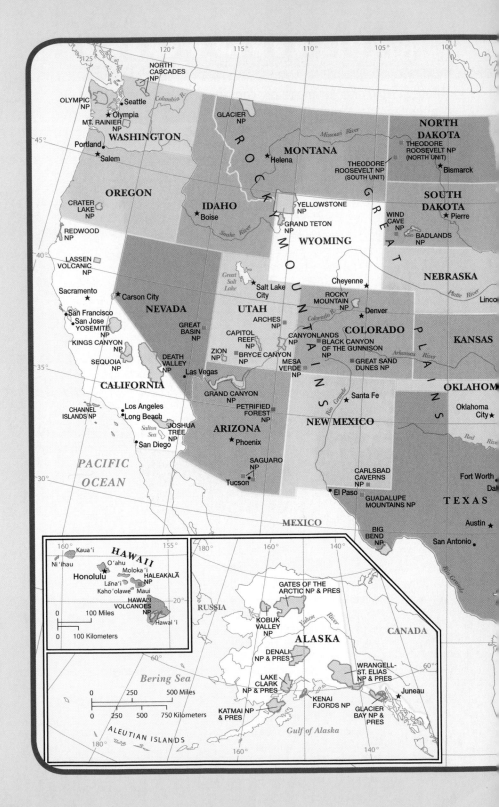

NORTH CASCADES NP

OLYMPIC NP
• Seattle
★ Olympia
MT. RAINIER NP
Portland •
★ Salem
WASHINGTON

Columbia R.

GLACIER NP

Missouri River

MONTANA
• Helena

NORTH DAKOTA
THEODORE ROOSEVELT NP (NORTH UNIT)
THEODORE ROOSEVELT NP (SOUTH UNIT)
• Bismarck

OREGON

CRATER LAKE NP

REDWOOD NP

IDAHO
★ Boise

Snake River

ROCKY

YELLOWSTONE NP

GRAND TETON NP

WYOMING

SOUTH DAKOTA
WIND CAVE NP
★ Pierre
BADLANDS NP

LASSEN VOLCANIC NP

Sacramento ★

★ Carson City

NEVADA

Great Salt Lake

• Salt Lake City

UTAH

ROCKY MOUNTAIN NP

Cheyenne •

NEBRASKA

Platte River

Linco

San Francisco •
San Jose •
YOSEMITE NP
KINGS CANYON NP

SEQUOIA NP

GREAT BASIN NP

DEATH VALLEY NP

ARCHES NP

CAPITOL REEF NP

ZION NP
BRYCE CANYON NP

Colorado R.

CANYONLANDS NP

MESA VERDE NP

Denver ★

COLORADO
BLACK CANYON OF THE GUNNISON NP
GREAT SAND DUNES NP

Arkansas River

KANSAS

OKLAHOM

CALIFORNIA

• Las Vegas

CHANNEL ISLANDS NP

Los Angeles •
Long Beach •

Salton Sea

JOSHUA TREE NP

San Diego •

GRAND CANYON NP

PETRIFIED FOREST NP

ARIZONA
★ Phoenix

SAGUARO NP

Tucson •

M O U N T A I N S

Santa Fe •

Rio Grande

NEW MEXICO

Oklahoma City ★

G R E A T   P L A I N S

Red River

PACIFIC OCEAN

CARLSBAD CAVERNS NP

• El Paso

GUADALUPE MOUNTAINS NP

T E X A S

Fort Worth
Dal

Austin ★

San Antonio •

MEXICO

BIG BEND NP

HAWAII
160°
Kaua'i
Ni'ihau
155°
O'ahu
Moloka'i
Honolulu
Lāna'i    Maui
Kaho'olawe
HAWAI'I VOLCANOES NP
HALEAKALĀ NP
Hawai'i

0    100 Miles
0    100 Kilometers

180°
160°
140°
GATES OF THE ARCTIC NP & PRES

RUSSIA

KOBUK VALLEY NP

Yukon River

ALASKA

CANADA

DENALI NP & PRES

WRANGELL-ST. ELIAS NP & PRES

60°

• Juneau

Bering Sea

LAKE CLARK NP & PRES

KENAI FJORDS NP

GLACIER BAY NP & PRES

0    250    500 Miles
0    250    500    750 Kilometers

KATMAI NP & PRES

Gulf of Alaska

ALEUTIAN ISLANDS

180°
160°
140°

290

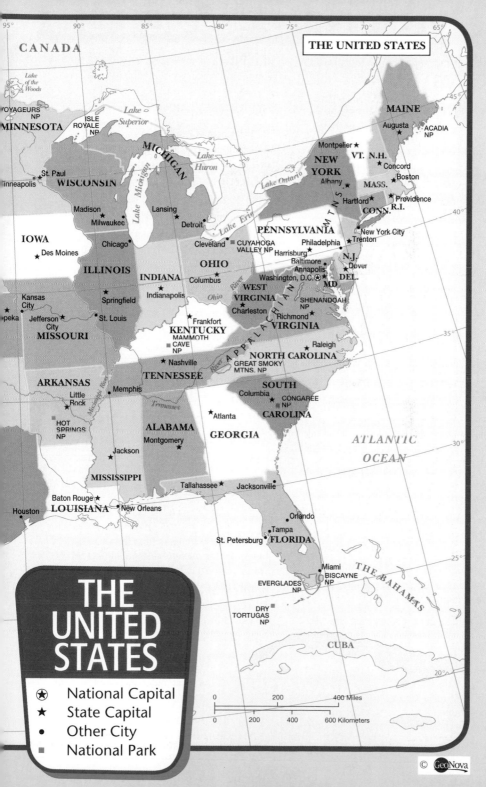

THE UNITED STATES

CANADA

95°  90°  85°  80°  75°  70°  65°

Lake of the Woods

VOYAGEURS NP

MINNESOTA

ISLE ROYALE NP

Lake Superior

45°

MAINE

Augusta ★

ACADIA NP

MICHIGAN

Lake Huron

Montpelier ★

VT. N.H.

Concord ★

WISCONSIN

St. Paul ★

Minneapolis ★

Madison ★
Milwaukee

Lansing ★

Detroit

Lake Erie

Lake Ontario

NEW YORK

Albany ★

Boston ★

MASS.

Hartford ★

Providence

CONN. R.I.

Lake Michigan

40°

PENNSYLVANIA

New York City

IOWA

Chicago

Cleveland

CUYAHOGA VALLEY NP

Harrisburg ★

Philadelphia

Trenton ★

Des Moines ★

OHIO

Columbus ★

Baltimore

N.J.

Dover ★

DEL.

ILLINOIS

INDIANA

Washington, D.C. ⊛

MD

Springfield ★

Indianapolis ★

Ohio River

WEST VIRGINIA

SHENANDOAH NP

Kansas City

St. Louis

Frankfort ★

Charleston ★

Richmond ★

VIRGINIA

peka

Jefferson City ★

MISSOURI

KENTUCKY

MAMMOTH CAVE NP

35°

APPALACHIAN MTNS

Raleigh ★

ARKANSAS

Nashville ★

TENNESSEE

GREAT SMOKY MTNS. NP

NORTH CAROLINA

Little Rock ★

Memphis

SOUTH

Columbia ★

CONGAREE NP

Mississippi River

Tennessee River

HOT SPRINGS NP

Atlanta ★

CAROLINA

ATLANTIC OCEAN

30°

ALABAMA

GEORGIA

Jackson ★

Montgomery ★

MISSISSIPPI

Tallahassee ★

Jacksonville

Baton Rouge ★

Houston

LOUISIANA

New Orleans

Orlando

25°

Tampa

St. Petersburg

FLORIDA

THE BAHAMAS

Miami

BISCAYNE NP

EVERGLADES NP

DRY TORTUGAS NP

CUBA

20°

THE UNITED STATES

⊛ National Capital
★ State Capital
• Other City
■ National Park

0   200   400 Miles

0   200   400   600 Kilometers

**ALABAMA** comes from an Indian word for "tribal town."

*Alaska*

**ALASKA** comes from *alakshak*, the Aleutian (Eskimo) word meaning "peninsula" or "land that is not an island."

**ARIZONA** comes from a Pima Indian word meaning "little spring place" or the Aztec word *arizuma*, meaning "silver-bearing."

**ARKANSAS** is a variation of Quapaw, the name of an Indian tribe. Quapaw means "south wind."

**CALIFORNIA** is the name of an imaginary island in a Spanish story. It was named by Spanish explorers of Baja California, a part of Mexico.

**COLORADO** comes from a Spanish word meaning "red." It was first given to the Colorado River because of its reddish color.

**CONNECTICUT** comes from an Algonquin Indian word meaning "long river place."

**DELAWARE** is named after Lord De La Warr, the English governor of Virginia in colonial times.

**FLORIDA**, which means "flowery" in Spanish, was named by the explorer Ponce de León, who landed there during Easter.

**GEORGIA** was named after King George II of England, who granted the right to create a colony there in 1732.

**HAWAII** probably comes from *Hawaiki*, or *Owhyhee*, the native Polynesian word for "homeland."

**IDAHO**'s name is of uncertain origin, but it may come from a Kiowa Apache name for the Comanche Indians.

*Hawaii*

**ILLINOIS** is the French version of *Illini*, an Algonquin Indian word meaning "men" or "warriors."

**INDIANA** means "land of the Indians."

**IOWA** comes from the name of an American Indian tribe that lived on the land that is now the state.

**KANSAS** comes from a Sioux Indian word that possibly meant "people of the south wind."

**KENTUCKY** comes from an Iroquois Indian word, possibly meaning "meadowland."

**LOUISIANA**, which was first settled by French explorers, was named after King Louis XIV of France.

**MAINE** means "the mainland." English explorers called it that to distinguish it from islands nearby.

*Maine*

**MARYLAND** was named after Queen Henrietta Maria, wife of King Charles I of England, who granted the right to establish an English colony there.

**MASSACHUSETTS** comes from an Indian word meaning "large hill place."

**MICHIGAN** comes from the Chippewa Indian words *mici gama*, meaning "great water" (referring to Lake Michigan).

**MINNESOTA** got its name from a Dakota Sioux Indian word meaning "cloudy water" or "sky-tinted water."

**MISSISSIPPI** is probably from Chippewa Indian words meaning "great river" or "gathering of all the waters," or from an Algonquin word, *messipi*.

**MISSOURI** comes from an Algonquin Indian term meaning "river of the big canoes."

# Got Their Names

**MONTANA** comes from a Latin or Spanish word meaning "mountainous."

**NEBRASKA** comes from "flat river" or "broad water," an Omaha or Otos Indian name for the Platte River.

**NEVADA** means "snow-clad" in Spanish. Spanish explorers gave the name to the Sierra Nevada Mountains.

**NEW HAMPSHIRE** was named by an early settler after his home county of Hampshire, in England.

**NEW JERSEY** was named for the English Channel island of Jersey.

New Mexico

**NEW MEXICO** was given its name by 16th-century Spaniards in Mexico.

**NEW YORK**, first called New Netherland, was renamed for the Duke of York after the English took it from Dutch settlers.

**NORTH CAROLINA**, the northern part of the English colony of Carolana, was named for King Charles I.

**NORTH DAKOTA** comes from a Sioux Indian word meaning "friend" or "ally."

**OHIO** is the Iroquois Indian word for "good river."

**OKLAHOMA** comes from a Choctaw Indian word meaning "red man."

**OREGON** may have come from *Ouaricon-sint,* a name on an old French map that was once given to what is now called the Columbia River. That river runs between Oregon and Washington.

**PENNSYLVANIA** meaning "Penn's woods," was the name given to the colony founded by William Penn.

**RHODE ISLAND** may have come from the Dutch "Roode Eylandt" (red island) or may have been named after the Greek island of Rhodes.

**SOUTH CAROLINA**, the southern part of the English colony of Carolana, was named for King Charles I.

**SOUTH DAKOTA** comes from a Sioux Indian word meaning "friend" or "ally."

**TENNESSEE** comes from "Tanasi," the name of Cherokee Indian villages on what is now the Little Tennessee River.

Texas

**TEXAS** comes from a word meaning "friends" or "allies," used by the Spanish to describe some of the American Indians living there.

**UTAH** comes from a Navajo word meaning "upper" or "higher up."

**VERMONT** comes from two French words, *vert* meaning "green" and *mont* meaning "mountain."

**VIRGINIA** was named in honor of Queen Elizabeth I of England, who was known as the Virgin Queen because she was never married.

**WASHINGTON** was named after George Washington, the first president of the United States. It is the only state named after a president.

**WEST VIRGINIA** got its name from the people of western Virginia, who formed their own government during the Civil War.

**WISCONSIN** comes from a Chippewa name that is believed to mean "grassy place." It was once spelled *Ouisconsin* and *Mesconsing.*

**WYOMING** comes from Algonquin Indian words that are said to mean "at the big plains," "large prairie place," or "on the great plain."

Pennsylvania

# FACTS About the STATES

A fter every state name is the postal abbreviation. The Area includes both land and water; it is given in square miles (sq mi) and square kilometers (sq km). Numbers in parentheses after Population, Area, and Entered Union show the state's rank compared with other states. City populations are for mid-2008, unless otherwise noted.

## ALABAMA (AL) Heart of Dixie, Camellia State

**POPULATION (2008):** 4,661,900 (23rd) **AREA:** 52,419 sq mi (30th) (135,765 sq km) 🌼 Camellia 🐦 Yellowhammer 🌲 Southern longleaf pine 🎵 "Alabama" **ENTERED UNION:** December 14, 1819 (22nd) ⭐ Montgomery **LARGEST CITIES (WITH POP.):** Birmingham, 228,798; Montgomery, 202,696; Mobile, 191,022; Huntsville, 176,645

⚙️ clothing and textiles, metal products, transportation equipment, paper, industrial machinery, food products, lumber, coal, oil, natural gas, livestock, peanuts, cotton

• Birmingham
⭐ Montgomery

*Montgomery was the capital of the Confederacy during the early months of the Civil War between February 18 and May 21, 1861. The Confederate capital then moved to Richmond, Virginia.*

## ALASKA (AK) The Last Frontier

**POPULATION (2008):** 686,293 (47th) **AREA:** 663,267 sq mi (1st) (1,717,854 sq km) 🌸 Forget-me-not 🐦 Willow ptarmigan 🌲 Sitka spruce 🎵 "Alaska's Flag" **ENTERED UNION:** January 3, 1959 (49th) ⭐ Juneau **LARGEST CITIES (WITH POP.):** Anchorage, 279,243; Fairbanks, 35,132; Juneau, 30,988; Wasilla, 10,256

⚙️ oil, natural gas, fish, food products, lumber and wood products, fur

Anchorage •
Juneau ⭐

*Travelers can use a plane, a boat, maybe even try a catapult, but Juneau is the only state capital that can not be reached by road.*

## ARIZONA (AZ) Grand Canyon State

**POPULATION (2008):** 6,500,180 (14th) **AREA:** 113,998 sq mi (6th) (295,253 sq km) 🌵 Blossom of the Saguaro cactus 🐦 Cactus wren 🌲 Paloverde 🎵 "Arizona" **ENTERED UNION:** February 14, 1912 (48th) ⭐ Phoenix **LARGEST CITIES (WITH POP.):** Phoenix, 1,567,924; Tucson, 541,811; Mesa, 463,552; Glendale, 251,522; Chandler, 247,170; Scottsdale, 235,371

⚙️ electronic equipment, transportation and industrial equipment, instruments, printing and publishing, copper and other metals

Phoenix ⭐
Tucson •

*You can find London Bridge in Lake Havasu City, AZ. Built in London, England, in the 1830s, the bridge was taken down and sold to Robert P. McCulloch in 1968. He re-assembled it on Lake Havasu in 1971.*

# ARKANSAS (AR) Natural State, Razorback State

**Little Rock**

**POPULATION (2008):** 2,855,390 (32nd) **AREA:** 53,179 sq mi (29th) (137,733 sq km) 🌼Apple blossom 🐦Mockingbird 🌲Pine 🎵"Arkansas" **ENTERED UNION:** June 15, 1836 (25th) ⭐Little Rock **LARGEST CITIES (WITH POP.):** Little Rock, 189,515; Fort Smith, 84,716; Fayetteville, 73,372; Springdale, 68,180

⚙ food products, paper, electronic equipment, industrial machinery, metal products, lumber and wood products, livestock, soybeans, rice, cotton, natural gas

*The only working diamond mine in the U.S. is located in Murfreesboro, AR, at Crater of Diamonds State Park. It is also the only diamond-producing site in the world that is open to the public. Visitors can keep whatever diamonds they find.*

# CALIFORNIA (CA) Golden State

**POPULATION (2008):** 36,756,666 (1st) **AREA:** 163,696 sq mi (3rd) (423,971 sq km) 🌼Golden poppy 🐦California valley quail 🌲California redwood 🎵"I Love You, California" **ENTERED UNION:** September 9, 1850 (31st) ⭐Sacramento **LARGEST CITIES (WITH POP.):** Los Angeles, 3,833,995; San Diego, 1,279,329; San Jose, 948,279; San Francisco, 808,976; Fresno, 476,050; Sacramento, 463,794; Long Beach, 463,789; Oakland, 404,155

⚙ transportation and industrial equipment, electronic equipment, oil, natural gas, motion pictures, milk, cattle, fruit, vegetables

**Sacramento**
**San Francisco**
**Los Angeles**
**San Diego**

*The iconic "Hollywood" hillside sign in Los Angeles was built as an advertisement for an upscale real estate development in 1923. It originally said "Hollywoodland" and was lit by 4,000 light bulbs. The "land" was removed by the city in 1949.*

# COLORADO (CO) Centennial State

**POPULATION (2008):** 4,939,456 (22nd) **AREA:** 104,094 sq mi (8th) (269,602 sq km) 🌼Rocky Mountain columbine 🐦Lark bunting 🌲Colorado blue spruce 🎵"Where the Columbines Grow" **ENTERED UNION:** August 1, 1876 (38th) ⭐Denver **LARGEST CITIES (WITH POP.):** Denver, 598,707; Colorado Springs, 380,307; Aurora, 319,057; Lakewood, 140,989; Fort Collins, 136,509

**Denver**
**Colorado Springs**

⚙ instruments and industrial machinery, food products, printing and publishing, metal products, electronic equipment, oil, coal, cattle

*The Anasazi Indians built entire cities into cliffsides across the American southwest. The settlements built between 1100 and 1300 at Mesa Verde in southwestern Colorado are the largest and best preserved.*

**Key:** 🌼Flower 🐦Bird 🌲Tree 🎵Song ⭐Capital ⚙Important Products

# CONNECTICUT (CT) Constitution State, Nutmeg State

**Hartford**

**POPULATION (2008):** 3,501,252 (29th) **AREA:** 5,543 sq mi (48th) (14,356 sq km) 🌼Mountain laurel 🐦American robin 🌳White oak 🎵"Yankee Doodle" **ENTERED UNION:** January 9, 1788 (5th) ⭐ Hartford **LARGEST CITIES (WITH POP.):** Bridgeport, 136,405; Hartford, 124,062; New Haven, 123,669; Stamford, 119,303; Waterbury, 107,037

⚙ aircraft parts, helicopters, industrial machinery, metals and metal products, electronic equipment, printing and publishing, medical instruments, chemicals, dairy products, stone

**did you know?** *The Hartford Courant is the country's oldest newspaper in continuous publication. It started as a weekly in 1764. George Washington once placed an ad in the paper to rent out some of his land in Mount Vernon, VA.*

# DELAWARE (DE) First State, Diamond State

**Dover**
⭐

**POPULATION (2008):** 873,092 (45th) **AREA:** 2,489 sq mi (49th) (6,446 sq km) 🌼Peach blossom 🐦Blue hen chicken 🌳American holly 🎵"Our Delaware" **ENTERED UNION:** December 7, 1787 (1st) ⭐Dover **LARGEST CITIES (WITH POP.):** Wilmington, 72,592; Dover, 36,107; Newark, 29,886

⚙ chemicals, transportation equipment, food products, chickens

**did you know?** *The Mason-Dixon line is an L-shaped border that separates Delaware, Pennsylvania, and Maryland. Charles Mason and Jeremiah Dixon drew it in the 1760s to settle a dispute between the colonies. The border is marked to this day with stones about every 1,000 feet.*

# FLORIDA (FL) Sunshine State

**Tallahassee**
⭐
**Jacksonville**

**Miami •**

**POPULATION (2008):** 18,328,340 (4th) **AREA:** 65,755 sq mi (22nd) (170,305 sq km) 🌼Orange blossom 🐦Mockingbird 🌳Sabal palmetto palm 🎵"Old Folks at Home" **ENTERED UNION:** March 3, 1845 (27th) ⭐Tallahassee **LARGEST CITIES (WITH POP.):** Jacksonville, 807,815; Miami, 413,201; Tampa, 340,882; St. Petersburg, 245,314; Orlando, 230,519 Hialeah, 210,542; Ft. Lauderdale, 183,126

⚙ electronic and transportation equipment, industrial machinery, printing and publishing, food products, citrus fruits, vegetables, livestock, phosphates, fish

**did you know?** *The Daytona 500, NASCAR's most prestigious race, was first run in 1959. The race is run each February at Daytona International Speedway.*

# GEORGIA (GA) Empire State of the South, Peach State

**POPULATION (2008):** 9,685,744 (9th) **AREA:** 59,425 sq mi (24th) (153,910 sq km) 🌸Cherokee rose 🐦Brown thrasher 🌲Live oak 🎵"Georgia on My Mind" **ENTERED UNION:** January 2, 1788 (4th) ⭐Atlanta **LARGEST CITIES (WITH POP.):** Atlanta, 537,958; Augusta, 199,486; Columbus, 186,984; Savannah, 132,410

⚙ clothing and textiles, transportation equipment, food products, paper, chickens, peanuts, peaches, clay

⭐ Atlanta

**did you know?**
*Hartsfield-Jackson Atlanta International Airport is one of the busiest in the world. Nearly a million planes land or depart from it every year.*

# HAWAII (HI) Aloha State

**POPULATION (2008):** 1,288,198 (42nd) **AREA:** 10,931 sq mi (43rd) (28,311 sq km) 🌸Yellow hibiscus 🐦Hawaiian goose 🌲Kukui 🎵"Hawaii Ponoi" **ENTERED UNION:** August 21, 1959 (50th) ⭐Honolulu **LARGEST CITIES (WITH POP.):** Honolulu, 374,676; (2000 census): Hilo, 40,759; Kailua, 36,513; Kaneohe, 34,970

⭐ Honolulu

⚙ food products, pineapples, sugar, printing and publishing, fish, flowers

**did you know?**
*The most massive volcano in the world, Mauna Loa ("Long Mountain"), is located on the island of Hawaii, the "Big" island. About four-fifths of the volcano lies underwater, but its peak reaches 13,681 feet above sea level.*

# IDAHO (ID) Gem State

**POPULATION (2008):** 1,523,816 (39th) **AREA:** 83,570 sq mi (14th) (216,445 sq km) 🌸Syringa 🐦Mountain bluebird 🌲White pine 🎵"Here We Have Idaho" **ENTERED UNION:** July 3, 1890 (43rd) ⭐Boise **LARGEST CITIES (WITH POP.):** Boise, 205,314; Nampa, 80,362; Meridian, 66,916; Pocatello, 54,901; Idaho Falls, 54,334

⚙ potatoes, hay, wheat, cattle, milk, lumber and wood products, food products

⭐ Boise

**did you know?**
*In 1951, an experimental nuclear reactor built near Arco, ID became the first to produce electricity that was usable in homes and buildings. In 1955, Arco became the world's first town to have all of its power generated by a nuclear reactor.*

**Key:** 🌸Flower 🐦Bird 🌲Tree 🎵Song ⭐Capital ⚙Important Products

# ILLINOIS (IL) Prairie State

Chicago

Springfield

**POPULATION (2008):** 12,901,563 (5th) **AREA:** 57,914 sq mi (25th) (149,997 sq km) ⚜️Native violet 🐦Cardinal 🌳White oak 🎵"Illinois" **ENTERED UNION:** December 3, 1818 (21st) ⭐Springfield **LARGEST CITIES (WITH POP.):** Chicago, 2,853,114; Aurora, 171,782; Rockford, 157,272; Joliet, 146,125; Naperville, 143,117; Springfield, 117,352; Peoria, 114,114

⚙️ industrial machinery, metals and metal products, printing and publishing, electronic equipment, food products, corn, soybeans, hogs

**did you know?** *The Chicago River, which today flows away from Lake Michigan, used to flow in the opposite direction. Between 1898 and 1900, engineers dug what became known as the Sanitary and Ship Canal, or Main Canal, connecting the Chicago River to the Mississippi River. This caused the water to reverse its flow.*

# INDIANA (IN) Hoosier State

Indianapolis

**POPULATION (2008):** 6,376,792 (16th) **AREA:** 36,418 sq mi (38th) (94,322 sq km) ⚜️Peony 🐦Cardinal 🌳Tulip poplar 🎵"On the Banks of the Wabash, Far Away" **ENTERED UNION:** December 11, 1816 (19th) ⭐Indianapolis **LARGEST CITIES (WITH POP.):** Indianapolis, 808,466; Fort Wayne, 251,591; Evansville, 116,309; South Bend, 103,807; Gary, 95,920

⚙️ transportation equipment, electronic equipment, industrial machinery, iron and steel, metal products, corn, soybeans, livestock, coal

**did you know?** *Two main routes of the Underground Railroad, a movement that helped free black slaves, went through Indiana. From 1827 to 1847, the Coffins ran a stop, in Newport (now Fountain City). They helped more than 2,000 runaway slaves escape.*

# IOWA (IA) Hawkeye State

Des Moines

**POPULATION (2008):** 3,002,555 (30th) **AREA:** 56,272 sq mi (26th) (145,744 sq km) ⚜️Wild rose 🐦Eastern goldfinch 🌳Oak 🎵"The Song of Iowa" **ENTERED UNION:** December 28, 1846 (29th) ⭐Des Moines **LARGEST CITIES (WITH POP.):** Des Moines, 197,052; Cedar Rapids, 128,056; Davenport, 100,827; Sioux City, 82,807

⚙️ corn, soybeans, hogs, cattle, industrial machinery, food products

**did you know?** *The only member of the Lewis and Clark expedition to die was Sgt. Charles Floyd. He died from peritonitis near present-day Sioux City, IA. A monument stands where he was buried.*

## KANSAS (KS) Sunflower State

**POPULATION (2008):** 2,802,134 (33rd) **AREA:** 82,277 sq mi (15th) (213,096 sq km) 🌻Native sunflower 🐦Western meadowlark 🌳Cottonwood 🎵"Home on the Range" **ENTERED UNION:** January 29, 1861 (34th) ⭐Topeka **LARGEST CITIES (WITH POP.):** Wichita, 366,046; Overland Park, 171,231; Kansas City, 142,562; Topeka, 123,446

Topeka ⭐

Wichita ●

⚙ cattle, aircraft and other transportation equipment, industrial machinery, food products, wheat, corn, hay, oil, natural gas

The pioneers of flight Amelia Earhart and Clyde Cessna were both from Kansas. The state is still one of the world's major airplane builders.

## KENTUCKY (KY) Bluegrass State

**POPULATION (2008):** 4,269,245 (26th) **AREA:** 40,409 sq mi (37th) (104,659 sq km) 🌻Goldenrod 🐦Cardinal 🌳Tulip poplar 🎵"My Old Kentucky Home" **ENTERED UNION:** June 1, 1792 (15th) ⭐Frankfort **LARGEST CITIES (WITH POP.):** Louisville, 713,877; Lexington-Fayette, 282,114; Owensboro, 55,516; Bowling Green, 55,097

⭐ Frankfort

Louisville ●

⚙ coal, industrial machinery, electronic equipment, transportation equipment, metals, tobacco, cattle

More than 360 miles of natural caves and underground passageways have been mapped under Mammoth Cave National Park. It's the largest network of natural tunnels in the world and extends up to 1,000 miles.

## LOUISIANA (LA) Pelican State

**POPULATION (2008):** 4,410,796 (25th) **AREA:** 51,840 sq mi (31st) (134,265 sq km) 🌻Magnolia 🐦Eastern brown pelican 🌳Cypress 🎵"Give Me Louisiana" **ENTERED UNION:** April 30, 1812 (18th) ⭐Baton Rouge **LARGEST CITIES (WITH POP.):** New Orleans, 311,853; Baton Rouge, 223,689; Shreveport, 199,729; Lafayette, 113,656

Baton Rouge ⭐

New ●
Orleans

⚙ natural gas, oil, chemicals, transportation equipment, paper, food products, cotton, fish

Louisiana is the only state whose legal system comes from Napoleonic Code, the system put into place in France by Napoleon Bonaparte. This is because Louisiana used to belong to France. The law codes of the other 49 states are based on English common law, which was practiced in England. The differences are minor.

**Key:** 🌻Flower 🐦Bird 🌳Tree 🎵Song ⭐Capital ⚙Important Products

# MAINE (ME) Pine Tree State

**POPULATION (2008):** 1,316,456 (40th) **AREA:** 35,385 sq mi (39th) (91,647 sq km) ✿White pine cone and tassel 🐦Chickadee 🌲Eastern white pine 🎵"State of Maine Song" **ENTERED UNION:** March 15, 1820 (23rd) ⭐Augusta **LARGEST CITIES (WITH POP.):** Portland, 62,561; Lewiston, 35,131; Bangor, 31,756

⚙ paper, transportation equipment, wood and wood products, electronic equipment, footwear, clothing, potatoes, milk, eggs, fish, seafood

*did you know?*

*Georgeana, now the town of York, was the first city in America to be chartered by England in 1641.*

Augusta ⭐

# MARYLAND (MD) Old Line State, Free State

Baltimore •

Annapolis ⭐

Washington, D.C. ⭐

**POPULATION (2008):** 5,633,597 (19th) **AREA:** 12,407 sq mi (42nd) (32,134 sq km) ✿Black-eyed susan 🐦Baltimore oriole 🌲White oak 🎵"Maryland, My Maryland" **ENTERED UNION:** April 28, 1788 (7th) ⭐Annapolis **LARGEST CITIES (WITH POP.):** Baltimore, 636,919; Rockville, 60,734; Frederick, 59,213; Gaithersburg, 58,744; Bowie, 52,544

⚙ printing and publishing, food products, transportation equipment, electronic equipment, chickens, soybeans, corn, stone

*did you know?*

*Maryland's official state sport is jousting. Competitors on horseback ride through a course and use their lances to collect rings. Competitors are called either "knights" or "maids."*

# MASSACHUSETTS (MA) Bay State, Old Colony

Boston ⭐

**POPULATION (2008):** 6,497,967 (15th) **AREA:** 10,555 sq mi (44th) (27,337 sq km) ✿Mayflower 🐦Chickadee 🌲American elm 🎵"All Hail to Massachusetts" **ENTERED UNION:** February 6, 1788 (6th) ⭐Boston **LARGEST CITIES (WITH POP.):** Boston, 609,023; Worcester, 175,011; Springfield, 150,640; Cambridge, 105,596; Lowell, 103,615

⚙ industrial machinery, electronic equipment, fish, instruments, printing, publishing, metal products, flowers, shrubs, cranberries

*did you know?*

*Pink flamingos, the tacky plastic lawn ornaments, were first made by a young sculptor named Don Featherstone in 1957. Every "authentic" pink flamingo was made by Union Products, of Leominster, from 1957 until the factory closed in 2006.*

# MICHIGAN (MI) Great Lakes State, Wolverine State

**POPULATION (2008):** 10,003,422 (8th) **AREA:** 96,716 sq mi (11th) (250,493 sq km) ✿Apple blossom 🐦Robin 🌲White pine 🎵"Michigan, My Michigan"
**ENTERED UNION:** January 26, 1837 (26th) ⭐Lansing
**LARGEST CITIES (WITH POP.):** Detroit, 912,062; Grand Rapids, 193,396; Warren, 133,939; Sterling Heights, 127,160; Ann Arbor, 114,386; Lansing, 113,968; Flint, 112,900

⚙ automobiles, industrial machinery, metal products, office furniture, plastic products, chemicals, food products, milk, corn, natural gas, iron ore, blueberries

 *Battle Creek, the headquarters for Kellogg's, Ralston Foods, and the Post Cereal division of Kraft Foods, is known as the Cereal Capital of the World.*

Lansing ⭐ Detroit •

# MINNESOTA (MN) North Star State, Gopher State

**POPULATION (2008):** 5,220,393 (21st) **AREA:** 86,939 sq mi (12th) (225,171 sq km) ✿Pink and white lady slipper 🐦Common loon 🌲Red pine 🎵"Hail! Minnesota" **ENTERED UNION:** May 11, 1858 (32nd) ⭐St. Paul **LARGEST CITIES (WITH POP.):** Minneapolis, 382,605; St. Paul, 279,590; Rochester, 100,413; Duluth, 84,284; Bloomington, 81,280

⚙ industrial machinery, printing and publishing, computers, food products, scientific and medical instruments, milk, hogs, cattle, corn, soybeans, iron ore

Minneapolis •
St. Paul ⭐

 *The "Land of 10,000 Lakes" has 11,842 lakes bigger than 10 acres within its borders. One out of every six Minnesotans owns a boat, the highest rate of any state.*

# MISSISSIPPI (MS) Magnolia State

**POPULATION (2008):** 2,938,618 (31st) **AREA:** 48,430 sq mi (32nd) (125,433 sq km) ✿Magnolia 🐦Mockingbird 🌲Magnolia 🎵"Go, Mississippi!" **ENTERED UNION:** December 10, 1817 (20th) ⭐Jackson **LARGEST CITIES (WITH POP.):** Jackson, 173,861; Gulfport, 70,055; Hattiesburg, 51,993; Biloxi, 45,670

⚙ transportation equipment, furniture, electrical machinery, lumber and wood products, cotton, rice, chickens, cattle

⭐
Jackson

*In 1902, President Theodore "Teddy" Roosevelt went bear hunting in Mississippi. He refused to shoot a bear that had been tied to a tree by his companions. The story inspired some toy makers to create a stuffed toy bear, which they called "Teddy's Bear." That's how the teddy bear was born.*

Key: ✿Flower 🐦Bird 🌲Tree 🎵Song ⭐Capital ⚙Important Products

# MISSOURI (MO) Show Me State

**POPULATION (2008):** 5,911,605 (18th) **AREA:** 69,704 sq mi (21st) (180,533 sq km) ✿Hawthorn ♫Bluebird ♣Dogwood ♪"Missouri Waltz" **ENTERED UNION:** August 10, 1821 (24th) ★Jefferson City **LARGEST CITIES (WITH POP.):** Kansas City, 451,572; St. Louis, 354,361; Springfield, 156,206; Independence, 110,440

⚙ transportation equipment, electrical and electronic equipment, printing and publishing, food products, cattle, hogs, milk, soybeans, corn, hay, lead

*The waffle cone for ice cream was first sold at the 1904 World's Fair in St. Louis.*

# MONTANA (MT) Treasure State

**POPULATION (2008):** 967,440 (44th) **AREA:** 147,042 sq mi (4th) (380,837 sq km) ✿Bitterroot ♫Western meadowlark ♣Ponderosa pine ♪"Montana" **ENTERED UNION:** November 8, 1889 (41st) ★Helena **LARGEST CITIES (WITH POP.):** Billings, 103,994; Missoula, 68,202; Great Falls, 59,251; Bozeman, 39,442

⚙ cattle, copper, gold, wheat, barley, wood and paper products

*The capital, Helena, was started by miners who found gold in a creek, or gulch, in 1864. It was first called Crabtown after one of the miners, John Crab. The city's main street, Last Chance Gulch, covers the length of the gulch.*

# NEBRASKA (NE) Cornhusker State

**POPULATION (2008):** 1,783,432 (38th) **AREA:** 77,354 sq mi (16th) (200,346 sq km) ✿Goldenrod ♫Western meadowlark ♣Cottonwood ♪"Beautiful Nebraska" **ENTERED UNION:** March 1, 1867 (37th) ★Lincoln **LARGEST CITIES (WITH POP.):** Omaha, 438,646; Lincoln, 251,624; Bellevue, 49,699; Grand Island, 45,801

⚙ cattle, hogs, milk, corn, soybeans, hay, wheat, sorghum, food products, industrial machinery

*Nebraska has the only unicameral (one-house) state legislature in the U.S. It is called the Nebraska Unicameral. The members are called senators, and they serve four-year terms. The leader of the legislature is called the Speaker.*

# NEVADA (NV) Sagebrush State, Battle Born State, Silver State

**POPULATION (2008):** 2,600,167 (35th) **AREA:** 110,561 sq mi (7th) (286,352 sq km) 🌸Sagebrush 🐦Mountain bluebird 🌲Single-leaf piñon, bristlecone pine 🎵"Home Means Nevada" **ENTERED UNION:** October 31, 1864 (36th) ⭐Carson City **LARGEST CITIES (WITH POP.):** Las Vegas, 558,383; Henderson, 252,064; North Las Vegas, 217,253; Reno, 217,016

⚙ gold, silver, cattle, hay, food products, plastics, chemicals

*Extending for about 110 miles, Lake Mead is the largest artificial lake in the U.S. It provides water for Nevada, Arizona, California, and northern Mexico. It was formed on the Colorado River when the Hoover Dam was built in 1936.*

Carson City

Las Vegas

# NEW HAMPSHIRE (NH) Granite State

**POPULATION (2008):** 1,315,809 (41st) **AREA:** 9,350 sq mi (46th) (24,216 sq km) 🌸Purple lilac 🐦Purple finch 🌲White birch 🎵"Old New Hampshire" **ENTERED UNION:** June 21, 1788 (9th) ⭐Concord **LARGEST CITIES (WITH POP.):** Manchester, 108,586; Nashua, 86,576; Concord, 42,255

⚙ industrial machinery, electric and electronic equipment, metal products, plastic products, dairy products, maple syrup and maple sugar

*New Hampshire was the first colony to declare its independence from England and start its own government in 1776—six months before the Declaration of Independence was signed.*

Concord

# NEW JERSEY (NJ) Garden State

**POPULATION (2008):** 8,682,661 (11th) **AREA:** 8,721 sq mi (47th) (22,587 sq km) 🌸Purple violet 🐦Eastern goldfinch 🌲Red oak 🎵none **ENTERED UNION:** December 18, 1787 (3rd) ⭐Trenton **LARGEST CITIES (WITH POP.):** Newark, 278,980; Jersey City, 241,114; Paterson, 145,643; Elizabeth, 124,755; Trenton, 82,883

⚙ chemicals, pharmaceuticals/drugs, electronic equipment, nursery and greenhouse products, food products, tomatoes, blueberries, and peaches

*The city of Paterson is one of the birthplaces of the Industrial Revolution in America. In the 1790s, the Society for Establishing Useful Manufacturers built a factory on the Passaic River. Until the early 20th century, Paterson produced many types of goods, including large amounts of silk fabric, inspiring the nickname "Silk City."*

Newark

Trenton

**Key:** 🌸Flower 🐦Bird 🌲Tree 🎵Song ⭐Capital ⚙Important Products

# NEW MEXICO

**(NM)** Land of Enchantment

Santa Fe ★

● Albuquerque

**POPULATION (2008):** 1,984,356 (36th) **AREA:** 121,589 sq mi (5th) (314,914 sq km) ❁Yucca ♫Roadrunner ❀Piñon ♪"O, Fair New Mexico" **ENTERED UNION:** January 6, 1912 (47th) ★Santa Fe **LARGEST CITIES (WITH POP.):** Albuquerque, 521,999; Las Cruces, 91,865; Rio Rancho, 79,655; Santa Fe, 71,831

⚙ electronic equipment, foods, machinery, clothing, lumber, transportation equipment, hay, onions, chiles

**did you know?** *In 1950, the town of Hot Springs renamed itself Truth or Consequences, NM, after a popular game show of the time.*

# NEW YORK

**(NY)** Empire State

Albany ★

● Buffalo

New York City ●

**POPULATION (2008):** 19,490,297 (3rd) **AREA:** 54,556 sq mi (27th) (141,299 sq km) ❁Rose ♫Bluebird ❀Sugar maple ♪"I Love New York" **ENTERED UNION:** July 26, 1788 (11th) ★Albany **LARGEST CITIES (WITH POP.):** New York, 8,363,710; Buffalo, 270,919; Rochester, 206,886; Yonkers, 201,588; Syracuse, 138,068

⚙ books and magazines, automobile and aircraft parts, toys and sporting goods, electronic equipment, machinery, clothing and textiles, metal products, milk, cattle, hay, apples

**did you know?** *New York City is the largest city in the U.S. and was the nation's first capital. It was also the home of another major first in American history—the first pizza restaurant in the U.S. opened there in 1895.*

# NORTH CAROLINA

**(NC)** Tar Heel State, Old North State

Raleigh ★

● Charlotte

**POPULATION (2008):** 9,222,414 (10th) **AREA:** 53,819 sq mi (28th) (139,391 sq km) ❁Dogwood ♫Cardinal ❀Pine ♪"The Old North State" **ENTERED UNION:** November 21, 1789 (12th) ★Raleigh **LARGEST CITIES (WITH POP.):** Charlotte, 687,456; Raleigh, 392,552; Greensboro, 250,642; Durham, 223,284; Winston-Salem, 217,600; Fayetteville 174,091

⚙ clothing and textiles, tobacco and tobacco products, industrial machinery, electronic equipment, furniture, cotton, soybeans, peanuts

**did you know?** *The Outer Banks, a line of offshore sandy islands, were full of pirates and smugglers in the early 1700s. The most notorious, Blackbeard, terrorized sailors along the coast before the crews of two British ships sent him to his watery grave there in 1718.*

# NORTH DAKOTA (ND) Peace Garden State

**POPULATION (2008):** 641,481 (48th) **AREA:** 70,700 sq mi (19th) (183,112 sq km) 🌸Wild prairie rose 🐦Western meadowlark 🌲American elm 🎵"North Dakota Hymn" **ENTERED UNION:** November 2, 1889 (39th) ⭐Bismarck **LARGEST CITIES (WITH POP.):** Fargo, 93,531; Bismarck, 60,389; Grand Forks, 51,313; Minot, 35,419

⭐ Bismarck

⚙ wheat, barley, hay, sunflowers, sugar beets, cattle, sand and gravel, food products, farm equipment, high-tech electronics

**did you know?** *During their expedition, Lewis and Clark spent the winter of 1804–05 in North Dakota. They named their fort after the Mandan tribe that lived nearby. They met Sacagawea, who gave birth to her son at Fort Mandan.*

# OHIO (OH) Buckeye State

**POPULATION (2008):** 11,485,910 (7th) **AREA:** 44,825 sq mi (34th) (116,096 sq km) 🌸Scarlet carnation 🐦Cardinal 🌲Buckeye 🎵"Beautiful Ohio" **ENTERED UNION:** March 1, 1803 (17th) ⭐Columbus **LARGEST CITIES (WITH POP.):** Columbus, 754,885; Cleveland, 433,748; Cincinnati, 333,336; Toledo, 293,201; Akron, 207,510; Dayton, 154,200

Cleveland
Columbus ⭐
Cincinnati

⚙ metal and metal products, transportation equipment, industrial machinery, rubber and plastic products, electronic equipment, printing and publishing, chemicals, food products, corn, soybeans, livestock, milk

**did you know?** *Though it was admitted to the Union in 1803, Ohio didn't technically become a state until 1953. Because of an oversight, Congress didn't formally vote on the resolution to admit Ohio as a state until August 7, 1953, when it made Ohio's statehood official, retroactive to 1803.*

# OKLAHOMA (OK) Sooner State

**POPULATION (2008):** 3,642,361 (28th) **AREA:** 69,898 sq mi (20th) (181,035 sq km) 🌸Mistletoe 🐦Scissor-tailed flycatcher 🌲Redbud 🎵"Oklahoma!" **ENTERED UNION:** November 16, 1907 (46th) ⭐Oklahoma City **LARGEST CITIES (WITH POP.):** Oklahoma City, 551,789; Tulsa, 385,635; Norman, 106,957; Broken Arrow, 92,931; Lawton, 90,091

Tulsa
⭐ Oklahoma City

⚙ natural gas, oil, cattle, nonelectrical machinery, transportation equipment, metal products, wheat, hay

**did you know?** *The American Indian nations called the Five Civilized Tribes (Cherokee, Chickasaw, Choctaw, Creek, and Seminole) were resettled in eastern Oklahoma by the federal government between 1817 and 1842.*

**Key:** 🌸Flower 🐦Bird 🌲Tree 🎵Song ⭐Capital ⚙Important Products

# OREGON (OR) Beaver State

• **Portland**

⭐ **Salem**

**POPULATION (2008):** 3,790,060 (27th) **AREA:** 98,381 sq mi (9th) (254,806 sq km) 🌸Oregon grape 🐦Western meadowlark 🌲Douglas fir 🎵"Oregon, My Oregon" **ENTERED UNION:** February 14, 1859 (33rd) ⭐Salem **LARGEST CITIES (WITH POP.):** Portland, 557,706; Salem, 153,435; Eugene, 150,104; Gresham, 101,221

⚙ lumber and wood products, electronics and semiconductors, food products, paper, cattle, hay, vegetables, Christmas trees

**did you know?** *The name Portland was settled by a coin toss between two founders, Asa Lovejoy and Francis Pettygrove, who both wanted to name the city after their home towns. Pettygrove, from Portland, Maine, won the toss. Lovejoy, from Boston, Massachusetts, lost.*

# PENNSYLVANIA (PA) Keystone State

**Harrisburg**
• **Pittsburgh** ⭐
**Philadelphia** •

**POPULATION (2008):** 12,448,279 (6th) **AREA:** 46,055 sq mi (33rd) (119,282 sq km) 🌸Mountain laurel 🐦Ruffed grouse 🌲Hemlock 🎵"Pennsylvania" **ENTERED UNION:** December 12, 1787 (2nd) ⭐Harrisburg (population, 47,196) **LARGEST CITIES (WITH POP.):** Philadelphia, 1,447,395; Pittsburgh, 310,037; Allentown, 107,250; Erie, 103,817

⚙ iron and steel, coal, industrial machinery, printing and publishing, food products, electronic equipment, transportation equipment, stone, clay and glass products

**did you know?** *An enormous fire has been burning since 1962 in the coal mines below the town of Centralia. Fewer than 20 people remain in the town. Surface temperatures have been measured at over 700°F.*

# RHODE ISLAND (RI) Little Rhody, Ocean State

**Providence**

⭐

**POPULATION (2008):** 1,050,788 (43rd) **AREA:** 1,545 sq mi (50th) (4,002 sq km) 🌸Violet 🐦Rhode Island red 🌲Red maple 🎵"Rhode Island" **ENTERED UNION:** May 29, 1790 (13th) ⭐Providence **LARGEST CITIES (WITH POP.):** Providence, 171,557; Warwick, 84,483; Cranston, 79,980; Pawtucket, 71,765

⚙ costume jewelry, toys, textiles, machinery, electronic equipment, fish

**did you know?** *A third of Rhode Island's area is water. Narragansett Bay is the largest in New England and contains about 35 islands. Close to 20 million tourists visit the tiny state each year to boat, fish, and bask along its 384 miles of sandy coast. The smallest state also has a big fishing industry.*

# SOUTH CAROLINA (SC) Palmetto State

**POPULATION (2008):** 4,479,800 (24th) **AREA:** 32,020 sq mi (40th) (82,931 sq km) 🌼Yellow jessamine 🐦Carolina wren 🌲Palmetto 🎵"Carolina" **ENTERED UNION:** May 23, 1788 (8th) ⭐Columbia **LARGEST CITIES (WITH POP.):** Columbia, 127,029; Charleston, 111,978; North Charleston, 94,407; Rock Hill, 67,339

Columbia ⭐

🔧 clothing and textiles, chemicals, industrial machinery, metal products, livestock, tobacco, Portland cement

*Gullahs are descendants of West African slaves who have chosen to live a traditional African life along the coast and islands of South Carolina, Georgia, and Florida. They have their own language, arts, crafts, religious beliefs, and foods that have been passed down for generations.*

# SOUTH DAKOTA (SD) Mt. Rushmore State, Coyote State

**POPULATION (2008):** 804,194 (46th) **AREA:** 77,116 sq mi (17th) (199,730 sq km) 🌼Pasqueflower 🐦Chinese ring-necked pheasant 🌲Black Hills spruce 🎵"Hail, South Dakota" **ENTERED UNION:** November 2, 1889 (40th) ⭐Pierre **LARGEST CITIES (WITH POP.):** Sioux Falls, 154,997; Rapid City, 65,491; Aberdeen, 24,460

⭐ Pierre

🔧 food and food products, machinery, electric and electronic equipment, corn, soybeans

*The Corn Palace in Mitchell is redecorated every year with themed murals made from corn, grains, and grasses by local artisans. When winter comes, birds and squirrels munch away the exterior.*

# TENNESSEE (TN) Volunteer State

**POPULATION (2008):** 6,214,888 (17th) **AREA:** 42,143 sq mi (36th) (109,150 sq km) 🌼Iris 🐦Mockingbird 🌲Tulip poplar 🎵"My Homeland, Tennessee"; "When It's Iris Time in Tennessee"; "My Tennessee"; "Tennessee Waltz"; "Rocky Top" **ENTERED UNION:** June 1, 1796 (16th) ⭐Nashville **LARGEST CITIES (WITH POP.):** Memphis, 669,651; Nashville-Davidson, 626,144; Knoxville, 184,802; Chattanooga, 170,880

⭐ Nashville
Memphis ●

🔧 chemicals, machinery, vehicles, food products, metal products, publishing, electronic equipment, paper products, rubber and plastic products, tobacco

*The Grand Ole Opry, the world's longest-running live radio program, was first broadcast from Nashville in 1925. It was originally called the WSM Barn Dance, but the name changed to the Grand Ole Opry in 1927.*

**Key:** 🌼Flower 🐦Bird 🌲Tree 🎵Song ⭐Capital 🔧Important Products

# TEXAS (TX) Lone Star State

**POPULATION (2008):** 24,326,974 (2nd) **AREA:** 268,581 sq mi (2nd) (695,622 sq km) ✿Bluebonnet 🐦Mockingbird 🌰Pecan 🎵"Texas, Our Texas" **ENTERED UNION:** December 29, 1845 (28th) ⭐Austin **LARGEST CITIES (WITH POP.):** Houston, 2,242,193; San Antonio, 1,351,305; Dallas, 1,279,910; Austin, 757,688; Fort Worth, 703,073; El Paso, 613,190; Arlington, 374,417; Corpus Christi, 286,462; Plano, 267,480

⚙ oil, natural gas, cattle, milk, eggs, transportation equipment, chemicals, clothing, industrial machinery, electrical and electronic equipment, cotton, grains

*Texas is the only state that is allowed by law to split into smaller states if its people want it to.*

# UTAH (UT) Beehive State

**POPULATION (2008):** 2,736,424 (34th) **AREA:** 84,899 sq mi (13th) (219,887 sq km) ✿Sego lily 🐦Seagull 🌲Blue spruce 🎵"Utah, This is the Place" **ENTERED UNION:** January 4, 1896 (45th) ⭐Salt Lake City **LARGEST CITIES (WITH POP.):** Salt Lake City, 181,698; West Valley City, 123,447; Provo, 118,581; West Jordan, 104,447

⚙ transportation equipment, medical instruments, electronic parts, food products, steel, copper, cattle, corn, hay, wheat, barley

*Early white settlers in Utah were saved from starvation by seagulls, the state bird. In 1848, hordes of locusts came into the Salt Lake Valley and began devouring the settlers' crops. All seemed lost before a flock of seagulls flew in and ate the locusts, saving the crops.*

# VERMONT (VT) Green Mountain State

**POPULATION (2008):** 621,270 (49th) **AREA:** 9,614 sq mi (45th) (24,900 sq km) ✿Red clover 🐦Hermit thrush 🌲Sugar maple 🎵"These Green Mountains" **ENTERED UNION:** March 4, 1791 (14th) ⭐Montpelier **LARGEST CITIES (WITH POP.):** Burlington, 38,897; South Burlington, 17,574; Rutland, 16,742

⚙ machine tools, furniture, scales, books, computer parts, foods, dairy products, apples, maple syrup

*The Green Mountain Boys who famously fought against the British during the American Revolution were originally formed in 1770 to fight off New York settlers. When the revolution broke out, the Vermonters and New Yorkers set aside their differences and united against the British.*

## VIRGINIA (VA) Old Dominion

**POPULATION (2008):** 7,769,089 (12th) **AREA:** 42,774 sq mi (35th) (110,784 sq km) 🌸Dogwood 🐦Cardinal 🌲Dogwood 🎵"Carry Me Back to Old Virginia" **ENTERED UNION:** June 25, 1788 (10th) ⭐Richmond **LARGEST CITIES (WITH POP.):** Virginia Beach, 433,746; Norfolk, 234,220; Chesapeake, 220,110; Richmond, 202,002; Newport News, 179,614

Alexandria
Richmond ⭐
Norfolk

⚙ transportation equipment, textiles, chemicals, printing, machinery, electronic equipment, food products, coal, livestock, tobacco, wood products, furniture

*Nancy Langhorne Astor in 1919 became the first woman to serve in the British House of Commons. She was born and raised in Virginia.*

## WASHINGTON (WA) Evergreen State

**POPULATION (2008):** 6,549,224 (13th) **AREA:** 71,300 sq mi (18th) (184,666 sq km) 🌸Western rhododendron 🐦Willow goldfinch 🌲Western hemlock 🎵"Washington, My Home" **ENTERED UNION:** November 11, 1889 (42nd) ⭐Olympia **LARGEST CITIES (WITH POP.):** Seattle, 598,541; Spokane, 202,319; Tacoma, 197,181; Vancouver, 163,186; Bellevue, 123,771

Seattle
Olympia

⚙ aircraft, lumber, pulp and paper, machinery, electronics, computer software, aluminum, processed fruits and vegetables

*Mount Rainier is the tallest volcano in the lower 48 states. It hasn't erupted in centuries. However, another volcano in Washington, Mount St. Helens, had a huge eruption on May 18, 1980. It lasted 9 hours and destroyed 230 square miles of woods. It is still active today.*

## WEST VIRGINIA (WV) Mountain State

**POPULATION (2008):** 1,814,468 (37th) **AREA:** 24,230 sq mi (41st) (62,755 sq km) 🌸Big rhododendron 🐦Cardinal 🌲Sugar maple 🎵"The West Virginia Hills"; "This Is My West Virginia"; "West Virginia, My Home Sweet Home" **ENTERED UNION:** June 20, 1863 (35th) ⭐ Charleston **LARGEST CITIES (WITH POP.):** Charleston, 50,302; Huntington, 49,185; Parkersburg, 31,611; Morgantown, 29,642; Wheeling, 28,913

Charleston

⚙ coal, natural gas, fabricated metal products, chemicals, automobile parts, aluminum, steel, machinery, cattle, hay, apples, peaches, tobacco

*The Golden Delicious variety of apple is the state fruit. It grew by chance on a family farm about 1900. It is now one of the most popular types of apples.*

**Key:** 🌸Flower 🐦Bird 🌲Tree 🎵Song ⭐Capital ⚙Important Products

# WISCONSIN (WI) Badger State

**POPULATION (2008):** 5,627,967 (20th) **AREA:** 65,498 sq mi (23rd) (169,639 sq km) ✿Wood violet ♫Robin ♣Sugar maple ♪"On, Wisconsin!" **ENTERED UNION:** May 29, 1848 (30th) ★Madison **LARGEST CITIES (WITH POP.):** Milwaukee, 604,477; Madison, 231,916; Green Bay, 101,025; Kenosha, 96,950; Racine, 82,196

⚙ paper products, printing, milk, butter, cheese, foods, food products, motor vehicles and equipment, medical instruments and supplies, plastics, corn, hay, vegetables

**Madison ★**
**Milwaukee ●**

 *The first ever ice cream sundaes were served in the towns of Manitowoc and Two Rivers in 1851.*

# WYOMING (WY) Cowboy State

**POPULATION (2008):** 532,668 (50th) **AREA:** 97,814 sq mi (10th) (253,337 sq km) ✿Indian paintbrush ♫Western meadowlark ♣Plains cottonwood ♪"Wyoming" **ENTERED UNION:** July 10, 1890 (44th) ★Cheyenne **LARGEST CITIES (WITH POP.):** Cheyenne, 56,915; Casper, 54,047; Laramie, 27,664

⚙ oil, natural gas, petroleum (oil) products, cattle, wheat, beans

**Cheyenne**
**★**

 *Dude ranches offer "tenderfeet" the opportunity to live the ropin' and ridin' way of the cowboy. Three brothers, Howard, Willis, and Alden Eaton, received so many guests at their ranch (including Pres. Theodore Roosevelt) that they opened the first dude ranch near Sheridan in 1904.*

# COMMONWEALTH OF PUERTO RICO (PR)

**★**
**San Juan**

**HISTORY:** Christopher Columbus landed in Puerto Rico in 1493. Puerto Rico was a Spanish colony for centuries, then was ceded (given) to the United States in 1898 after the Spanish-American War. In 1952, still associated with the United States, Puerto Rico became a commonwealth with its own constitution. **POPULATION (2008):** 3,954,037 **AREA:** 5,324 sq mi (13,789 sq km) ✿Maga ♫Reinita ♣Ceiba **NATIONAL ANTHEM:** "La Borinqueña" ★San Juan **LARGEST CITIES (WITH POP.; 2000 census):** San Juan, 421,958; Carolina, 168,164; Ponce, 155,038; Caguas, 88,680

⚙ chemicals, food products, electronic equipment, clothing and textiles, industrial machinery, coffee, sugarcane, fruit, hogs

 *Puerto Ricans have most of the same rights as other Americans, but they cannot vote in U.S. presidential elections and they have no voting representatives in the federal government. They don't have to pay federal taxes.*

# WASHINGTON, D.C.
## The Capital of the
# UNITED STATES

**LAND AREA:** 61 square miles  **POPULATION (2008):** 591,833
**FLOWER:** American beauty rose  **BIRD:** Wood thrush

**WEB SITE** *www.dc.gov • www.washington.org*

**HISTORY** The District of Columbia, or Washington, D.C., became the capital of the United States in 1800, when the federal government moved there from Philadelphia. The city of Washington was designed and built to be the capital. It was named after George Washington. Many of its major sights are on the Mall, an open grassy area that runs from the Capitol to the Potomac River.

**CAPITOL**, which houses the U.S. Congress, is at the east end of the Mall on Capitol Hill. Its dome can be seen from far away.

**JEFFERSON MEMORIAL**, a circular marble building located near the Potomac River, is partly based on a design by Thomas Jefferson for the University of Virginia.

**LIBRARY OF CONGRESS**, research library for Congress and the largest library in the world, is on Independence Avenue across the street from the Capitol.

**LINCOLN MEMORIAL**, at the west end of the Mall, is built of white marble and styled like a Greek temple. Inside is a large, seated statue of Abraham Lincoln. His Gettysburg Address is carved on a nearby wall.

**NATIONAL ARCHIVES**, on Constitution Avenue, holds the Declaration of Independence, Constitution, and Bill of Rights.

**NATIONAL WORLD WAR II MEMORIAL**, located between the Lincoln Memorial and the Washington Monument at the Mall, honors the 16 million Americans who served during the war.

**SMITHSONIAN INSTITUTION** has 18 museums (2 of them are in New York City), including the new National Museum of the American Indian, the National Air and Space Museum and the Museum of Natural History. The National Zoo is part of the Smithsonian.

**U.S. HOLOCAUST MEMORIAL MUSEUM** presents the history of the Nazis' murder of more than six million Jews and millions of other people from 1933 to 1945. The exhibit *Daniel's Story* tells the story of the Holocaust from a child's point of view.

**WASHINGTON MONUMENT** is a white marble pillar, or obelisk, standing on the Mall and rising to more than 555 feet. From the top there are wonderful views of the city.

**WHITE HOUSE**, at 1600 Pennsylvania Avenue, has been the home of every U.S. president except George Washington.

**WOMEN IN MILITARY SERVICE FOR AMERICA MEMORIAL,** stands near the entrance to Arlington National Cemetery in Virginia. It honors the 2 million women who have served in the U.S. armed forces.

**VIETNAM VETERANS MEMORIAL**, located near the Lincoln Memorial, includes a wall with all the names of those killed or missing in action during the conflict.

◄ Jefferson Memorial

311

# Weather

What is a mistral? ➡ see page 312

## How to Read a Weather Map

Meteorologists around the world basically use the same set of symbols to show weather conditions. This allows them to quickly and easily communicate with one another. The symbols in a newspaper or TV weather map might vary somewhat from the ones shown below.

By examining this map, meteorologists can predict what the weather might be like in the future. They are able to do this because they know how the weather usually changes. For example, dry, calm weather typically occurs in high-pressure areas while precipitation is seen in low-pressure areas. Storms usually come before a cold front. As a cold front passes through an area, its temperature drops. Light rain might herald a warm front. As a warm front moves through an area, it gets warmer.

Because so many things—big and small—can influence the weather, only forecasts of up to five days tend to be accurate.

### Selected Weather Symbols

| Sky Cover | | Fronts | | Weather | |
|---|---|---|---|---|---|
| ◯ | Clear | ▲▲▲ | Cold front | ▪ Rain | ═ Fog |
| ◓ | Scattered | ●●● | Warm front | ✳ Snow | ∞ Haze |
| ● | Overcast | ▲●▲ | Stationary front | ⚡ Thunderstorm | |

**Wind:** ◎ Calm   —— 1-2 knots (1-2 mph)   —➤ 3-7 knots (3-8 mph)

**L** Low Pressure Center       **H** High Pressure Center

# WEIRD WEATHER FACTS

**Winds** are known by specific names in certain parts of the world. Here is a sample:

**Föhn, or foehn**—Warm, dry wind that travels down a mountain's leeward side, or the side of the mountain facing away from the wind. This occurs after a cool, moist wind travels up and over the side of the mountain facing the wind. Originally used to refer to a wind in the Alps.

**Chinook**—A föhn wind common in the Rocky Mountains. Named after a Native American tribe.

**Mistral**—Strong, cold, dry wind that blows from the north across southern France and into the Mediterranean. It can reach speeds of up to about 85 miles per hour.

**Sirocco**—Warm, humid wind that originates as a hot, dry wind in North Africa. It picks up moisture as it crosses the Mediterranean and brings rain to Europe.

A **sundog**, or parhelia, is a phenomenon caused by light passing through or reflecting off of ice crystals in the atmosphere. Sundogs appear as bright spots of light on either side of the Sun. If you drew a line through sundogs and the Sun, the line would be parallel to the horizon.

# RECORD TEMPERATURES BY STATE (Through mid-2009)

**Coldest Temperature** →

**Hottest Temperature** →

| STATE | Lowest | | Highest | |
|---|---|---|---|---|
| | °F | Latest date | °F | Latest date |
| Alabama | −27 | Jan. 30, 1966 | 112 | Sept. 5, 1925 |
| Alaska | −80 | Jan. 23, 1971 | 100 | June 27, 1915 |
| Arizona | −40 | Jan. 7, 1971 | 128 | July 5, 2007 |
| Arkansas | −29 | Feb. 13, 1905 | 120 | Aug. 10, 1936 |
| California | −45 | Jan. 20, 1937 | 134 | July 10, 1913 |
| Colorado | −61 | Feb. 1, 1985 | 118 | July 11, 1888 |
| Connecticut | −32 | Jan. 22, 1961 | 106 | July 15, 1995 |
| Delaware | −17 | Jan. 17, 1893 | 110 | July 21, 1930 |
| Florida | −2 | Feb. 13, 1899 | 109 | June 29, 1931 |
| Georgia | −17 | Jan. 27, 1940 | 112 | Aug. 20, 1983 |
| Hawaii | 12 | May 17, 1979 | 100 | Apr. 27, 1931 |
| Idaho | −60 | Jan. 18, 1943 | 118 | July 28, 1934 |
| Illinois | −36 | Jan. 5, 1999 | 117 | July 14, 1954 |
| Indiana | −36 | Jan. 19, 1994 | 116 | July 14, 1936 |
| Iowa | −47 | Feb. 3, 1996 | 118 | July 20, 1934 |
| Kansas | −40 | Feb. 13, 1905 | 121 | July 24, 1936 |
| Kentucky | −37 | Jan. 19, 1994 | 114 | July 28, 1930 |
| Louisiana | −16 | Feb. 13, 1899 | 114 | Aug. 10, 1936 |
| Maine | −48 | Jan. 16, 2009 | 105 | July 10, 1911 |
| Maryland | −40 | Jan. 13, 1912 | 109 | July 10, 1936 |
| Massachusetts | −35 | Jan. 12, 1981 | 107 | Aug. 2, 1975 |
| Michigan | −51 | Feb. 9, 1934 | 112 | July 13, 1936 |
| Minnesota | −60 | Feb. 2, 1996 | 114 | July 6, 1936 |
| Mississippi | −19 | Jan. 30, 1966 | 115 | July 29, 1930 |
| Missouri | −40 | Feb. 13, 1905 | 118 | July 14, 1954 |
| Montana | −70 | Jan. 20, 1954 | 117 | July 5, 1937 |
| Nebraska | −47 | Dec. 22, 1989 | 118 | July 24, 1936 |
| Nevada | −50 | Jan. 8, 1937 | 125 | June 29, 1994 |
| New Hampshire | −47 | Jan. 29, 1934 | 106 | July 4, 1911 |
| New Jersey | −34 | Jan. 5, 1904 | 110 | July 10, 1936 |
| New Mexico | −50 | Feb. 1, 1951 | 122 | June 27, 1994 |
| New York | −52 | Feb. 18, 1979 | 108 | July 22, 1926 |
| North Carolina | −34 | Jan. 21, 1985 | 110 | Aug. 21, 1983 |
| North Dakota | −60 | Feb. 15, 1936 | 121 | July 6, 1936 |
| Ohio | −39 | Feb. 10, 1899 | 113 | July 21, 1934 |
| Oklahoma | −27 | Jan. 18, 1930 | 120 | June 27, 1994 |
| Oregon | −54 | Feb. 10, 1933 | 119 | Aug. 10, 1898 |
| Pennsylvania | −42 | Jan. 5, 1904 | 111 | July 10, 1936 |
| Rhode Island | −25 | Feb. 5, 1996 | 104 | Aug. 2, 1975 |
| South Carolina | −19 | Jan. 21, 1985 | 111 | June 28, 1954 |
| South Dakota | −58 | Feb. 17, 1936 | 120 | July 15, 2006 |
| Tennessee | −32 | Dec. 30, 1917 | 113 | Aug. 9, 1930 |
| Texas | −23 | Feb. 8, 1933 | 120 | June 28, 1994 |
| Utah | −69 | Feb. 1, 1985 | 117 | July 5, 1985 |
| Vermont | −50 | Dec. 30, 1933 | 105 | July 4, 1911 |
| Virginia | −30 | Jan. 22, 1985 | 110 | July 15, 1954 |
| Washington | −48 | Dec. 30, 1968 | 118 | Aug. 5, 1961 |
| West Virginia | −37 | Dec. 30, 1917 | 112 | July 10, 1936 |
| Wisconsin | −55 | Feb. 4, 1996 | 114 | July 13, 1936 |
| Wyoming | −66 | Feb. 9, 1933 | 115 | Aug. 8, 1983 |

Record temperatures may have occurred on earlier dates. Dates listed here are for most recent occurrence of a record temperature.

# Weights & Measures

At what temperature does water boil? ➡ page 315

**M**etrology isn't the study of weather. (That's meteorology.) It is the science of measurement. Almost everything you use every day is measured—either when it is made or when it's sold. Materials for buildings and parts for machines must be measured carefully so they will fit together. Clothes have sizes so you'll know which to choose. Many items sold in a supermarket are priced by weight or by volume.

## EARLIEST MEASUREMENTS

The human body was the first "ruler." An "inch" was the width of a thumb; a "hand" was five fingers wide; a "foot" was—you guessed it—the length of a foot! A "cubit" ran from the elbow to the tip of the middle finger (about 20 inches), and a "yard" was the length of a whole arm.

Later, measurements came from daily activities, like plowing. A "furlong" was the distance an ox team could plow before stopping to rest (now we say it is about 220 yards). The trouble with these units was that they were different from person to person, place to place, and ox to ox.

## MEASUREMENTS WE USE TODAY

The official system in the U.S. is the customary system (sometimes called the imperial or English system). Scientists and most other countries use the International System of Units (metric system). The Weights and Measures Division of the U.S. National Institute of Standards and Technology (NIST) makes sure that a gallon of milk in California is the same as one in New York. When the NIST was founded in 1901, there were as many as eight different "standard" gallons in the U.S. and four different legal measures of a "foot" in Brooklyn, New York, alone.

ANCIENT MEASURE

**1 foot =**
length of a person's foot

**1 yard =**
from nose to fingertip

**1 acre =**
land an ox could plow in a day

12 inches

3 feet or 36 inches

4,840 square yards

MODERN MEASURE

# TAKING TEMPERATURES

There are two main systems for measuring temperature. One is **Fahrenheit** (abbreviated F). The other is **Celsius** (abbreviated C). Another word for Celsius is Centigrade.

Zero degrees (0°) Celsius is equal to 32 degrees (32°) Fahrenheit.

## To convert from Celsius to Fahrenheit:

Multiply by 1.8 and add 32.
($°F = 1.8 \times °C + 32$)

**Example:** $20°C \times 1.8 = 36; 36 + 32 = 68°F$

## To convert from Fahrenheit to Celsius, reverse the process:

Subtract 32 and divide by 1.8.

**Example:** $68°F - 32 = 36; 36 \div 1.8 = 20°C$

**Boiling Point of Water**
212°F   100°C

**Normal Room Temperature**
68°F    20°C

**Freezing Point of Water**
32°F    0°C

212°
68°
32°
−40°

100°
20°
0°
−40°

← Fahrenheit

Celsius →

F    C

# HOTTEST and COLDEST Places in the World

| Continent | Highest Temperature | Lowest Temperature |
|---|---|---|
| AFRICA | El Azizia, Libya, 136°F (58°C) | Ifrane, Morocco, −11°F (−24°C) |
| ANTARCTICA | Vanda Station, 59°F (15°C) | Vostok, −129°F (−89°C) |
| ASIA | Tirat Tsvi, Israel, 129°F (54°C) | Verkhoyansk, Russia, and Oimekon, Russia, −90°F (−68°C) |
| AUSTRALIA | Cloncurry, Queensland, 128°F (53°C) | Charlotte Pass, New South Wales, −9°F (−23°C) |
| EUROPE | Seville, Spain, 122°F (50°C) | Ust'Shchugor, Russia, −67°F (−55°C) |
| NORTH AMERICA | Death Valley, California, 134°F (57°C) | Snag, Yukon Territory, Canada, −81°F (−63°C) |
| SOUTH AMERICA | Rivadavia, Argentina, 120°F (49°C) | Sarmiento, Argentina, −27°F (−33°C) |

**did you know?**

Through 2008, six of the ten warmest years on record for the contiguous U.S. have occurred since 1998, according to the National Climatic Data Center. Annual temperature records date back to 1895.

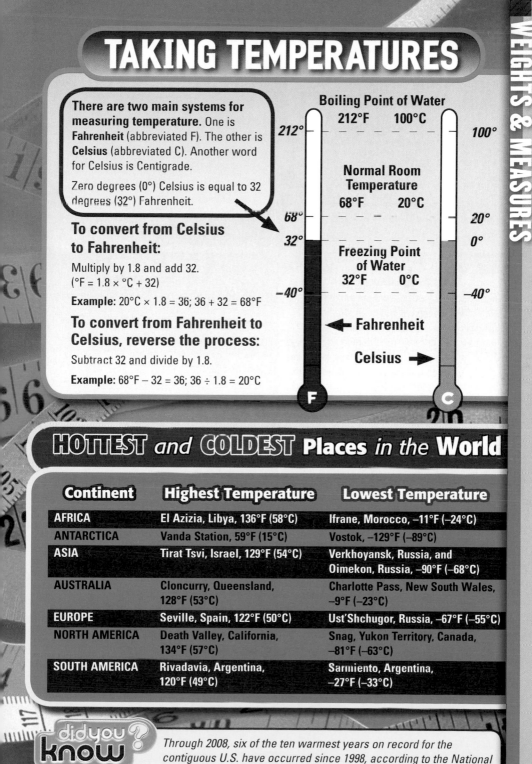

# LENGTH

The basic unit of **length** in the U.S. system is the **inch**. Length, width, and thickness all use the inch or larger related units.

1 foot (ft) = 12 inches (in.)

1 yard (yd) = 3 feet = 36 inches

1 rod (rd) = 5½ yards

1 furlong (fur) = 40 rods = 220 yards
= 660 feet

1 mile (mi) (also called statute mile) =
8 furlongs = 1,760 yards = 5,280 feet

1 nautical mile = 6,076.1 feet = 1.15 statute miles

1 league = 3 miles

# AREA

**Area** is used to measure a section of a two-dimensional surface like the floor or a piece of paper. Most area measurements are given in **square units**. Land is measured in **acres**.

1 square foot (sq ft) = 144 square inches
(sq in.)

1 square yard (sq yd) = 9 square feet =
1,296 square inches

1 square rod (sq rd) = 30¼ square yards

1 acre = 160 square rods = 4,840 square yards
= 43,560 square feet

1 square mile (sq mi) = 640 acres

# CAPACITY

Units of **capacity** are used to measure how much of something will fit into a container. **Liquid measure** is used to measure liquids, such as water or gasoline. **Dry measure** is used with large amounts of solid materials, like grain or fruit. Although both liquid and dry measures use the terms "pint" and "quart," they mean different amounts and should not be confused.

## Dry Measure

1 quart (qt) = 2 pints (pt)
1 peck (pk) = 8 quarts
1 bushel (bu) = 4 pecks

## Liquid Measure

1 gill = 4 fluid ounces (fl oz)
1 pint (pt) = 4 gills = 16 ounces (oz)
1 quart (qt) = 2 pints = 32 ounces
1 gallon (gal) = 4 quarts = 128 ounces

For measuring most U.S. liquids,
1 barrel (bbl) = 31½ gallons

For measuring oil, 1 barrel = 42 gallons

## Cooking Measurements

The measurements used in cooking are based on the **fluid ounce**.
1 teaspoon (tsp) = ⅙ fluid ounce (fl oz)
1 tablespoon (tbsp) = 3 teaspoons
= ½ fluid ounce
1 cup = 16 tablespoons = 8 fluid ounces
1 pint = 2 cups
1 quart (qt) = 2 pints (pt)
1 gallon (gal)= 4 quarts

# VOLUME

The amount of space taken up by a three-dimensional object (or the amount of space available within an object) is measured in **volume**. Volume is usually expressed in **cubic units**. If you wanted to buy a room air conditioner and needed to know how much space there was to be cooled, you could measure the room in cubic feet.

1 cubic foot (cu ft) = 12 inches x 12 inches
x 12 inches = 1,728
cubic inches (cu in.)
1 cubic yard (cu yd) = 27 cubic feet

# DEPTH

Some measurements of length are used to measure ocean depth and distance.

1 fathom = 6 feet (ft)
1 cable = 120 fathoms = 720 feet

# WEIGHT

Although 1 cubic foot of popcorn and 1 cubic foot of rock take up the same amount of space, it wouldn't feel the same if you tried to lift them. We measure heaviness as **weight**. Most objects are measured in **avoirdupois weight** (pronounced a-ver-de-POIZ):

1 dram (dr) = 27.344 grains (gr)
1 ounce (oz) = 16 drams = 437.5 grains
1 pound (lb) = 16 ounces
1 hundredweight (cwt) = 100 pounds
1 ton = 2,000 pounds (also called short ton)

# THE **METRIC** SYSTEM

The metric system was created in France in 1795. Standardized in 1960 and given the name International System of Units, it is now used in most countries and in scientific works. The system is based on 10, like the decimal counting system. The basic unit for length is the **meter**. The **liter** is a basic unit of volume or capacity, and the **gram** is a basic unit of mass. Related units are made by adding a prefix to the basic unit. The prefixes and their meanings are:

milli- $= \dfrac{1}{1,000}$

**centi-** $= \dfrac{1}{100}$

deci- $= \dfrac{1}{10}$

deka- = **10**

**hecto-** = **100**

kilo- = **1,000**

## For Example

milli**meter (mm)** $= \dfrac{1}{1,000}$ of a meter

kilo**meter (km)** = 1,000 meters

milli**gram (mg)** $= \dfrac{1}{1,000}$ of a gram

kilo**gram (kg)** = 1,000 grams

To get a rough idea of measurements in the metric system, it helps to know that a **liter** is a little more than a quart. A **meter** is a little over a yard. A **kilogram** is a little over 2 pounds. And a **kilometer** is just over half a mile.

## Homework Tip Converting Measurements

| From: | Multiply by: | To get: | From: | Multiply by: | To get: |
|---|---|---|---|---|---|
| inches | 2.5400 | centimeters | centimeters | 0.3937 | inches |
| inches | 0.0254 | meters | centimeters | 0.0328 | feet |
| feet | 30.4800 | centimeters | meters | 39.3701 | inches |
| feet | 0.3048 | meters | meters | 3.2808 | feet |
| yards | 0.9144 | meters | meters | 1.0936 | yards |
| miles | 1.6093 | kilometers | kilometers | 0.6210 | miles |
| square inches | 6.4516 | square centimeters | square centimeters | 0.1550 | square inches |
| square feet | 0.0929 | square meters | square meters | 10.7639 | square feet |
| square yards | 0.8361 | square meters | square meters | 1.1960 | square yards |
| acres | 0.4047 | hectares | hectares | 2.4710 | acres |
| cubic inches | 16.3871 | cubic centimeters | cubic centimeters | 0.0610 | cubic inches |
| cubic feet | 0.0283 | cubic meters | cubic meters | 35.3147 | cubic feet |
| cubic yards | 0.7646 | cubic meters | cubic meters | 1.3080 | cubic yards |
| quarts (liquid) | 0.9464 | liters | liters | 1.0567 | quarts (liquid) |
| ounces | 28.3495 | grams | grams | 0.0353 | ounces |
| pounds | 0.4536 | kilograms | kilograms | 2.2046 | pounds |

# World History

What was the Silk Road? ➡ page 322

**E**ach of the five sections in this chapter tells the history of a major region of the world: the Middle East, Africa, Asia, Europe, or the Americas. Major events from ancient times to the present are described under the headings for each region.

# THE ANCIENT MIDDLE EAST

**4000–3000 B.C.** The world's first cities are built by the Sumerian peoples in Mesopotamia, now southern Iraq. Sumerians develop a kind of writing called **cuneiform**. Egyptians develop a kind of writing called **hieroglyphics**.

▲*hieroglyphics*

**2700 B.C.** Egyptians begin building the great pyramids in the desert.

**1792 B.C.** Some of the first written laws are created in Babylonia. They are called the Code of Hammurabi.

**1200 B.C.** Hebrew people settle in Canaan in Palestine after escaping from slavery in Egypt. They are led by the prophet Moses.

**1000 B.C.** King David unites the Hebrews in one strong kingdom. ▶

### ANCIENT PALESTINE
Palestine was invaded by many different peoples after 1000 B.C., including the Babylonians, Egyptians, Persians, and Romans.

**336 B.C.** Alexander the Great, King of Macedonia, builds an empire from Egypt to India.

## ISLAM: A RELIGION GROWS IN THE MIDDLE EAST A.D. 610–632
Around 610, the prophet Muhammad starts to proclaim and teach Islam. This religion spreads from Arabia to all the neighboring regions in the Middle East and North Africa. Its followers are called Muslims.

### THE KORAN
The holy book of Islam is the Koran. It was related by Muhammad beginning in 611.

▲ *The Koran*

### THE SPREAD OF ISLAM
The Arab armies that went across North Africa brought great change:
• The people who lived there were converted to Islam.
• The Arabic language replaced many local languages as an official language. North Africa is still an Arabic-speaking region today, and Islam is the major faith.

**63 B.C.** Romans conquer Palestine and make it part of their empire.

**Around 4 B.C.** Jesus Christ, the founder of the Christian religion, is born in Bethlehem. He is crucified about A.D. 29.

**A.D. 632** Muhammad dies. By now, Islam is accepted in Arabia as a religion.

**641** Arab Muslims conquer the Persians.

**Late 600s** Islam begins to spread to the west into Africa and Spain.

▼ *The pyramids at Giza*

# THE MIDDLE EAST

**THE UMAYYAD AND ABBASID DYNASTIES** The Umayyads (661-750) and the Abbasids (750-1256) are the first two Muslim-led dynasties. Both empires stretch across northern Africa and the Middle East into Asia.

**711–732** Umayyads invade Europe but are defeated by Frankish leader Charles Martel in France. This defeat halts the spread of Islam into Western Europe.

**1071** Muslim Turks conquer Jerusalem.

**1095–1291** Europeans try to take back Jerusalem and other parts of the Middle East for Christians during the Crusades.

**1300-1900s** The Ottoman Turks, who are Muslims, create a huge empire, covering the Middle East, North Africa, and part of Eastern Europe. European countries take over portions of it beginning in the 1800s.

**1914-1918** World War I begins in 1914. Most of the Middle East falls under British or French control.

**1921** Two new Arab kingdoms are created: Transjordan and Iraq. The French take control of Syria and Lebanon.

**1922** Egypt becomes independent from Britain.

**JEWS MIGRATE TO PALESTINE** Jews began migrating to Palestine in the 1880s. In 1945, after World War II, many Jews who survived the Holocaust migrated to Palestine.

**1948** The state of Israel is created.

**THE ARAB-ISRAELI WARS** Arab countries near Israel (Egypt, Iraq, Jordan, Lebanon, and Syria) attack the new country in 1948 but fail to destroy it. Israel and its neighbors fight wars again in 1956, 1967, and 1973. Israel wins each war. In the 1967 war, Israel captures the Sinai Desert from Egypt, the Golan Heights from Syria, and the West Bank from Jordan.

**1979** Egypt and Israel sign a peace treaty. Israel returns the Sinai to Egypt.

◄ *Anwar al-Sadat, Jimmy Carter, Menachem Begin celebrate signing of peace treaty.*

**THE MIDDLE EAST AND OIL** About 20% of the oil we use to drive cars, heat homes, and run machines comes from the Middle East. Many countries rely on oil imports from the region, which has more than half the world's crude oil reserves.

**The 1990s and 2000s**

• In 1991, the U.S. and its allies go to war with Iraq after Iraq invades Kuwait. Iraq is defeated and signs a peace agreement but is accused of violating it. In 2003, the U.S., Britain, and other allies invade Iraq and remove the regime of Saddam Hussein. Free elections are held and a democratic government is formed, but violence there continues.

• Tensions between Israel and the Palestinians increase. In 2005, Israel pulls out from Gaza. In 2006, Palestinian elections in the West Bank and Gaza bring Hamas, an organization that has historically been dedicated to eliminating the state of Israel, to power.

*Dome of the Rock and the Western Wall, Jerusalem* ▼

319

# ANCIENT AFRICA

**ANCIENT AFRICA** In ancient times, northern Africa was dominated by the Egyptians, Greeks, and Romans. However, we know very little about the lives of ancient Africans south of the Sahara Desert. They did not have written languages. What we learn about them comes from weapons, tools, and other items from their civilization.

**2000 B.C.** The Nubian Kingdom of Kush, rich with gold, ivory, and jewels, arises south of Egypt. It is a major center of art, learning, and trade until around A.D. 350.

**1000 B.C.** Bantu-speaking people around Cameroon begin an 1,800-year expansion into much of eastern and southern Africa.

**500 B.C.** Carthage, an empire centered in Tunisia, becomes rich and powerful through trading. Its ports span the African coast of the Mediterranean Sea. Rome defeats Carthage and its most famous leader, ◄Hannibal, during the second Punic War (218-201 B.C.).

• The Nok in Nigeria are the earliest users of iron for tools and weapons south of the Sahara Desert. They are also known for their terracotta sculptures.

• The Christian Kingdom of Aksum in northern Ethiopia becomes a wealthy trading center on the Red Sea for treasures like ivory. It makes its own coins and monuments, many of which survive today.

**By A.D. 700** Ghana, the first known empire south of the Sahara Desert, takes power through trade around the upper Senegal and Niger Rivers. Its Mande people control the trade in gold from nearby mines to Arabs in the north.

**By 900** Arab Muslim merchants bring Islam to the Bantu speakers along the east coast of Africa, creating the Swahili language and culture. Traders in Kenya and Tanzania export ivory, slaves, perfumes, and gold to Asia.

**1054-1145** Islamic Berbers unite into the Almoravid Kingdom centered at Marrakech, Morocco. They spread into Ghana and southern Spain.

**1230-1400s** A Mande prince named Sundiata (the "Lion King") forms the Mali Kingdom where Ghana once stood. Timbuktu becomes its main city.

**1250-1400s** Great Zimbabwe becomes the largest settlement (12,000-20,000 Bantu-speaking people) in southern Africa.

**1464-1591** As Mali loses power, Songhai rises to become the third and final great empire of western Africa.

**1481** Portugal sets up the first permanent European trading post south of the Sahara Desert at Elmina, Ghana. Slaves, in addition to gold and ivory, are soon exported.

**1483-1665** Kongo, the most powerful kingdom on central Africa's west coast, provides thousands of slaves each year for Portugal. Portugal's colony Angola overtakes the Kongo in 1665.

*Camel train moving across the Sahara*

# AFRICA

**1650-1810** Slave trading peaks across the "Slave Coast" from eastern Ghana to western Nigeria as competing African states sell tens of thousands of captured foes each year to competing European traders.

## THE AFRICAN SLAVE TRADE

African slaves were taken to the Caribbean to harvest sugar on European plantations. Later, slaves were taken to South America and the United States. The ships from Africa were overcrowded and diseased. About 20% of the slaves died during the long journey.

**1652** The Dutch East India Company sets up a supply camp in southern Africa at the Cape of Good Hope (later Cape Town). Dutch settlers and French Protestants called Huguenots establish Cape Colony. Their descendants are known as the Boers or Afrikaners and develop a distinct language and culture.

**1792** Freed slaves, mostly from Britain and the Americas, found Freetown in Sierra Leone.

**1803** Denmark is the first European country to ban slave trading. Britain follows in 1807, the U.S. in 1808. Most European nations ban the trade by 1820, but illegal trading continues for decades.

**1814** Britain purchases the Dutch South African colony at Cape Town. British colonists arrive after 1820.

**1816-28** The Zulus, ruled by the chieftain Shaka, dominate eastern South Africa.

**1835-43** The "Great Trek" (march) of the Boers away from British Cape Town.

**1884-85** European nations meet in Berlin and agree to divide control of Africa. No African states are invited to the agreements. The "Scramble for Africa" lasts until World War I. Only Ethiopia and Liberia remain independent.

**1899-1902** Great Britain and the Boers fight in South Africa in the Boer War. The Boers accept British rule but are allowed a role in government.

**1948** The white Afrikaner-dominated South African government creates the policy of apartheid ("apartness"), the total separation of races. Blacks are banned from many restaurants, theaters, schools, and jobs. Apartheid sparks protests, many of which end in bloodshed.

**1957** Ghana gains independence from Britain, becoming the first territory in Africa below the Sahara to regain freedom from European rule. Over the next 20 years, the rest of Africa gains independence.

**1990-94** South Africa abolishes its policy of apartheid. In 1994, Nelson Mandela becomes South Africa's first black president. ▶

**1994** Fighting between Hutu and Tutsi ethnic groups in Rwanda leads to the massacre of more than 800,000 civilians.

**1998-2004** Fighting in the Democratic Republic of the Congo involves 9 nations. About 4 million die, mostly from starvation and disease. While the war is officially over by 2003, fighting continues.

▼ **2006** Ellen Johnson-Sirleaf becomes president of Liberia, and Africa's first elected female leader.

**2009** Conflict that began in 2003 continues in the Darfur region of Sudan, although there is some evidence that the level of violence is declining.

*A savanna in Kenya*

321

**3500 B.C.** People settle in the Indus River Valley of India and Pakistan and the Yellow River Valley of China.

**2500 B.C.** Cities of Mohenjo-Daro and Harappa in Pakistan become centers of trade and farming.

**Around 1523 B.C.** Shang peoples in China build walled towns and use a kind of writing based on pictures. This writing develops into the writing Chinese people use today.

**Around 1050 B.C.** Chou peoples in China overthrow the Shang and control large territories.

**563 B.C.** Siddhartha Gautama is born in India. He becomes known as the Buddha—the "Enlightened One"—and is the founder of the Buddhist religion (Buddhism).

**551 B.C.** The Chinese philosopher Confucius is born. His teachings—especially rules about how people should treat each other—spread throughout China and are still followed today.

**320–232 B.C.**
• Northern India is united under the emperor Chandragupta Maurya.
• Asoka, emperor of India, sends Buddhist missionaries throughout southern Asia to spread the Buddhist religion.

**221 B.C.** The Chinese begin building the Great Wall. Its main section is more than 2,000 miles long and is meant to keep invading peoples out.

**202 B.C.** The Han people of China win control of all of China.

**A.D. 320** The Gupta Empire controls northern India. The Guptas, who are Hindus, drive the Buddhist religion out of India. They are well known for their many advances in mathematics and medicine.

**618** The Tang dynasty begins in China. The Tang dynasty is well known for music, poetry, and painting. They export silk and porcelains as far away as Africa.

**THE SILK ROAD** Around 100 B.C., only the Chinese knew how to make silk. To get this light, comfortable material, Europeans sent fortunes in glass, gold, jade, and other items to China. The exchanges between Europeans and Chinese created one of the greatest trading routes in history—the Silk Road. Chinese inventions such as paper and gunpowder were also spread via the Silk Road. Europeans found out how to make silk around A.D. 500, but trade continued until about 1400.

**960** The Northern Sung dynasty in China makes advances in banking and paper money. China's population of 50 million doubles over 200 years, thanks to improved ways of farming that lead to greater food production.

*The Forbidden City*

# ASIA

**1000** The Samurai, a warrior people, become powerful in Japan. They live by a code of honor known as *Bushido*. ▶

**1180** The Khmer Empire in Cambodia becomes widely known for its beautiful temples.

**1206** The Mongol leader Genghis Khan creates an empire that stretches from China to India, Russia, and Eastern Europe.

**1264** Kublai Khan, grandson of Genghis Khan, rules China as emperor from his new capital at Beijing.

**1368** The Ming dynasty comes to power in China. The Ming drive the Mongols out of the country.

**1526** The Mughal Empire in India begins under Babur. The Mughals are Muslims who invade and conquer India.

**1644** The Ming dynasty in China is overthrown by the Manchu peoples.

**1839** The Opium War takes place in China between the Chinese and the British. The British and other Western powers want to control trade in Asia. The Chinese want the British to stop selling opium to the Chinese. Britain wins the war in 1842.

**1858** The French begin to take control of Indochina (Southeast Asia).

**1868** In Japan, Emperor Meiji comes to power. Western ideas begin to influence the Japanese.

---

**THE JAPANESE IN ASIA** Japan became a powerful country during the early 20th century. In the 1930s, Japan began to invade some of its neighbors. In 1941, the United States and Japan went to war after Japan attacked the U.S. Navy at Pearl Harbor, Hawaii.

▼ *Statues from Angkor Wat temple, Cambodia*

**1945** Japan is defeated in World War II after the U.S. drops atomic bombs on the Japanese cities of Hiroshima and Nagasaki.

**1947** India and Pakistan become independent from Great Britain.

**1949** China comes under the rule of the Communists led by Mao Zedong. The Communist government abolishes private property and takes over all businesses. ▶

**1950–1953** **THE KOREAN WAR** North Korea, a Communist country, invades South Korea. The U.S. and other nations join to fight the invasion. China joins North Korea. The fighting ends in 1953. Neither side wins.

**1954–1975** **THE VIETNAM WAR** The French are defeated in Indochina in 1954 by Vietnamese nationalists. The U.S. sends troops in 1965 to fight on the side of South Vietnam against the Communists in the North. The U.S. withdraws in 1973. In 1975, South Vietnam is taken over by North Vietnam.

**1989** Chinese students protest for democracy, but the protests are crushed by the army in Beijing's Tiananmen Square.

**The 1990s** Britain returns Hong Kong to China (1997). China builds its economy, but does not allow democracy.

**The 2000s** U.S.-led military action overthrows the Taliban regime in Afghanistan (2001) and seeks to root out terrorists there. North Korea admits it has been developing nuclear weapons, and Iran is believed to be developing them.

A powerful earthquake in the Indian Ocean in December 2004 sets off huge waves (tsunamis) that kill more than 225,000 people in Indonesia, Sri Lanka, and other countries.

In August 2008, for the first time China hosts the Summer Olympic Games in Beijing.

In 2009, the United States sends additional troops to Afghanistan to fight the Taliban, which has regained strength.

# ANCIENT EUROPE

**4000 B.C.** People in Europe start building monuments out of large stones called megaliths, such as Stonehenge in England.

**2500 B.C.–1200 B.C.**
### The Minoans and the Mycenaeans
- People on the island of Crete (Minoans) in the Mediterranean Sea build great palaces and become sailors and traders.
- People from Mycenae invade Crete and destroy the power of the Minoans.

**THE TROJAN WAR** The Trojan War was a conflict between invading Greeks and the people of Troas (Troy) in Southwestern Turkey around 1200 B.C. Although little is known today about the real war, it has become a part of Greek mythology (pages 134-135). According to legend, a group of Greek soldiers hid inside a huge wooden horse. The horse was pulled into the city of Troy. Then the soldiers jumped out of the horse and conquered Troy.

**900-600 B.C.** Celtic peoples in Northern Europe settle on farms and in villages and learn to mine for iron ore.

**600 B.C.** Etruscan peoples take over most of Italy. They build many cities and become traders.

## SOME ACHIEVEMENTS OF THE GREEKS
The early Greeks were responsible for

- the first governments that were elected by people,
- great poets such as Homer, who composed the *Iliad* and the *Odyssey*,

▲ *Socrates*

- great thinkers such as Socrates, Plato, and Aristotle,
- great architecture, like the Parthenon and the Temple of Athena Nike on the Acropolis in Athens.

**431 B.C.** The Peloponnesian Wars begin between the Greek cities of Athens and Sparta. The wars end in 404 B.C. when Sparta wins.

**338 B.C.** King Philip II of Macedonia in northern Greece conquers all of Greece.

**336 B.C.** Philip's son Alexander the Great becomes king. He makes an empire from the Mediterranean Sea to India. For the next 300 years, Greek culture dominates this vast area.

**264 B.C.– A.D. 476**
### THE ROMAN EMPIRE
The city of Rome in Italy begins to expand and capture surrounding lands. The Romans gradually build a great empire and control all of the Mediterranean region. At its height, the Roman Empire includes Western Europe, Greece, Egypt, and much of the Middle East. It lasts until A.D. 476.

*Stonehenge*

# ANCIENT **EUROPE**

## ROMAN ACHIEVEMENTS

- Roman law; many of our laws are based on Roman law.
- Great roads to connect their huge empire; The Appian Way, south of Rome, is a Roman road that is still in use today.
- Aqueducts to bring water to the people in large cities.
- Great sculpture; Roman statues can still be seen in Europe.
- Great architecture; The Colosseum, which still stands in Rome today, is an example.
- Great writers, such as the poet Virgil, who wrote the *Aeneid*.

**49 B.C.** A civil war breaks out that destroys Rome's republican form of government.

**45 B.C.** Julius Caesar becomes the sole ruler of Rome but is murdered one year later by rivals.

**27 B.C.** Octavian becomes the first emperor of Rome. He takes the name Augustus. A peaceful period of almost 200 years begins.

**THE CHRISTIAN FAITH** Christians believe that Jesus Christ is the Son of God. The history and beliefs of Christianity are found in the New Testament of the Bible. Christianity spread slowly throughout the Roman Empire. The Romans tried to stop the new religion and persecuted the Christians. They were forced to hold their services in hiding, and some were crucified. Eventually, more and more Romans became Christian.

*A painting of Jesus Christ*

**THE BYZANTINE EMPIRE**, centered in modern-day Turkey, was the eastern half of the old Roman Empire. Byzantine rulers extended their power into western Europe; the Byzantine Emperor Justinian ruled parts of Spain, North Africa, and Italy. Constantinople (now Istanbul, Turkey) became the capital of the Byzantine Empire in A.D. 330.

**A.D. 313** The Roman Emperor Constantine gives full rights to Christians. He eventually becomes a Christian himself.

**410** The Visigoths and other barbarian tribes from northern Europe invade the Roman Empire and begin to take over its lands.

▲ *Constantine*

**476** The last Roman emperor, Romulus Augustus, is overthrown.

**768** Charlemagne becomes king of the Franks in northern Europe. He rules a kingdom that includes parts of France, Germany, and northern Italy.

**800** Feudalism becomes important in Europe. Feudalism means that poor farmers are allowed to farm a lord's land in return for certain services to the lord.

**896** Magyar peoples found Hungary.

**800s–900s** Viking warriors and traders from Scandinavia begin to move into the British Isles, France, and parts of the Mediterranean.

**989** The Russian state of Kiev becomes Christian.

▼ *The Colosseum, Rome*

# EUROPE

**1066** William of Normandy, a Frenchman, successfully invades England and makes himself king. He is known as William the Conqueror.

**1096–1291 THE CRUSADES** In 1096, Christian leaders send a series of armies to try to capture Jerusalem from the Muslims. In the end, the Christians do not succeed. However, trade increases greatly between the Middle East and Europe.

**1215** The Magna Carta is a document agreed to by King John of England and the English nobility. The English king agrees that he does not have absolute power and has to obey the laws of the land. The Magna Carta is an important step toward democracy.

▲ *King John*

**1290** The Ottoman Empire begins. It is controlled by Turkish Muslims who conquer lands in the eastern Mediterranean and the Middle East.

**1337** The Hundred Years' War begins in Europe between France and England. The war lasts until 1453 when France wins.

**1348** The bubonic plague (Black Death) begins in Europe. As much as one-third of the whole population of Europe dies from this disease, caused by the bite of infected fleas.

**1453** The Ottoman Turks capture the city of Constantinople and rename it Istanbul.

**1517 THE REFORMATION** The Protestant Reformation splits European Christians apart. It starts when German priest Martin Luther breaks away from the Roman Catholic pope.

▲ *Martin Luther*

**1534** King Henry VIII of England breaks away from the Roman Catholic church. He names himself head of the English (Anglican) church.

**1558** The reign of King Henry's daughter Elizabeth I begins in England.

**1588** The Spanish Armada (fleet of warships) is defeated by the English Navy as Spain tries to invade England.

**1600s** The Ottoman Turks expand their empire through most of eastern and central Europe.

**1618** Much of Europe is destroyed in the Thirty Years' War, which ends in 1648.

**1642** The English Civil War begins. King Charles I fights against the forces of the Parliament. The king is defeated, and executed in 1649. His son, Charles II, returns as king in 1660.

**1789 THE FRENCH REVOLUTION** The French Revolution ends the rule of kings in France and leads to democracy there. At first, however, there are wars and times when dictators take control. Many people are executed. King Louis XVI and Queen Marie Antoinette are overthrown in the Revolution, and both are executed in 1793.

◄ *Arc de Triomphe, Paris*

# EUROPE

**1762** Catherine the Great becomes Empress of Russia. She extends the Russian Empire.

**1799** Napoleon Bonaparte, an army officer, becomes dictator of France. Under his rule, France conquers most of Europe by 1812.

**1815** Napoleon's forces are defeated by the British and German armies at Waterloo (in Belgium). Napoleon is exiled to a remote island and dies there in 1821.

**1848** Revolutions break out in countries of Europe. People force their rulers to make more democratic changes.

**1914–1918 WORLD WAR I IN EUROPE**
At the start of World War I in Europe, Germany, Austria-Hungary, and the Ottoman Empire oppose England, France, Russia, and, later, the U.S. (the Allies). The Allies win in 1918.

▼ *Tsar Nicholas II*

**1917** The Tsar is overthrown in the Russian Revolution. The Bolsheviks (Communists) under Vladimir Lenin take control. Millions are starved, sent to labor camps, or executed under Joseph Stalin (1929-1953).

**THE RISE OF HITLER** Adolf Hitler became dictator of Germany in 1933. He joined forces with rulers in Italy and Japan to form the Axis powers. In World War II (1939-1945), the Axis powers were defeated by the Allies—Great Britain, the Soviet Union, and the U.S. During his rule, Hitler's Nazis killed millions of Jews and other people in the Holocaust.

▲ *Italy's Benito Mussolini and Adolf Hitler*

**The 1990s** Communist governments in Eastern Europe are replaced by democratic ones. Divided Germany becomes one nation, and the Soviet Union breaks up. The European Union (EU) forms. The North Atlantic Treaty Organization (NATO) bombs Yugoslavia in an effort to protect Albanians driven out of the Kosovo region.

**2005** Riots in Paris suburbs express the discontent of France's large minority Muslim population, which numbers 5-6 million.

**2009** Europe suffers through major economic recession, and unemployment surges.

## All About >> AUSTRALIA

Australian aborigines (native peoples) have lived there for more than 60,000 years. In the 17th century, Portuguese, Dutch, and Spanish expeditions explored Australian coasts. In the 1770s, Capt. James Cook of Britain made three voyages to the continent, cementing Britain's claims of ownership. On May 13, 1787, Capt. Arthur Phillip brought 11 ships from Britain, carrying convicts and guards. Although the first communities were prison colonies, regular immigrants settled around the continent over the 19th century. Wool and mining were major industries. Australia was established as a commonwealth of Great Britain on January 1, 1901. Today, Australia is a country of more than 21 million people. It is famous for exotic animals like kangaroos and koalas. It is also the home of actors Russell Crowe and Nicole Kidman. The Sydney Opera House is a world-famous landmark.

*Sydney Opera House* ▶

# THE AMERICAS

**10,000-8000 B.C.** People in North and South America gather plants for food and hunt animals using stone-pointed spears.

**Around 3000 B.C.** People in Central America begin farming, growing corn and beans for food.

**1500 B.C.** Mayan people in Central America begin to live in small villages.

**500 B.C.** People in North America begin to hunt buffalo to use for meat and for clothing.

**100 B.C.** The city of Teotihuacán is founded in Mexico. It becomes the center of a huge empire extending from central Mexico to Guatemala. Teotihuacán contains many large pyramids and temples.

**A.D. 150** Mayan people in Guatemala build many centers for religious ceremonies. They create a calendar and learn mathematics and astronomy.

**900** Toltec warriors in Mexico begin to invade lands of Mayan people. Mayans leave their old cities and move to the Yucatan Peninsula of Mexico.

**1000** Native Americans in the southwestern United States begin to live in settlements called pueblos. They learn to farm.

**1325** Mexican Indians known as Aztecs create the huge city of Tenochtitlán and rule a large empire in Mexico. They are warriors who practice human sacrifice.

**1492** Christopher Columbus sails from Europe across the Atlantic Ocean and lands in the Bahamas, in the Caribbean Sea. This marks the first step toward the founding of European settlements in the Americas.

*Christopher* ▲
*Columbus*

**1500** Portuguese explorers reach Brazil and claim it for Portugal.

**1519** Spanish conqueror Hernán Cortés travels into the Aztec Empire in search of gold. The Aztecs are defeated in 1521 by Cortés. The Spanish take control of Mexico. ▶

**WHY DID THE SPANISH WIN?** How did the Spanish defeat the powerful Aztec Empire in such a short time? One reason is that the Spanish had better weapons. Another is that many Aztecs died from diseases brought to the New World by the Spanish. The Aztecs had never had these illnesses before, and so did not have immunity to them. Also, many neighboring Indians hated the Aztecs as conquerors and helped the Spanish to defeat them.

**1534** Jacques Cartier of France explores Canada.

**1583** The first English colony in Canada is set up in Newfoundland.

**1607** English colonists led by Captain John Smith settle in Jamestown, Virginia. Virginia becomes the oldest of the original thirteen colonies that will form the United States.

**1619** First African slaves arrive in English-controlled America.

**1682** The French explorer René Robert Cavelier, sieur de La Salle, sails down the Mississippi River. The area is named Louisiana after the French King Louis XIV.

*Chac Mool, Mayan Figure* ▶

# THE AMERICAS

**EUROPEAN COLONIES** By 1700, most of the Americas are under the control of Europeans.

**Spain:** Florida, southwestern United States, Mexico, Central America, western South America

**Portugal:** eastern South America

**France:** central United States, parts of Canada

**England:** eastern U.S., parts of Canada

**Holland:** eastern U.S., West Indies, eastern South America

**1700s** European colonies in North and South America grow in population and wealth.

**1775–1783 AMERICAN REVOLUTION**
The American Revolution begins in 1775 when the first shot is fired in Lexington, Massachusetts. The thirteen original British colonies in North America become independent under the Treaty of Paris, signed in 1783.

## Becoming Independent

Most countries of Latin America gained independence from Spain in the early 1800s. Others weren't liberated until much later.

| COUNTRY | YEAR OF INDEPENDENCE |
|---|---|
| Argentina | 1816 |
| Bolivia | 1825 |
| Brazil | 1822[1] |
| Chile | 1818 |
| Colombia | 1819 |
| Ecuador | 1822 |
| Guyana | 1966[2] |
| Mexico | 1821 |
| Paraguay | 1811 |
| Peru | 1824 |
| Suriname | 1975[3] |
| Uruguay | 1825 |
| Venezuela | 1821 |

[1] from Portugal  [2] from Britain  [3] from the Netherlands

**1867** The Canadian provinces are united as the Dominion of Canada.

**1898 THE SPANISH-AMERICAN WAR** Spain and the U.S. fight a brief war in 1898. Spain loses its colonies Cuba, Puerto Rico, and the Philippines.

**U.S. POWER IN THE 1900s** During the 1900s, the U.S. sent troops to various countries, including Mexico (1914; 1916–1917), Nicaragua (1912–1933), Haiti (1915–1934; 1994–1995), and Panama (1989). In 1962, the U.S. went on alert when the Soviet Union put missiles on Cuba.

**1994** The North American Free Trade Agreement (NAFTA) increases trade between the U.S., Canada, and Mexico.

**2001** Radical Muslim terrorists crash planes into U.S. targets, killing about 3,000 people; the U.S. launches a "war on terrorism."

**2003** U.S.-led forces invade Iraq and overthrow the regime of Saddam Hussein.

**2009** Barack Obama is sworn in as president of the United States. He is the country's first African American president.

**SIMÓN BOLÍVAR: LIBERATOR OF SOUTH AMERICA** In 1810, Simón Bolívar began a revolt against Spain. He fought against the Spanish and in 1924 became president of the independent country of Greater Colombia. As a result of his leadership, ten South American countries became independent from Spain by 1830.

**1810–1910 MEXICO'S REVOLUTION** In 1846, Mexico and the United States go to war. Mexico loses parts of the Southwest and California to the U.S. A revolution in 1910 overthrows Porfirio Díaz.

*Porfirio Diaz* ▶

# THEN & NOW
## FROM 2009

## 10 Years Ago–1999

**Then:** After overcoming cancer, Lance Armstrong wins his first Tour de France, the world's best-known bicycle race. He goes on to win the race a record seven times, from 1999 to 2005.

**Now:** In September 2008, Armstrong announces he will come out of retirement, and he finishes third in the 2009 Tour de France.

**Then:** On December 31, the US turns over the administration of the Panama Canal to the Panamanian Government. Completed by the United States in 1914, the Panama Canal is 48 miles long and joins the Pacific and Atlantic Oceans.

**Now:** In 2007, Panama breaks ground to expand the Canal with a third set of locks. The project should be complete between 2014 and 2015.

## 50 Years Ago–1959

**Then:** Alaska and Hawaii are admitted as the 49th and 50th states in the United States.

**Now:** Both states begin 2009 with their first woman governors: Sarah Palin, Governor of Alaska, and Linda Lingle, Governor of Hawaii. Palin, the vice-presidential candidate on the unsuccessful 2008 Republican Party ticket, resigns as governor in July 2009.

**Then:** Fidel Castro comes to power in Cuba.

**Now:** Castro is the leader of Cuba until February 2008. His brother Raul Castro is chosen as his successor as President of Cuba.

## 100 Years Ago–1909

**Then:** The National Association for the Advancement of Colored People (NAACP) is founded on February 12, Lincoln's birthday. Led by W. E. B. Du Bois, the NAACP includes both prominent black and white intellectuals.

**Now:** As one of its guiding mission objectives, the NAACP continues to work "to ensure the political, educational, social, and economic equality of all citizens."

**Then:** Einar Dessau of Denmark becomes the first ham radio operator to broadcast using a short-wave radio transmitter.

**Now:** Amateur radio, or "ham radio," continues to be a popular hobby throughout the world. Radio amateurs have access to a range of wave bands that allow them to transmit and communicate with each other.

**Then:** Karl Landsteiner discovers that all blood is not alike. He classifies blood into four main groups, or types: A, B, AB, and O. Landsteiner wins the Nobel Prize in Medicine for this discovery in 1930.

**Now:** Blood tests are used to test for a wide variety of conditions, including infection, cholesterol levels, and disease.

## 500 Years Ago–1509

In 1509, at the age of 17, Henry VIII became the King of England. He is one of England's most famous kings. Henry's divorce from his first wife led to the formation of his own church, the Church of England. He eventually had six wives, two of whom he had executed. His daughter with Anne Boleyn (his second wife), Elizabeth I, eventually succeeded her father and became one of the most powerful monarchs in England.

Henry VIII remains a popular figure in film and television. He is portrayed in *The Other Boleyn Girl*, a film from 2008, and the TV series *Tudors* from 2007.

# THEN & NOW FROM 2010

## 10 Years Ago–2000

**Then:** George W. Bush is elected president of the United States. Bush loses the popular vote but wins the Electoral College vote after the U.S. Supreme Court rules that there will not be a recount of disputed ballots in Florida.

**Now:** After moving back to Texas with his wife, Laura, in 2009, former President Bush stays out of the spotlight. He works on setting up his presidential library at Southern Methodist University in Texas.

**Then:** Suicide bombers attack the USS Cole while it is in harbor in Yemen, killing 17 sailors and wounding 36 more.

**Now:** The United States continues its efforts to locate and capture terrorists in the Middle East and elsewhere.

## 50 Years Ago–1960

**Then:** Four black students sit down at a "whites only" Woolworth's lunch counter in Greensboro, N.C. The restaurant allows them to stay but refuses to serve them. This is one of the events that launches the civil rights movement of the 1960s.

**Now:** Today any kind of discrimination in public places, schools, employment, or any other area of public life is against the law, and major legislation and court decisions exist to protect the rights of all minorities.

**Then:** About 38 percent of all U.S. women age 16 and up are in the labor force, and women make up about 33 percent of the labor force overall.

**Now:** As of 2008, almost 60 percent of U.S. women age 16 and up have jobs, and women make up about 47 percent of the labor force. Of the women with jobs, the largest percentage have managerial or professional jobs.

## 500 Years Ago–1510

In 1510, Martin Luther began the Protestant Reformation when he nailed his 95 Theses to the door of a cathedral in Wittenberg, Germany. His criticism of the Catholic Church led to the formation of a new religion, called Protestantism. Today, about 53 percent of Americans describe themselves as Protestants.

## 100 Years Ago–1910

▲ **Then:** Halley's Comet appears on schedule as predicted by the astronomer Edmond Halley, who, using Newton's Laws of Motions, announced in 1705 that the comet would reappear about every 76 years.

**Now:** The comet makes its predicted reappearance in 1986. Its next sighting will occur in 2061, so mark your calendar.

**Then:** The Boy Scouts of America is founded by a Chicago publisher. The organization's goal is to teach the values of honesty, responsibility, and personal fitness to young boys.

**Now:** There are nearly 3 million Boy Scouts in the United States, led by more than 1 million adult volunteer leaders.

**Then:** The first "Morris Plan" bank to make consumer loans to customers opens in Norfolk, Virginia. People no longer have to borrow from family or friends or borrow at outrageous interest rates from "loan sharks."

**Now:** As of 2007, Americans owe about $2.5 trillion in all kinds of consumer debt, or about $8,365 per person. This includes mortgages, credit card debt, personal loans, and similar borrowing.

# WOMEN IN HISTORY

The following women played important roles in shaping some of history's biggest events.

## CLEOPATRA

**CLEOPATRA** (69-30 B.C.), queen of Egypt famous for her association with Roman leaders Julius Caesar and Mark Antony. After her father's death, Cleopatra, at the age of about 17, and her 12-year-old brother Ptolemy jointly ruled. By custom, they were forced to marry each other. A few years later, she was sent away, but came back to rule when Caesar defeated her enemies. For a time, she lived with Caesar in Rome until his assassination in 44 B.C. She later went back to Egypt, where she met and married Antony.

## JOAN OF ARC

**JOAN OF ARC** (1412-1431), heroine and patron saint of France, known as the Maid of Orléans. She led French troops to a big victory over the English in the Battle of Orléans (1429), a turning point in the Hundred Years' War. Joan believed she was guided by voices from God, and she dressed like a male soldier. In 1431, she was burned at the stake as a heretic. The Catholic Church later declared her innocent, and she was made a saint in 1920. She is the subject of many monuments, paintings, and works of literature.

## CATHERINE THE GREAT

**CATHERINE THE GREAT** (1729-1796), empress of Russia (1762-1796). Catherine made Russia a European power and greatly expanded the territory of the Russian Empire. She raised the status of the nobles by granting them privileges such as freedom from military service and legal control over their serfs. She promoted culture as well as the education of women and religious tolerance.

## SOJOURNER TRUTH

**SOJOURNER TRUTH** (c. 1797-1883), abolitionist and women's rights activist (born Isabella Baumfree). She was raised as a slave on an estate in upstate New York. She escaped in 1826. In 1843, she became a traveling preacher and took the name Sojourner Truth. She traveled widely, speaking out against slavery and for women's rights. Her famous speech, "Ain't I a Woman?" was about how women were as smart and strong as men.

## FLORENCE NIGHTINGALE

**FLORENCE NIGHTINGALE** (1820-1910), British nurse and founder of modern nursing. She was a superintendent of female nurses during the Crimean War in Turkey, where she trained nurses and helped set up field hospitals, saving many lives. In 1860 she founded the first professional nursing school, at Saint Thomas's Hospital in London. In 1907, she became the first woman to receive the British Order of Merit.

## HARRIET TUBMAN

**HARRIET TUBMAN** (1821-1913), born Arminta Ross, escaped slavery when she was in her twenties. Before the Civil War, she repeatedly risked her life to lead hundreds of slaves to freedom by way of a network of homes and churches called the "Underground Railroad." During her nineteen trips back into the south, none of the fugitive slaves she guided was ever captured. She became known as the "Moses of her people" for her courage. During the Civil War, Tubman acted as a scout, spy, and nurse for the Union troops in South Carolina.

**MARIE CURIE** (1867-1934), Polish-French physical chemist known for discovering the radioactive element radium, which is used to treat some diseases. She also discovered the rare element polonium (named after Poland, her country of birth). She won the Nobel Prize for chemistry in 1911. She and her husband, Pierre Curie, also won the Nobel Prize for physics in 1903 for their work on radiation. Sadly, her work led to her death—she died from radiation poisoning.

**ANNE FRANK** (1929-1945), young German born Jewish girl whose diary of her family's two years in hiding--in the back rooms of an Amersterdam office

building--during the German occupation of The Netherlands, became a worldwide classic in literature. The Gestapo arrested the occupants of the secret annex after acting on a tip. Frank died in the Bergen-Belsen concentration camp in 1945. Her diary was saved by office worker Miep Gies and presented to Frank's father Otto when he was the only family member to return from the camps. Published in 1947 as *Het Achterhuis* (The House Behind), it appearred in the U.S. in 1952 as *Anne Frank: The Diary of a Young Girl.*

**VALENTINA TERESHKOVA** (born 1937), Russian cosmonaut and the first woman in space. During her 3-day spaceflight in June 1963 aboard the *Vostok 6,* she orbited Earth 48 times. Five months later, she married cosmonaut Andrian Nikolayev. In 1964, she gave birth to a daughter, the first child born to parents who had both flown in space.

**BILLIE JEAN KING** (born 1943), American tennis player who became a symbol for women's equality. King won 12 Grand Slam singles titles. But her most famous victory may have been in

the 1973 "Battle of the Sexes" match, when she beat male player Bobby Riggs in three straight sets. King helped start the first women's pro tennis tour in 1970. In 1971, she became the first woman athlete to win more than $100,000 in one season.

**JODY WILLIAMS** (born 1950) Activist who helped found the International Campaign to Ban Landmines. A landmine is a weapon which is placed in the ground and explodes when triggered by a vehicle or person. More than 15,000 people are injured or killed by landmines each year. Williams travels the world, speaking about how landmines kill and injure innocent civilians and working with governments to create a worldwide ban. Williams and her organization won the 1997 Nobel Peace Prize for their work.

**▲ DR. MAE JEMISON** (born 1956) The first African-American woman to go into space. She flew on the 1992 space shuttle *Endeavour* as a science mission specialist. She was born in Decatur, Alabama, and grew up in Chicago, Illinois. Dr. Jemison is a medical doctor who also has degrees in chemical engineering and African and African-American studies.

# Answers

## Buildings Quiz, p. 50

1. Eiffel Tower
2. The Great Sphinx
3. Transamerica Pyramid Building
4. Stonehenge
5. Space Needle

## Environment, p. 79

```
P L A S T I C   B O T T L E
      A L U M I N U M   C A N
              G L A S S
          C A R D B O A R D
        P A P E R
    B A T T E R I E S
        C O M P O S T
```

## Matching Game, p. 83

Lederhosen (short pants with suspenders): **Germany**

Pien-fu (2-piece robe): **China**

Kikoi (sarong-type skirt): **Uganda**

Chamanto (knee-length poncho): **Chile**

Kamiks (watertight boots): **Arctic Inuit people**

Kaftan (belted shirt-dress): **Morocco**

# Jokes and Riddles, p. 114–115

**1** The President **2** One combined bale **3** Your eardrum **4** Add a g and it's gone. **5** Your lap **6** You take your feet off the floor. **7** For beating the eggs **8** They're both the capital of England. **9** It gets wet. **10** It's too far to walk. **11** Language **12** Don't look, I'm changing. **13** The shoppers are a woman, her daughter, and her granddaughter. **14** Grow older **15** A hole **16** With an asteroid belt **17** Your word **18** A newspaper **19** A garbage truck **20** Any dog—skyscrapers can't jump. **21** The letter M **22** To measure how long he slept. **23** Your breath **24** I'm telling motherboard on you. **25** Because if they flew over a bay, they would be bagels! **26** One **27** All of them **28** His breath **29** Nine **30** Because he's living. **31** Mississippi **32** Umbrellas **33** A bird that gets up at the quack of dawn! **34** Nightmares **35** Time to get a new fence. **36** When it turns into a driveway. **37** A chair **38** You're the bus driver, how old are you? **39** There are no stairs, it's a one-story house. **40** A Whale of a Tale

# Word Connect, p. 115

```
F A N T A S T I C
    C       O       A
    T I P   A       N
    O   A G R E E
O A R     S
P       S T O R Y
T A B     R
I   A   A N G R Y
O   B   V       E
N   Y   E       L
        L E V E L
```

## Movies & TV Match-Up, p. 127

Mac & Blooregard: *Foster's Home for Imaginary Friends*
Katara & Sokka: *Avatar: The Last Airbender*
Will & Elizabeth: *Pirates of the Caribbean*
Tony and Pepper: *Iron Man*

Susan & Reed: *Fantastic Four*
Simon & Ryan: *American Idol*
Alex & Justin: *Wizards of Waverly Place*
Quinn & Lola: *Zoey 101*

## Roman Numerals, p. 181

2010 = MMX

50,000 = MMMMMMMMMMMMMMMMMMMMMMMMMMMMMMMMMMMMM MMMMMMMMMMMMMMMM

## Sudoku, p. 183

| 9 | 2 | 7 | 8 | 5 | 1 | 3 | 6 | 4 |
| 6 | 8 | 1 | 4 | 7 | 3 | 5 | 9 | 2 |
| 5 | 4 | 3 | 2 | 9 | 6 | 7 | 8 | 1 |
| 7 | 9 | 5 | 6 | 3 | 2 | 4 | 1 | 8 |
| 1 | 6 | 8 | 7 | 4 | 5 | 2 | 3 | 9 |
| 2 | 3 | 4 | 9 | 1 | 8 | 6 | 5 | 7 |
| 8 | 1 | 2 | 3 | 6 | 7 | 9 | 4 | 5 |
| 3 | 5 | 9 | 1 | 2 | 4 | 8 | 7 | 6 |
| 4 | 7 | 6 | 5 | 8 | 9 | 1 | 2 | 3 |

## Sports Scramble, p. 238

Tampa Bay Rays: **Carl Crawford**
Orlando Magic: **Dwight Howard**
Minnesota Vikings: **Adrian Peterson**

Arizona Cardinals: **Larry Fitzgerald**
Los Angeles Sparks: **Candace Parker**

# INDEX

# Photo Credits

**FRONT COVER**: Jeter, Cyrus: AP Images; snowboarder, wind turbines, Olympic flag, Vancouver, screen, baseball, Smartphone: Shutterstock.com. **BACK COVER**: Bolt, Swift, Wii console: AP Images; Obama, Panda: Shutterstock. **3**: Swift: AP Images. Military: U.S. Navy photo by Photographer's Mate 1st Class Bart A. Bauer. **4**: President Dollars: United States Mint. White: AP Images. **6-7**: *Gossip Girl*: The CW/Photofest. **6**: Idol: AP Images for Fox. **7**: Cyrus: AP Images; *Ugly Betty*: ABC/Photofest; *Glee*: Carin Baer/© Fox Television/Courtesy: Everett Collection. **8-9**: *New Moon*: ©Summit Entertainment/Courtesy Everett Collection. **9**: *Harry Potter and the Half-Blood Prince*: ©Warner Bros./courtesy Everett Collection; *Star Trek*: © Paramount/courtesy Everett Collection. **10-11**. *Up*: © Walt Disney Co./courtesy Everett Collection. **10**: *X-Men Origins*: *Wolverine*: James Fisher, TM and © Copyright 20th Century Fox Film Corp. All rights reserved./courtesy Everett Collection. **11**: *Transformers 2: Revenge of the Fallen*: Jaimie Trueblood. © Paramount/courtesy Everett Collection; *Fame*: Saeed Adyani/© MGM/courtesy Everett Collection. **12**: Swift: Getty Images; Jackson: AP Images. **13**: Lovato: Getty Images; Jonas Brothers: AP Images. **14-15**: Roethlisberger: AP Images. **14**: UCONN: NCAA Photos/AP Images. **15**: AP Images. **16**: Bryant: AP Images; Fiolek: Getty Images. **17**: AP Images. **18**: Anglerfish: Norbert Wu/Getty Images. **31**: Van Gogh: © SuperStock, Inc./SuperStock; "Poppy," Georgia O'Keeffe, 1927. Courtesy of the Museum Of Fine Arts, St. Petersburg. **34**: King: Consolidated News Pictures/Hulton Archive/Getty Images; Fanning: AP Images; Chavez: Department of Labor. **35**: Washington: Courtesy of the Library of Congress, LC-USZ62-49568; Ride: Shutterstock.com; Phelps: AFP/Getty Images. **36**: Elliott: PHIL MCCARTEN/UPI/Landov; Key: Courtesy of the Library of Congress, LC-USZ62-53017; Stewart: Chad Buchanan/Getty Images. **37**: Lin: AP Images; Heigl: WireImage/Getty Images; Barton: Courtesy of the Library of Congress, LC-USZ62-108565. **39**: Roshaade, Azeez & Azeezie Malouf, 1915: Courtesy of Edward A. Thomas. **40**: Cover from THE HOUSE IN THE NIGHT by Susan Marie Swanson, pictures by Beth Krommes. Jacket art copyright © 2008 by Beth Krommes. Used by permission of Houghton Mifflin Harcourt Publishing Company. All rights reserved; BIRD: LEW & LOW BOOKS. **41**: Lewis: John Chillingworth/Picture Post/Getty Images; Paulsen: AP Images. **42**: THE HOUSE WITH THE CLOCK IN ITS WALLS by John Bellairs, illustrated by Edward Gorey. Used courtesy of Penguin Books for Young Readers; Book Cover from THE LITTLE PRINCE by Antoine de Saint-Exupery, copyright 1943 by Harcourt, Inc. and renewed 1971 by Consuelo de Saint-Exupery, English translation copyright © 2000 by Richard Howard, reproduced by permission of Houghton Mifflin Harcourt Publishing Company; Jacket Cover from TALES OF A FOURTH GRADE NOTHING by Judy Blume. Used by permission of Random House Children's Books, a division of Random House Inc.; SOUNDER: Cover Illustration Copyright © 1989 by Daniel Maffia. Used by Permission of HarperCollins Publishers. **43**: DIARY OF A WIMPY KID by Jeff Kiney/Amulet Book; Cover from LINCOLN: A PHOTOBIOGRAPHY by Russell Freedman. Jacket copyright © 1987 by Houghton Mifflin Company. Reprinted by permission Clarion Books, an imprint of Houghton Mifflin Harcourt Publishing Company. All rights reserved. **44**: Library of Congress, LC-USZ62-10610. **47**: Steel framed building: Courtesy of the Library of Congress, LC-USZ62-69629. **48**: The Glass House: Ron Blunt Photography. **60**: Booth: Courtesy of the Library of Congress, LC-USZ62-25166; James, Capone: AP Images. **66**: Hindenburg: Naval Air Engineering Station (NAES) Lakehurst, NJ. **67**: *Lusitania*: Library of Congress, LC-USZC4-10986; Blizzard of 1888: National Oceanic and Atmospheric Administration/Department of Commerce. **75**: Polar ice cap: NASA/NRDC; Polar ice caps reflecting sun rays: NASA/GSFC. **80**: Edwardian: Hulton Collection/Getty Images; **81**: Travolta: © Paramount Pictures; *Gossip Girl*: KC BAILEY/THE CW/Landov. **82**: Native American: © Anders Ryman/Alamy. **84**: The Beatles: Rock Band: MTV Games/Harmonix. **85**: SCRIBBLENAUTS: © 2009 WB Games Inc. (see bottom of p. 351 for detail). **88**: Library of Congress, LC-USZ62-25351. **89**: AP Images. **94**: Carly Simon: Edward A. Thomas. **106**: iPhone: AP Images.

**107**: Jacket covered with burrs: Dr. Richard Kessel & Dr. Gene Shih/Getty Images; Flying microbot: Randi Silberman/IEEE Spectrum. **116**: American Revolution: Library of Congress, LC-USZC4-2135; U.S.S. *Constitution*: U.S. Navy photo by Photographer's Mate Chief John E. Gay; Civil War: Library of Congress, LC-B8184-10086; Spanish-American War: Library of Congress, LC-USZ62-26060. **117**: Uncle Sam: Library of Congress, LC-USZC4-3859; Yalta: National Archives; A-10A Thunderbolt II: U.S. Air Force. **118**: Afghanistan War: Department of Defense; Iraq War: U.S. Navy photo by Photographer's Mate 1st Class Bart A. Bauer. **119**: Medal of Honor: National Archives; Operation Iraqi Freedom: AP Images. **120**: AP Images. **121**: President Dollars: United States Mint. **122**: U.S. Dollar bill: © 2008 The United States Treasury Bureau of Engraving and Printing. **123**: iStockphoto. **124**: *The Simpsons*: Fox/Photofest. **125**: *American Idol*: AP Images for Fox; *The Princess and the Frog*: © Walt Disney Co./courtesy Everett Collection. **126**: *The Wizard of Oz* (film): MGM/Photofest; *The Wizard of Oz* (book): Library of Congress, 03032405; *Charlie and the Chocolate Factory*: Warner Bros./Photofest; **127**: *Harry Potter and the Half-Blood Prince*: © Warner Bros./ courtesy Everett Collection; *The Chronicles of Narnia: Prince Caspian*: Walt Disney Pictures/ Photofest. **128**: Smithsonian: Keith Stanley; American Museum of Natural History: American Museum of Natural History. **129**: Jamestown Settlement: Jamestown-Yorktown Foundation; Temple of Dendur: Bob Krist/Corbis. **130**: Keys: AP Images; Allen: Getty Images for Fox. **131**: Getty Images. **133**: *Dancing with the Stars*: ABC/Photofest; Kids dancing: Photofest. **136**: Ban Ki-Moon: UN Photo/Mark Garten. **178**: Totem pole: © Edward A. Thomas. **179**: Navajo Nation: 127-MN-69889-B; Navajo Indian Code Talkers Henry Bake and George Kirk, Dec. 1943; Department of Defense. Department of the Navy. U.S. Marine Corps; National Archives and Records Administration; Seneca: AP Images. **188**: Library of Congress, LC-B2- 5202- 12. **190**: Obama: The Obama-Biden Transition Project; von Suttner: Library of Congress, LC-B2- 1377-8. **191**: AP Images for Nickelodeon. **193**: Duct tape: Duck® brand duct tape Stuck at PromContest®; hot dog eating: AP Images. **197**: Ali al-Sistani: Reuters /Landov. **199**: ®LifeStraw, Vestergaard Frandsen. **201**: Paracelsus: iStockphoto. **202**: Soundwaves: Loren Winters/Visuals Unlimited, Inc. **205**: Anton van Leeuwenhoek: courtesy History of Science Collections, University of Oklahoma Libraries; Amoebas: Wim van Egmond/ Visuals Unlimited, Inc.; DNA: AP Images. **206**: Oil and water: Environmental Protection Administration. **207**: Kepler: courtesy History of Science Collections, University of Oklahoma Libraries; Darwin: Library of Congress, LC-USZ62-2709; Goodall: AP Images. **208**: Sun and planets: The International Astronomical Union/Martin Kornmesser. **209**: Saturn ring: NASA/ JPL/GSFC/Ames. **211**: Pluto: NASA/Hubble Space Telescope Collection; Ceres: NASA, ESA, J. Parker (Southwest Research Institute), P. Thomas (Cornell University), L. McFadden (University of Maryland, College Park), and M. Mutchler and Z. Levay (STScI). **213**: Moon: NASA/JPL. **214**: Phoenix landing on moon: NASA/JPL-Calech/University of Arizona; New Horizons spacecraft: NASA/Johns Hopkins University Applied Physics Laboratory/ Southwest Research Institute. **216**: Virgin Galactic SpaceShipOne: AP Images; Mars rover: NASA/JPL-Caltech. **217**: M100 Spiral Galaxy: NASA/Space Telescope Science Institute; Comet Hale-Bopp: NASA/JPL. **218**: Girl soccer: iStockphoto. **219**: Bicycle Polo: Bill Matheson & Scott Jordan, © Norm Carr; Lincecum: AP Images. **221**: Phelps: Al Bello/Getty Images. **223**: Liukin: Jed Jacobsohn/Getty Images; Van der Weijden: AP Images. **224-227**: AP Images. **228**: Crawford: AP Images; Gehrig: Getty Images. **229**: Hulton Archive/Getty Images. **230**: Naismith Memorial Hall of Fame; Basketball, Bryant: AP Images. **231-232, 234**: AP Images. **235**: Sloan: AP Images. **236**: Ovechkin: NHLI/Getty Images. **237**: Altidore: AP Images; Marta: Getty Images. **239**: AP Images. **244**: Viking ship: Courtesy of Project Guttenberg. **245**: Stagecoach: Library of Congress, LC-USZC4-3266; hot air balloon: Library of Congress, LC-USZ62-43058; Fulton steamboat: Library of Congress, LC-D4-22602. **246**: Transcontinental Railroad: Andrew J. Russell Collection/Oakland Museum of California; Wright plane: Library of Congress, LC-USZ62-6166A. **247**: Apollo 11 & shuttle: NASA; hybrid car: AP Images. **248**: Space Needle: Getty Images. **249**: Maverick roller coaster: courtesy of Cedar Point Amusement Park. **250**: H. Nelson Jackson: Special Collections, University of Vermont Library; lunchboxes: Courtesy of The Lunchbox Museum. **252**: Grand Canyon: AP Images. **256**: U.S. Constitution: National Archives and Records Administration. **259**: Congress: National Archives and Records Administration. **261**: AP Images. **262**: Obama: AP Images. **263, 265**: AP Images.

# THE WORLD ALMANAC FOR KIDS 2010

>>>> **#1** for **Facts** and **Fun**

> You'll find amazing facts about the world around you on every page of The World Almanac for Kids. Here are just a few...

Where is the world's tallest roller coaster? **see page 249** >

What is the largest animal on Earth? **see page 22**

◄ How many monthly users does Twitter have? **see page 240**

What is the most popular pet in the United States? **see page 24**

How many calories do you burn up each minute jogging? **see page 97** >

Why can't Scuba divers go to the bottom of the ocean? **see page 206**

◄ What U.S. city has been hit by the most tornadoes? **see page 63**

What is the host city for the 2010 Winter Olympics? **see page 224**

Where is the hottest place on Earth? **see page 316**

When is National Ice Cream Day? **see page 59** >